The Cost of Loyalty

The Cost of Loyalty

Dishonesty, Hubris, and Failure in the U.S. Military

Tim Bakken

BLOOMSBURY PUBLISHING

NEW YORK · LONDON · OXFORD · NEW DELHI · SYDNEY

BLOOMSBURY PUBLISHING
Bloomsbury Publishing Inc.
1385 Broadway, New York, NY 10018, USA

BLOOMSBURY, BLOOMSBURY PUBLISHING, and the Diana logo are trademarks
of Bloomsbury Publishing Plc

First published in the United States 2020

ISBN: HB: 978-1-63286-898-5; eBook: 978-1-63286-899-2

LIBRARY OF CONGRESS CATALOGING-IN-PUBLICATION DATA IS AVAILABLE

2 4 6 8 10 9 7 5 3 1

Typeset by Westchester Publishing Services
Printed and bound in the U.S.A. by Berryville Graphics Inc., Berryville, Virginia

To find out more about our authors and books visit www.bloomsbury.com and sign up
for our newsletters.

Bloomsbury books may be purchased for business or promotional use. For information on
bulk purchases please contact Macmillan Corporate and Premium Sales Department at
specialmarkets@macmillan.com.

CONTENTS

The Collapse

On the final evening of the academic year at West Point, the computer system collapsed. This incident, in May 2019—the third such breakdown in just over two months—came hours before the last day of classes at what the U.S. Army calls the "preeminent leadership institution in the world," and was accompanied by a complete loss of internet connections. The army colonel responsible for the system admitted at the time that the shutdown "had a crippling impact on cadets," though he managed to skirt all responsibility. It was a failure on his watch, and entirely not his fault.

In some ways, he was correct. The failure of that system was not his doing inasmuch as the failure of the entire system was not. His denial of responsibility was a sign of the large creeping problem inside America's military and the schools that feed it. Breakdowns and malfunctions with far greater ramifications had been rampant long before the colonel became the chief information officer, and even before he was a student in the same place, decades earlier.

The colonel attributed the system "outages" to "management, process, and technology failures [and] clumsy maintenance" by the Pentagon's Defense Research and Engineering Network (the DREN), the greater computer system that supports research and development for the entire U.S. military. After shifting and dispersing blame instead of accepting it, the colonel repeated another dubious and grandiose army mantra, reminding some in the West Point community, "We are and will remain the #1 public university in the United States."

This kind of hubris in the face of inarguable failure is neither rare here nor mysterious. It is central to military officers' bearing, as they try to project an image of competence, surety, and expertise, optimism over logic. The bragging, however, is not a harmless "hooah," the guttural cheer uttered by soldiers to express their camaraderie and enthusiasm. Inside the U.S. military, such mantras and public relations adages can metastasize into falsity that may be used to justify interventions and wars, including those in Korea, Vietnam, Afghanistan, and Iraq.

The geopolitical consequences of those wars could not be more significant. Communist, totalitarian North Korea possesses atomic weapons. Communist China fought the Americans on behalf of the North Koreans and supported the North Vietnamese, and China is now the second most influential nation in the world. Vietnam is completely Communist. Afghanistan's sovereignty is threatened daily by the Taliban. Iraqi society, heavily influenced by Iran, which is another potential atomic threat, is in turmoil. Arising from the war in Iraq, ISIS is an international threat, including in Afghanistan. The Middle East is more dangerous than when the United States invaded Iraq under false pretenses in 2003. No one knows for sure, but probably three to six million people were killed in these wars, including over one hundred thousand U.S. soldiers. Inside America, the last seventy-five years of military intervention have unleashed a flood of incompetence, hubris, and denial.

I have been living at the headwaters.

West Point has graduated just about every top general in every war since 1861. It has been and remains one of the most critical institutions in America. Now completing my twentieth year teaching there, I've had a front-row seat to a culture that has led to great losses. I've observed how the thinking and behavior taught at West Point, mirrored in the other academies, overwhelmingly influences military culture at large and contributes to or creates catastrophes thousands of miles away.

The variables that lead to the military's failure are numerous and complex, but lack of support is surely not one of them. Public polling regularly shows that the military is overwhelmingly the most popular institution in America. It is the most well resourced, technologically advanced, and highly weaponized force in world history. These immense advantages are a product of America's democracy, economy, and system of taxation. What America creates, builds, and achieves becomes what its military should be able to create, build, and achieve. Why does it lose?

Along the way, the military, of its own volition, has separated from the civilian society that was supposed to be overseeing it and caused the nation irreparable damage. This separation has occurred slowly, but unabated, since the end of World War II, which, not coincidentally, was the military's last clear-cut victory. The public's deference toward America's perceived military prowess solidified in 1945 and, despite seventy-five years of losses, has hardened into place. Under the watch of an executive branch that has ceded more and more authority to military generals—who now on their own often decide whom to attack around the world—and a Congress united by little except the fear of challenging war, the U.S. military has become an island. It has completely severed its culture, mores, and legal system from the basic tenets of civilian society and constitutional government.

After winning several critical Supreme Court cases in the 1970s and 1980s, the military successfully codified this separation into law. The highest court in the land deferred to the generals' contention that they needed more leeway to create "good order and discipline." As a result, legal and moral authority was delegated to the military chain of command, essentially depriving soldiers of constitutional liberties enjoyed by all U.S. citizens. The institution tasked with defending our freedoms was no longer required to offer these liberties. Within this insular world, unaccountable to outside authority, the U.S. military developed one value that eats away at all others: loyalty.

The military's disassociation from civilian society has led to an institution that is larger and more independent than some nations, a sovereign entity within America, opaque and secretive. It is led by self-protective officers who can go decades without ever having to reckon with a contrary opinion. Conformity is not only valued but also treated as an end in itself. As in an authoritarian state, free speech, independent thought, and creativity are stifled and smothered. The individual gains nothing and risks everything by engaging in dissent. Compliance equals survival.

In this closed system, the generals do not develop the ingenuity necessary to win modern wars or the capacity to understand whether a war is even winnable in the first place. This leads to a consideration that is almost too disturbing to acknowledge: some generals may indeed understand but remain silent because there is no mechanism in the military for them to express their individual ideas or opinions. Men and women die because other men and women do not have the reasoning, or the ability, or the courage to speak truthfully.

Of course, a computer meltdown at a military academy is not a failed foreign intervention, but it does illustrate a military institution more focused on large machinery than on computer hardware and software, which are the modern tools that will determine success or failure in war. Along with an absence of adequate ingenuity, the conditions for individual and organizational failure are pervasive inside the military: loyalty over truth; isolation; censorship; control over everyone; manipulation of the media; narcissism; retaliation; and callousness. The military's separation reinforces its worst instincts, especially its penchant for violence. This is a grave matter, and it is present every day at the three military academies. Statistics from studies by the Pentagon and Department of Justice show that women students attending the academies are five times more likely to be sexually assaulted than women students attending other colleges in the United States. The moderating influences and voices of reason that are inescapable in civilian society don't make their way inside the academies.

In a place where loyalty is the top value, change is almost scientifically impossible. In any number of instances over the past two decades, I experienced the futility of relying on the most well educated officers in the military when urging basic modern practices. Civilian professors and I proposed that West Point should permit all faculty members, rather than exclusively army officers, to apply for academic leadership positions at West Point. This was rejected. Another time, I argued against what I believed was favoritism, a prohibited practice under federal law. This was met by immediate retaliation, a common response inside the military. I notified the top two officials in the U.S. Army, the civilian secretary of the army and the chief of staff, a four-star general, about conditions at West Point.

According to the federal agency where I litigated and won a case against the army, it was the head of the Department of Law, a colonel and military lawyer, who was responsible for the retaliation. From this case, I became a legally recognized whistleblower working under a corrective order issued by a federal administrative judge to West Point. When the army promoted the colonel to brigadier general, it was only the latest example of what I've come to expect from the "world's preeminent leadership institution." It is a malfunctioning system, and the consequences are the most dire imaginable.

The cost of loyalty is far too high, and we, for the safety of our nation, have to pay the bill that has come due.

INTRODUCTION

Breaking the Myth

Americans' love for the military is embedded in their collective identity, as much a part of who they are as their affection for football, big cars, and fast food. Many are convinced of the military's invincibility and that men and women in uniform personify the highest ideals of service and honor. Remarking on the catastrophic U.S. invasion of Iraq in 2003, journalist George Packer wrote, "Like the President, [Vice President] Cheney maintained an almost mystical confidence in American military power and an utter incuriosity about the details of its human consequences."[1] Despite the public's unceasing adulation, there is one overarching consideration that shadows the military's seeming strength and reliability: it has not won a war in seventy-five years.

That the U.S. military is the best and most moral fighting force in history is embedded in the American psyche. In the *Atlantic*, James Fallows characterized this kind of idealization as "overblown, limitless praise, absent the caveats or public skepticism we would apply to other American institutions, especially ones that run on taxpayer money."[2] Politicians fight to one-up each other in flattery for the military, and the armed forces' unquestioned reputation for near omnipotence is enjoyed by generals despite great military losses. Dissenters who harbor doubt or speak against the prevailing perception are so maligned that staying quiet seems the wiser position.

One simply has to observe weekend pastimes to spot rituals that are akin to worship. Sporting events, particularly football games, are soaked in military symbolism, as though the gladiators on the field should personify the courage and aggressiveness of armed servicemen and women. Military power is fetishized before the games with the unfurling of giant flags and flyovers by airborne weapons of war, displays that became more firmly entrenched after the September 11 attacks. The spectacles have been recently revealed to be initiated by the military itself. The Pentagon signed seventy-two contracts with professional sports teams and spent $6.8 million to support patriotic displays of the teams, according to a Senate report, which condemned the practice as "paid patriotism."[3]

Though the Pentagon will not disclose how much it spends to influence opinions at home and abroad, the Associated Press found that the Department of Defense "spent at least $4.7 billion that year [2009] on a mix of public relations and propaganda campaigns."[4] In one year, the Pentagon "will employ 27,000 people just for recruitment, advertising, and public relations—almost as many as the total 30,000 person workforce in the State department."[5] Public spectacles are part of the U.S. military's recruitment infrastructure, a behemoth that obscures and romanticizes the violence of war.

With eight hundred bases in seventy countries and territories throughout the world (what former naval officer and author Chalmers Johnson pointedly called America's new colonies[6]) and always with over a million active-duty soldiers under arms, the U.S. military is the most widely dispersed and highly funded fighting force in history.[7] The military receives over 20 percent of every dollar the U.S. government spends.[8] The president's proposed 2020 military budget was $750 billion, up from $639 just two years earlier[9] and equal to that of the next fourteen countries combined.[10] The projected defense-related funding for 2021 stretches to $956.7 billion.[11]

With the military in possession of such enormous resources and staffed by highly trained soldiers, airmen, marines, and sailors, one critical question remains unanswered. Why does the American military keep losing wars? (A common definition of a war is that it is an international or civil conflict causing at least one thousand deaths yearly.[12]) A broad answer is that the U.S. military is deficient or broken. Against the North Koreans, who fought in mountainous terrain, or rural tribal fighters like the Vietcong, al-Qaeda, the Taliban, and ISIS, who possessed only small weapons, America's grand total of victories is zero. "In truth," former army colonel and conservative author Andrew Bacevich writes in *Breach of Trust*, "since 1945 the U.S. Army has not achieved anything approximating victory in any contest larger than policing exercises."[13]

One could argue that the wars in Korea, Vietnam, Afghanistan, and Iraq were difficult to win, or that the definition of winning is subjective or malleable. But if the generals believed the wars could not be won and remained silent, then they are complicit in America's failures. If the generals believed the wars were winnable, but they could not achieve victory, then they lacked the ability to outfight and outwit their enemies. Either circumstance is a colossal problem for America.

THE BALANCE SHEET

Clear victory was once the norm for America. Through World War II, the nation fought wars to obtain territory and defend itself, which included the protection of Europe. Its enemies were identifiable nations that could be overcome by superior numbers of soldiers, utilization of natural resources, or scientific and industrial ingenuity.

From the Revolutionary War through the German and Japanese surrenders in 1945, America possessed unrivaled resources—productive land protected by oceans; a strong economy; a populous nation through immigration; and democratic and constitutional decision-making. American resourcefulness spurred unmatched educational, economic, and industrial production. America's soft power—media, universities, technology, capitalism, and openness—more than military might, contributed to the end of the Cold War, which is enormously revealing. That the Cold War with the Soviet Union was never fought conventionally—military to military—is a likely reason that the United States won.

Meanwhile, the hot wars that the United States has fought in the last seventy-five years almost all fall into the category of civil war, virtually the only kind of war remaining on the planet. If not for the world's civil wars, "war could be on the verge of ceasing to exist as a substantial phenomenon," according to political science professor John Mueller.[14] After 1945, fighting in civil wars and ideological conflicts, which last longer than conventional wars and may be less likely to result in a settlement, became the American military's modus operandi.[15] The American rationale for war was to stop the spread of communism and, later, terrorism. Confident in the rightness of its own ideology, the United States waded into or invaded the Korean peninsula, Vietnam, Afghanistan, and Iraq—with disastrous results.

Even assuming that those wars were winnable—a big assumption—the generals needed to create novel strategies and adapt to the complex political structures that developed after World War II. This did not occur. "The U.S. military . . . has traditionally resisted adapting itself to stabilizing missions, preferring to plan for reruns of World War II," writes political science professor Dominic Tierney in *How We Fight: Crusades, Quagmires, and the American Way of War.*[16]

The problem was not only a lack of adaptation. It was—and continues to be—an inability or lack of desire to face a reality that may require adaptation. Historian John W. Dower writes that "after Vietnam the elite military academies that trained career officers actually expunged counterinsurgency from their regular curricula."[17] Similarly, Professor Tierney notes that the army's 1976 training manual "incredibly . . . didn't even mention counterinsurgency—even though the United States had just lost more than fifty thousand men battling insurgents for eight years in Vietnam. As if saying the name of the guerilla bogeyman might summon it again."[18] Former vice chief of staff for the army and retired general Jack Keane admitted, "After the Vietnam War, we purged ourselves of everything that had to do with irregular warfare or insurgency, because it had to do with how we lost that war. In hindsight, that was a bad decision."[19]

This is beyond an understatement. It is also one of the clearest representations of the monumental problem at hand. The U.S. military fights the wars it knows and wants to be fighting (some version of World War II), not what's on the ground—other countries' civil wars. The adversaries in civil wars are often motivated by ethnic, religious, tribal, or ideological identity, which may be more powerful motivators than nationalism. They fight on familiar terrain, in mountains, jungles, and valleys near their homes. They manufacture, purchase, or rig weaponry to fit their narrow circumstances. "To judge by the record of the past twenty years," Bacevich writes,

"U.S. forces win decisively only when the enemy obligingly fight on American terms."[20]

None of America's recent enemies has been doing us this favor. As Dower points out, the war on terror, launched in 2001 and ongoing still, is "almost antithetical to the high-tech, smart-weapon, rapid-deployment, small-footprint, in-and-out war [former defense secretary Donald Rumsfeld] and a legion of erstwhile defense experts in Washington had envisioned."[21] The U.S. military commissioned relatively generic weapons, for example, tanks with turrets that do not swoop low or high enough to counter insurgents who live and fight on undulating terrain.

Speaking at West Point in November 2018, two U.S. Army captains who were company commanders during the Battle of Mosul (Iraq) in 2017 described how old thinking and expensive weapons cannot win the day. They explained how "waiting seven years" for the U.S. Army and Pentagon to produce weapons and strategies to fight ISIS in Iraq was a losing proposition. In the dense urban environment of Mosul, population 600,000, a city reminiscent of antiquity, ISIS "thugs," one of the captains said, held the city for two years by dint of their ingenuity. The civilization surrounding Mosul dates to 2500 B.C.E., and the city today contains up to seven layers of old catacombs. Two or three ISIS snipers running back and forth through the catacombs and firing intermittently created the impression of a much larger force. Within the city, ISIS soldiers launched mortars from inside houses by cutting holes in the roofs and shuttering the holes after launch. Iraqi and U.S. soldiers could not locate the houses for days, by which time ISIS was gone.

On March 17, 2017, the United States dropped a five-hundred-pound bomb on a concrete building in a densely populated part of Mosul in an attempt to kill two ISIS snipers. For lack of intelligence and situational awareness, the Americans were unaware that over a hundred Iraqi civilians had taken refuge within the structure, almost all of whom were killed when the U.S. bomb ignited ISIS munitions. The final death toll might have been 141, because additional missing civilians were never found. The *New York Times* reported that a U.S. general said it was possible civilians had been held in the building (which one of the captains at West Point also said), "though there was no proof of that," according to the *Times*.[22]

When the Iraqi soldiers moved toward Mosul, ISIS, using "swarms" of commercial drones, quadcopters bought off the shelf, would hover the drones over soldiers and bomb them with jerry-rigged grenades. One captain observed that U.S. fighter planes were useless against the tiny drones. Because the Iraqi and American soldiers did not foresee the drone attacks and did not have assets (missiles or electromagnetic) to shoot down the drones, "ISIS controlled the airspace below 2,000 feet."

While these captains described the tactical conditions of war, American military leaders since World War II have been also unfamiliar with geographic, cultural, political, and social conditions in the regions where troops have fought. In modern wars, the generals have had to rely more on their intellect and less on weaponry, and they've been outgunned by their adversaries. The most critical reason for failure is the decline in the performance of U.S. military officers since World War II. Andrew Bacevich described broadly the most recent collapse of commanders in *The Limits of Power: The End of American Exceptionalism*: "The quality of American generalship since the end of the Cold War has seldom risen above the mediocre . . . This is one of the dirty little secrets to which the world's only super power has yet to own up. As the United States has come to rely ever more heavily on armed force to prop up its position of global preeminence, the quality of senior American military leadership has been consistently disappointing . . . First-rate generalship has been hard to come by."[23]

More specifically, in a 2017 book-length study, three social scientists on the faculty at West Point detailed for the Army War College the "intellectual" decline among the officers of the army over the past one hundred years, and the utter collapse since the end of World War II. Ominously, they found that political, social, and cultural influences will prevent America from finding better officers any time soon. Army officers, according to the scientists, used to come from a somewhat representative sample of Americans, from big and small towns and different social and cultural backgrounds. This changed as military service became less desirable and as the army deemphasized intellectual testing and individual performance in favor of malleable metrics that can be manipulated, like the "whole person score" used by West Point to admit "at risk" students. "In short," the scientists concluded, "contrary to popular opinion and scholarly assertion, the rigor of the Army's intellectual selection instruments has deteriorated over the last century ... [and] the trend has been toward declining standards and declining (relative) scores ... This difficult [operational] environment will require future Army officers to perform at a higher intellectual level than they presently do."[24] The scientists found that "this trend of deteriorating mental standards" led the army to abandon its attempt to retain officers with "abundant intelligence" because they refused to stay in the army, and that "motivation replaced intelligence as the most important consideration in officer selection."[25] The officers leading the military today appear not to have the ability to win modern wars, and almost nobody knows it.

KOREA

The results of the last four wars since 1945 should lead Americans to reassess their faith in military leaders. Those wars, in Korea, Vietnam, Afghanistan, and Iraq, illustrate recurring approaches that have led to failure. The operation called Desert Storm, in January and February of 1991, when the U.S. and thirty-eight allied nations expelled Iraq from Kuwait in a ground war lasting about one hundred hours, is not included in this evaluation because it was not a war under one common definition (one thousand dead yearly). This was certainly treated as a victory at the time. But hindsight has revealed a more nuanced picture. After the war, Saddam Hussein, the Iraqi president, slaughtered the Shiites and Kurds. His Republican Guard retained power. The U.S.-incited rebellion against Saddam failed. Shiites and Kurds in Iraq never forgot this, and they carried their anger and distrust with them in 2003 and onward when America needed their help. The lasting legacy of Desert Storm was that the civilian population couldn't trust America, a condition that contributed to the military's failure in Iraq after the U.S. invaded in 2003.

The Korean War, according to journalist Neil Sheehan, "was the first war in American history in which the leaders of the Army and the nation were so divorced from reality and so grossly underestimated their opponent that they brought disaster to the Army and the nation."[26] In the wake of World War II, the Korean peninsula had become a dangerous laboratory in which the dueling ideologies of communism and democracy contended. The North developed into a Communist state, while the South adopted western ideas. With the support of the Soviet Union and the Chinese Communists, the North, in 1950, attacked and took control of most of the South. In response, U.S. Army general Douglas MacArthur was called to command United Nations forces, of which U.S. troops comprised over 80 percent.

Throughout the Korean War, the United States possessed superior weapons and technology, particularly air power. (Neither the Chinese nor the North Koreans even had an air force.) When attacking, the Chinese used the noise from bugles and drums to confuse the UN and American forces. The U.S. military responded in a manner consistent with its technological superiority: brute force.

According to Dean Rusk, who served as the secretary of state in the Kennedy administration, the United States bombed "everything that moved in North Korea, every brick standing on top of another," including dams, which caused flooding and crop destruction when they burst.[27] The U.S. Air Force and Navy dropped 635,000 tons of bombs on North Korea—more than the total tonnage dropped in the Pacific theater of World War II—as well as 32,557 tons of napalm, a liquid chemical that destroys plant life and incinerates human skin. Approximately 3 million Koreans died in the war, about 12 to 14 percent of the country's total population. Of these deaths, about 1.9 million were North Koreans, possibly 20 percent of their population.[28]

The U.S. military's overreliance on technology contributed to overconfidence, from MacArthur all the way down the chain of command. Much of the failure in Korea (and later in Vietnam) was attributable to the generals' strategic misjudgment and moral unwinding. This is underscored by their self-defeating bombing of Korean population centers, as well as U.S. soldiers' abusive and sometimes murderous treatment of civilians, which only intensified their enemies' resolve. In 1951 President Harry Truman finally fired the duplicitous and incompetent General MacArthur, who had helped set the stage for defeat by motivating the Chinese to enter the conflict.

Because the Korean peninsula remained divided after the 1953 armistice, some argue that the Korean War remains a stalemate. But the results of the war contravene this notion. First, over 36,000 U.S. soldiers died in Korea. In addition, as South Korea developed as a nation, it was beset by authoritarianism, repression, martial law, presidential assassination, and a military coup. The Korean War's most dangerous legacy is that it contributed to North Korea's motivation to develop nuclear weapons. "Most Americans are completely unaware that we destroyed more cities in the North than we did in Japan or Germany during World War II," said historian Bruce Cumings. "Every North Korean knows about this, it's drilled into their minds."[29]

The military's failure to win set the stage for North Korea to become a nuclear threat to America. After U.S. bombers destroyed their population centers, the North Koreans came to loathe and distrust the United States. They believed that only nuclear-armed intercontinental ballistic missiles could counter America's technological superiority. After enduring political repression and starvation for nearly seventy years, the North Koreans developed their first nuclear weapon in 2009. Their next goal was met on July 4, 2017, when they successfully tested an intercontinental ballistic missile (ICBM) capable of reaching Hawaii.[30]

VIETNAM

Throughout the Cold War, in its fierce and nearly single-minded opposition to communism, America was willing to fight wars or support violent revolutions in Asia, Central America, South America, and Cuba. As in Korea, America's involvement in Vietnam began with the seeds of a civil war. French control over Vietnam ended in 1954, and, after meetings in Geneva that included France and the Soviet Union, China, Britain, and the United States, Vietnam was split into two zones. Communist leader Ho Chi Minh led the north, while the fervent anti-Communist Catholic Ngo Dinh Diem became president of South Vietnam. Hoping for a fully democratic Vietnam, the administration of Dwight D. Eisenhower sent military advisors to train the army of South Vietnam. In 1961 John F. Kennedy sent four hundred Green Berets to train the South Vietnamese army in counterinsurgency against Communist guerrillas.

When President Kennedy was assassinated in 1963, the United States had over 16,000 advisors in South Vietnam, many of whom were engaged in combat. By March 1965, at the constant urging of the U.S. military, President Lyndon Johnson ordered 82,000 troops to Vietnam, and then another

100,000 in both 1965 and 1966. A year later the total number of U.S. troops in Vietnam was over 500,000. By then, immersed in General William Westmoreland's strategy of attrition, over 15,000 U.S. soldiers had been killed and nearly 110,000 wounded. Desperate in 1970, and likely in violation of international law, President Richard Nixon ordered U.S. and South Vietnam forces to invade Cambodia in an attempt to cut the supply lines of the North Vietnamese, leading to more death and destruction but no path to victory.[31]

Defense Intelligence Agency reports that the U.S. military would not defeat the North Vietnamese were summarily rejected by army commanders, especially the most influential and longest-serving, General Westmoreland. For four years (1964–1968), Westmoreland claimed that victory was in sight if only America could kill more North Vietnamese. In *A Bright Shining Lie: John Paul Vann and America in Vietnam*, Neil Sheehan described the overconfidence and pretension possessed by U.S. generals: "By the second decade after World War II, the dominant characteristics of the senior leadership of the American armed forces had become professional arrogance, lack of imagination, and moral and intellectual insensitivity . . . The attributes were the symptoms of an institutional illness that might most appropriately be called the disease of victory, for it arose out of the victorious response to the challenge of Nazi Germany and imperial Japan."[32]

In Vietnam, as in Korea, American technology and its military leaders' judgment were outmatched by North Vietnamese motivation and ingenuity. By the war's end in 1975, 58,200 U.S. servicemen had been killed, among the 2.7 million U.S. soldiers who participated,[33] and over 300,000 had been wounded. North Vietnam and South Vietnam lost 1 to 3 million people, with 2 million wounded. By almost all accounts, the war was a black eye for the United States and a pointless sacrifice of a generation of young men.

AFGHANISTAN

"In fact war is often the undoing of a great power when wars begin to cost too much or go on longer than anticipated," wrote professor Neta Crawford in 2016.[34] As in Korea and Vietnam, America found itself embroiled in a civil war in Afghanistan just twenty-six years after the fall of Saigon. The U.S. military's quick removal of the Taliban from power in

November 2001 led to a prolonged and self-defeating stay in Afghanistan, a modern war that is nearing two decades. The continuing war there is particularly disturbing because as early as December 2001 the United States had achieved its prime objective, the removal of al-Qaeda and the Taliban from and establishment of a civilian government in Kabul.[35] A compelling argument can be made that the United States should have withdrawn, at the latest, by the end of 2003, when it had only 13,100 troops in Afghanistan. But the administration of George W. Bush and its neoconservative leaders had plans for Afghanistan: they wanted to turn it into a democracy.

Instead, the United States allowed Afghanistan eventually to become more unstable and violent than before the invasion. This seemed predictable; "nation building 'from the outside' is quite impossible and might delegitimize a state, rather than leading to its gradual rooting in the fabrics of society," according to professor Andreas Wimmer,[36] articulating a widely held analysis.

Even though Bush, as a presidential candidate, explicitly spoke out against the futility of nation building, his administration's policy was just that. In April 2002 he announced a reconstruction plan for Afghanistan, and Congress provided $39 billion to fund the initiative through the end of the decade. On May 1, 2003, Secretary of Defense Rumsfeld announced the end of "major combat" in Afghanistan, when only eight thousand U.S. troops were in the country.[37] In August 2003, in its first operational mission outside Europe, the North Atlantic Treaty Organization (NATO) took control of the International Security Forces (ISAF), which numbered only about five thousand troops.

On October 29, 2004, Osama bin Laden resurfaced and, in a video, explicitly claimed responsibility for the September 11 attacks. He had escaped to Pakistan on horseback during the Battle of Tora Bora in December 2001. Despite intelligence indicating his presence in the mountains, U.S. forces did not lead the assault, leaving it instead to ragtag Afghan fighters.[38] In 2005, after regrouping in Pakistan, the Taliban returned to Afghanistan to engage in widespread violence, successfully using buried improvised explosive devices (IEDS) and suicide bombings to attack U.S. troops and destabilize the U.S.-backed Afghan government. A National Intelligence Estimate released two years later showed that al-Qaeda had actually become stronger than it was six years prior, right before the U.S. invasion.[39]

The Taliban bounced back. The anti-American sentiment of Afghans increased. "Those feelings were nurtured by the sluggish pace of reconstruction, allegations of prisoner abuse at U.S. detention facilities, widespread corruption in the Afghan government, and civilian casualties caused by U.S. and NATO bombings," according to journalist Griff Witte.[40] A 2015 United Nations report indicated that the Taliban insurgency was then greater than at any time since the United States had attacked in 2001.[41] The next year, American military commanders estimated that the United States might have to "keep thousands of troops in . . . [Afghanistan] for decades."[42] By the end of 2003, when the U.S. had completed its stated objective of getting rid of al-Qaeda and the Taliban, seventy U.S. service members had died in the war in Afghanistan. Since then, more than 2,300 additional U.S. soldiers have been killed.

President Barack Obama increased the number of troops to a hundred thousand and then promised to reduce it to under ten thousand. In 2017 President Donald Trump added at least four thousand additional troops to Afghanistan, although a chief presidential aide, Steve Bannon, questioned the returns on the $850 billion in nonmilitary spending there.[43] Nonetheless, Trump announced later in 2017 an even more open-ended commitment of troops, which numbered fourteen thousand in 2019, because the soldiers "deserve a plan for victory."[44] The next day, retired general David Petraeus, speaking at West Point, said, "In Afghanistan, there's no path to victory that I know of."

The American commander in Afghanistan, General Austin "Scott" Miller, had said in February of 2019, "Neither side will win it militarily, and if neither side will win it militarily you have to move . . . towards a political settlement here." On April 9, 2019, H. R. McMaster, then a retired general and a former national security advisor for Trump, said in a discussion at West Point, "We have never sustained a sound strategy in Afghanistan." In October 2019, having obtained no concessions from the Taliban, the U.S. military, with no public announcement, began withdrawing several thousand troops from Afghanistan.

IRAQ

In 2003, when the United States could have exited Afghanistan after expelling the Taliban, the Bush administration instead turned its sights on Iraq.

In the year prior, the administration floated any number of justifications for invading the country. It claimed that Iraq and al-Qaeda had conspired in the September 11 attacks, which was not true. In a memorable formulation, former U.S. counterterrorism czar Richard Clarke offered, "Having been attacked by Al Qaeda, for us now to go bombing Iraq in response would be like our invading Mexico after the Japanese attacked us at Pearl Harbor."[45] The administration then claimed that Saddam Hussein was a brutal dictator who had to go. This truism, known to everyone in the world for over two decades, provided no legal or strategic basis for war. (In the previous decade, when U.S. airplanes were patrolling no-fly zones in Iraq, Saddam hadn't shot down a single plane.[46]) The final and most infamous claim was that Iraq was developing weapons of mass destruction. This, too, was false.

The invasion of Iraq became inevitable when, on February 5, 2003, a familiar face appeared at the United Nations: secretary of state Colin Powell, a former army general and chairman of the Joint Chiefs of Staff under George H. W. Bush. Powell, who regularly topped lists of "Most Admired Americans,"[47] held up a faux vial of anthrax in a theatrical presentation and testified that Iraq possessed or was developing weapons of mass destruction.

Years later, evidence showed that Powell believed the opposite to be true. (Iraq's nuclear weapons program had ended in 1991, and a 2004 report confirmed that the nation had no nuclear, chemical, or biological weapons programs.) Powell's reflexive obedience to President Bush was forged in a military culture that elevates loyalty over truth. "Clearly, Powell's loyalty to George Bush extended to being willing to deceive the world," writes Jonathan Schwarz in the *Huffington Post*. "He's never been held accountable for his actions, and it's extremely unlikely he ever will be."[48] Schwarz finds that Powell fabricated or lied repeatedly during his presentation at the United Nations, concluding that "Powell was consciously lying: he fabricated 'evidence' and ignored repeated warnings that what he was saying was false."[49]

"It was the old general's ultimate sacrifice as a good soldier," writes military commentator Tom Ricks, who notes that Powell's reputation may have been "the first casualty of the Iraq War."[50]

Even without weapons of mass destruction, Iraq's culture and society would make it a difficult place to conquer. Southern Iraq, Mesopotamia, was one of the birthplaces of civilization, where the Code of Hammurabi, possibly the first written code of law, was created prior to 1750 B.C.E. Introduced to Arab Islamic rule in the Middle Ages, Iraq would not quickly embrace Western values. Despite this history, vice president Dick Cheney claimed on television that "my belief is we will, in fact, be greeted as liberators."[51]

In Iraq, "the illusion of painless engagement . . . was short-lived," according to author Frank Rich.[52] The invasion destabilized Iraq and much of the Middle East and was accompanied by a bewildering lack of planning for running the country after Saddam Hussein was deposed.

"As the war planning had progressed over the nearly 16 months," writes Bob Woodward, "Powell had felt that the easier the war looked, the less Rumsfeld, the Pentagon and [General Tommy] Franks had worried about the aftermath. They seemed to think Iraq was a crystal goblet and that all they had to do was tap it and it would crack."[53]

"It now seems more likely," Ricks writes, "that the U.S. invasion of Iraq in the spring of 2003 was based on perhaps the worst war plan in American history . . . Its incompleteness helped create the conditions for the difficult occupation that followed. The invasion is of interest now mainly for its role in creating those problems."[54]

The Iraqis found it inconceivable that the world's remaining superpower could fail miserably in planning how to run their country. "The notion that bad planning, halfhearted commitment, ignorance, and incompetence accounted for the anarchy simply wasn't believable,"[55] explained George Packer. The failure to protect Iraq was one of the main reasons that the insurgency there proliferated. Iraqis suspected that it was malicious intent that allowed for the country to be mired in over a decade of fallout from the U.S. invasion. Melvin A. Goodman, a former U.S. intelligence officer, notes, "The U.S. military failed to understand that the lack of security provided to civilians in Iraq led to greater success and recruitment for militias and insurgent groups."[56]

The wars in Afghanistan and Iraq have taken the lives of more than 7,000 U.S. soldiers and 7,800 U.S. civilian contractors.[57] The deaths do not include the 53,300 additional U.S. troops wounded in action or the hundreds of thousands of local people who were killed.[58]

"Worst of all," writes Rosa Brooks, a former counselor in the Defense Department, "we caused untold suffering for the very population we so earnestly intended to help."[59] (The dead from Afghanistan and Iraq include six army officers who were my students in courses at West Point.[60])

As military strategy professor and fellow at the Council on Foreign Relations Richard K. Betts writes, "Even if the eventual outcome in Iraq proves reasonably stable"—and that's a colossal if—"the cost will have far exceeded the benefit."[61] Betts adds up the cost: "Thousands of American casualties, dozens of times more Iraqi casualties, prolonged economic dislocation in the country, hordes of refugees, increased Iranian influence in the region, expanded and inflamed anti-American Islamist movements throughout the world, and an astronomical bill . . . up to three trillion dollars."[62]

Today, Afghanistan and Iraq remain two of the most unstable and dangerous places on earth, with more unrest, death, and violence than in the years preceding the U.S. invasions. A 2013 study estimated that the final cost of both wars combined could be $6 trillion.[63] A poll around the same time found that close to 75 percent of Americans believe that the wars in Iraq and Afghanistan will be viewed as "more of a failure than a success" or "complete failures."[64] Indeed, young American adults today have no memory of peace, and the remainder have lived through three or four wars. War, for America, has become normal, and the toll continues to rise. In 2019, the Watson Institute at Brown University estimated that the wars in Afghanistan and Iraq, and the violent offshoots they spawned in Pakistan and Syria, will cost the United States $13.9 trillion, if the interest on the debt used to pay for the wars is included.

The war in Iraq unleashed another threat to America: Iran, an adversary with the capability of developing nuclear weapons. While U.S. armies were fighting on its eastern (Afghanistan) and western (Iraq) borders, Iran successfully exerted greater influence in the civil wars in Syria and Yemen, as well as the insurgency in Iraq. Shia militias, Sunni insurgents, and, through ISIS—which grew from the insurgency and al-Qaeda in Iraq—fighters throughout the world flowed into Iraq. As early as 2004, the U.S.

National Intelligence Council predicted an ISIS-like group by 2020 with "a powerful counter ideology that has widespread appeal."[65]

The U.S. invasion of Iraq was the most significant contributor to the violence and destabilization in the Middle East in the twenty-first century. Turkey renewed its attacks on the Kurds in southern Turkey, northern Iraq, and northern Syria. Civil war broke out in Syria, leading to Syrian refugees destabilizing the European political system and to Russia's military intervention in Syria. In 2014 Yemen fell into its third civil war since 1990, with Saudi Arabia and Iran supporting opposing sides, respectively the former government and the Houthi rebels. When President Donald Trump pulled the remaining U.S. troops from northern Syria in October 2019, Turkey attacked the Kurds, America's longtime ally. The Kurds then allied with the Syrian regime of Bashar al-Assad and Russia. Trump's action, an extension of the U.S. invasion of Iraq in 2003, gave the green light to Turkey to attack the Kurds and emboldened ISIS, whose members were imprisoned by the Kurds, and Iran, another U.S. adversary. Turkey and Russia then agreed jointly to control northern Syria.

The American military and political failure of these wars can be measured by the most appalling outcome: America's enemies—and possibly its future enemies—are far stronger now than when the United States entered or invaded their countries. The Communists remain in charge of Vietnam and also North Korea, which possesses nuclear weapons. The Taliban control half of Afghanistan. Iran, constantly threatening the United States and Israel, gained significant control over Iraq while America fought the war there.[66] Aside from the humanitarian crisis, the worst strategic result of the civil war in Syria is that Russian soldiers are now on the ground and in the air, using Russian planes and technology to help the Syrian army defeat the insurgents who were supported by the United States.

Individually and collectively, America's four major wars since 1945 should be considered enormous losses.

SEPARATE SOCIETIES

What can explain these losses? One answer lies in understanding that the U.S. military, especially the group of generals and admirals who graduate from the academies, is no longer representative of America. The military has become a separate society. It is unmoored from the values and practices that lead to excellence and success in a modern world. Along with separation, the cronyism, hubris, arrogance, and dishonesty that define the culture and which develop within individual officers have been major contributors to failure.

The military's social and cultural separatism began soon after World War II and was embodied by General Douglas MacArthur, who was relieved of his command by President Truman for his disdain of civilian authority over the military, a principle established in the Constitution. However, in a little-known moment in history, a monumental U.S. Supreme Court decision from 1974 effectively placed the U.S. military outside the Constitution. The fulcrum of the case, *Parker v. Levy*, was Captain Howard Levy, a dermatologist in the army. In 1967 Levy refused an order to train Special Forces soldiers on skin diseases. In public, Levy told soldiers, "The United States is wrong to be involved in the Vietnam War. I would refuse to go to Vietnam if ordered. I don't see why any colored soldier would go to Vietnam . . . because they are discriminated against and denied their freedom in the United States, and they are sacrificed and discriminated against in Vietnam by being given all the hazardous duty and they are suffering the majority of casualties . . . Special Forces personnel are liars and thieves and killers of peasants and murderers of women and children."[67]

Levy was court-martialed by the army for disobeying an order to train soldiers and for calling them "liars and thieves" and "killers." The army alleged that Levy's speech promoted "disloyalty and disaffection among the troops," and Levy was found guilty and sentenced to three years in prison. He served twenty-six months.

In upholding Captain Levy's conviction, the Supreme Court held that the military may withhold constitutional protections from soldiers to ensure "uniformity" and "good order and discipline." Writing for the majority, justice William Rehnquist reasoned that the military is "by necessity, a *specialized society separate from civilian society* . . . [and] that the military has, again by necessity, developed laws and traditions of its own during its long history" (emphasis mine).[68] This little-known decision by the court allowed the military legally to extract itself from American life. The court's decision effectively eliminated constitutional protections for soldiers when the military asserts a need for good order and discipline, which it will argue that it always needs.

It is no longer the Constitution but rather military officers, acting individually or collectively, who are authorized to determine what, if any, rights soldiers may possess. In three other cases, like *Levy*, all authored by the conservative Rehnquist, the Supreme Court permitted the military to create an impenetrable social, cultural, and legal wall between itself and American values. In *Rostker v. Goldberg*, from 1981, the court rejected a young man's equal protection claim that women should have to register with the selective service if men are required to register. In *Goldman v. Weinberger*, from 1986, Justice Rehnquist reasoned that the military may prohibit soldiers' religious practices, in this case wearing a yarmulke indoors, to "foster instinctive obedience, unity, commitment, and esprit de corps."[69] In *Solorio v. U.S.*, from 1987, the court, overturning its own precedent, found that the military may criminally prosecute soldiers for acts allegedly committed at any place in the world and at any time, not only while on military duty.[70]

One arrives at a sobering, frightening realization: the U.S. Constitution does not apply to members of the U.S. military the way it applies to everyone else. America's most consequential document does not constrain military leaders the way it constrains every other public official and institution. This has freed the military to promote the ethos of loyalty over truth within the institution, which necessarily pits the military against the civilian society that is supposed to oversee it. The rule of law has become less prevalent; individual officers make all the rules without being effectively constrained by legal doctrines or democratic norms. Where there is such discretion in authorities and lack of accountability, there are fertile grounds for corruption.[71]

A negative feedback loop has developed. The Constitution no longer effectively constrains the generals. Any military officer interested in career advancement will not speak freely, especially when it's most necessary, as when the nation must decide whether to engage in war, because then the officer will be more noticeable. (This was a huge issue in the faulty decision to invade Iraq in 2003.) To avoid antagonizing any of the officers higher in their chain of command, officers, including generals, remain silent or fall in line by parroting the positions of superior officers. Members of

Congress, whose voters work for military contractors in every congressional district, cannot muster the personal courage to overrule military leaders. When, through this process, an institution as powerful as the U.S. military becomes autonomous, authoritarian values have the potential to displace democratic values and practices.

The military has not achieved this separation on its own; civilian society has contributed to the military's isolation. A few generations ago, a nation at war acted like a nation at war. In a 1950 speech at the outset of the Korean War, President Truman explained the need for national sacrifice: "As an additional safeguard against inflation, and to help finance our defense needs, it will be necessary to make substantial increases in taxes."[72] Those days are behind us. As military historian Adrian Lewis has written, "The most significant transformation in the American conduct of war since World War II and the invention of the atomic bomb was not technological, but cultural, social, and political—the removal of the American people from the conduct of war."[73]

Weeks after the September 11 attacks, President George W. Bush implored Americans to vacation at Disney World and, infamously, to go shopping.[74] The president never asked the public to make any sacrifice in the way he asked the soldiers. Unlike Truman, who expected everyone to contribute, Bush successfully pushed large income tax cuts through Congress during the wars, which made it easier for him to sell military engagements to the public.

Andrew Bacevich points to a modern culture where wars like those in Afghanistan and Iraq "almost immediately became and thereafter remained a third-person-plural enterprise: *they* fought while *we* watched, uninvolved and seemingly unaffected. The fighting *they* were American soldiers, members of an institution that already existed at a considerable remove from the rest of society."[75]

This separation from mainstream society is not something the military shies away from or even denies. To the contrary, it often relies on this separation as a basis for resistance to civilian oversight. In a 2011 speech to the graduating class of West Point cadets, Admiral Mike Mullen, at the time the chairman of the Joint Chiefs, said of civilians, "I fear they do not know us. I fear they do not comprehend the full weight of the burden we carry or the price we pay when we return from battle."[76] According to commentator Rosa Brooks, "The *Military Times'* 2012 annual survey found that more than 75 percent of all active duty personnel and reservists believe 'The military community has little in common with the rest of the country and most civilians do not understand the military.'"[77]

To understand the dangers of the separation between the military and civilian societies, one must first consider the beginning of the assembly line, namely the military academies for the U.S. Army, Air Force, Navy, and Marines. These are the institutions where almost all of the top generals and admirals are educated and where, during their careers, they return to teach young students to think as they do. These future officers will also return to teach the same lessons and to model the same behavior before they are one day interred at the academies' cemeteries, which abut the classrooms where they began their careers.

CHAPTER 1

The Origins of the Separate World

Despite many external enemies, it is telling that America's founders were fearful of the threat posed by a standing army. The Founding Fathers "claimed an aversion to war and military power,"[1] and worried that a standing army could destroy democracy by enforcing the edicts of potential despots, consuming the nation's resources, and threatening peace by making war an easier option for politicians. In the Declaration of Independence, Thomas Jefferson and other patriots complained about the king of Britain's "Standing Armies without the Consent of our legislatures," and rendering "the Military independent of and superior to the Civil Power." It can be argued that the very rationale for the United States was freedom from autonomous military power.

Although the military today often receives uncritical adulation, this was not always the case. The colonists viewed armies as "nurseries of vice" and "the grand engine of despotism." A professional army is "always dangerous to the Liberties of the People," wrote famed rabble-rouser Samuel Adams in 1776.[2] At the Constitutional Convention in 1787, James Madison warned, "Oppressors can tyrannize only when they achieve a standing army, an enslaved press, and a disarmed populace."[3]

The fear of an army was rooted in the colonists' experience with the British. In 1770, two thousand British troops were stationed in Boston to enforce the king's taxation. The king's grant of a monopoly on the sale of tea to the East India Company led to the Boston Massacre three year later.[4] When George Washington became president in April of 1789, the Founders' aversion to armed authority resulted in an army of only several dozen soldiers who guarded munitions at West Point and Fort Pitt, in Pennsylvania, as well as 700 militia men who could be called on to protect America from Indians and the British.[5] From 1789 through 1939, with the exception of the years the United States fought the Civil War, the Spanish-American War, and World War I, the number of active-duty military personnel was small, befitting a nation fearful of its own army: 7,108 personnel in 1801; 20,699 in 1851; 112,322 in 1901; and 334,473 in 1939.[6] The number of active-duty personnel peaked at over 12 million in 1945.

Despite their deep differences, both Federalists and Anti-Federalists in early America were suspicious of an army for reasons that are germane today: a military can become a power center of its own, a separate sovereign not only at its bases in foreign nations but also within a constitutional government. Military officers' status, identity, and livelihoods depend on an authoritarian military ethos rather than on democracy. Military generals acquire more of everything when the nation is at war.

THE CONTINUED SEPARATION

Isolated soldiers may become more loyal to each other than to the Constitution. James Madison, although a proponent of a strong central government, argued that "the means of defense against foreign danger, have been always the instruments of tyranny at home ... Throughout all Europe, the armies kept up under the pretext of defending, have enslaved the people."[7]

As the Cold War accelerated following World War II, the U.S. military resumed its expeditionary nature on a grander scale.[8] Rationalized as a deterrent to the Soviets, an expedient military became a normal extension of U.S. domestic politics and foreign policy. Up to that point in history, the military had increased in size in response to emergencies, like the Civil War and the world wars, but now it was expanding as a matter of course. The number of active service members has ranged from 1 to 3.6 million every year since 1945, with spikes during the Korean and Vietnam War eras.[9] A larger and richer, and more independent, military has led to nearly ceaseless interventions. A 1999 report from the Congressional Research Service cited "hundreds of instances in which the United States has used its armed forces abroad."[10]

As the State Department has been weakened—a process that has sped up during the Trump administration—the military has assumed a role once filled by diplomats abroad. Journalist Ronan Farrow, in his 2018 book *War on Peace*, detailed the decline of professional diplomacy: "From Mogadishu to Damascus to Islamabad, the United States cast civilian dialogue to the side, replacing the tools of diplomacy with direct, tactical deals between our military and foreign forces."[11] The trend continued, as Farrow explained: "At home, White Houses filled with generals . . . uniformed officers [who] increasingly handled the negotiation, economic reconstruction, and infrastructure development for which we once had a devoted body of trained specialists. As a result, a different set of relationships has come to form the bedrock of American foreign policy. Where civilians are not empowered to negotiate, military-to-military dealings still flourish."[12]

With over three hundred military incursions from 1798 to 2017 "for other than normal peacetime purposes,"[13] the U.S. military has become possibly the largest employer in the world, now with 2.15 million service personnel (active and reserve) and over 730,000 civilians.[14] This does not include its vast network of private military contractors throughout America and the world, a behemoth that President Dwight D. Eisenhower in 1961 famously labeled "the military-industrial complex."

The U.S. military now operates a gigantic standing army (and navy and air force) on all continents, at nearly five thousand locations or sites in 160 to 170 nations.[15] This presence enables it to engage in nearly perpetual combat operations throughout the world. From just 2003 to 2019, U.S. military personnel died in seventy different countries in combat and training exercises, according to the Congressional Research Service.[16] Article I of the Constitution authorizes a declaration of war, but Congress has not issued one since 1942. Six of the eighteen congressional authorities in Article I relate specifically to Congress's control over the military. This expansive constitutional authority has not prevented presidents from urging the nation toward war. It has not limited how the generals run wars on behalf of presidents. It has not shortened the duration of wars.

As President Obama's chief of staff Bill Daley once bemoaned, getting things done domestically is difficult because "you must go to Congress," but actually "it is very easy to go to war."[17] In relinquishing control of the military, Congress passed vague, open-ended resolutions that authorized presidents to initiate or continue military actions in Vietnam, Afghanistan, and Iraq. In 1971 Congress repealed its Vietnam War resolution, but Richard Nixon disregarded the repeal and continued the war. The resolutions become statutes, just another federal law, when the presidents sign them. The practical effects of the resolutions are little different from those of declarations of war, but unlike declarations, the softer-sounding resolutions do not signal to Americans or the world that hundreds of thousands (Iraq) or millions (Korea and Vietnam) of people are about to die.

These American military actions turned into long wars with no expiration dates. It is chilling to compare Madison's explanation of his fear of a standing army with the conditions that have come to pass today: "Of all the enemies to public liberty war is, perhaps, the most to be dreaded, because it comprises and develops the germ of every other. War is the parent of armies . . . The same malignant aspect in republicanism may be traced in the inequality of fortunes, and the opportunities of fraud, growing out of a state of war, and in the degeneracy of manners and of morals engendered by both. *No nation could preserve its freedom in the midst of continual warfare*" (emphasis mine).[18]

In July 2018, detainees at Guantanamo Bay who had been imprisoned by the U.S. military without trial for sixteen years demanded a trial or resettlement overseas. The federal judge hearing the case referred to the Hundred Years' War in Europe in the Middle Ages and asked a Trump administration lawyer if the military possessed the authority to hold someone for one hundred years. "We could hold them for 100 years if the conflict lasted 100 years," responded the government's lawyer, who cited the continuing war in Afghanistan. "You cannot tell when hostilities end until they have ended."[19]

GOING THROUGH THE MOTIONS

West Point represents two hundred years of tradition unhampered by progress.

—Colonel Joseph Adamczyk

In many ways, the military's separate world begins at the United States Military Academy at West Point, an hour's drive north of New York City. In examining any institution, one of the significant challenges is to describe how practices and attitudes lay the foundation for important decisions and actions in the future. The inquiry can be difficult because closed institutions defend and hide their inner values beneath traditions and ceremonies. At West Point, army officers who have been ordered to preside at funerals for veterans, for example, practice folding the flag and handing it to grieving families, and then practice how to deceive the families at the height of their mourning, during the playing of "Taps."

The Pentagon, despite employing over 6,500 soldiers in 137 military bands at a cost of $437 million a year, does not have enough musicians to meet the requests of the families of veterans.[20] As a workaround, the military outfits the funeral officers with realistic-looking bugles that contain concealed digital recordings. At the funerals, the officers secretly activate the recordings and then inhale, extend their bellies, puff their cheeks, and blow, pretending to be riffing a melodious and heartfelt version of "Taps" for the families.

At one funeral, a family member told an officer that his playing of "Taps" was "beautiful."

The officer smiled and accepted the accolades. "The only thing I could say was 'thanks.' I just didn't want to get caught," he said.

The bugle deceit is a curious practice because West Point's most fundamental rule is that "a cadet will not lie, cheat, steal, or tolerate those who do." While the bugle fabrication doesn't seem all that monumental, why would the military not tell the truth? The families would understand that a recording instead of a soldier-musician playing "Taps" at the funerals might mean more support for soldiers serving now on the ground somewhere in the world. Though families know that real musicians and bugles are playing at the funerals of deceased generals, the presence of an officer in a dress uniform expressing the thanks of a grateful nation, even if he plays "Taps" on a recording device, would still mean everything to them. The military's bugle fabrication is designed to comfort grieving Americans and is not a gross injustice. But it is an apt metaphor of the world inside the military and at West Point because the deceit, directed toward fellow Americans, is a trickle in a tidal wave, one small surge of dishonesty that spreads outward to all corners of the military establishment.

In September 2015, General Vincent Brooks traveled from Hawaii, where he commanded U.S. forces in the Pacific and Asia, to celebrate his thirty-five-year class reunion at West Point. Addressing military faculty members late one afternoon in a building with glass walls high atop a granite palisade, the black Hudson River and the green highlands behind him, Brooks appeared to the lower-ranking officers in front of him to meld with nature and reign above them. "West Point is the exemplar," Brooks told the officers. "You are an exemplar around the world."

A STREAM THROUGH HISTORY

America's wars are first won and lost at West Point. More than seventy-six thousand men and women have graduated from the academy since it produced its first graduate in 1802. It is a remarkably insular place, with a culture and value system all its own. As the first civilian promoted to professor of law at West Point, in 2004, I have been in a unique position to get a look at what goes on there, to see what kind of people America is sending out into the world, with what kind of character and values, and with what education and training.

Looking back at the school's history, one begins to understand why it continues to be treated as a noble and near faultless institution, even as the evidence pours in against it. West Point is a child of America's vaunted founding, associated with the nation's proclaimed independence and revolutionary victory, and first conceived by a beloved founding father. Though many other poisonous things from America's adolescence have fallen away—the haloed status of that particular founding father among them—West Point's reputation remains resilient.

West Point was one of the most important redoubts during the Revolutionary War and is America's longest continuously running military reservation. It was commanded in 1780 by famed traitor Benedict Arnold, who plotted to surrender the fort to the British. Arnold's coconspirator, a British major named John Andre, was captured in civilian clothes with the architectural plans to West Point, which he had received from Arnold. George Washington and his staff charged Andre with espionage, gave him a short trial, and then hanged him. Arnold, however, escaped to Virginia and then to Britain, where he lived out the remainder of his life.

In 1802, West Point was founded as an engineering school by President Thomas Jefferson.[21] It remains the place from which almost all of America's top generals are educated and spend the most formative years of their lives.[22]

The Civil War alone is a prime example of how thoroughly West Point runs through the American military's bloodstream. Jefferson Davis (Class of 1828) was president of the Confederacy. Robert E. Lee, considered by some modern historians to be a mediocre general,[23] graduated from West Point the next year and later served as West Point's superintendent. Stonewall Jackson, the Confederacy's other leading general, graduated from West Point in 1846. An 1838 graduate, P. G. T. Beauregard, was the superintendent briefly in 1861 and became the first general officer (brigadier) for the South in the Civil War. He commanded the Confederate forces that started the war by firing at the U.S. Army post at Fort Sumter, in South Carolina, in April 1861.

In fact, nearly all the prominent generals for the North and the South were West Point graduates, including Ulysses S. Grant (Class of 1843), William Tecumseh Sherman (Class of 1840), and Abner Doubleday (Class of 1842). The graduates' influence on America expanded significantly during that defining point in American history.

"The Civil War was a West Point war," said Mark Greenbaum, writing in the *New York Times*:

> West Point graduates dominated the general staff from Fort Sumter to Appomattox. Out of the approximately 560 Union generals to serve during the war, about 220 were West Point graduates (in the Confederacy, the ratio was a little lower but still significant, 140 out of 400). Given how rapidly and large the two armies grew, the dominance by West Point graduates of the top leadership positions is striking . . . The military's thinking at the outset of the Civil War was perhaps best delineated by Confederate Gen. Richard Ewell (Class of 1840) who purportedly noted that West Point "taught officers of the 'old army' everything they needed to know about commanding a company of fifty dragoons on the western plains against the Cheyenne Indians, but nothing else."[24]

Southern officers would long have an outsize influence at West Point. The academy would respond to the civil rights movement of the 1960s by creating Lee Barracks, named for the Confederate general, and commemorating other Confederate officers. In 2001 West Point dedicated Reconciliation Plaza, a walkway in front of Lee Barracks and Grant Hall, to commemorate graduates who died in wars, with a particular focus on the Civil War and Vietnam War.[25] Reconciliation Plaza makes no mention of slavery and provides equal billing to Union and Confederate officers. The Civil War is treated there like an all-star game, where both sides represent the best America had to offer.

After the Civil War, in the late nineteenth and early twentieth centuries, West Point graduated George Armstrong Custer, Douglas MacArthur, and Omar Bradley. In World War I, General John Pershing (Class of 1886) commanded the American Expeditionary Force. In World War II, General Dwight Eisenhower (Class of 1915) was the Supreme Allied Commander. He is the last general who graduated from West Point to win a war.

In many respects, after World War II, the modern world raced past West Point, as well as the U.S. Naval Academy, which was founded in 1845.[26] Bruce Fleming, a professor at the Naval Academy, wrote in 2010, "The service academies are holdovers from the 19th century, when they were virtually the only avenue for producing an officer corps for the nation's military and when such top-down institutions were taken for granted. But the world has changed, which the academies don't seem to have noticed, or to have drawn any conclusions from."[27]

Much of West Point's anachronistic culture and operations today, including its educational curriculum, can be traced to the insularity, isolation, and near complete separation from American society that is promoted there. It is arguably one of the most consequential fraternities in the world, yet one in which membership is largely limited to West Point graduates. From 1812 to 2020, for example, a span of 208 years, of the 150 military officers who have served as superintendent (58 of 58), commandant (74 of 78), and dean (13 of 14), the top three positions, 145 of them, or almost 97 percent, have been graduates of West Point.[28] All but three have been white males.

DRAGGED RELUCTANTLY INTO THE FUTURE

In the early 1990s senators John Glenn (D-OH) and Sam Nunn (D-GA) became concerned with West Point's insularity and inflexibility and pressed the army to hire civilian professors, which it began to do a few years later. Until that time, with the exception of a few specialist instructors in foreign languages and physical education, all the instructors had been military officers. The civilians at West Point today are the only instructors to have worked outside the army and now comprise about 25 percent of the faculty. However, many of those professors are actually retired military officers who were hired by the military administrators, their friends. Over the years, those military administrators have worked diligently and effectively to marginalize and control the civilians and the new ideas they offer. To the administrators, there is even a hierarchy among the civilian professors, with the retired army officers at the top.

Change and reform could, conceivably, come from the generals and colonels who, over the generations, have been superintendents, deans, and department heads. They could effortlessly propose statutory changes or establish regulations that would open their positions to those who are not army officers. They could provide professors with job security comparable to that in higher education, which would promote freedom of speech and professionalism. Instead, they tell the professors that a contract implies distrust, and as long as you're doing a good job, it shouldn't be a concern. The culture itself is one that resists change. Perhaps most tellingly, no civilians, whether at West Point or from any place in the country, are even permitted to apply for the positions of superintendent, dean, and department head. With rules in place preventing any civilian authority or leadership, it's easy to see how entrenched the old culture has become.

This is, of course, the intention of the military administrators. The hierarchy and attendant subservience are baked into daily living. Many of the civilian professors feel compelled to address the superintendent and dean, as well as department heads, who almost always have far less professional experience, as "sir" or "ma'am," just like military officers of lower rank.

When I arrived at West Point in June 2000, it was my general impression that the academy was a top institution, one that had democratized and modernized by opening its classrooms to civilian faculty. I thought of it as an opportunity, a step toward progress in which I wanted to participate. It was my belief that the academy's wanton favoritism and discrimination were falling away, making room for an open meritocracy. Within hours of arriving, I realized that it was not true, that something was not right at West Point.

On that first day, three new military instructors, a captain and two lieutenant colonels, and I met with the head of the law department, Colonel Patrick Finnegan (Class of '71), who had been one of the most respected lawyers in the army's Judge Advocate General's (JAG) Corps. In a brief introduction, Finnegan, who was most responsible for hiring me, told us that we all had the freedom to speak. We were granted "academic freedom," he said, but were prohibited from telling lawyer jokes because he didn't like those kinds of jokes.

As part of a tour of the campus, Finnegan took us to the Cadet Store, which sold trinkets, candy, clothes, and paper goods, all emblazoned with West Point's name, just like any store on any college campus in America. The five of us filed casually through the turnstiles. I was the only member of our group in civilian attire, a business suit, while Finnegan and the other new teachers were in military uniform. After a few whispers among the store's employees, we were met by the manager, who put her hand up like a stop sign. Finnegan and the other officers, she explained, were allowed inside the store, but I, a civilian, was not.

"We're not buying anything," Finnegan protested on my behalf, but it was to no avail. Despite the all-civilian workforce, the manager reiterated the rule: civilians were not allowed inside the store, even to view the merchandise. One could wonder about the practical reason for this rule; that the store would not take civilians' money seems counterintuitive. The real reason is that the segregated store was another accouterment of an exclusionary club.

I worked around these kinds of issues (e.g., free flu immunizations for military, but not civilian, personnel; two-semester research sabbaticals at full pay for military instructors and only one semester for civilian instructors) and taught criminal law and constitutional and military law, courses in which I emphasize why the rule of law should be preeminent, above the decrees of presidents and the orders of high-ranking military officers. (All the students at the military academies are undergraduates.) Sadly, as we will see, some of the greatest errors in U.S. history occurred when officers and presidents held themselves above the law. My personal experience has shown how officers disregard law in favor of loyalty.

In 2005 Finnegan became the academic dean of West Point, a position that is accompanied by a military promotion to brigadier general. Colonel Maritza Sáenz Ryan, who had been Finnegan's deputy, then became head of the department. I believe that most of the officers feared Ryan, and she seemed to embrace the control she had over them. On many days, one or both of her two top aides, full colonels, rode the elevator with her and escorted her to her car, parked in a reserved space about a hundred feet from the exit door. Once in a meeting with Ryan present, one of the car-walking colonels said, "Commander. Commander. She's in charge . . . When Colonel Ryan comes into my office I stand up."

Ryan told me once that, except for teaching classes, every faculty member should be in his office every day from 9:00 A.M. to 5:00 P.M. The reason, she said, was so she could check on us to be sure we were safe in case of a terrorist attack or a nuclear accident at the Indian Point Energy Center, over twenty miles away. These were clumsy pretexts she used to try to exert control and enhance her status. I told Ryan that the nine-to-five office rule was unfair because it did not comport with the more flexible standards in the faculty manual, much of which I had drafted while on a committee. Ryan reported me to Finnegan, who, as dean, had approved the faculty manual. However, in a meeting attended by me, Ryan, Finnegan, and his administrative assistant, Finnegan said that the interpretation of the rule was actually up to the discretion of the department head.

I reminded Finnegan that his favorite civilian professor, who had received acclaim for writing a book romanticizing West Point and the military, came to West Point every other day. Finnegan explained to me how everybody is different. He and Ryan eventually backed down. It seemed to me that Finnegan believed Ryan was wrong, but he still supported her, a fellow officer, over an outsider.

Immediately prior to coming to West Point, most of the military officers who become temporary teachers attend graduate school for a year or two. Many of the army lawyers who are headed for the law department obtain a master's degree in law (LL.M.) prior to beginning their teaching stints. The army pays for all the officers' tuition, salaries, and benefits, while also fully supporting their families. One officer left West Point for parts of two days every week to teach at a college that paid him an additional $20,000.

Another time, the officer was allowed to leave West Point for a year to study for the LL.M. degree.

In March 2011, I asked Ryan to relieve me from one course in the fall semester so that I could study for the LL.M. degree. (Unlike the military faculty, I had to pay my own tuition.) Ryan refused, though there was no logical reason for her refusal. Many new instructors would have gladly wanted the experience of teaching a new course; alternatively, I could have taught an additional course the following semester.

In April, I went up the chain of command and complained about Ryan to the new dean, Brigadier General Tim Trainor, Ryan's longtime colleague. I believed West Point engaged in favoritism, a prohibited personnel practice under federal law, to the benefit not only of military faculty but also of former officers who, after retirement or resignation, were (and are) hired by West Point to become civilian professors or administrators. Trainor commissioned an "investigation," headed by his and Ryan's colleague, Colonel Rick Kerin. Unsurprisingly, in August 2011 Kerin found that Ryan had done nothing wrong. Trainor rejected my complaint.

During and after the investigation, Ryan's retaliation became overt. She began disparaging me in writing and in front of others. Then, without reason, she suddenly changed my teaching schedule, which had given me late classes every other day for seven years.[29] Under the new schedule, I was required to teach early classes every day, making it almost impossible for me to study for the LL.M. degree. To those who work in academia, this kind of change is significant. Success in the profession is heavily dependent on research and writing, which require flexible schedules and uninterrupted periods of work. A teacher's schedule can literally make or break a career. (I ended up completing the LL.M. degree at Columbia Law School by taking night classes.)

Ryan's schedule change constituted illegal retaliation, a violation of federal law. To prove this, I filed a complaint with the U.S. Merit Systems Protection Board. This is the route that most federal employees must take when they claim they've been adversely affected by a job action. During the litigation, before an administrative judge, I determined that West Point officials were withholding documents, which they continued to do, despite my discovery requests. The judge ordered West Point's lawyers to hand over what turned out to be a twenty-nine-page memorandum written by Ryan, in which she baselessly and falsely disparaged me personally and professionally.

After a hearing in 2012, the federal administrative judge concluded that I was a whistleblower, siding with me and finding retaliation. In her decision, the judge gave short shrift to Ryan's credibility.[30] "Colonel Ryan made various negative statements about the appellant [Bakken]—statements which were wholly inconsistent with what she and [her deputy] had written in the appellant's performance evaluations,"[31] she wrote, and "Colonel Ryan testified that she was planning to change the schedule since she became the department chairperson in 2006. However, she could not give a coherent explanation as to why it took until 2011 to implement the change."[32]

The judge rescinded Ryan's schedule change and ordered West Point to pay my legal fees.[33] The army inspector general then investigated the actions—or lack of actions—of the superintendent of West Point, Lieutenant General David Huntoon, and concluded that he should have disciplined Ryan.[34] In a prior investigation, the Pentagon inspector general had concluded that Huntoon misused federal employees at West Point. Huntoon and Ryan retired in 2013 and 2015, and both received commendations from the army. It was the next superintendent, Lieutenant General Robert Caslen, who presided over Ryan's retirement ceremony, where he, on behalf of the army, advanced her to brigadier general. In yet another investigation, the Pentagon inspector general had found that Caslen committed an ethics violation (religious proselyting in uniform) when he worked as a brigadier general at the Pentagon.

Although I won the case, this experience led me to search for larger patterns across the military culture as a whole. A separate society depends on retaliation to coerce people into silence and maintain a corrupt order. The retaliation ensures that the highest virtue is "taking care of our own," to the detriment of everyone and everything else. What initially seemed difficult—identifying the thinking and practices at the academies and in the military that contribute to failure—became more obvious. The kinds of violence used by the cadets at the military academies, for example, especially sexual assault, can be observed in soldiers' abuse and killing of innocent civilians in all the wars.

Almost everyone knows the abuse is illegal, and that most people will not arbitrarily hurt others. This indicates that there is a condition within the military that leads soldiers to abuse other people, or that some who join the military are prone to abuse. When they feel they've lost control, officers especially, because they're the enforcers of loyalty, will try to hurt whomever they can label as a scapegoat or characterize as a threat. This is part of the American military ethos.

THE MOST SHAMEFUL EPISODE

The danger in arguing that law can protect individuals and democracy from the military's overreaching is that law can be co-opted to provide a cloak for abuse and immunity to the abusers. In Korea, Vietnam, Afghanistan, and Iraq, for instance, the U.S. military bombed the enemy relentlessly from the air. (Only Iraq had a semblance of an air force.) The military claimed that any civilian deaths were unavoidable and not violations of the laws of war. Even if this were true, the excessive bombing boomeranged. The North Koreans responded by developing atomic bombs and missiles capable of carrying them to the United States.

Citizens enable such counterproductive strategies when they defer important decisions to generals. Even former secretary of defense Donald Rumsfeld, as controlling a civilian leader as the military has known, admitted that there was only "a thin layer of civilian control" over the military.[35] How thin that layer is can be illustrated by one of the most shameful episodes in America's history.

During World War II, U.S. Army general John L. DeWitt was the military commander for the United States' West Coast. On February 14, 1942, he issued a report, *Japanese Evacuation from the West Coast*, which the army and the Roosevelt administration used to intern 120,000 Japanese Americans who had been born in the United States. Citing no evidence of sabotage or espionage, DeWitt justified the incarceration of innocent Americans through blatant racism: "The Japanese race is an enemy race and while many second and third generation Japanese born on United States soil, possessed of United States citizenship, have become Americanized, the racial strains are undiluted . . . There are indications that these [Japanese Americans] are organized and ready for concerted action at a favorable opportunity. The very fact that no sabotage has taken place to date is a disturbing and confirming indication that such action will be taken."[36] General DeWitt's reasoning, of course, was preposterous, arguing that innocence indicates future guilt. Judicial and societal deference to this kind of backward thinking because it comes from the military often permits the military to do just about anything it wants.

The internment of the Japanese Americans was followed by one of the most disturbing decisions in the Supreme Court's checkered history. In 1944, in *Korematsu v. U.S.*, a Japanese American challenged his criminal conviction for not leaving a military exclusion zone in California. In its decision upholding the conviction, the court laid the groundwork for providing almost unlimited deference to the military. *Korematsu* foreshadowed the diminution of constitutional rights for military personnel in *Parker v. Levy*, in 1974. In *Korematsu*, the court concluded that it "could not reject" the military's determination that it was unable to identify disloyal Americans. Finding a threat where none existed, the military asked for the authority to imprison Americans, and the civilian government and the court acquiesced. This pattern would arise again and again over the next seventy-five years as the legislative branch relinquished more of its war powers and the executive branch proved all too willing to give the military the authority it wanted.

GROWING THE BEAST

Since World War II, the U.S. "standing army" has ballooned and spread, slowly becoming a sovereign force of its own, far beyond what any civilian command can control—even if it wanted to. As its size and power have grown, the military's fortunes have become entangled with all kinds of outside forces, including big business and politics. In 1951 President Truman mustered the political will to relieve the incompetent and bombastic MacArthur from command in Korea, but this was "probably the last classic assertion of the constitutional principle that the president and the civilians appointed by him control the military," according to Chalmers Johnson.[37] Nevertheless, Truman was still subservient to another growing force at work: military as business.

Truman's successor, Dwight Eisenhower, was in a unique position, having led both the military and civilian government. He recognized the growing problem of business's influence on military decisions. Three days before he relinquished the presidency, when he was answerable to no one, he finally spoke up. In his farewell address, he warned against this dangerous melding of the military and big business, saying it represented a domestic threat to peace: "This conjunction of an immense military establishment and a large arms industry is new in the American experience. The total influence—economic, political, even spiritual—is felt in every city, every State house, every office of the Federal government . . . In the councils of government, we must guard against the acquisition of unwarranted influence, whether sought or unsought, by the military industrial complex. The potential for the disastrous rise of misplaced power exists and will persist."[38] Eisenhower understood the dangerous incentive structure at work: as long as war remains profitable for large and powerful organizations—which are free to lobby, make campaign contributions, and otherwise influence policy—there will always be forces trying to instigate, support, or perpetuate military conflict.

Even without wars, corporations profit handsomely through building fearsome weapons in response to a U.S. military strategy and foreign policy of deterrence. The irony is that deterrence—which is enforced through the most advanced technology and weapons money can buy—provides relatively little bang for the buck. America's battlefield enemies of the last seventy-five years—North Koreans, Chinese, Vietnamese, Taliban, ISIS, and al-Qaeda—could not be defeated with superior weaponry. Instead the United States needed superior strategy, which was not forthcoming. Nonetheless, in recent decades, huge amounts of money have shifted from the taxpayers to the Pentagon and then to the corporations, whose high-tech tentacles stretch throughout the entire economy.

The military-industrial complex is an incredibly sophisticated world that makes powerful people a lot of money and which is exceedingly difficult to track, making effective oversight and inquiry near impossible. The experts are often the generals and admirals who approve the contracts with the weapons companies. Then they retire and, while still acting as civilian advisors for the Pentagon, take jobs within the industry, a revolving door that incentivizes the purchase and use of weapons.[39] As a 2010 *Boston Globe* report explained, "such apparent conflicts are a routine fact of life at the lucrative nexus between the defense procurement system, which spends hundreds of billions of dollars a year, and the industry that feasts on those riches. And almost nothing is ever done about it."[40]

In the twenty-first century, the military costs over $700 billion a year, and its budget is 3 to 4 percent of the United States' gross domestic product (GDP).[41] By way of comparison, the budget for the National Cancer Institute is only about $5 billion per year,[42] when over 609,000 people in the United States die from cancer each year.[43] Dina Rasor, who founded what is now the Project on Government Oversight, explains that "after these high-ranking generals retire with generous pensions, many of them still seek out lucrative jobs with defense contractors, either as employees or as consultants. This is furthering the corruption of the weapons procurement budget as they work to subtly influence the military brass who used to be at a rank lower than them . . . This is disastrous for the troops below these generals and breeds a cynicism to any of the honest officers below them and encourages others to follow in their footsteps."[44]

The burgeoning cost of the military and the ballooning profits for defense contractors create priorities that adversely impact military tactics, strategy, and the overall prosecution of wars. The U.S. armed forces spend lavishly on hardware, and they have a vested interest in using it. But what they really need is better intellectual software, notably deep learning among officers and a culture that promotes a freedom to speak up and disagree. As veteran war reporter James McCartney writes in *America's War Machine: Vested Interests, Endless Conflicts*, "The record of the last twenty-plus years [through 2015] strongly suggests that the Cold War produced economic and political forces that today are beyond our control, creating a militaristic culture and institutions, many parts of which have vested interests in war."[45]

Nearly sixty years after Eisenhower first coined the term, the influence of the military-industrial complex became even more embedded and influential with the 2010 Supreme Court decision in *Citizens United*. The court determined that corporations have a First Amendment right to speak and, therefore, to spend unlimited amounts of money on political advocacy. In a recent article, "The Tragedy of the American Military," James Fallows rightly asked, "Why does civilian technology grow ever cheaper and more reliable while military technology does the opposite?"[46] The underlying reason is not complicated. There's an entire industry that depends on the generals deciding to choose and use bigger and more expensive weapons.

The arms industry is pervasive, and expert at exerting its soft power across the country. As James McCartney writes, "It is fair to suggest that right-wing ideologues with close ties to military contractors may be relied upon to find an enemy."[47] Lockheed Martin, for instance, is a giant defense contractor and major contributor to the Heritage Foundation, which aggressively lobbied the Pentagon and Congress in 2009 not to curtail funding for Lockheed's F-22 Raptor fighter jet.[48] Before canceling the F-22 in 2012, the Pentagon spent a total of $67.3 billion for 188 planes. Still in service, the F-22 has never been used in air-to-air combat. The Pentagon replaced the F-22 with the F-35 program, which will cost "more than $1 trillion during its 60-year lifespan," according to a 2019 *New York Times* report.[49]

A few Russian cyber agents did more to destabilize the 2016 presidential election and American democracy than all the weapons of the Cold War put together, and the U.S. military was helpless to stop them. It was stuck in a different mode of thinking, one that worked seventy-five years ago. As McCartney noted, "We are building weapons to fight enemies that do not exist."[50]

Even President Eisenhower would be surprised at the ingenuity of today's military-industrial complex, which targets its customers early, while they're still students at West Point. The scene on game day at Michie Stadium, which seats thirty-eight thousand for football games, is exhibit A. Reminiscent of a huge discotheque from the 1970s, with garish multi-colored neon corporate banners in the end zones and pulsating advertisements on the mega television screen (when it's not broken), the football games are a giant advertisement for the arms industry. The logos of major defense contractors adorn every area inside the stadium.

The generals who will authorize billions of dollars of weapons purchases from Lockheed Martin, Boeing, Northrop Grumman, and Jeep enjoy the game in luxury suites or on the field. Other sponsors have included Exxon-Mobil and General Dynamics, which makes aerospace and combat vehicles and is one of the many corporate sponsors of one of the most important days of the academic year, Projects Day, when the seniors present their capstone projects to the younger cadets, faculty members, and other corporate titans. Raytheon and General Electric are sponsors. One government contractor, Great Lakes Systems and Technology, exclaims, "GLS&T, as a US Army . . . prime contractor . . . participated in West Point cadet project day . . . USMA is one of six GLS&T partners currently advancing . . . software for logistics automation."[51] This transactional insider relationship is designed to influence the current generals and the college students who will one day take their place.

As the action unfolds on the gridiron, after every West Point (Army) first down, the public-address announcer howls, "Another . . . Army . . ."

The announcer conditions the cadets, the future generals, to howl with him for several seconds, "First Down!"

After the roar and glee dissipate into silence before the next play, the announcer repeats happily, "Brought to you by EMCOR!"

A major defense and government contractor, EMCOR and its CEO, Anthony J. Guzzi (Class of '86), understand that sponsorship of first downs is an opportunity to give something back to the nation. Meanwhile the nation and its current and future military leaders are expected to give a lot more back to EMCOR.

WAR AND THE BALLOT BOX

As the Vietnam War illustrated all too clearly, military leaders who are the first to obtain on-the-ground information are free to conceal or reveal facts to buttress their positions. This gives them the ability to control perception of the war's progress. But the military, where dissenters are ostracized and punished, is not structured to communicate even basic truths. We need only to examine how Lyndon Johnson sunk his entire presidency into the quagmire of Vietnam to see how dangerous that problem has been—and continues to be.

As the war in Southeast Asia dragged on and began to eat away at his presidency, Johnson felt huge pressure from the public, indeed from the eyes of history. As the Pentagon Papers would reveal, John McNaughton, Defense Secretary Robert McNamara's top assistant, admitted that "70%" of the reason to stay in Vietnam was "To avoid a humiliating U.S. defeat."[52] Johnson was in too deep and had committed too much to lose the war. His military advisors and generals (specifically Maxwell Taylor and William Westmoreland) continually lied to him—lies that Johnson was all too willing to believe and amplify—to make victory seem possible. They just needed to keep the money and soldiers flowing into Vietnam until America eventually won.

With his administration under constant criticism, Johnson decided not to run for re-election. By 1969, when he left office, three hundred Americans were dying each week in Vietnam.[53] Richard Nixon claimed publicly and privately before he was inaugurated, "I'm going to stop the war. Fast. I mean it."[54] But as president he would go on to expand it. Four years later, in 1973, American forces left Vietnam after failure. When Saigon fell in 1975, the entire American excursion in Vietnam proved to be a colossal waste of human life, time, and money.

"The war was a lie from the first," wrote journalist Robert Scheer in 2011. "It never had anything to do with the freedom of the Vietnamese (we installed one tyrant after another in power), but instead had to do with our irrational Cold War obsession with 'international communism.'"

The presidents and their generals, if they could see what was happening, did not report truthfully to the public what they saw. "Johnson and Nixon make it quite clear on their White House tapes," Scheer continued, "that the mindless killing, McNamara's infamous body count, was about domestic politics and never security."[55] Vietnam is the ultimate lesson in what happens when autonomous generals and politically minded leaders become detached from the leavening effects of American society.

Johnson's and Nixon's political calculus and their military leaders' failure to speak truthfully had grave and long-lasting consequences. "When presidents and generals speak clearly to one another," writes Tom Ricks in *The Generals*, "in an atmosphere of candor and trust, wars tend to be fought more effectively than when officials mislead one another or simply do not deal among themselves in a straightforward manner."[56] What's most shocking about the debacle in Vietnam is that those lessons were never learned or internalized within the military.

Right out of the gate, the Iraq War was marred by political motivations, with some believing that the war itself was part of George Bush's plan to win a second term in 2004.[57] Despite the politics, the secretary of state,

Colin Powell, single-handedly could have stopped a war. A former army colonel, Lawrence Wilkerson, was Powell's chief of staff at the State Department. Wilkerson described a meeting prior to Powell's monumental February 5, 2003, speech at the United Nations. Wilkerson said that Powell "walked over to the window and said 'I wonder what will happen when we put 500,000 troops into Iraq and . . . [comb] the country from one end to the other and find nothing.'" Wilkerson continued, "Though neither Powell nor anyone else in the State Department team intentionally lied, we did participate in a hoax."[58] It's a strange word choice—*hoax*, which implies something inconsequential, the very opposite of what Powell and Co. did.

A career military man, Powell was doing what his superiors needed him to do—a habit that we need not wonder where he learned. In 2004, as the insurgency in Iraq gained strength, both the military and civilian command continued to sell the lie: the military sold it to the Bush administration, which sold it to the public. As Frank Rich memorably posited, "The problem with Bush was not that he was stupid but that he thought everyone else was stupid."[59]

There was no insurgency in 2004 because there couldn't be: it was an election year. With the assistance of the military, the administration cooked the books in Iraq, and eventually in Afghanistan as well. In May 2004 Bush said the "daily life" of Afghans was improving.[60] Three months later, he said, "And as a result of the United States military, [the] Taliban is no longer in existence."[61]

Of course, the wars did not end anytime soon, as civilian and military leaders pretended. In 2018 the Taliban controlled 59 districts in Afghanistan, the government controlled 229, and 119 were up for grabs. Additional U.S. troops did not turn the tide and, for the first time, the United States requested to speak directly to the Taliban instead of insisting on the Afghan government leading peace talks.[62] It was a clear admission of failure after seventeen years of war. By 2019, when the U.S. troop level in Afghanistan was fourteen thousand, the total number of U.S. soldiers killed in Iraq and Afghanistan was over seven thousand and counting.[63] Then the Taliban controlled half of the country.

In the early years of the wars in Afghanistan and Iraq, no military leader high-ranking enough to have Bush's ear would tell him what he needed to hear, least of all the leader of Central Command, Tommy Franks. Franks wouldn't risk jeopardizing his career. The general would not get the full truth either because of his tendency "to berate subordinates, frequently shouting and cursing at them,"[64] according to Tom Ricks in the fittingly titled *Fiasco: The American Military Adventure in Iraq, 2003 to 2005.* "Central command is two thousand indentured servants whose life is consumed by the whims of Tommy Franks," an officer who worked with Franks told Ricks. "I am convinced that much of the information that came out of Central Command is unreliable because he demands it instantly, so people pull it out of their hats. It's all SWAGs [scientific wild-assed guesses]. Also, everything has to be good news stuff . . . You would find out you can't tell the truth."[65]

Franks retired from the army in 2003 and embarked on a career of lucrative speeches and a book for which he received a "multimillion-dollar contract."[66] The general was the beneficiary of a career that was marked by hearing what he wanted from his officers and passing on to his civilian leaders what they wanted to hear. In short, like Powell, he was a "good soldier," and was rewarded handsomely.

ECHO CHAMBERS

The broad influence of the military makes the paeans about the checks of civilian control seem comical, naïve, or dishonest. Any superficial control that exists is either too thin to matter or too politically motivated to allow for free thinking and honesty about the military organization. Either circumstance allows the closed military system to remain tightly sealed. Officers' careerism and their commitment to loyalty above all else ensure that everyone toes the line.

It's not a coincidence that the selling of the Iraq War happened within this closed system. When the case for war had to be made, the introduction occurred at West Point's graduation ceremony on June 1, 2002, fewer than ten months before the invasion. President Bush tried to scare Americans senseless about future terrorist attacks and laid the groundwork for war with Iraq. "In defending the peace, we face a threat with no precedent," Bush warned.[67]

It was at the VFW's national convention in Nashville three months later that Vice President Cheney was tasked with beginning to "educate the public" on the threat from Saddam, the link with al-Qaeda and 9/11, and Iraq's supposed WMD, none of which would prove to be correct.[68] It was on the USS *Abraham Lincoln* in May 2003 that Bush landed, in full flight uniform, to declare "mission accomplished" in Iraq in a conflict that had only just begun.

Despite the lack of victory in Afghanistan and the misguided invasion of Iraq, Bush and Cheney are still hailed as heroes within this closed system. The vice president came to West Point in 2007 to give the graduation speech and feed back into the echo chamber, continuing to saber-rattle about the need for leadership in these wars that had gone wrong for him. In the waning days of his imperial vice presidency, he could still rouse an audience—of impressionable military men and women. Bush would also return to West Point in his final year as president and even be honored there again with the academy's highest award in 2017. The man responsible for getting over seven thousand soldiers (and a total of five hundred thousand people[69]) killed over a lie would be welcomed with open arms inside this separate world. Bush and Cheney returned to the one place where they could stand proud behind their failed wars, the place where even MacArthur's reputation remains untainted, the place where the military and its people are never wrong.

As champions of the U.S. military's infallibility, Bush, who served stateside in a National Guard unit, and Cheney, who did not serve at all, would be loyally venerated in military circles, long after the rest of the world had recognized their folly. The feedback loop did its work. The politicians in the executive branch lean on military power to back up their policies, and the generals feed back to these titular civilian bosses what they want to hear. In return, the generals are allowed to operate with little scrutiny. As long as the military brass are helping to sell the president's message, they get all the deference in the world. These political motives poison the honesty of the military, while the gap between what the public knows and what is actually going on widens, and the separate society only grows stronger.

EXECUTIVE DEFERENCE

There is a common attitude among military brass that the civilian overseers are "temporary help," Tom Ricks explains. "After all, the military rationale goes, in a few years the civilians will all be gone from this Pentagon—but those in uniform will still be in those uniforms."[70]

Combine this cynicism with an executive who is hesitant to overrule military commanders "for fear of appearing irresolute and weak,"[71] writes professor Richard Betts, and you have a recipe for a growing and dangerous separate society in charge of America's foreign policy.

President Barack Obama, who was known to butt heads with his military commanders, found an environment where he was often pressured to side with the generals. Obama's lack of military experience—like President Clinton's—brought a general disdain from the military at the top, which as a whole worked against him. For Obama, "going against the military would make the president look weak,"[72] according to Ronan Farrow, something no commander in chief can afford. Nevertheless, Obama still "surrounded himself with retired generals or other military officers in senior positions."[73]

President Donald Trump, who "idolizes swaggering commanders," is perhaps the strongest example yet of how civilian command bows to military authority. Trump's drastic swing from adamantly opposed to strongly in favor of sending additional troops to Afghanistan was no mystery. It's what the generals urged him to do. And it is the military ethos that now saturates America's civilian leadership.[74]

Trump's worship of the military spilled over into his choices for the most important positions in civilian government. James Mattis, the first secretary of defense, John Kelly, the second White House chief of staff, and Michael Flynn, the first national security advisor, were all former generals. (Trump's second [acting] secretary of defense was Patrick M. Shanahan, who had worked for thirty-one years for Boeing, a major defense contractor.) His next secretary of defense was Mark Esper (Class of '86), a former army officer and corporate lobbyist. The second national security advisor, H. R. McMaster (Class of '84), whose two top aides were former generals, was a current general. Trump's second secretary of state, Mike Pompeo, was an army captain (Class of '86) and Esper's classmate at West Point. (Before his election to Congress in 2010, Pompeo was an executive for Koch Industries, a large federal contractor.[75]) Attorney general Jeff Sessions (captain), energy secretary Rick Perry (captain), and interior secretary Ryan Zinke (commander) had been officers in the army, air force, and navy. Trump's second director of national intelligence (acting) was Joseph Maguire, who had been a navy admiral. Maguire, in September 2019, refused to transmit to Congress the complaint of a whistleblower, a CIA officer, who claimed correctly that Trump, in a telephone call in July 2019, asked the president of Ukraine to investigate a chief political rival in the 2020 presidential campaign, former vice president Joe Biden. After the White House, under pressure, released a partial transcript of the call, Maguire said he was no longer covered by "executive privilege" and sent the complaint to Congress.

Members of Congress, even from the opposition party, expressed little concern for the military influence over Trump. Referring to Mattis, Kelly, and McMaster, senator Richard Blumenthal (D-Conn.) said, "They are standouts of dependability in the face of rash and impulsive conduct." More incredibly, Senator Brian Schatz (D-Hawaii) said, "I feel like the concern about the need to maintain civilian oversight of the military is a totally legitimate one, but *that concern should be addressed at a later time*" (emphasis mine).[76]

At its own request, the military—just the generals who rose to high positions—got an even freer hand from President Trump, who "appears to be going back to a model of greater delegation of authority," according to former under secretary of defense for policy Michèle A. Flournoy. "But there is a risk if there is inadequate oversight and the president stops paying close attention. It can be detrimental, even dangerous, if a commander in chief does not feel ownership of the campaign or loses touch with how things are evolving on the ground."[77]

Trump shifted responsibility for tactical decisions from the White House's National Security Council to the Pentagon.[78] He then let the secretary of defense, retired General Mattis, set troop levels in Afghanistan[79] and reduced the limits on drone strikes, to eliminate unnecessary "bureaucracy" remaining from the Obama administration.[80] After just five days in office, at a time when the public could imagine that a new president might be extra cautious, Trump approved a Special Forces raid in Yemen, not from the Situation Room but rather while eating dinner at the White House residence.[81]

"Trump approved his first covert counterterrorism operation without sufficient intelligence, ground support, or adequate back up preparations," according to a Reuters account backed by military officials.[82] One Navy SEAL was killed, and five other U.S. service members were wounded;

fourteen militants were killed; twenty-five civilians were killed, including nine children under thirteen; and one $70 million aircraft was destroyed. Despite White House and Pentagon claims to the contrary, the raid "yielded no significant intelligence," according to senior officials.[83]

Even in the face of continued failure, America's deference to the military is a trend that will not end any time soon, nor will the pendulum swing back toward civilian control. As Madison and Jefferson understood, a standing army will not give back its power voluntarily. The separate society of the U.S. military continues to grow stronger, more powerful, and freer from oversight, producing a dangerous and unfounded confidence in military solutions. Perhaps the attitude is best illustrated by former White House chief of staff John Kelly, who had been a four-star general in the marines. During his confirmation hearing for secretary of homeland security, a Republican operative offered Kelly an American flag pin.

The general's response captures perfectly military officers' hubris and the automatic respect they believe they deserve.

"I am an American Flag," he said.[84]

CHAPTER 2

Unfounded Hubris

A powerful parallel society like the military is well positioned to reject the foundational values of mainstream society. Distant from civilian oversight and in possession of seemingly limitless resources, the military, after World War II, became certain that its values were superior to those of the civilian world. The military has worked effectively to gain the trust of Americans, who, in polls, place it at the top of the institutions in which they have the most confidence.[1] Former marine and author Phil Klay recently pointed out that "almost every other major institution of American life is in the red: 12 percent approval for Congress, 27 percent for newspapers, 40 percent for the Supreme Court, and 41 percent for organized religion. Meanwhile, 27 percent of Democrats and 36 percent of Republicans see the opposing party as a threat to the nation."[2] In contrast, public approval of the military remains steadily in the mid-70s year after year, no matter how it's doing on the battlefield.[3] This combination of praise and autonomy has contributed to a remarkably sturdy sense of hubris in the armed forces.

In a 2015 study from the Army War College, *Lying to Ourselves: Dishonesty in the Army Profession*, retired lieutenant colonel Leonard Wong and retired colonel Stephen Gerras, both West Point graduates, recognized the gap between perception and reality in the military. "The effusive public adulation and constant professional self-talk," they write, "can also lead to excessive pride and self-exaltation. Overconfidence can leave officers—especially those at the senior level—vulnerable to the belief that they are unimperiled by the temptations and snares found at the common level of life."[4]

Arrogance breeds an assumption that experience in the military is like a superpower that guarantees success and excellence in all walks of life. The authors of *Freakonomics* call this tendency "domain transfer,"[5] and it's common among high-ranking military officers. Joan Johnson-Freese, a civilian professor at the Naval War College, writes that U.S. "military institutions believe that military expertise is interchangeable with any level of other expertise,"[6] an issue that is apparent not just at the war colleges but also at the military academies, which rely predominantly on military officers as instructors. Everyone would think it absurd, and harmful to the country, to hire a college president with no military experience to be an infantry commander. But the army, navy, and air force hire officers from infantry, artillery, and other branches to be the presidents (superintendents) of the military academies.

A large majority of these officers who teach at the academies do not have terminal degrees (a doctorate) in an academic discipline, nor do they have any experience teaching, researching, or practicing in their disciplines prior to being assigned to teach at the academies. When they leave for other assignments—which translates into about 60 percent of all instructors leaving after only two or three years—the West Point administration calls them the "second graduating class." Treating faculty turnover as though it is something to celebrate is backward, and it sacrifices something important—the opportunity for the cadets to receive an education from actual education professionals.

Having obtained respect and deference, the military developed the attitude that it should be left alone to run its own affairs and prosecute wars. Scrutiny, if any, should come from internal voices.

In the major wars in which America has been entangled since World War II (Korea, Vietnam, Afghanistan, and Iraq), the generals acted as though they would win if they poured more technology, soldiers, and weaponry into the fight, all the while believing they could impose democratic values on uncooperative populaces through force of weapons. They assumed, with disastrous results, that what once worked would always work. It was the military culture of hubris that reinforced their mistaken assumptions. And after the expulsion of Iraq from Kuwait in January and February of 1991, this false confidence only spread through the military ranks. As Andrew Bacevich posits, "Senior military leaders left unasked questions of fundamental importance. What if the effect of projecting U.S. military power was not to solve problems but to exacerbate them?"[7] The twentieth century offers a litany of military generals whose own hubris only aggravated the problems that U.S. military intervention was supposed to alleviate.

MACARTHUR IN KOREA

As journalist Neil Sheehan noted, in the 1950s "the dominant characteristics of the senior leadership of the American armed forces had become professional arrogance, lack of imagination, and moral and intellectual insensitivity."[8] There is no better illustration of this trend than General Douglas MacArthur (Class of 1903), a former superintendent of West Point. Portrayed as a hero after World War II, MacArthur carried his accolades with him into the Korean War, where he commanded the United Nations forces. His decision to push his troops to the Chinese border, certain the Chinese would not enter the war, was catastrophic. Over three hundred thousand Chinese troops attacked the U.S. Eighth Army in North Korea and ensured the eventual division of the Korean peninsula. Mao Zedong himself said of MacArthur, "The more arrogant and more stubborn he is the better. An arrogant enemy is easy to defeat."[9]

MacArthur "surrounded himself" with men who "would not disturb the dreamworld of self-worship in which he chose to live," according to historian William Stueck.[10] Absent reliable advisors, MacArthur's promise in 1950 to President Truman that the Korean War would be over in a matter of months was a mix of arrogance and cluelessness about the enemy he was fighting. "MacArthur illustrates that when a general believes he cannot be removed," writes Tom Ricks, "the quality of strategic discourse with his superiors—both military and civilian—tends to suffer, and with it the effectiveness of their collective decision-making process."[11]

MacArthur was famously and frequently clouded by his overconfidence. The reason was not just natural arrogance, although he had plenty of it. The carefully constructed world around the general—which had protected him for over thirty years—was also to blame. The information he received came from fawning military aides who reported what he wanted to hear, rather than the facts. Their tone "was almost wholly simpering and reverential, and I have always held the view that this sycophancy was what tripped him up in the end,"[12] reported famed newspaper columnist Joseph Alsop. MacArthur's staff in Tokyo, from where he managed the Korean War, was "proof of the basic rule of armies at war: the farther one gets from the front, the more laggards, toadies and fools one encounters," according to Alsop. MacArthur dictated strategy from Tokyo and slept nightly there during all of his Korean command, further isolating him from his troops, the war, and the enemy.

British journalist Malcolm Muggeridge interviewed General MacArthur in Tokyo and found him entirely out of touch with reality:

> His inconceivable theme was that the U.S. Army had brought democracy and Christianity to Japan, and had thereby wrought a revolution unique in history. He spoke of the Sermon on the Mount, producing an exceptionally large number of clichés ("Freedom is heady wine," etc.). I was bored and embarrassed. He seemed to me like a broken-down actor of the type one meets in railway trains or boarding houses in England . . . With relief he made his way back to his military billet, where trays of highballs were brought in from 4 P.M. onwards, and the only interruption was an occasional shriek as some Japanese girl resorted to Jujitsu in self-defense against the more intimate assaults of some American apostle of democracy and Christianity.[13]

MacArthur's stereotypes about the nature of his allies and enemies illustrated his misguided sense of destiny and superiority. He considered Asians "obedient, dutiful, childlike, and quick to follow resolute leadership," according to historian Bruce Cumings.[14] After U.S. forces occupied Pyongyang, the capital of North Korea, in 1950, MacArthur asked, "Any celebrities here to greet me?" Referring to the first leader of North Korea, Kim Il Sung, he asked, "Where is Kim Buck Tooth?"[15]

In *The Generals*, Tom Ricks described how MacArthur "abused his subordinates, always insisting on glory himself and denying it to underlings,"[16] and assigned cronies to combat commands because of their personal loyalty. The general even accepted the Distinguished Flying Cross from one of them for flying back to his home base in Tokyo on a passenger plane, even though they saw no enemy ground troops or aircraft during the flight.[17] "MacArthur's rhetoric, rarely measured, veered toward the hysterical," writes Ricks. "His statements lacked any sense that competing views might hold merit. He cast minor policy differences in the most absolute and extreme terms."[18]

Though Truman fired MacArthur in 1951, much of the damage was done. By the time of MacArthur's ouster, the North Koreans and Chinese had gained a foothold on half the peninsula. The Korean War dragged on for another two years, and although the fighting ended with a truce in 1953, America's most lasting failure is that it could not prevent North Korea from building a nuclear arsenal that is now capable of striking the United States. History has not been kind to MacArthur—but, as Ricks notes, there is one place where MacArthur's reputation, like Bush's and Cheney's, remains unblemished. "In the Army, MacArthur is remembered, if at all, as a bit of an embarrassment, except perhaps at West Point."[19]

WESTMORELAND IN VIETNAM

On his way to assume command in Vietnam in late 1963, General William Westmoreland stopped at West Point to address the cadets. He then made a stop in New York City to see Douglas MacArthur at his retirement home, a suite at the Waldorf Astoria Hotel. Westmoreland (Class of '36), like MacArthur, had also been West Point's "first captain"—the highest-ranking cadet there—as well as a former superintendent of the academy.

In his Manhattan suite, surrounded by the gilded accoutrements he no doubt felt he deserved, MacArthur—who was a few months from death—advised Westmoreland to treat the South Vietnamese officers "as you did your cadets. Do not overlook the possibility that in order to defeat the guerrilla you may have to resort to a scorched earth policy." Westmoreland registered no disagreement.[20] Like MacArthur, Westmoreland, who was the U.S. commander in Vietnam from 1964 to 1968, compensated for his lack of curiosity with an enormous amount of hubris and misrepresentation.

Historians have derided Westmoreland for his performance during the Vietnam War and for his lies to President Johnson regarding its progress, as well as his futile "body-count" approach to combat. "Men of limited imagination who rise as high as Westmoreland had tended to play blindly to their strength, no matter what its relevance to the problem at hand," writes Neil Sheehan of Westmoreland. "Political and social action . . . were areas that did not attract the general, because he did not understand them."[21]

If Westmoreland had a strength, it wasn't subtlety or nuance. He was the ultimate exemplar of the idea that a hammer sees everything as a nail. What he knew was brute force, and he was certain that it would lead to victory in Southeast Asia. According to Westmoreland biographer Lewis Sorley (Class of '56), the general had a "perspective so widely off the mark that it raises fundamental questions of [his] awareness of the context in which the war was being fought."[22]

Men like Westmoreland "expect their enemies to behave stupidly, and they perceive their own behavior as farsighted generalship," writes Sheehan.[23] Bombing rural areas constantly, Westmoreland believed that the North Vietnamese, enduring daily death and hardship, would give up and concede defeat. But his "free-fire" strategy, unrestrained shooting and bombing into a zone, backfired: it strengthened the enemy's resolve and turned even ambivalent Vietnamese civilians against the Americans. Westmoreland did not learn from MacArthur's failure in North Korea, where unprecedented aerial bombardment could not lead to victory and only deepened Korean hatred for the United States. Westmoreland repeated his predecessor's mistakes.

In war after war, the U.S. military's misuse or overuse of its superior weapons, disregard for the civilian population, and abuse of enemy soldiers have strengthened the enemy: in Korea and Vietnam, where U.S. soldiers committed mass killings of civilians, and more recently at the Abu Ghraib prison in Iraq and at the detention facility at Guantanamo Bay, Cuba. Where the U.S. military has ignored social or legal norms—or more precisely, where the U.S. military has applied its own social and legal norms—the results have been predictably poor.

Westmoreland was unaware that his attrition strategy—kill more troops than the enemy can replace—betrayed his own personal callousness toward human life. His approach, followed by and passed down to his soldiers, was reminiscent of that of General John L. DeWitt, who helped justify the detention of Japanese Americans in World War II because the "Japanese race is an enemy race."

Westmoreland, like DeWitt and MacArthur, was similarly prone to racial prejudice. "The Oriental doesn't put the same high price on life as does the Westerner," Westmoreland said in a 1974 documentary film, *Hearts and Minds*. "Life is plentiful, life is cheap in the Orient. And as the philosophy of the Orient expresses it life is not important."[24] If Westmoreland really believed this racist stereotype, then his strategy of attrition made little sense; if it were true, the North Vietnamese could not be deterred, no matter how many casualties were inflicted among their ranks.

Despite Westmoreland's narrow-minded strategy, he considered himself a student of counterinsurgency warfare. The self-impression was not hindered by the actual evidence, because, according to biographer Sorley, Westmoreland "had missed out on all the major military schools, had published no articles relating to military history in professional journals, was not known as much of a reader, and seemed unaware of commonplace matters in even such recent history as World War II."[25]

Air force general Robert Beckel said Westmoreland "seemed rather stupid. He didn't seem to grasp things or follow the proceedings very well." Army general Charles Simmons agreed, noting that "General Westmoreland was intellectually very shallow and made no effort to study, read, or learn. He would just not read anything. His performance was appalling."[26] It's unlikely that the first captain of his class at West Point, who would go on to become superintendent of the military academy and then leader of American forces, would ever have any reason to doubt his own counsel.

Westmoreland is not just considered a failure in hindsight. There was contemporaneous evidence everywhere. When Westmoreland was the commander in Vietnam, a study directed by the army chief of staff, General Harold Johnson, indicated that Westmoreland's approach to the war was not working. Colonel Herbert Schandler, who wrote Westmoreland's response to the study, believed that it was sound. "We all thought [the study] was great stuff, but we couldn't say that," said Schandler. "We had to write things like 'there are some good ideas here for consideration' and so on. And we said 'we are implementing many of these programs already.' We had to say that—General Westmoreland wanted to show he was ahead of the game."[27] Sorley writes, "Westmoreland's headquarters was obliged to reject out-of-hand the PROVN [Program for the Pacification and Long-Term Development of Vietnam] findings, because they of course repudiated everything Westmoreland was doing."[28]

Recognizing the staggering depth of MacArthur's and Westmoreland's obtuseness leads to a clearer understanding of the deficiencies in the military and how America can lose wars. Military academy administrations in different generations selected these men to lead all the other cadets at West Point. The military leadership in Washington selected them to prosecute two major wars. Yet Sorley found that Westmoreland was "limited in his understanding of complex situations, entirely dependent on conventional solutions, and willing to shade or misremember or deny the record when his perceived interests were at risk. Westmoreland's strengths eventually propelled him to a level beyond his understanding and abilities. The results were tragic, not just for him but for the Army and the nation he served, and most of all of course for the South Vietnamese, who sacrificed all and lost all," as well as the North Vietnamese, who lost just as much.[29] Sorley notes a widespread problem in the military: those who rise to the top are not necessarily the most qualified, but rather those who understand how to navigate the politics and culture of the military.

In *A Bright Shining Lie*, Neil Sheehan describes how Westmoreland's dull thinking and quest for glory prevented adjustments to his overall plan even as evidence poured in that it was not working. Westmoreland refused to create a joint command to integrate U.S. and South Vietnamese soldiers because "a U.S. Army officer could not win acclaim at the head of native troops. For him, glory and professional fulfillment could come only by leading American soldiers in war."[30]

Like MacArthur, Westmoreland's legend lived on at his alma mater, where his obtuseness and incompetence were inverted. The academy's chief of American history, Colonel Greg Daddis (Class of '89), wrote *Westmoreland's War: Reassessing American Strategy in Vietnam*, a book that even Daddis calls "a work of historical revisionism."[31] Contravening most accounts of the general, Daddis claims that Westmoreland "was not the unthinking officer who is presented so contemptuously in many history books."[32] Daddis blames the loss of the war on a failed "grand strategy" of civilian leaders and a tenacious enemy, all the while heaping fawning praise on Westmoreland and his leadership, characterizing his strategy as "sound" and "well-conceived."[33]

The closed society of West Point helps to create this kind of dysfunctional feedback loop. Daddis believes that Westmoreland, the former cadet and superintendent, was a heroic, competent leader.

POMPOUS CIRCUMSTANCE

Despite their dismal records, MacArthur and Westmoreland have always been hailed as heroes at their alma mater, a place where their reputation looms large. (West Point's parade field, its most prominent public space, is bookended by statues of Eisenhower and MacArthur.) The closed system secured their legacies. The hubris began during their time at the academy, when military leaders told them they were among America's best and brightest. They carried this self-satisfaction on their missions out into the world, and then it was reflected back to them upon their return to the academy, where they were treated as demigods. Both men spent decades never having directly to hear someone doubt or dispute their opinions, which is the very last thing we should ever want from military leaders. Despite recent examples of similar failures on the battlefield, America's military leaders are still treated, everywhere they go, with the pomp and circumstance of heroes just returning from victory in war.

Four-star generals and admirals today are flown on jets not just for work but also to ski, vacation, and golf resorts (234 military golf courses) operated by the U.S. military around the world,[34] accompanied by a dozen aides, drivers, security guards, gourmet chefs, and valets to carry their bags. In 2011 General David Petraeus, for example, had twenty-eight motorcycles escort him from Central Command in Tampa, Florida, to the nearby house of a socialite. While in the military, "Petraeus instructed aides to hand him bottles of water at precise intervals during his jogging routine and have fresh, sliced pineapple available during business trips before his bedtime," according to the *Washington Post*.[35]

Generals don't fly commercial and are not relegated to a small corporate jet. Each four-star general who heads a regional command has a military C-40, equal to a Boeing 737, outfitted with beds, business-class seating, and two galleys. Former secretary of defense Robert Gates, who'd be in a position to know, said of generals, "There is something about a sense of entitlement and of having great power that skews people's judgment."[36] When military officers with poor judgment are responsible for life and death, as well as the health of the republic, a nation that does not discern its vulnerability from their decisions is at great risk.

The overconfidence and misjudgment are inevitable because the generals and other officers project their entitlements onto the students of the military academies. In January 2017, General John W. Nicholson (Class of '82), the commander in Afghanistan, addressed the senior cadets at West Point. Gushing, Nicholson said Winston Churchill's praise of the Royal Air Force, which saved Britain from the Nazis in World War II, could also be applied to the young cadets, fresh from their free lunch in the mess hall and appreciative of the chance to doze prior to afternoon classes. "Never was so much owed by so many to so few," he said, referring to these cadets.

The generals are inculcating in these young men and women a sense of infallibility and superiority before they have accomplished anything. If they believe they are worthy of this treatment upon enrollment, imagine how they feel about themselves once they get out into the world. And those who rise to the top of the armed forces continually believe they are deserving of this special treatment. They are never presented with any reason to doubt it. Conflicting views are disregarded or maligned as unpatriotic. In this separate society, doubters are dismissed as irrelevant and dissenters are silenced with systematic retaliation. As veteran journalist Seymour Hersh pointedly writes, "To prove a general wrong is a career-ending move for more junior officers."[37]

Dina Rasor described in 2012 the generals' superficial regality. Over the years, Rasor attended many hearings at the U.S. Capitol and observed employees from government agencies arriving routinely to testify before Congress. She found it "darkly humorous" to watch the entrances and productions of the four-star generals, who were aided by three or four lower-ranking generals and other officers "scurrying ahead to set up the presentation and charts . . . It was known on the Hill as the flotilla, and it was actually sad to see full-bird colonels masquerading as chart bunnies for the four star. Nobody [in Congress] wants to be seen beating up on a distinguished top officer in uniform, even if, in reality, he is just another obfuscating bureaucrat under those stars on his shoulders. This allows the DoD to get away with more fraud than other agencies."[38]

In his speech to the graduating West Point class of 2002, when he was making the case for war in Iraq, President Bush encapsulated the way the young cadets are supposed to feel about themselves. "In every corner of America," the commander in chief told the graduating cadets, "the words 'West Point' command immediate respect. This place where the Hudson River bends is more than a fine institution of learning. The United States Military Academy is the guardian of values that have shaped the soldiers who have shaped the history of the world."

Most of the officers who graduated from West Point have long held their alma mater, and by extension themselves, in such high esteem. In a 2012 promotional video for a company that trains executives, Colonel Bernard Banks (Class of '87), a former head of the Department of Behavioral Sciences and Leadership at West Point, noted that civilians—who are prone to shortcuts, he believed—do not meet the high standards of West Point and the Army. Banks claimed that civilian "individuals grew up in a culture of if you're not cheating you're not trying . . . I'm glad to have been part of something that's much larger than myself . . . [West Point] represents the absolute best."[39]

Lieutenant General Sean MacFarland (Class of '81)—considered "a legend in army circles"[40]—was similarly suspicious of outsiders. In 2011 MacFarland, then a brigadier, wrote in a military journal, "Four words largely sum up what it means to be a soldier: fight, kill, die, and buddy. No other job, occupation, career, or profession entails the intimacy wrapped up in those four words . . . Our soldiers have their ethos, one that compares to the best that have existed in the history of civilization."[41]

The military promotes and fosters cohesion in a way that creates a strict moral hierarchy, one with officers like Banks and McFarland at the top.

Retired air force major general Charles Dunlap, now a professor at Duke Law School, told the *Atlantic*, "I think there is a strong sense in the military that it is indeed a better society than the one it serves. And there is some rationality for that."[42] Dunlap later wrote that he was more certain that civilian society pales when compared with the military: "The magnificent altruism, courage, and dedication that the troops typically illustrate starkly contrasts with what [Secretary of Defense] appointees so often see elsewhere in American society."[43]

Lieutenant General Robert Caslen (Class of '75), West Point's superintendent from 2013 to 2018, was as certain as his brethren about the virtues of his alma mater. Citing former army chief of staff General Ray Odierno (Class of '76), Caslen frequently recounted that "West Point is the world's preeminent leader development institution" and proclaimed, "If the great American public wants to see what's right in our nation, they want to see that occurring within the military academy. They see us and the military academy as standing in the gap between the evil that's out there and protecting America."[44] The cadets quickly accept these claims of preeminence. The feeling of superiority becomes embedded in these impressionable young men and women, affecting how they see themselves, the institution that has created them, and the rest of the world. Every place is beneath West Point. Every person is beneath a graduate of West Point.

THE FALLING GRAY LINE

This self-reinforcing cycle of praise is not based in reality—both in regard to the military's performance and the quality of the academies themselves. In October 2017, retired lieutenant colonel Robert M. Heffington, a former history professor at West Point, wrote a scathing open letter regarding what he had witnessed at his alma mater, where graduates refer to themselves as members of the "long gray line," after the color of one of their uniforms. Considering the intense feelings Heffington expressed in his letter, that he waited until retirement to report what he believed was a grave matter illustrates the lack of opportunity for dissent and the ever-present fear of retaliation in the military. The final straw seems to have been the recent graduation of a cadet who was "an avowed Communist and sworn enemy of the United States," according to Heffington.[45]

Among Heffington's targets were the plummeting standards. "First and foremost," writes Heffington, "standards at West Point are nonexistent. The Superintendent [Robert Caslen at the time] refuses to enforce admissions standards or the cadet Honor Code, the Dean refuses to enforce academic standards, and the Commandant refuses to enforce standards of conduct and discipline. Cadets know this, and it has given rise to a level of cadet arrogance and entitlement the likes of which West Point has never seen in its history . . . I have personally taught cadets who are borderline illiterate and cannot read simple passages from the assigned textbooks."[46]

The unbounded hubris that plagues America's military leaders is not only the result of being puffed up once they've reached the top. Through the entitlements the military students receive when entering the academies and the unearned praise they receive from generals, the students are taught that they and their forebears are superior.

These feelings are buttressed by the government's lavish spending on the military academies. The Government Accounting Office, in apparently its most recent complete report of the academies, found that West Point's total operating expenditures in just one year, 2002, were $365 million[47] (over $500 million in 2019 when adjusted for inflation)—for a school that graduates only about 950 to 990 cadets a year.[48]

To put this massive expenditure in context, the National Cancer Institute received less money in the same year for research into brain cancer ($95.2 million), ovarian cancer ($93.5 million), cervical cancer ($67.6 million), or a slew of other ailments.[49] Remarkably, in 2002, the operating expenditures for the three military academies were $991 million, which exceeded the federal research funding for thirteen of the most deadly cancers combined. A single six-story dormitory at West Point, Davis Barracks, completed in 2017, cost the government more than $186 million.[50] In January 2019, the garrison commander at West Point estimated that it would spend $2 billion on forty-five building projects over the next five years.

According to the promotional materials from West Point's admissions office, the return on investment is priceless. "The U.S. Military Academy is the world's preeminent institution for leadership development and higher education—it's where America cultivates leaders for our nation's future generations. Being accepted for admission into West Point is an exceptional honor and—in every regard—a degree earned from West Point speaks volumes about your abilities."[51] Although this seems almost too good to true, a poll of West Point students found that "overall reputation" was the number-one reason that students gave for attending the school.[52]

For many who enter the academy, their chute sparkles with special opportunity. To be admitted to a military academy, most high school students must be nominated by a member of Congress. But an investigation in 2014 by *USA Today* found that some congressional nominations for admission to the academies went to "children of well-connected families, friends, and campaign contributors."[53] From 2012 to 2014, U.S. "representatives and senators . . . accepted more than $171,000 in campaign contributions from the families of students they've nominated to military service academies over the past two years."[54] The students learn the importance of political influence early, and that factors other than merit will propel their careers.

The qualifications of the students at the military academies are inflated and misrepresented by military administrators, and then misperceived by Congress and the public.[55] This is largely because each of the academies falsifies the difficulty of obtaining admission. One of the prime factors in determining the desirability and prestige of a college is the percentage of applicants who are accepted, which is based on the number who apply for admission. The academies' administrators, all high-ranking military officers who graduated from the same academies, exaggerate low acceptance rates to boost their rankings and prestige. This helps their students obtain valuable scholarships and opportunities that should go to more deserving students at more rigorous colleges. The falsity gives the graduates of the academies, once they've become officers, advantages over the officers who entered the military via another route, such as ROTC or officer candidate school. It is possible that misrepresenting these statistics may constitute criminal offenses relating to conspiracy and fraud.[56]

One reason the academies are ranked among the top colleges is that the rankings are based heavily on the amount of money spent on educating students, and the government's money flows freely to the academies. The rankings often cite financial aid, student debt, job placement, and faculty resources, all of which disproportionately favor the military academies. The academies are free—in fact, all military students actually receive salaries, over $12,000 a year—so the "financial aid" for every student is 100 percent. At graduation, 100 percent of the students have jobs (in the military) and 100 percent have no debt. With ample resources, the academies do not hire adjunct professors, so the percentage of full-time faculty members is also 100.

In 2018, *Forbes* ranked West Point and the Naval Academy at 27 and 31, respectively, among all the nation's "top colleges."[57] The *Forbes* rankings are tailor-made for the resource-rich academies, whose students must graduate in four years, who must work in the military upon graduation, and who do not have any student debt. *Forbes*'s rankings are based on postgraduate success, including salary (35 percent); student debt (20 percent); student experience (20 percent); graduation rate (12.5 percent); and academic success (12.5 percent).[58] But a 2014 study for *Psychology Today* found that West Point and the Naval Academy were ranked 111 and 112 on their students' average SAT scores.[59]

The academies' admissions misrepresentations cause Congress, accreditation bodies, and publications that rank colleges to buy wholesale into the perception that the academies are selective institutions. The opposite is true. One West Point civilian instructor (a retired military officer) who took leave to teach at a leading university said upon his return, "My best student at West Point would be the worst student in my classes" at the university.

Bruce Fleming, a civilian English professor who sat on the Naval Academy's admissions board, explains the admissions process in "Let's Abolish West Point," a 2015 article in *Salon*. "Our military academies aren't filled with best and brightest," writes Fleming. "They are a boondoggle, on your dime, and serve no one."[60] Fleming describes how the Naval Academy fabricated upward the number of applicants to lower its admissions rate, thereby increasing its prestige:

> In fact we count all 7,500 applicants to a week-long summer program for 11th graders, that enrolls 2,500, as Naval Academy applicants, as well as anybody who fills out enough information to create a candidate number. It was just last year we stopped counting

the 3,000 applicants to ROTC programs at civilian schools as Naval Academy applicants . . . when a reporter discovered it, but when I was on the admissions board for a year a decade ago we considered nothing close to the 20,000 applicants they claim. It was actually fewer than 5,000 candidates for 1,800 admits.[61]

The admissions misrepresentation is similar at West Point, which reports an acceptance rate in the single or low double digits. But, in fact, the actual acceptance rate every year is over 50 percent, a gigantic discrepancy. Here's how the process works. For the graduating class of 2016, for example, West Point reported 15,171 "applicants." In reality, the academy counted as an applicant anyone who expressed interest in West Point and on whom it started a file. A "file started" (West Point's term) can be based on nothing more than West Point's sending the student informational materials.

These high schoolers are in no way applicants based on any common definition or understanding of the term. An "applicant," according to the National Center for Education Statistics, part of the U.S. Department of Education, is "an individual who has fulfilled the institution's requirements to be considered for admission (including payment or waiving of the application fee, if any) and who has been notified of one of the following actions: admission, nonadmission, placement on waiting list, or application withdrawn by applicant or institution."[62]

Obviously, a high school student who makes an inquiry is not an applicant under this (or any) definition. West Point claims to use this standard definition of applicant. But it does not. Top administrators, all of whom are generals, colonels, and admirals and who graduated from the academies, must know this, but they continue to report these swollen, and false, numbers. In the 2019 rankings of *U.S. News and World Report*, the most prominent rater, the academies received extraordinary credit for their hefty government funding and their admissions misrepresentations. Faculty and financial "resources" account for 30 percent of a college's total score, and a college's undergraduate academic reputation among college administrators comprises 20 percent of a college's score.[63] Thus, 50 percent of the military academies' ranking is based on the large amounts of money they receive from the government and the perception of a high academic reputation and selectivity, which arise from their misrepresentations about the difficulty in obtaining admission.

The data show that for the graduating class of 2016 West Point had only 2,394 applicants who were "fully qualified and nominated" by a member of Congress (or other source). The academy accepted 1,358 of these applicants—for an actual acceptance rate of 56.7 percent. The evidence shows further that the same strategy is used every year to massively misrepresent acceptance rates, and every year the academies apparently report the false rates to the Department of Education. In 2018, for example, the Department of Education listed the admission rates as 11, 9, and 11 percent, for West Point, Navy, and Air Force, respectively. The Education Department indicated over 12,000 applicants for West Point, over 16,000 for the Naval Academy, and over 10,000 for the Air Force Academy.[64] On June 24, 2019, West Point's public affairs office, in a press release, claimed that "the incoming class [of 2023] was selected from a pool of nearly 12,300 applicants."

As a member of a committee that was evaluating West Point's admissions process in 2015, I told the other members that West Point was incorrectly calculating its acceptance rate. Another civilian professor, Thomas Sherlock, backed me up, telling the committee, "In my opinion, we need an authoritative statement as to the process that arrives at the [reported] 9 percent acceptance rate."

Another member of the committee, Colonel Bernard Banks, told the director of admissions, Colonel Deborah McDonald (Class of '85), "Some team members have expressed angst . . . that reporting files opened versus files completed (and subsequently people offered admission) presents a skewed perception of how difficult it is to gain admission. I invite you to share your perspective on the issue." Banks' attribution of "angst" to "team members" is the peculiar way the military attributes a problem to the people who identify it, rather than to its own corrupt system. (Banks was the officer who claimed on a promotional video that civilian society was not up to par with West Point.)

McDonald responded by claiming that she was not responsible for reporting the trumped-up numbers. "I believe OPA/OIR [Office of Institutional Research] completes the forms . . . on acceptance rates for institutional research and unsure if they use files started versus qualified applicants. I do concur . . . that the acceptance rate should not be tied to files opened since that really is a meaningless number."

In response, Colonel Holly West (Class of '91), from the Office of Institutional Research, did not want credit for the numbers. West attributed to the director of admissions—McDonald—the characterization of files opened as applicants, noting, "From USMA Director of Admissions: 'The number of applicants is the number of files opened.'"

Another member of the committee, Lieutenant Colonel Pete Kilner (Class of '90), resorted to a common army ploy to try to quash my and Professor Sherlock's inquiry. He suggested that those who questioned the process—two civilians—were not team players. "I really do not understand the level of distrust for Academy leaders," alleged Kilner. He noted that he had shared our concerns with the academic dean, Brigadier General Tim Trainor, who was confident that West Point's reporting was "in accordance with standardized definitions" and would respond to the committee in writing. Trainor's certainty masks a basic fact: the number of applicants and the acceptance rates reported by West Point and the other academies are far different, wildly so, from the real number of applicants and acceptance rates. Trainor's response never arrived.

By counting "files started" or summer-seminar participants as applicants, all three military academies vastly misrepresent their actual acceptance rates.[65] This, in turn, misrepresents upward the quality of the students, and the selectivity, desirability, and quality of the academies. This would be an academic scandal at any school, but since these academies are feeding the military, the potential consequences of the apparent fraud are far more consequential. The fabrications lay the foundation for the military's overconfidence and the public's blind trust in the military, all of which have very real, disastrous effects.

The admission fabrication allows military administrators to portray themselves and the other officers who graduated from the academies as possessing qualifications, competence, and expertise they do not have. The misrepresentations inflate the reputations of academy graduates on which the government relies when selecting its future military leaders. Academy students and graduates (including current military officers and those working outside the military) are receiving tangible and intangible benefits based on intentional misrepresentations.[66] Where honesty is not valued, there is no incentive to report correct numbers; everyone in authority benefits from the falsity.

This kind of blatant cronyism at the military academies, which will be addressed in the next chapter, cascades from one generation to the next. Insiders, often the children of academy graduates (especially current military officers), know that admissions standards are low, and those children will be more likely to apply, be admitted, and become officers (aside from the advantages accrued from nepotism). It's the very opposite of the highly selective process that West Point and the other military academies advertise.

High school students with no inside knowledge will view the (false) low acceptance rates at the academies as barriers to entry and believe that it is hopeless to apply. In the 2019 edition of the *U.S. News* college ratings, acceptance rates for the academies were listed as 8, 10, and 12 percent (for Navy, West Point, and Air Force). As a consequence, many capable, public-service-minded high school students will never consider the military academies or the military at all. Year in and year out, they will be replaced by students with lower qualifications who know the game. "More than a quarter of our students have SAT scores [in math or verbal] in the 400s and 500s," said Bruce Fleming about the Naval Academy. "Yes, our top quarter is comparable to the top half of Ivies . . . [and] we have some bright kids, but they're the exception."[67]

THE PREP SCHOOL BACKDOOR

The quality of West Point (and Naval and Air Force Academy) students has proven to be considerably lower than advertised, and a main reason is that the schools have many methods through which to favor applicants for nonacademic reasons, including through free government-funded "prep schools." These boarding schools permit academically deficient high school students—especially those who are good athletes—to take a gap year prior to entering the academies. The students take remedial courses and play the sport for which they were recruited—and receive a salary of over $12,000 per year from the U.S. government. In December of 2016, one former student at the Naval Academy's prep school told the *New York Times*, "It was like another year of high school. We had cars, we could visit friends, and we were flush with cash. It was high school kids getting paid."[68]

The prep schools were designed during World War I to help enlisted soldiers and sailors gain admission to West Point and the Naval Academy. But since the late 1960s, the prep schools have become the back doors the academies use to admit unqualified students who are recruited by athletic coaches and "children of alumni or politicians who didn't have the grades or SAT scores to be admitted into the Naval Academy [for example] directly from high school," according to the *New York Times*. In a "major shift," West Point in 1995 began to use its prep school to meet "class composition goals regarding minorities and recruited athletes," according to Dr. Joel Jebb (Class of '82), the director of English at West Point's prep school.[69]

After one year, the prep schoolers are virtually guaranteed admission to the academies. At a cost of over $50,000 per year per student, the prep schools provide a "thirteenth year" of remedial education.[70] Completed in 2012, the new West Point prep school cost over $142 million.[71] In addition to the three government-funded prep schools, West Point has special relationships with private prep schools throughout the country.[72] Its alumni office uses money from private donors to pay for high school graduates to attend these schools, which provide another back door for deficient students to enter the academy.[73]

But even the remedial courses for prep-school students do not put them in a position to match the regularly admitted students. In his 2016 PhD dissertation, Jebb, the director of English, summarizes the marginal qualifications of students admitted to the academy through the prep school. "By almost any measure that can be made," he writes, "such as standardized test scores, high school grades, high school class rank, quality of high school, leadership potential, and extracurricular activities," the prep schoolers in English 101 'begin the journey to that first day . . . quite far off the pace of their Direct Admit classmates."[74] The prep schoolers, once they are admitted, also maintain a GPA that is ".3 lower on a four point scale" (one-third of a letter grade) than the non-prep-school students in a first-year English course used as a basis of comparison.[75] Jebb expressed "surprise . . . followed by dismay"[76] at the discrepancy between the two groups.

To be eligible for the prep school in the first place, a high school student must be so deficient that he or she would be ineligible even to be considered for regular ("direct") admission. This means that a student-applicant could not meet even the lowest acceptable admission standard, mainly the "prescribed minimum scores on the SAT or ACT," according to Jebb. That is, the student must fall below the line under which any student in the regular admissions process would be summarily rejected. It seems impossible, but the prep schoolers are less qualified than the applicants who were considered but rejected during the regular admissions process.[77]

West Point's reasoning is that the prep school is reserved for truly "at risk" students and those in need of remedial education. This, of course, begs the question of why the academies would ever create a pipeline to admission for such poor students. Academically, an at-risk student admitted by West Point after a year at the prep school has a math or reading and writing score on the SAT below 500, far below the average (527 for math and 533 for reading and writing) for all students in the country who take the SAT. This means that 25 percent of the students at West Point and the academies are in the bottom 40 percent of all the high school students who take the SAT, and many of those test-takers do not ever attend college.[78]

The prep schoolers themselves also have a low success rate once they arrive at the prep schools. "Of the 256 students who entered the [Naval Academy] preparatory school in fall 2006," according to the *Washington Post*, "155 stayed on to graduate in spring 2011 . . . a graduation rate of 61 percent."[79] The prep-school "graduates" comprise about 25 percent of about 3,600 first-year cadets and midshipmen. This means that a large percentage of the graduates of the military academies who are officers in the army, navy, air force, and marines (who come from the Naval Academy) displaced applicants who were more qualified on all criteria and more likely to become higher-performing officers. The primary reason the academies bend over backward to admit that many unqualified students can be found on the field.

THE PROBLEM OF SPORTS

Today the primary purpose of the prep schools is to provide a broken back door into the academies for students who are unqualified for regular admission, so they can play for the athletic teams.[80] Every year, over 50 percent of the football and men's basketball and lacrosse players, for example, enter West Point through its prep school. Having played four years of college basketball, I appreciate how athletic competition helps develop people and provides a source of energy and pride for communities. But allowing into the academies students who are unqualified excludes far stronger all-around students who would more likely have greater success in the military.

A former head of the history department at West Point, retired brigadier general Lance Betros (Class of '77), could not justify the prep schools. In his book about West Point, *Carved from Granite*, he found that the "candidates who enter West Point via USMAPS [U.S. Military Academy Prep School] displace an equal number of candidates who, on average, have far greater potential for officership."[81] The data that West Point's administration provided to Betros showed that the academic qualifications of the cadets on West Point's athletic teams were far below those of other cadets. For one, the SAT scores of the cadets on the men's basketball, football, and baseball teams were 132, 131, and 126 points,[82] respectively, below cadets who were not recruited athletes.[83] (The College Board, which creates and administers the SAT, tells students that a "difference of at least 60 points between two students' scores indicates a true difference in ability."[84])

Betros concluded:

> The preferment of recruited athletes in the Academy's admission system was hard to explain objectively. It was not justified by their performance as cadets; although there were many exceptions, athletes generally ranked at or near the bottom of the class. Nor was the preferment justified by athletes' retention on active duty once commissioned . . . [because] overall the attrition of recruited athletes exceeded virtually every other population. Finally, it was not justified by the athletes' contributions as officers, as measured by attainment of high rank; army studies completed in the early 1950s suggested that high academic achievement was far more contributory to becoming a general officer than high athletic achievement. More recent evidence confirms the deleterious effect of athletic recruiting

on the quality of the Corps of Cadets and, by extension, the officer corps . . . The data revealed that only 13.5 percent of the colonels and generals in those classes [who graduated from 1978 to 1989] were recruited athletes [who comprised 19 to 24 percent of the classes].[85]

Colonel Michael L. Jones, a former director of admissions (Class of '70), once proudly reported to the faculty that West Point rejected a high school student who had a 4.0 grade point average because the student was not sufficiently physically fit. This was rich with irony because, remarkably, officers working under the commandant, who is responsible for the cadets' work outside the academic realm, report that about 50 percent of fourth-year cadets have *lower* scores on the Army Physical Fitness Test than they did in their first year at West Point. In September 2019 the West Point physician for occupational health reported that studies show 10 to 15 percent of first-year cadets use tobacco or nicotine products, but this increases to 20 to 30 percent of fourth-year cadets (graduating seniors). The physician lamented that soldiers may suffer from nicotine withdrawal while on missions. Even those with little awareness of the academies would presume that cadets would be smoking or vaping less and have greater physical fitness when they graduate and become officers. The opposite appears to be true.

Many high-ranking officers promote the idea that athletics help build a robust culture, and that would be fine if it were true. Year after year, the superintendents argue that a winning football team improves morale throughout the army, especially if the West Point team beats its main rivals, the air force and navy teams. Improved morale is difficult to measure, but from 1997 through 2015 the West Point football team was singularly dismal, winning only 27 percent of its games,[86] with losing records, 2–17, against both Air Force and Navy, and the worst single season in college football history, 0–13. The losing prompted the military administration at West Point to lower academic and character standards further so that what they termed "at risk" high school students who excelled in one sport could be easily admitted.

Their plan worked on the athletic field, but it harmed the nation. In 2016, the West Point football team ended the season with an 8–5 record, the best record in two decades, including a win over Navy, the first in fifteen years. That was followed by a 2017 season of 10–3, including a second consecutive win over Navy and a shutout win over Air Force, as well as wins over Navy and Air Force in 2018 and a record of 11–2.

West Point's commitment to winning football games while lowering academic and character standards came at a significant cost. If some of today's at-risk athletes and underperforming students become high-ranking officers and generals who determine wartime strategies, the real-world effect could be profound. But the athletic culture at West Point has already had tragic consequences. At 1:50 A.M. on September 11, 2016, a twenty-year-old star cornerback on the football team, Brandon Jackson, with a blood-alcohol level of 0.12 percent, crashed his car, going ninety-seven miles per hour, police estimated, into a guardrail and died instantly, about fifteen miles from West Point. "While his death was 100% the result of his own open, deliberate, and knowing malfeasance," an army investigator wrote, "the institutional-cultural lens is important because Cadet Jackson's actions were treated as ambiguous offenses by . . . [West Point] personnel who witnessed his misconduct" (underage drinking, keeping a car at West Point, and leaving post). Two months later another football player was arrested for drunk driving. From August to December of 2017, eight football players enrolled in a substance abuse program, according to the *Daily Beast*.[87] (Any information about students comes from published media reports.)

The star quarterback Ahmad Bradshaw seemed to epitomize the low-performing, "at risk" student who matriculates at the academies through the prep schools. The circumstances surrounding Bradshaw would have been unknown except for a confidential source that was identified by the *Daily Beast* as "a high-ranking, highly decorated soldier." The soldier said that his "decision to disclose the files [regarding Bradshaw] was based on his belief that Bradshaw's documented honor code and behavior violations, negative observation reports, and below-average performance . . . [showed] he does not have the integrity to lead men and women into potential combat or wear the uniform of a U.S. Army officer."[88]

Bradshaw, after a year at West Point's prep school—where Jackson, the deceased cornerback, had been a student—was first enrolled at the academy in the summer of 2014. Several weeks into his first semester, Bradshaw was accused of rape by a female cadet. He denied any sexual contact with the accuser. A West Point investigation by Major Damon M. Torres found there was a consensual sexual relationship between Bradshaw and the accuser. Bradshaw was disciplined for improperly using government facilities for sexual activity and did not play football in the 2014 season. A second investigation, by army lawyers and investigators, found that Bradshaw should not be charged with sexual assault due to "insufficient evidence." The superintendent, Lieutenant General Robert Caslen, a former West Point football player himself, did not authorize any charges against Bradshaw.

Bradshaw starred on the football team for three seasons (2015–2017) despite repeatedly being cited for misconduct or poor performance in other areas, according to the *Daily Beast*. Of twenty observations reports of Bradshaw, fifteen—by fellow cadets as well as three army majors—were negative.[89] In addition, Bradshaw was "disciplined" in the summer of 2016 (apparently by not being permitted to attend the first day of football practice) for misconduct that West Point and its head football coach, Jeff Monken, refused to identify.

Then, in November 2016, an honor board comprised of fellow cadets found that Bradshaw had violated the honor code by cheating on an assignment the previous semester, according to the *Daily Beast*. After the finding of an honor violation, almost all other cadets are prohibited from participating in any activity in which they represent West Point, but not Bradshaw. Superintendent Caslen decided not to act until after the football season ended, conveniently allowing Bradshaw to play in the Army-Navy game in December 2016. Bradshaw was "suspended" from playing games from February to August, when there are no intercollegiate football games, and he became eligible again just in time for the 2017 season. Speaking to staff and faculty about the reports on the football players, Caslen called the *Daily Beast* a "tabloid newspaper that likes to publish sensational articles" and accused the officer who leaked the documents of being a criminal, a textbook example of West Point's—and the military's—favorite response to complaints: attacking the complainant.

CELEBRATING MEDIOCRITY

Even prior to recent incidents of misconduct and the lowering of standards for at-risk cadets, West Point embodied and bizarrely celebrated (and continues to celebrate) a culture of mediocrity. Cadets' informal mantra for getting over and getting by is "cooperate and graduate." Soon after Bradshaw's cheating incident, U.S. vice president Joe Biden gave the 2016 commencement address as 952 cadets awaited formal graduation and the oath that would transform them into second lieutenants in America's army. Biden, Superintendent Caslen, and McDonald, the admissions director, looked on approvingly and smiled at one cadet on the main stage as he received a standing ovation from all the other cadets. The exalted cadet was grinning widely, his arms raised high in jubilation, his diploma in one hand and a large wad of cash in the other.

Referring to the young man, the *Pointer View*, the newspaper published by West Point's Public Affairs Office, reported, "Second Lt. Alex Fletcher is ecstatic about being the 'Goat,' which goes to the last ranked cadet to graduate [lowest and last in his class]. Outside of the cheers and adulation from the Class of 2016, Fletcher received a dollar from each member of the class as part of [the] tradition of honoring the 'Goat.'" (The term is a reference to the mascot of the Naval Academy, and thus a jab at West Point's rivals.)

Of his accomplishment, Fletcher said, "I am beyond ecstatic . . . I have been wanting this day since I was a freshman. I remember when I was in the stands as a freshman, I saw the goat, everybody just started cheering, and I knew that's what I wanted." Fletcher, proudly last in his class, is currently defending America in the U.S. Army's Field Artillery Branch.[90] There's not a person alive who would want an operation performed by a surgeon who brags about finishing last in her or his graduating class in medical school, yet at West Point, such a graduate merits congratulations and a cash payment.

Just a few months before Fletcher became the goat, General Joseph L. Votel (Class of '80), formerly the commander of U.S. Special Operations, returned to his alma mater to speak with cadets who were in their third year. Votel told the "Cows"—what West Point calls its third-year students—"I wasn't all that great of a cadet and while I was on the Dean's list—it wasn't the Dean's List you really wanted to be on. I did, however, rally my last couple semesters and managed to graduate in the 35th percentile of my class—thank you very much! For those of you out there in that same academic 'band of averageness'—take heart . . . the Army is run by C+ students . . . at least

USSOCOM [U.S. Special Operations Command] is." Two months later, Votel became the head of Central Command, where he oversaw the U.S. wars in Afghanistan and Iraq.

CONTAGIOUS HUBRIS

The 2017 study by the social scientists at West Point confirmed the intellectual decline of army officers.[91] But even prior to the study, Jason W. Warren, a major in the army, zeroed in on a lack of respect for intelligence as pervasive in the institution. In a 2015 article, he concluded that the army is decidedly anti-intellectual and promotes officers based on their tactical experience, not on their strategic thinking. Citing commentators, Warren recounted how John Abizaid, George Casey, Tommy Franks, and Ricardo (Rick) Sanchez, commanding generals in Iraq, did not "grasp the situation."[92] "Without leaders capable of developing an intellectual framework for winning," Major Warren concluded, "the Army will continue to produce disappointing results."[93]

Army general Tommy Franks oversaw the beginning of the wars in both Afghanistan and Iraq. "Most generals get the opportunity to lose, at worst, one war. Franks, who from mid-2000 to mid-2003 oversaw the U.S. Central Command, the headquarters for operations in the Middle East, bungled two," according to Tom Ricks.[94] Even Franks's "success" in the first weeks of the Iraq War was illusory; the prompt toppling of Saddam Hussein's regime allowed many high-ranking Iraqis to escape or "to melt away into the population or go into hiding and fight another day," writes George Packer.[95] President Bush blamed the subsequent Iraqi insurgency on U.S. forces' early "catastrophic success."[96]

Tom Ricks captures Franks's mix of arrogance and incompetence, which seem de rigueur for those atop the military hierarchy: "Gen. Franks sometimes makes assertions that are wildly inaccurate, but he offers them with great certitude."[97] Franks also lacked a basic understanding of what victory would mean in these two modern wars, with assumptions based on previous and dated conceptions. "Sean Naylor of the *Army Times*," Ricks writes, "noted how Franks failed to grasp in waging the Afghan war that taking the enemy's capital wasn't the same as winning the war, a conceptual error he would repeat in Iraq."[98]

Daniel Bolger, a retired army lieutenant general and graduate of the Citadel, concluded in his 2014 book *Why We Lost: A General's Inside Account of the Iraq and Afghanistan Wars* that "we faltered due to a distinct lack of humility. Certain we knew best, confident our skilled troops would prevail, we persisted in a failed course for far too long and came up well short, to the detriment of our trusting country-men."[99] To put a finer point on it, when you're not smart enough to fear the underdog then you will not survive, referencing the lyrics of the rock group Spoon.

Beginning at the academies, the U.S. military fosters disrespect for intelligence and outside opinions and hostility to any learning that would upset the status quo. Officers are like-minded and fall in line behind old thinking and practices. The effect is a recurring, debilitating sameness, the self-selection and then the self-sorting of those who think and act alike, constancy and conformity without growth, as we will see now.

CHAPTER 3

Conformity and Cronyism—
One and the Same

I n the twenty-first century, the disconnection of the military and its academies from American society—where at any one time less than 1 percent
of the population serves in the armed forces[1]—has become complete. When
forced to leave West Point for poor grades or misconduct, a cadet is
described as being "separated," a literal and metaphorical term that signifies
exclusion from a way of thinking and living. Cadets who enter the academy
may come from every state, but they in no way represent a cross-section of
the nation. The idea that when a cadet arrives he or she is a blank slate, "a
nobody . . . literally a bag of underwear,"[2] as one cadet told author David
Lipsky, is necessarily not true. The cadet is bringing a worldview and a
mindset that represent a very narrow segment of America.

The graduates of West Point are solidly on the conservative side of
American political thought. A 2013 study by the Alumni Factor showed
how the perspectives of West Point graduates diverge from the perspectives of the graduates of other colleges. The numbers are eye-opening. Of
the West Pointers, 74 percent reported being on the conservative spectrum, compared with 45 percent of all college graduates; 95 percent
believed that "America is the best country in the world," compared with

77 percent of all college graduates; 96 percent agreed that "capitalism is a positive force in our world today," compared with 78 percent of all college graduates; 71 percent agreed that "affirmative action is unfair," compared with 48 percent of all college graduates; 36 percent agreed that "abortion should be illegal," compared with 21 percent of all college graduates; 83 percent agreed that "children should be allowed to pray in school," compared with 66 percent of all college graduates; 16 percent agreed that "capital punishment is immoral," compared with 47 percent of all college graduates; and 44 percent agreed that "guns should be more controlled than they are," compared with 73 percent of all college graduates.[3]

The absence of moderating perspectives produces narrow thinking and tunnel vision, like seeing only one color in a rainbow, and creates fertile ground for groupthink. This helps solidify an attitude that separation from mainstream society is necessary to sustain the superior, and necessarily fewer, values inside the military. Packing an institution with the same type of people and thinking hardens into place the same behavior. As Harvard Law professor Cass Sunstein examined in *Going to Extremes: How Like Minds Unite and Divide*, the more like-minded a group, the more its beliefs imprint back onto the group.

Sunstein's work shows that a "predisposition in a particular direction would be exaggerated, sometimes substantially, when people were in a group with others who share the predisposition,"[4] explains author David Aaronovitch. The divisions between the military and academia are particularly stark. Joan Johnson-Freese, professor at the Naval War College, explains in *Educating America's Military* that "academics . . . tend to be liberal, while military officers tend to be conservative—the empirical evidence on that is indisputable. Both cultures tend to be insular and spend considerable time talking to people much like themselves."[5]

When the results of the Alumni Factor survey were presented to Lieutenant Colonel Pete Kilner, among others, his response reinforced the findings. Kilner held an influential position in the army as an academy professor at West Point and the director of leader development and organizational learning. When Kilner retired from the military, West Point—which means the military officers he knew—made him the chair for character development of the cadets. But of course Kilner brought his old military ideas into his new civilian job. As an officer, he was confident he could explain why conservative people attend or graduate from West Point. West Pointers, he said, are just "more patriotic, more willing to engage in selfless service, and more willing to die for our country." To me, Kilner seems to come pretty close to just coming out and saying what he thinks: he and they are just better people.

The military should be relying on the academies to produce new knowledge and teach its future officers how to adapt to new problems. Instead, the academies are dominated by a military-training ethos that has been churning in its own isolated sphere for generations, taught by the officers who received the same time-worn information from their predecessors. To illustrate, the brigade tactical officer (BTO) at West Point is always a colonel who is responsible for drug-sniffing dogs that search cadets' rooms for contraband, for planning and regulating how cadets dress, for determining whether cadets' rooms are in proper order, and for evaluating whether their marching at parades is satisfactory.

These are enormously time-consuming practices that do not exist elsewhere in American society, and they lead to virtually no new learning. Nonetheless, one West Point–educated BTO recently complained to other colonels that cadets' academic pursuits, including day-long trips to conferences or events to nearby New York City, prevented him from fielding fifty-person cadet units for marching practice on the parade field. Another colonel, one of the few in high positions who was not a graduate of West Point, was baffled. "Why don't you just reduce the fifty-cadet units to a smaller number, like forty?" he asked. The BTO responded incredulously but gratefully, "We never thought of that."

This is the same system that produced General Douglas MacArthur, who created a cult of personality around himself; he "assigned cronies— picked not for their competence but for their personal loyalty—to combat commands, despite their glaring lack of experience [and] encouraged sycophantism among his subordinates."[6] This isolation around MacArthur contributed to his inept belief that the Chinese would never get involved in the Korean War and then, after they did, that attacking with nuclear weapons was a good idea.

The system allows Major General Samuel Koster, who lied about and covered up his soldiers' murders of five hundred civilians—children, women, and old men—at My Lai, in the Vietnam War, to become the superintendent of West Point in his next job. The system permitted General William Westmoreland to lie to his president to induce him to send hundreds of thousands of soldiers to Vietnam when the war was lost. The system then rewarded Westmoreland by making him army chief of staff, its top officer.

It produced General David Petraeus, who disclosed the nation's most highly sensitive classified information to impress a lover, and he went on to lie about it to federal agents. In 2015, U.S. soldiers and airmen in an aerial gunship fired cannons on a hospital in Kunduz, Afghanistan, for thirty to sixty minutes and, while receiving no return fire, killed forty-two innocent doctors, nurses, and patients. The four-star generals in overall command, John Campbell in Afghanistan and Joseph Votel at Central Command, concluded that no soldier should be charged with any crime.

These generals, all graduates of West Point, joined the armed forces with little awareness of their own limitations. They entered West Point believing in their superiority, and everything they encountered reinforced their feelings. Today, the U.S. military recruits the same type of people and trains them to conform fully to the generals' notions of what are proper forms of thinking and behavior. In their hubris and isolated mindsets, the generals do not attract a cross-section of Americans and then adapt the institution to intellectually diverse students' and soldiers' collective strengths. From the outside, the military's purpose is to protect America, but the spine of day-to-day life in the military is self-protection: advance your career; help your friends; don't say bad things about the military, especially to outsiders; retaliate against dissenters; at all times and under all circumstances, maintain appearances; and, above all, remain loyal to the institution and your superiors, regardless of their wrongdoing.

From time to time, any institution will produce deficient leaders, but the military's poor record in this regard—spanning generations—is impossible to ignore. Incredibly, the last U.S. general to win a war, Dwight Eisenhower, graduated in 1915. Over the past seventy-five years, all of America's top commanders have displayed remarkably similar incompetence, narrow thinking, and self-assuredness. The personality traits and approaches of the top military leaders are replicated time and time again, and examining West Point's role in this is instructive. At the academies, no outside air is let in, and the vacuum inside has sacrificed the quality of the cadets' education.

Military officers rotate in and out of the academies to teach at their alma maters and inculcate in a new generation of students the same thinking, values, and back-scratching loyalty toward fellow academy graduates. Novelist Lucian K. Truscott IV (Class of '69) explains a particularly degrading point in this process in the late 1960s: "The honor code broke down before our eyes as staff and faculty jobs at West Point began filling with officers returning from Vietnam. Some had covered their uniforms with bogus medals and made their careers with lies—inflating body counts, ignoring drug abuse, turning a blind eye to racial discrimination, and worst of all, telling everyone above them in the chain of command that we were winning a war they knew we were losing. The lies became embedded in the curriculum of the academy, and finally in its moral DNA."[7]

A CERTAIN TYPE

In almost every measure, today's military officers come from the same places, literally and metaphorically. In personality tests, they are "traditionalists" who "value words like dependability, reliability, thoroughness, responsibility, duty, trustworthiness and service to society." They embrace operations over creativity and work in a bureaucracy that rewards conformity.[8] They are prone to perceiving threats among ambiguous stimuli.

In a 2010 dissertation, "Civil-Military Relations in a Time of War," military officer Heidi Urben found that "in 1976, 63% of military elites [primarily colonels and lieutenant colonels at the Army War College or the Pentagon] professed to have conservative political views; by 1996, the percentage increased to 73%. Meanwhile the percentage of senior military officers who described their political ideology as liberal dropped from 16% to 3%."[9]

The military brass are also out of step with civilians of comparable class; "while 67% of senior officers claimed affiliation with the Republican Party," Urben notes, "only 34% of a comparable civilian elite did."[10] As *Time* magazine explained, the sorting happened exponentially; between

1976 and 1996, "the share of senior military officers identifying . . . as Republican jumped from one-third to two-thirds, while those claiming to be moderates fell from 46% to 22% . . . Urben found that younger officers leaving the Army were far more likely to identify themselves as Democrats than those opting to stay, which would tend to make the more senior ranks increasingly Republican."[11]

Surveys from 1980 to 2004 showed that from 64 to 77 percent of military officers identify themselves as conservative and 3 to 9 percent identify themselves as liberal, according to data collected by author Jason Dempsey.[12] Similarly, Urben found that nearly 69 percent of army colonels (the highest rank in her survey) identify themselves on the conservative spectrum, and only 10 percent on the liberal spectrum.[13]

The familial background of people who join the military is similarly monochromatic. Surveys show that about 80 percent of the people serving in the military come from families where a sibling or parent is also in the military.[14] Remarkably, nearly half (49 percent) of active-duty military personnel are concentrated in just five states: California, Georgia, North Carolina, Texas, and Virginia. Four of the five states that are the highest-rate contributors of eighteen-to-twenty-four-year-olds in the military are from the South: Georgia, Florida, South Carolina, and Virginia.[15]

Any ideology that dominates an institution the way conservatism dominates the U.S. officer corps will produce stagnation, groupthink, and isolation. For example, studies show that conservatives and liberals can view the same set of problems and facts but arrive at very different solutions. Without the leavening effect of intellectual balance, decades of one-sided thinking will produce the same kinds of narrow responses.

In a 2014 study published in *Behavioral and Brain Sciences*, "Differences in Negativity Bias Underlie Variations in Political Ideology," researchers John Hibbing, Kevin Smith, and John Alford summarized decades of studies into the characteristics of conservatives and liberals. They found that conservatives are likely quicker to focus on the negative because of their instinctive need for protection and security.

According to the researchers, "Mounting empirical evidence suggests that, compared to liberals, conservatives are more responsive and attuned to negative stimuli, patterns consistent with their tendency to advocate political solutions designed to protect against threats and disorder—real or perceived."[16] The researchers suggest that conservatives' responsiveness to negative stimuli, which might have been necessary to protect people and groups as they evolved, may not be as valuable in resolving modern problems.[17]

The variables, interactions, and relationships in the modern world are so numerous and complex that a single-minded response—bombing population centers in North Korea, conducting a war of attrition in Vietnam, or attacking every nation that may pose an abstract or potential threat—is likely to fail. Hibbing and his colleagues explain that just as "virtually all species benefit from having individuals with different immune systems . . . human groups benefit from having members who are differentially responsive and attentive to negative stimuli."[18] Whether in thinking or practice, polarization is doomed to be less effective than openness and intellectual diversity. With the absence of varied viewpoints or any dissent, an isolated group is in danger of both misperceiving threats and erring in response to them.

Moreover, conservative beliefs are more likely to lead to dynamic action (as opposed to sensible inaction). Sometimes not acting is the more prudent form of action, but the conservative mind is less likely to accept this paradox. "Environmental stimuli that are unexpected, ambiguous, uncertain, or disorderly," Hibbing and his colleagues found, "also appear to generate more response and attention from conservatives than liberals at a variety of levels, including brain activation patterns, sympathetic nervous system response, cognitive behaviors, and self-reports."[19] Simply put, the conservative brain or thinking is more likely to spot conflict where there may or may not be any.

Immediate responses, sometimes violence, were perhaps once necessary to preserve segregated groups that possessed only limited defenses and resources. In ancient times and in agrarian America, where communities were isolated, any outside threat posed a significant danger to an entire group. But today, given its nuclear weapons and vast armaments, as well as an extensive internal policing apparatus, America faces no threat of invasion. Under all indices, war should be far less likely than in the past; in fact, it has become less likely for countries throughout the world, with one exception: the United States.

In the absence of dissent, decision-making in the U.S. military is not suited for confrontations with modern enemies, which depend much more on winning hearts and minds than hills and land. The U.S. military needs far more intellectual capacity and flexibility than it is currently getting. According to almost all research, people who hold conservative values— which dominate the officer corps of the American military—are more authoritarian, conventional, conformist, traditional, and submissive to authority. Such fundamentalism leads to scorn of compromise and a persistent type of anti-intellectualism, exactly the opposite of what is needed to resolve the complex problems that face today's armed forces.[20]

The army's intellectual inflexibility was described in a 2013 study, *Changing Minds in the Army: Why It Is So Difficult and What to Do About It*, by Stephen Gerras and Leonard Wong, the authors of the 2015 study *Lying to Ourselves: Dishonesty in the Army Profession*, referenced in chapter 2. "Personality data gathered at the U.S. Army War College (USAWC) from lieutenant colonels and colonels who were students," they found, "show the most successful officers score lower in openness than the general U.S. population . . . To make matters worse, though, those USAWC students selected for brigade command score even lower than the overall USAWC average. This raises an interesting paradox: The leaders recognized and selected by the army to serve at strategic levels—where uncertainty and complexity are the greatest—tend to have lower levels of one of the attributes most related to success at strategic level."[21] "Interesting paradox" is an understatement, to say the least. The result has been downright fatal. Those who rise to the top of the military hierarchy are particularly suited— even selected—for their lack of nuanced thinking.

The U.S. Army is placing unqualified officers into its highest ranks. In assessing military campaigns throughout the world over the past two hundred years, a Rand study from 2014 found "strategic blunders" when decision-makers relied "on defective cognitive models of reality." Too often U.S. generals are fighting the wars they would rather be fighting or they are fighting previous wars, unable to adapt to conditions in front of them. The Rand study elaborates, "This can at once result from and aggravate faulty intuition, egotism, arrogance, hubris, grand but flawed strategic ideas, underestimating the enemy and the difficulties and duration of conflict, overconfidence in war plans, ignoring what could go wrong, stifling debate, shunning independent advice, and penalizing dissent—conditions that can be especially dangerous if accompanied by excessive risk taking based on an overestimation of the ability to control events."[22]

Since World War II, the disabling characteristics highlighted in the Rand study have been inherent in the daily work and methods of the U.S. military. These characteristics are reinforced through the recruitment and promotion of narrow-thinking officers and misguided decisions by U.S. commanders who do not understand the enemy and stubbornly refuse to learn. The resulting errors among officers are compounded by their blind loyalty and desire to advance their careers. As Bob Woodward pointed out, this is part of their makeup and training: "Military men have always known they have to adapt to their superiors, adaptability having much in common with both subservience and survival."[23] But "survival" in this context doesn't mean living; it means career advancement.

According to Admiral James G. Stavridis, former NATO Supreme Allied Commander in Europe, "The enormous irony of the military profession is that we are huge risk takers in what we do operationally . . . we are happy to take personal risk or operational risk, but too many of us won't take career risk."[24] War college professor Joan Johnson-Freese pointed out this same tendency in promoted officers who "went on to successful careers where risk-averse answers to their boss's questions are standard."[25]

Through a type of artificial selection, where the best do not join or do not remain in the military, the military command is not where the nation puts its smartest or most forward-thinking people. To make it to the top of the pyramid, officers are expected to carry out orders, conform their thinking and behavior to what superior officers desire, and never question up the chain of command. In the military ranks, George Packer explained, "intellectual candor . . . [makes] professional advancement less likely."[26] The result is a type of natural selection, survival of the loyalist.

It was silence and acquiescence in the ranks that led to the U.S. decision to attack Iraq in 2003, according to the Rand study. A "group of neoconservatives in and out of government" sought "opportunity in danger," a chance to bring democracy to the Middle East. The Pentagon was willing to "cherry-pick selective intelligence." A "sense of prowess and hubris" helped create "dysfunctional and opaque" decision-making.[27] The remedies to the problems are independent analysis, objectivity and balance, and modern technology-enhanced computer analyses, according to the study.[28]

Such positive change is unlikely to occur anytime soon because these attributes are not rooted anywhere inside the U.S. military. Instead, the Rand study described a theme in military losses: "Individuals and institutions faced with complex strategic choices rely on simplified representations of reality . . . without which complexity could overwhelm them."[29] Uncomfortable with complexity and the questions that arise during open discussions, the U.S. military—as represented by its officers—has hatched a separate world. It is one where officers emphasize loyalty, patriotism, and fidelity, qualities that have little to do with—and in some cases are counterproductive to—creating winning strategies.

This penchant for simplicity, the military's isolation from civil society, and its resistance to intellectual diversity comprise the model at the military academies, from which most of the top generals and admirals graduate. These are places that have many deficient students who are admitted only because they are proficient in one sport or whose parent (or other relative) graduated from the academies; narrow curriculums focused on engineering and vocational accreditation; a large majority of instructors (military officers) who have master's instead of doctoral degrees and little or no teaching or practical experience; administrator jobs filled only by military officers; and threats of termination and criminal prosecution of instructors who do not submit their speeches and writings to censors for "clearance." America's generals and admirals are educated and formed in an environment that echoes the military itself—and the two devour and perpetuate each other in a destructive feedback loop.

THE CURRICULUM

The overseers of the cadets and curriculum at West Point are always military officers who have little experience in education, almost no experience practicing within a professional discipline, and never any professional employment experience outside the army. They have spent all their time in the army's branches, and for over two hundred years almost all of them have shared a single characteristic: they have been graduates of West Point. This applies to the superintendents, commandants, and deans; 145 of 150 of these officers since 1812 have been graduates of West Point.

Throughout the army today, West Point graduates are ubiquitous, especially among the higher ranks, and are sometimes identified by nonacademy graduates as "ring knockers" for the large, expensive (up to $11,000) class rings many of them wear ostentatiously throughout their careers. From year to year 50 to 60 percent of the instructors are army captains and majors. They do not have doctoral degrees in the courses they teach and become instructors after working in an army branch (such as infantry) and one or two years in a master's degree program. Cadets are receiving a very expensive "community college education," according to Tom Ricks in his *Washington Post* op-ed "Why We Should Get Rid of West Point."[30] Because these military instructors do not have the experience necessary to engage in the normal professional activities of college professors (such as research and publication), they teach most of the courses at West Point. In two or three years they will leave and go back to their army branches and be replaced by others like them.

Soon after its founding in 1802, West Point was organized around civil engineering because its graduates were responsible for helping to build America's infrastructure. As political science professor Dominic Tierney explains, "[Early] American soldiers dug canals and erected bridges. They built roads, dredged harbors, and explored and surveyed the land."[31] In the twenty-first century, this is no longer the case. Though civilian contractors are almost always hired today to do the military's engineering work, from 40 to 50 percent of the students at all three academies still study some type of engineering, such as civil, mechanical, or electrical. Additionally, all students must take several engineering courses at the expense of a more well-rounded education. The most critical infrastructure of the twenty-first century is not physical infrastructure at all: it is an understanding of societies and cultures, which these graduates lack and the academies devalue.

Engineering is "an educational discipline where right and wrong answers prevail; something works, or it doesn't,"[32] writes war college professor Joan Johnson-Freese in *Educating America's Military*. The military academies should be producing broad-thinking leaders, especially because generals have to be strategic thinkers and lower-ranking officers have to be the "mayors" of towns in Afghanistan and Iraq and elsewhere. But the creativity in engineering is in building hard structures, whereas a different creativity, keen emotional intelligence, is needed to understand the behavior of foreign civilian populations and modern adversaries.

Johnson-Freese concludes that the narrowness of the education found at the war colleges and academies has failed to prepare their students by not helping them understand "the context and processes of their operating environment . . . In fact, failed leaders have often failed because they did not understand the political or social ramifications of their actions." She points to the well-known litany of failed generals who have risen to the top and have plagued America's performance in battle: "MacArthur's misreading the Chinese in Korea, Westmoreland thinking he could win a war of attrition in Vietnam, and failing to plan for reconstruction in Iraq and Afghanistan are among many errors in judgment that can be cited as rooted in failure to understand the environment."[33]

In a startling study from 2009, two European researchers, Diego Gambetta from the University of Oxford and Steffen Hertog from Sciences Po, explained why they believe a disproportionate number of violent Islamic radicals they identified, 78 of 178 (44 percent), studied engineering. "We can conjecture that engineering as a degree might be relatively more attractive to individuals seeking cognitive 'closure' and clear-cut answers as opposed to more open-ended sciences—a disposition which has been empirically linked to conservative political attitudes. Engineering is a subject in which individuals with a dislike for ambiguity might feel comfortable."[34]

A 1984 study by the Carnegie Foundation, the most relevant one according to Gambetta and Hertzog, found that among 5,057 faculty-member respondents to a survey at undergraduate colleges and universities in the United States "the proportion of [male] engineers who declare themselves to be on the right of the political spectrum is greater than in any other disciplinary group: 57.6 % of them are either conservative or strongly conservative [compared to 18.6 percent of social scientists, for example] . . . Perhaps this is an uncanny coincidence, but the four fields at the top of the conservatism scale—engineering, economics, medicine, and science—are the same four secular fields we found at the top of our main jihadist sample."

Gambetta and Hertzog found that religion and conservativism lead to narrow political positions. "The Carnegie survey reveals an even more surprising fact, hitherto unnoticed, that strengthens the suspicion that the engineers' mindset may play a part in their proneness not only to radicalise to the right of the political spectrum, but do so with a religious slant: engineers turn out to be by far the most religious group of all academics—66.5 %, followed again by 61.7 % in economics, 49.9 % in sciences, 48.8 % of social scientists, 46.3 % of doctors and 44.1 % of lawyers."[35] Regarding violent groups, Gambetta and Hertog observed: "The only other case in which we find a trace of engineers' prominence outside of Islamic violent groups is . . . among the most extreme right-wing movements, especially in the U.S. and in Germany."[36]

Referencing Friedrich von Hayek, a 1974 Nobel Prize winner in economics, the researchers conclude that engineering education does not lead students "to understand individuals and their world as the outcome of a social process in which spontaneous behaviours and interactions play a significant part. Rather, it fosters on them a script in which a strict 'rational' control of processes plays the key role: this would make them on the one hand less adept at dealing with the confusing causality of the social and political realms and the compromise and circumspection that these entail, and on the other hand inclined to think that societies should operate in an orderly way akin to well-functioning machines—a feature which is reminiscent of the Islamist engineers in [one] account."[37] In a repressive, authoritarian environment, this mindset can lead to radicalization.[38]

Engineering is the last discipline around which a broad education should be based. But it's the primary discipline at each of the three U.S. military academies. At the academies, many lessons of wars are ignored in favor of the narrow engineering curriculum. Forgoing an opportunity for a broader education, all cadets at West Point must take at least three engineering courses, and almost half of them (those majoring in engineering) must take twelve to fifteen engineering courses. While killing is the most sobering activity in war, cadets do not receive any instruction on the mental or psychological processes used in deciding whether to kill an enemy combatant or how it feels to have a fellow soldier killed.

The absence of broader lessons in the curriculum is not an oversight. It is the specific intent of a culture that does not traffic in doubt or self-reflection. Failure in Vietnam "was not a question senior military leadership cared to explore," according to George Packer, so why would military instructors at West Point teach the war through that lens? Why would officers design a curriculum around seeking remedies to events they do not understand or which they do not consider to be failures at all?

West Point, for example, has one course in military history, which deals with wars since 1945. (In 2017 West Point dropped another military history course, which concerned lessons from older wars.) When he taught at West Point (2010–2015), Colonel Greg Daddis, known for his "revisionist history" and fawning book about General Westmoreland, was considered the resident expert on Vietnam. The current military history course has four lessons on Vietnam, and U.S. soldiers' massacre of civilians at My Lai is not part of the curriculum. There is no course on counterinsurgency, the type of strategy necessary in modern wars.

Only 30 percent of the military instructors have doctoral degrees.[39] In contrast, 91 percent of the civilian instructors have doctoral degrees, a percentage comparable to that at similar colleges.

At the Air Force Academy, 86 percent of the civilian instructors but only 33 to 40 percent of the military instructors possessed doctorates.[40] Nearly *four dozen* instructors taught courses for which they did not hold a related master's degree. According to *Truthout*, "An instructor with a master's degree in exercise physiology teaches mathematical science. Another instructor with a master's degree in meteorology teaches geopolitics. But maybe the most bizarre examples have to do with language courses. An instructor with a master's degree in business administration teaches Arabic. Another with a master's degree in educational leadership teaches Chinese. And another instructor with a master's degree in public administration teaches Russian."[41]

A longitudinal study of teaching at the Air Force Academy showed the consequences of hiring military instructors without doctorates.[42] The 2010 study found that "students with instructors without PhDs do well in that instructor's class, which translates into good student evaluations for the instructor, but go on to perform poorly in more advanced classes."[43] This is a microcosm of what ails the military. Underlings become expert at giving their bosses what they want, but they perform poorly when confronted with ambiguity or complicated problems.

Despite having far lower qualifications than civilians with doctoral degrees (who could be hired in their place), military instructors cost the government twice as much as civilian professors.[44] Part of the massive expense for military instructors is that the government pays for their educations, their families' homes and health care, their children's K–12 educations, and other benefits not available to civilian professors.

According to former Air Force Academy economics professor David Mullin, the motivation to hire military instructors who are more costly and less qualified than civilian instructors is privilege.[45] Military officers are a privileged class at the academies, rewarded beyond their merit, and the cadets who observe and internalize this fact understand that the same will be true for them. While more qualified civilian professors are not hired, and those who are hired are treated as inferior, the most significant repercussion is that cadets suffer from a subpar education.

About 80 percent of all the military instructors at West Point and the Air Force Academy are officers with a master's degree who "rotate" in and out after staying only two or three years. That kind of turnover alone is destructive to any institution. Further, a consequence of this practice is that it ensures that the old ways of doing things never die. The long-term military instructors control every aspect of the academies and cannot be challenged because most officers are far inferior in rank and civilian instructors are prohibited from ever moving into the top administrative positions, from which they could initiate change. (The Naval Academy allows civilian professors to become a department head or dean.) Teaching at the academies is universally thought by officers to be a great gig: a free master's degree at a civilian university; a few years away from less regal military bases; and the automatic acquisition of the title "assistant professor," bestowed by some academic departments on the instructors when they leave the academy. The academies function as a popular stop on a military career carousel. Everything works out for the officers, and there is no incentive to change. The loop continues circling, rewarding military officers with teaching jobs for which they aren't qualified and sacrificing the education and readiness of yet another generation of cadets.

THE POWER OF CONFORMITY

I never had a thought of my own until I left the service.

—Marine major general Smedley Butler (1881–1940)

In *Absolutely American*, a book that tracks a cohort of cadets through four years at the academy, David Lipsky writes, "Daily life at West Point is organized the way people in the Middle Ages believed God oversaw the universe: every encounter is supposed to develop the cadets in some way."[46] This is a fundamental fact about life at West Point, with its emphasis on cadets' shiny shoes, properly tucked shirts, table manners, and marching expertise. "The terms of success at West Point," Lipsky writes, "are belonging and not-belonging. The official word for expulsion is separation: you're nosed out, cut off from the pack, shipped far away from the brotherhood."[47] While Lipsky's book is mostly respectful, at times fawning, he recognizes that the culture at West Point is carefully designed to replicate itself. It's a laboratory that churns out a product, with little room for growth outside the model.

This happens on both a macro and a micro scale. New officers teaching the same course at West Point may be expected to use the same colored chalk on blackboards (whiteboards are rarely used) to emphasize the same point in order to ensure "uniformity" among impressionable new cadets. You can walk down a row of classrooms in an academic building and see the same PowerPoint slide on a screen at almost exactly the same time. The chalk technique comes from the Thayer method of the early 1800s, named after Sylvanus Thayer, who became superintendent in 1817 and was a prime reason West Point became organized around engineering. As part of the Thayer method, when cadets hear from their instructors the dog whistle "Take boards!," they are trained to stand and write formulas, equations, or diagrams on blackboards.

To some outsiders, uniformed cadets squeaking at the blackboard seems traditional, even quaint, as the military instructor walks from cadet to cadet to comment on their work. But this routine hides flaws and gaps in the ability of the instructors, who are not equipped to offer meaningful feedback to individual cadets during a fifty-five-minute class. The two-hundred-year-old method, cast as active learning, is little more than a tool to control cadets' time in the classroom and relieve inexperienced instructors from shouldering the more difficult burden of facilitating discussion and deeper learning when students are interacting in a larger group.

The inexperienced instructors do not create any part of the courses they teach. Unlike professors at other colleges, they receive the course syllabus, administrative guide, quizzes, exams, PowerPoint slides, textbook, and project and paper assignments from the long-term instructors. In most courses, the number of "graded events" each semester can range from ten to fifteen (when the number is two or three at other colleges), with up to fifteen hundred points for the semester. This is a vocational training or physical-fitness model, like soldiers getting together each day to exercise repetitiously and uniformly, implanted into what should be a higher education setting.

As for the leadership and faculty makeup, West Point is almost certainly the least diverse institution, public or private, in the history of America. Since 1812, all fifty-eight superintendents, thirteen of the fourteen academic deans, and seventy-four of the seventy-eight commandants have been graduates of West Point.[48] With similarly narrow backgrounds, the dean, a brigadier general, and twenty-eight colonels control the academic program. Upon their selection, these colonels became known as Professors, United States Military Academy (PUSMAs), although none of them ever worked as a professor prior to arriving at West Point.

In 2010, the academy's dean, Brigadier General Pat Finnegan, issued a new rule: that "Professors USMA serve with the academic rank of Professor," which he claimed was justified because of "their statutory leadership responsibilities." Their new title was not based on any academic accomplishment but solely on the fact that they already possessed the title "Professor, USMA," as listed in a federal statute. All the PUSMAs today have doctoral degrees, albeit through abbreviated three-year PhD graduate programs (and one has a law degree). Because the PUSMAs come only from the army, there are only several officers with a PhD who are eligible to apply for each position, when the number of applicants at any other college could be in the hundreds.

This too works in the officers' favor and against the cadets. Anywhere else, the new PUSMAs would be among the least experienced assistant professors in the academic world. However, at West Point, they (along with the dean) run the entire academic program. First arriving at West Point in their late thirties or early forties, the PUSMAs may hold their positions until mandatory retirement at sixty-four. (Except for generals, mandatory retirement for all other officers in the military is sixty-two.) They are always replaced by new PUSMAs, and, in written correspondence, they address each other as "Leaders" or "Leader Team." The PUSMAs are less likely than civilian professors to qualify for academic promotion because they may spend twenty years in the army prior to obtaining their positions, often rarely working in their disciplines, and almost never having published articles or books or participated in other scholarly activity. They know how to receive and dispatch orders. This is what they are rewarded for doing, and it is what they reward the cadets for learning how to do.

Under West Point's rules, the PUSMAs, at retirement, may even receive the academic title of professor emeritus. This title is based in part on their automatic academic rank of professor, which is based on their automatic title of "professor, USMA." Who votes on whether retiring PUSMAs receive the title of professor emeritus? It's their longtime friends and colleagues, the other PUSMAs, who make up the Academic Board.

Further, a federal statute provides that a retiring PUSMA may be advanced to brigadier general in retirement without ever working as a brigadier general.[49] The PUSMA's justification is that they are entitled to be called generals because they might have earned that promotion if they had not *sacrificed* by volunteering to work at West Point. The PUSMAs will be listed in army records as a brigadier general and may wear a star on their uniforms in postretirement ceremonies and parades. In sum, the PUSMAs who enter West Point will accrue up to four titles they would not likely attain in the army or at any other educational institution.

Any threat from the outside regarding this entrenched system is met with fierce resistance. In 2015 the civilian faculty senate at West Point proposed that civilian professors should have the opportunity to compete for the positions of dean, department head, and deputy department head. (Later, after he rejected the proposal, the superintendent, Lieutenant General Robert Caslen, decided that "senate" projected too much autonomy and stripped the word from the title, making the group the Superintendent's Civilian Advisory Committee.) Widening the field of applicants would seem to be a positive development, but not to the officers at West Point.

The dean, Brigadier General Tim Trainor, appointed the head of the Department of Foreign Languages, Greg Ebner, to cochair the committee designated to issue a report on whether the administrative positions should be open to civilians, which Ebner opposed. At a faculty council meeting, Ebner essentially made an argument for cronyism. "If you take away the department head position and give it to a civilian faculty member that means a military faculty member is not going to get that position," said Ebner, ignoring the importance of merit-based promotions. "I would argue that if we made a civilian faculty member the department head then we just limited the career development of Academy [military] Professors . . . Because of their careers in the Army PUSMAs have extensive exposure to the Army staff. Their classmates, their friends, and colleagues are all in positions that allow us to get things done for West Point." Ebner summarized how cronyism works and why it's essential to the PUSMAs.

Then the new dean, Brigadier General Cindy Jebb, read the minutes of a civilian senate meeting held after Ebner's address to the faculty. A civilian professor who was the chair of the senate and had worked more than twenty years at West Point, Dr. Gary Washington, commented on Ebner's response to questions. Washington, according to the minutes, viewed Ebner's behavior as "bullying." Jebb summoned Washington to her office and directed him to apologize to Ebner, which he did.

After Democratic senators John Glenn and Sam Nunn pressured West Point into hiring civilian professors in the mid-1990s, the PUSMAs evaded the purpose of hiring civilians (bringing new ideas to the academy) and ensured continued obedience and conformity. They hired retired military officers, many of whom were their friends then working with them at West Point, to fill many of the civilian professor positions. This practice, which continues, allows former officers, often colonels, to collect some of the highest civilian salaries at the academy while working as civilian professors or administrators. In one department, eleven of the fifteen civilian professors have been former or current (reserve) military officers. At the same time, the retired officers are also collecting their military pensions, about $100,000 yearly for a full colonel.

Among the approximately 550 faculty members at West Point, about 425 of them are military officers, who fall into three groups. The dean and PUSMAs control the academic program. The next group consists of "academy professors," majors, lieutenant colonels, and colonels who will finish their thirty-year careers at West Point. The third group contains the captains and majors who stay for two or three years and then leave for other assignments in the army. Some of these short-term captains and majors, from 50 to 60 percent of the faculty, will return to West Point to become the academy professors. Some of the academy professors will become the PUSMAs, who together (academy professors and PUSMAs) comprise about 15 percent of the faculty. One of the PUSMAs will then become the dean. The regular civilian instructors (those not limited to one to three years) number about one hundred, of whom about twenty-five are former military officers.

This is a cycle that creates perpetual conformity. The academies accept over 50 percent of their actual applicants, a large portion of whom are low-performing or at-risk high school students. Some of them—often the least independent-minded because of the nature of military promotions—become colonels and generals. Then they return to West Point as superintendent, dean, department heads, or instructors. They recycle the same conformist thinking and behavior, which becomes the basis for military tactics and strategies in war.

FAULTY PRODUCTION

What kind of military officers is the system of cronyism and title-gifting actually producing? Rather than creating more flexible, broad-minded officers—despite how vigorously they claim to want to do this—the academies are headed in the opposite direction. They are focusing more on discrete vocational and technological training. A key reason for this is that the academies, no matter what they pronounce publicly, are actually preparing their students for jobs in private industry. They know that most of their graduates, despite the stated "mission" of a "lifetime of service," a hollow public-relations mantra the academies know is false, will not have careers as officers at all and will leave active duty in under ten years, usually sooner, just as fast as they can fulfill their contractual obligations.

According to a Rand study, 56 percent of West Point graduates will leave the army within eight years of graduation. This is the highest attrition rate among the four sources that provide officers to the army: West Point; ROTC scholarship candidates; ROTC nonscholarship candidates; and officer candidate school. The retention of junior officers is "lowest for the individuals in whom the Army has made the largest investment," reported Rand, referring to the West Point and ROTC students who have their educations paid by the government.[50]

The other major reason for the narrow academic curriculum is that the academies want an outside body to certify their engineering programs. As a result, the academies participate in an accreditation process administered by the Accreditation Board for Engineering and Technology (ABET). This is a good idea at a college with a more qualified faculty and more course offerings to compensate for the narrow engineering courses, and where graduating students will join the engineering profession. But the nation is paying top dollar for the academies to produce military officers, not entry-level workers for corporations.

ABET is, in effect, directing the curriculum at every military academy. In 2017, the engineering departments at West Point gained an even tighter hold over the curriculum to better ensure that engineering cadets could more easily complete their ABET-designed curriculum. West Point dropped four general-education courses that had been required of all cadets, one course each in the math, English and philosophy, chemistry and life sciences, and history departments. The dropped course in the history department was—incredibly—in military history. This change gave the engineering departments the opportunity to mandate that their cadets replace the four liberal arts courses—critical to a broad education—with one to three additional engineering courses (or other courses mandated by the engineering departments).

All cadets were required to add a course called Officership, which has no connection to any academic discipline and is comprised mainly of considering anecdotal situations encountered in the military. The curriculum was narrowed further in the fall of 2019. The army required cadets to drop a course in either American history or a regional history course (on Europe or Asia, for example) and mandated that they take a course on "history of the army."

By its own standards, ABET declares that it is designed to produce "graduates prepared to enter a global workforce."[51] Ten West Point academic programs, within five of the thirteen academic departments (consisting of about 50 percent of the cadets), are accredited by ABET: chemical engineering; civil engineering; computer science; electrical engineering; engineering management; environmental engineering; information technology; mechanical engineering; nuclear engineering; and systems engineering.[52] ABET requires reaccreditation every six years, which means the most senior professors are perpetually preparing paperwork for ABET instead of devoting time to teaching and scholarship and the creation of knowledge.

The reason for the narrow engineering focus at West Point—a vestige of the 1800s—becomes clearer when one considers that while most professional degrees (law and medicine, for example) consume three or four years of study following a four-year college degree, a student can become a professional engineer with an undergraduate degree. Because West Point and the other academies require their students to graduate in four years, it is difficult or impossible for military students to complete both the required ABET courses and the liberal arts courses necessary for a broad education. As a result, West Point has never created or has done away with a full range of diverse liberal arts and humanities courses.

From the perspective of the military officers who run the academies, the ultimate goal of an ABET-accredited program is to ensure that cadets graduate with a professional degree and improve their postmilitary civilian job prospects, as well as the job prospects of the military instructors who resign or retire. The irony is that after the students at the academies graduate and fulfill their commitments of five years of active-duty military service and three years of reserve service, they are no longer competent to assume even entry-level jobs in engineering.

The rejection of a broad curriculum and the complete adoption of an ABET-accredited curriculum at the academies has had enormous direct and indirect costs. One study, from 2014, concluded that "engagement with public welfare concerns is not highly valued in [engineering] students' professional identities as engineers and that this engagement declines over the course of their engineering education. Among respondents who enter engineering jobs, interest in public welfare concerns does not return after they leave college."[53] The most important work of army officers in Afghanistan and Iraq or anywhere in the world, working with the local populations on the ground level, is not a major part of the curriculum.

In addition, the curriculum is designed so that cadets and midshipmen make as few individual choices as possible. As one West Point cadet told David Lipsky in *Absolutely American*, "I have a lot of choices made for me, and I kinda like that."[54] The Naval Academy even mandates students' career choices by requiring 65 percent of them to major in science, technology, engineering, or math.[55] At West Point, the majority of the thirteen to fifteen courses cadets must take to obtain a major are selected for them by the PUSMAs. All twenty-seven of the remaining courses outside their majors are also selected for them by the PUSMAs through the Academic Board. Some of the twenty-seven courses have alternatives for more academically driven cadets (Advanced General Chemistry or Advanced Literature). Overall, the structure at the military academies leads to a narrow band of knowledge for students and inhibits their ability to develop decision-making skills and judgment about important matters, including their own futures.

This training model, a focus on skill development and rote learning, with black-or-white answers, is yet another layer underneath the traditional practice of controlling every aspect of cadets' lives. Cadets ask instructors to give them the "takeaways" and "approved solutions" after class discussion. The military officers, who learned this way, are happy to comply. Cadets do not learn how to make decisions about even the most basic and mundane matters, such as whether and when to eat. All four-thousand-plus cadets at West Point, for example, are required to be in "formation" at 6:50 A.M., standing outdoors in straight lines and rows. They are then inspected by their tactical officers before everyone marches to breakfast and lunch—every day during a cadet's four college years. After the prelunch formation, the West

Point Band (comprised of full-time enlisted soldiers who spend their careers playing music at West Point) plays martial music in sync with the marching cadets. On the weekends when they have "leave," cadets are required to be back in formation for "recall" at 7:00 P.M. on Sunday night.

This regimen begins before the cadets' first classes, when they are required to practice during the summer to ensure that they will march into the football stadium in uniform splendor to attend the mandatory autumn games. The punishment meted out by the BTO (brigade tactical officer, a colonel) for the rare cadet who does not show up for a game or leaves at halftime to study is "restriction" to the cadet's room, where the cadet will remain when not on "duty" attending class; the cadet, perversely, may be prohibited from visiting the library. Another favorite punishment of the officers is to require cadets to walk in silence for hours with dummy long guns slung over their shoulders, back and forth on a blacktop tarmac.

In the early 2000s, one tactical officer, an army captain, told me that the enormous amount of time consumed by the formations, marching, and mandatory meals was beneficial because it allowed him the opportunity to see the "whites of the cadets' eyes" every day to be sure he wasn't missing anything. In addition to the daily formations outside, at 11:30 every night, tactical officers or upper-class cadets enter other cadets' rooms without notice, opening shut doors, to be sure everyone is present. Each cadet is also required to certify through a website that he or she is present in her or his assigned room. In a meeting in 2018, about fifteen years after the tactical officer's explanation, I asked the current BTO, the supervising colonel, why he mandated "formations" at all, but particularly why he would mandate a lunch formation after having a breakfast formation only a few hours earlier. The BTO said, "I like to see the whites of cadets' eyes at least once a day."

In this culture, no matter how lacking in usefulness, practices like formations and marching and the reasoning behind them never really evolve. In fact, they never change. Over the years, tactical officers, without notice and often accompanied by drug-sniffing dogs, are allowed to enter the cadets' rooms—no warrant required—for "inspections." While looking for contraband, they sift through the contents of dressers, closets, lockers, bags, books, and personal papers. It's akin to living in a police state but more restrictive, with the mandatory formations and meals and nighttime bed checks more numerous than daily roll calls in prisons.

The tactical officers, who learned these practices when they were cadets, characterize this type of control as "mentorship" or "leadership" to ensure "accountability," the word used by the BTO to justify the formations. The West Point system, with cadets treated like inmates and subject to perpetual punishment on the whims of officers, is working against the young cadets' personal and professional development. It ends up producing officers who are emotionally immature, needy, and dependent on others to make even mundane decisions for them.

CRONYISM

One primary reason why institutions collapse is that they engage in favoritism and cronyism, which prevent the most efficient use of resources and degrade the morale of those who are the most competent. Unlike at a merit-based institution, where weaker personnel are eventually overtaken by the more qualified, West Point and the military at large are weighed down by the heaviness of their back-scratching practices. At the academies, the top job of superintendent is always held by a lieutenant general or vice admiral, although there is no reason why a civilian, like the secretaries of the army, navy, and air force, could not hold this position. Since 1812, all fifty-eight West Point superintendents have been white male graduates of West Point, except for one African American man, Lieutenant General Darryl A. Williams, who was hired in 2018.[56]

Similarly, since 1881, every Naval Academy superintendent (fifty-two of fifty-two), all white males, has been a graduate of the Naval Academy. Since 1954, when the Air Force Academy was founded (based on West Point's model), every academy superintendent except two (eighteen of twenty) has been a graduate of West Point or the Air Force Academy, and all have been white males except for one white female. From 1802 to 2003 (the most recent year of counting by a historian), approximately 213 of the 273 department heads at West Point were graduates of West Point.[57] Until the mid-1990s, nearly 100 percent of the academic instructors were military officers. In recent decades, 66–75 percent of the military instructors have been graduates of West Point.[58]

The dean and colonels who head the academic departments even hire the spouses of other high-ranking officers as civilian teachers. In recent years, at least four spouses of full colonels at West Point were hired as civilian teachers (three assistant professors and one instructor). Unlike apparently all the other civilians in their departments, not one of them had a PhD. One of the spouses did not have a master's degree in the academic discipline of the department.

THE CORPORATE LADDER

Not only practiced at the academies, favoritism, cronyism, and conformity infect the entire personnel and promotion system in the military. In the army, 90 percent of lieutenants are promoted to captain, and 80 percent of captains are promoted to major. Even when a captain is not promoted to major or a major is not promoted to lieutenant colonel (a 70 percent promotion rate), the army "may selectively continue" nonpromoted captains for a total of twenty years and nonpromoted majors for a total of twenty-four years.[59] One of the army's reasons for the subsequent long period of retention after nonpromotion is to ensure that the officers will serve a total of twenty years, when they are eligible for a pension. The rationale for retention is loyalty, not merit, and it does nothing to weed out poor officers or, by extension, serve the nation.

A 2010 survey of 250 West Point graduates found that 93 percent of them believed that "half or more of 'the best officers leave the military early rather than serving a full career.'"[60] Those who believe in merit-based promotion are alienated and find no reason to stay. This system does not just elevate those with minimal qualifications; by design, it turns off those who wish to succeed inside a merit-based system. This is where cronyism does perhaps its most lasting damage.

The army requires an officer to serve twenty-seven years before promotion to brigadier general (one star). Under extraordinary circumstances, a "below-the-zone" promotion could elevate an officer to brigadier after twenty-five or twenty-six years.[61] But most officers who are promoted through the normal process will become brigadier generals at about age forty-nine or fifty, and a general (four stars) at about age sixty or a couple years younger. This is probably about fifteen or twenty years later than when a high performer in nearly any other profession would first assume a comparable role in an organization.

The most competent officers resign early rather than face careers mired in a dysfunctional bureaucracy run by entitled and low-performing generals. A 2010 study for the Army War College concluded, "Since the late 1980s . . . prospects for the Officer Corps' future have been darkened by an ever-diminishing return on this investment, as evidenced by plummeting company grade officer [lieutenant, captain, and major] retention rates. Significantly, this leakage includes a large share of high-performing officers, many of them developed via a fully-funded undergraduate education [West Point]."[62] Lavish, free educations cannot prevent high achievers from leaving the army as soon as they satisfy their legal obligations.

As a U.S. soldier in Iraq told journalist George Packer, "The reason why morale sucks is because of . . . the brigade and division commanders, and probably the generals at the Pentagon and Central Command too, all of whom seem to be insulated from what is going on at the ground level. Either that or they are unwilling to hear the truth of things, or (and this is the most likely), they do know what is going on, but they want to get promoted so badly that they're willing to screw over soldiers by being unwilling to face the problem of morale . . . These people are like serious alcoholics unwilling to admit there even is a problem."[63]

In 2007 Lieutenant Colonel Paul Yingling, who joined the army through ROTC, described in the *Armed Forces Journal* how the military promotion system depends on inside dealing and favoritism:

> The system that produces our generals does little to reward creativity and moral courage. Officers rise to flag rank [generals and admirals] by following remarkably similar career patterns. Senior generals, both active and retired, are the most important figures in determining an officer's potential for flag rank. The views of subordinates and peers play no role in an officer's advancement; to move up he must only please his superiors. In a system in which senior officers select for promotion those like themselves, there are powerful incentives for conformity. It is unreasonable to expect that an officer who

spends 25 years conforming to institutional expectations will emerge as an innovator in his late forties.[64]

After twenty-seven years in the army and five combat tours in Bosnia, Afghanistan, and Iraq, Yingling explained why he retired as a colonel in 2012 and became a high school social studies teacher. "Behind closed doors in Washington," he writes, "there is widespread recognition that while our troops are remarkable, the great majority of our generals are not. In private meetings with senior leaders, I explain how parochialism, ambition and greed have corrupted our national security apparatus. Bad advice and bad decisions are not accidents, but the results of a system that rewards bad behavior."[65]

BLIND LOYALTY

An illustrative example is useful to show how conformity in the army stamps out independent thought to the detriment of the institution and nation. Under a former superintendent, West Point implemented a rule that requires civilian instructors who are traveling to conferences outside the United States to complete about twelve hours of online training, the same training that soldiers deploying to combat zones are required to complete.

In a discussion with a civilian staff member who had been in the army, I asked whether the training was a productive use of time for routine academic trips, pointing to one eight-hour training video that describes what to do if you are on the run, alone, behind the lines, in enemy territory. The video details what information to provide and how to act if you become a hostage or prisoner of war, and what kinds of grubs, bugs, caterpillars, tree bark, and plant roots are edible if you are on your own. I explained to him that though this is helpful information in the right circumstances, it is unlikely to be useful on a trip from New York to London. The staff member's response: everyone is treated the same way in the army.

I tried to engage him on what I thought was a common-sense issue, but he continued to look at me blankly and said the rules have to be enforced "because that's what *my* superintendent and country want."

After a few minutes, I thought I had a winning question, one that surely couldn't be answered with the same robotic response. "What if your super-intendent wanted you to commit war crimes? Would you do it?"

"I do what *my* superintendent orders me to do. And that's why you have to take the training." He was hitched so tightly to the concept of following orders that he wouldn't even answer a basic question that all soldiers know the answer to.

It's possible he was only trying to impress and puff himself up to show that he was more patriotic than other civilians because he would follow a commander's order without questioning whether the order is legal. He is far from alone in this commitment. To some soldiers, this is part of loyalty. Their lack of inquiry, the refusal to challenge even the most archaic or objectionable principles, and an aversion to any kind of internal conflict harden a culture into place. As author Megan McArdle writes in the *Atlantic*, "Even a dysfunctional culture, once well established, is astonishingly efficient at reproducing itself."[66]

The irony is that no one in the military is ever ultimately treated the same, according to baseline principles. The arbitrariness inherent in officers making and enforcing their own rules requires all personnel to accept external decision-making by the "boss," the ingratiating way in which lower-ranking officers, when speaking to a group of people, refer to a commander when the commander is present. The freedom to speak, the most necessary and valuable component of internal decision-making—and democracy—is discouraged. In everyday military life, speech is punished formally and through social exclusion. For that kind of system to remain solidly in place, its members must favor loyalty over honesty, a plague in the military that we turn to next.

CHAPTER 4

Supreme Values—How Loyalty Creates Dishonesty

T ruth is not included in the Seven Core Army Values, which are, in order, loyalty, duty, respect, selfless service, honor, integrity, and personal courage.[1] The first value, loyalty, has come to crowd out all the others. The army's description of loyalty reads like a rule of separation: "A loyal soldier is one who supports the leadership and stands up for fellow soldiers."[2] Experience shows that this leads to soldiers who believe they must overlook the misconduct committed around them. Between the world wars, from 1920 to 1940, the "cardinal [American] military virtue" became loyalty, which encompassed "virtue, honor, patriotism, and subordination," according to former Harvard professor Samuel P. Huntington. "The other significance of the military devotion to loyalty was in the extent to which it reflected the separation between the military values and the popular civilian values," writes Huntington.[3]

In today's military, patriotism and loyalty are valued more than competence. The army defines loyalty as "true faith and allegiance to the U.S. Constitution, the Army, your unit and other Soldiers."[4] It does not mention fellow citizens. At its core, loyalty involves choosing sides; anyone outside the circle is viewed suspiciously or, often, as a threat. When loyalty is the supreme virtue, then everything that is done in aid of it, including lying, becomes more easily accepted, even sanctioned.

In the early twentieth century, the U.S. Army could punish insubordination with death,[5] and even today insubordination, which includes being "disrespectful in language or deportment" toward an officer, remains a criminal offense.[6] In a statement accompanying his report on U.S. soldiers' murders of civilians at My Lai during the Vietnam War, Lieutenant General William Ray Peers delivered a confidential memorandum to General William Westmoreland. "Peers had come to believe that the Army officer corps had drifted far from its stated values," writes Tom Ricks. "It had become an organization in which lying and hypocrisy were widespread and tolerated, perhaps encouraged and required."[7]

What Peers may have missed, and what Ricks recognized, is that the army's emphasis on loyalty made lying and covering up for each other normal and expected. Soldiers formally swear an oath to the Constitution, but in practice their first commitment is to each other, not to the principles enshrined in America's founding document, and not to fellow citizens. In the fifty years since the My Lai Massacre, the cult of loyalty has led its offspring, dishonesty, to become a bedrock layer in the military.

The authors of the 2015 study *Lying to Ourselves: Dishonesty in the Army Profession*, Leonard Wong and Stephen Gerras, a retired lieutenant colonel and retired colonel and both graduates of West Point, found that lying and a culture of protecting lies permeate the army. Lies and deception regarding bureaucratic requirements are common and accepted. Officers have a variety of names for satisfying bureaucratic standards without meeting them: "pencil whipping, checking the block, making priorities, meeting the intent, or getting creative."[8] According to Wong and Gerras, army officers have become "ethically numb" from "repeated exposure to the overwhelming demands and the associated need to put their honor on the line to verify compliance."[9]

The rationale that officers use to justify false statements is that they do not have enough time to fulfill bureaucratic requirements. They might, for example, approve completion-of-training certificates for soldiers who have not taken the training. Many of the fabrications are encouraged and endorsed, as subordinates are forced to prioritize which requirements will actually be done to standard and which will only be reported as done to standard. As Wong and Gerras describe it, "When asked if units are submitting inaccurate data, one staff officer bluntly replied, 'Sure, I used to do it when I was down there.' Another staff officer added, 'Nobody believes the data; [senior leaders] take it with a grain of salt . . . The data isn't valued, probably because they know the data isn't accurate.' One officer summed up the situation, 'We don't trust our compliance data. There's no system to track it. If we frame something as compliance, people "check the block." They will quibble and the Army staff knows it.'"[10]

Wong and Gerras conducted scores of discussions with army officers and some marine officers.[11] They cited a variety of common lies, including an example of two-way falsity, where officers asserted on evaluations that overweight noncommissioned officers (NCOs) were taller than their actual heights to ensure that they could remain in the army despite an apparent lack of physical fitness.[12] The lying creates a domino effect; when one officer does it (or accepts it), the soldiers below the officer do not want to appear to be insubordinate by dissenting. This is how a culture of deception becomes commonplace. In the absence of truth as a higher value, loyalty becomes the immovable firmament.

One officer described to Wong and Gerras what happens to the dissenter who tells the truth: "We're all kind of vultures. The one guy [who told the truth]—get him. He exposed himself. And no one wants to stand out . . . If you're looking to do this [stay in the army] for a long period of time, your intent is to appease the person above you. Just like the person you're appeasing made that decision a long time ago."[13]

Of course, these deceptions do not remain in the bureaucratic world. They frequently carry over into combat operations. "One might expect that ethical boundaries are more plainly delineated in a combat environment—the stakes are higher, and the mission is more clearly focused," write Wong and Gerras. "Discussions with officers, however, revealed that many of the same issues in the garrison environment also emerge in combat. For example, a senior officer described how the combat mission can lead to putting the right 'spin' on reports: 'We got so focused on getting bodies to combat that we overlooked a lot of issues like weight control, alcohol, or PT' [physical training]."[14]

According to the study, senior U.S. Army officers fabricate the readiness of coalition forces, a deception that recently deployed officers consistently report. When the new senior officers arrive at their commands, they rate the coalition forces as deficient so that they have cover when something goes wrong after their arrival. When the officers leave their commands a year later, they invariably rate the coalition forces as competent and well trained. "I show up and [the readiness assessments] go yellow or green to red," one army colonel said. "I'm ready to leave—they go from yellow to green. We went through the reports with the CG [commanding general] every ninety days. Everyone wanted to believe what they wanted to believe."[15] It's akin to a teacher failing the entire class at the start of the year and then giving A's across the board at the end to create the illusion of learning. The difference, in this case, is that lives and the security of the nation are at stake.

Wong and Gerras believe that the "gravest peril" of dishonesty is "the facilitation of hypocrisy in Army leaders" because they "learn to talk of one world while living in another."[16] Officers then become tentative and indecisive; without knowing what is real, they cannot identify the best solution to a problem. At the strategic level, the officers' hypocrisy leads to more serious corruption and wasting of government resources. Army leaders "unconcernedly shift a billion dollars to overseas contingency operations funding to minimize the base budget or to brief as fact the number of sexual assault response coordinators when the data are obviously suspect."[17] Presumably, commanders move money to try to show they are doing more with less and to justify their request or receipt of additional money.

"Ethical fading and rampant rationalizations have allowed leaders to espouse lofty professional values while slogging through the mire of dishonesty and deceit," the study concluded. These habits and disregard for the truth create a "corrosive ethical culture that few acknowledge and even fewer discuss or work to correct."[18] The study illustrated a near total devaluation of truth among army officers. "The end result," Wong and Gerras concluded, "is a profession whose members often hold and propagate a false sense of integrity that prevents the profession from addressing—or even acknowledging—the duplicity and deceit throughout the formation."[19]

Ironically, in an institution whose practices are bent on control, intellectual chaos has erupted amid the apparent order of pressed uniforms, tight formations, and marching bands. One army captain explained, "I think a real danger . . . is [that] we're requiring every single person at every single level to make their own determination on what they want to lie about. Because we're all setting a different standard and because we can't talk about it, we're obviously going to have the potential for the guys who take it too far."[20]

The devaluation of truth and the ascent of loyalty—the replacement of the rule of law with the predilections of individual officers—have created a significant threat to democracy in that this condition has suppressed the creation and dissemination of knowledge. Through the officers' duplicity, Americans are deprived of the facts and arguments necessary to exercise good judgment. Loyalty is the linchpin that keeps a decrepit intellectual machine running. Even the most virtuous dissenter will be buried after raising the most important issue, creating a culture of silence and retaliation. Ultimate decisions no longer devolve to the people.

Without truth, there is little trust, which itself is necessary for an institution like the military to operate effectively. "'White' lies and 'innocent' mistruths have become so commonplace in the U.S. Army that there is often no ethical angst, no deep soul-searching, and no righteous outrage when examples of routine dishonesty are encountered," according to Wong and Gerras. "Mutually agreed deception exists in the Army because many decisions to lie, cheat, or steal are simply no longer viewed as ethical choices."[21] Once that ethical line is blurred, it becomes very difficult to draw it back into existence, because no one knows where the line is supposed to be.

Like Wong and Gerras, two other retired military officers, Joe Doty (lieutenant colonel) and Pete Hoffman (colonel), open their 2014 *Army Magazine* article "Front and Center: Admit It—Lying Is a Problem in the Military" by recognizing the problem of lying, but they do not identify any specific solutions. "It can be argued," they write, "that lying, quibbling (small lies), half-truths, stretching the truth, partial truths, and so on, within the military are becoming normalized or tacitly acceptable. Recent notable examples include recruiters lying and encouraging lying to receive bonuses, officers cheating on nuclear certification exams, and fraudulent travel claims."[22]

This culture of dishonesty does not just appear fully formed in enlisted soldiers or officers in garrison. As with many of the ingrained habits in the military, the seeds germinate in the thinking and practices at the military academies.

On May 16, 2019, Lieutenant General Darryl A. Williams, West Point's superintendent, and Brigadier General Cindy Jebb, its academic dean, convened the civilian professors and announced that, according to West Point's top civilian attorney, Lori Doughty, they would become "permanent" employees, after working the previous twenty-five years as temporary help. Williams introduced Doughty, who said that the professors could claim, once the change was final, that they were "tenured" faculty members. This would allow West Point to obtain better civilian professors, because it would advertise to prospective professors that it now provides tenure. Everyone in the academic profession recognizes that real academic tenure, in the form of a long-term contract, is desirable because it limits the grounds for termination, thus promoting freedom in research, speaking, and writing and, thereby, the search for truth.

I told Doughty that this plan was not professional tenure as it is known in the academic world. I explained that the new plan provided even less job security than what the professors had under the current faculty manual, which Doughty claimed was not legally valid. At best, their plan offered the civil-service standards that are applicable to the two million federal employees who are termed "tenured" because they are no longer temporary. I told Doughty that if West Point advertised "tenure" to prospective professors, this would "not be forthright."

Doughty said, "Acknowledged."

CHEATING SCANDAL

From 1945 to 1949, Maxwell Taylor was the superintendent at West Point, which named its main administration building, Taylor Hall, in his honor. Despite General Taylor's creation of an honor code at West Point when he was the superintendent, cadets apparently engaged in rampant cheating. It culminated in an infamous scandal in 1951, when ninety cadets, including a majority of the football team, were dismissed for exchanging future examinations.[23] A generation later, in 1976, West Point found itself submerged in scandal again after dismissing 152 cadets for cheating.[24] Nearly 20 percent of the cadets on a standard course in electrical engineering collaborated on a take-home examination that did not permit collaboration;[25] by another account, 75 percent of the class cheated on the examination.[26] A commission empaneled to examine the origins of the cheating concluded that "the Academy must now acknowledge the causes of the breakdown and devote its full energies to rebuilding an improved and strengthened institution."[27] West Point deemed 148 of the dismissed cadets eligible for return,[28] and ultimately 90 of them did.[29]

On the same day in 1976 that the first dispositions of the West Point cheating scandal were announced, six cadets from the Coast Guard Academy were asked to resign for cheating.[30] This came two years after a major cheating incident at the Naval Academy, where 125 midshipmen were implicated in cheating, including stealing an exam. In 1984 the Air Force Academy expelled nineteen cadets for cheating on a physics test.[31] The students who were educated in the shadow of cheating became generals and admirals in the twenty-first century.

General Ray Odierno (Class of '76), a former army chief of staff (2011–15), was a commander in Iraq, where his inspector general, now a colonel, was one of the cadets who had been expelled from West Point for cheating on the electrical engineering test in 1976. He returned to West Point after his dismissal and graduated in 1978.

Michael M. O'Brien (Class of '77) worked in Iraq for a private contractor for fourteen months during the Iraq war, beginning in the summer of 2006. In his book *America's Failure in Iraq*, O'Brien describes filing a complaint with that inspector general about one month before he left Iraq. "Allowing cadets to return to West Point after having been kicked out for an honor violation had never been done before," writes O'Brien. "Now here he was a full bird colonel and the Inspector General for the entire Multi-National Forces-Iraq, commanded by a 4-star general. And what does the IG do? It investigates, among other things, lying and cheating."[32]

THE GULF OF TONKIN

After championing the honor code at West Point ("a cadet will not lie, cheat, steal, or tolerate those who do"), Maxwell Taylor became the chairman of the Joint Chiefs of Staff in 1962, at the outset of the Vietnam War. According to Tom Ricks, "American memory scapegoats William Westmoreland as the general who lost the Vietnam War, but Taylor should bear much of the blame for getting the country into it."[33]

Through his friendship with President John Kennedy and his brother, Robert Kennedy, General Taylor probably influenced the U.S. intervention in Vietnam more than any other military officer. He pushed the idea of intervention and then shaped the military strategy.[34] "Taylor tugged the Joint Chiefs of Staff into supporting American involvement in a ground war in Vietnam," writes Ricks. "Before Taylor was involved, the Joint Chiefs had concluded that Vietnam was at the periphery of American interests."[35]

In his book *Dereliction of Duty*, future national security advisor H. R. McMaster finds the most fault with Taylor, who misled the press, the other joint chiefs, and the National Security Council. "Ever loyal to the president," McMaster writes, "Taylor shielded him from the views of his less politically sensitive colleagues while telling the Chiefs that their recommendations had been given full consideration. To keep the Chiefs from expressing dissenting views, he helped to craft a relationship based on distrust and deceit in which the president obscured the finality of decisions and made false promises that the JCS conception of the war might one day be realized."[36]

President Lyndon Johnson's—and his military commanders'—deceptions during the Vietnam War are perhaps the most illustrative and destructive early examples of the culture of lying, both at the highest levels of the military and also its civilian command. The very impetus for the war itself, the Gulf of Tonkin "incident," was essentially a fraud that the president and his military leaders perpetrated on the American people. As historians Lloyd Gardner and Marilyn Young write in their book *Iraq and the Lessons of Vietnam*, Johnson was a trailblazer in that he "set the example for fixing intelligence around policy"[37] rather than the other way around.

The incident that catalyzed the Vietnam War—North Vietnamese patrol boats allegedly attacking a U.S. destroyer in the Gulf of Tonkin on August 4, 1964—never even occurred, according to a previously top-secret report released by the National Security Agency in 2007. "It is not simply that there is a different story as to what happened," the NSA report concluded; "it is that *no attack* happened that night."

The NSA report explained the intentional and unintentional forces that coalesced around the false story: "Through a compound of analytic errors and an unwillingness to consider contrary evidence, American SIGINT [signals intelligence] elements in the region and at NSA HQs reported Hanoi's plans to attack the two ships of the Desoto patrol. Further analytic errors and an obscuring of other information led to publication of more 'evidence.' In truth, Hanoi's navy was engaged in nothing that night but the salvage of two of the boats damaged on 2 August."[38]

In intentionally considering a limited number of facts, the Pentagon and the Johnson administration willingly created a version of events that supported their story about a North Vietnamese attack. The phantom attack helped them justify a new war, which they believed would be short and victorious for the United States. In 1965, a year after he ordered massive military action in Vietnam, President Johnson confided to an aide about the Tonkin incident, "For all I know, our Navy was shooting at whales out there."[39] Even Secretary of Defense Robert McNamara himself would eventually admit that there had been no attack.[40]

The deception surrounding the Gulf of Tonkin was possible only because a large number of people in the military and civilian bureaucracy remained silent. "Later statements by various intelligence and Defense Department officials suggest that there was a large group who simply did not believe that the attack had happened or that the evidence even pointed to an attack," writes NSA analyst Robert Hanyok in 2017.[41]

Obviously, according to Hanyok, there was no mechanism in place or even a culture of permission anywhere in the government to allow for any of them to speak up:

> Many high-ranking officials from CIA, the Department of State, and the Pentagon could not see the evidence assembled by McNamara as supporting a Vietnamese attack. Some of them were skeptical (or claim to have been so) from almost the beginning of the incident. This group of doubters included the then U.S. Army's deputy chief of staff for military operations, General Bruce Palmer Jr. [West Point Class of '36], Ray Cline, the CIA's deputy director for intelligence, the heads of the Department of State's Intelligence and Far Eastern Divisions, as well as a host of staffers on the National

Security Council and in the Defense Department, who, in years to come, would become notable: Daniel Ellsberg [who leaked the Pentagon Papers in 1971], Alvid [*sic*] Friedman [presumably Alvin Friedman, deputy assistant secretary of defense for international affairs], and Alexander Haig [West Point Class of '45, a future general and secretary of state].[42]

The NSA report from 2002 noted that Ray Cline had said, "We knew it was bum dope that we were getting from the Seventh Fleet, but we were told only to give the facts with no elaboration on the nature of the evidence. Everyone knew how volatile LBJ was. He did not like to deal with uncertainties."[43] That's the problem with blind loyalty: it supersedes duty to everything and everyone else, and it leads to wars.

LYING IN VIETNAM

I was a witness in Vietnam. I spent half my time in a helicopter traveling around the country. I was a witness to the decimation of my West Point Class. And I knew we were decimated for a lie.

—Captain John Wheeler (Class of '66)

Much of the responsibility for the failure in Vietnam should be attributed not just to General Westmoreland's "body count" strategy, but also to his penchant for exaggeration and fabrication, which prolonged the war. In his March 1965 commander's evaluation, Westmoreland claimed that "current trends are highly encouraging and the GVN [government of South Vietnam] may have actually turned the tide at long last."[44] But just three months later, Westmoreland insisted he needed more U.S. troops, writing, "The struggle has become a war of attrition. Short of decision to introduce nuclear weapons against sources and channels of enemy power, I see no likelihood of achieving a quick, favorable end to the war." (In November 1965, despite the clear evidence, Westmoreland denied that he ever contemplated nuclear weapons.[45])

President Johnson recognized that there were two fronts to the Vietnam War: the war itself and the public perception of the war. In 1967 he initiated a "Progress Offensive," a presidential plan to convince the public of something that isn't true, that the war was being won when everyone at the top knew it probably would be lost.

As part of the "offensive," a telling term in that it characterized an attempt to manipulate Americans rather than an enemy force, Westmoreland traveled back to the United States to speak and to brief politicians. Prior to these trips, in early 1967, Westmoreland sent statistics to General Earle Wheeler (Class of '32), chairman of the Joint Chiefs, indicating that the enemy, not the U.S. and South Vietnamese forces, was initiating most of the battles. "If these figures should reach the public domain," Wheeler replied, "they would, literally, blow the lid off Washington. Please do whatever is necessary to insure these figures are not repeat not released to news media or otherwise exposed to public knowledge."[46]

Two days later, having learned that about two-thirds of the 385 engagements with enemy battalions over the previous twelve months had been initiated by the enemy, Wheeler became frantic. "I must say I find this difficult to believe and certainly contrary to my own impressions of how the war has been going during the past six to eight months," he wrote. "I can only interpret the new figures to mean that, despite the force buildup, despite our many successful spoiling attacks and base area searches, and despite the heavy interdiction campaign in North Vietnam and Laos, VC/NVA [Vietcong and North Vietnamese Army] combat capability and offensive activity through 1966 and now in 1967 has been increasing steadily."[47] But in August 1967 Wheeler, apparently jumping on board Johnson's Progress Offensive, hailed the effectiveness of the U.S. bombing of North Vietnam and disagreed with negative intelligence assessments, according to the NSA report on the Vietnam War.[48]

Wheeler then urged they cover up the bad news and lie to the president. "I cannot go to the President and tell him that, contrary to my reports and those of the other Chiefs as to the progress of the war in which we have laid great stress upon the thesis that you [Westmoreland] have seized the initiative from the enemy, the situation is such that we are not sure who has the initiative in South Vietnam." Rather than speaking the truth to LBJ, Wheeler instead sent a special assistant to Vietnam to work with Westmoreland on fabricating numbers.[49]

In order to create a more favorable narrative, Westmoreland changed his method of counting. He sent to his superior, Admiral Ulysses S. Grant

Sharp Jr., the commander in the Pacific, a cable that described his maneuver of developing "terms of reference in the form of new definitions, criteria, formats and procedures related to the reporting of enemy activity which can be used to assess effectively significant trends in the organized combat initiative."[50] Mixed in with the jargon and military-speak is a clear directive and strategy: we don't like the facts, so we're changing them.

Later that year, in November 1967, Westmoreland told the National Press Club in Washington, "I am absolutely certain that whereas in 1965 the enemy was winning, today he is certainly losing,"[51] because the "enemy's 'losses [are] above his input capacity.'"[52] For Westmoreland, the "crossover point" and harbinger of success would be when American troops killed more enemy soldiers than the North Vietnamese could replace, the basis for his entire strategy in Vietnam: killing. But there never was any crossover point. Westmoreland's number padding was designed not only to burnish his own ego and his reputation in the public sphere, but also to ensure that the war would continue until America somehow won. But events on the ground refused to cooperate with Westmoreland's lies.

On January 30, 1968, two months after Westmoreland's boasts at the National Press Club, the Communists launched a massive offensive throughout South Vietnam during the Vietnamese New Year holiday, known as Tet. Although the Americans and South Vietnamese repelled almost all the attacks, the surprise of the offensive and the fact that the enemy reached the grounds of the U.S. embassy, after Westmoreland's reassurances, made it seem like a loss.[53] During the offensive a field grade officer, Zeb Bradford, said, "I remember Westmoreland saying: 'Everything I have worked for is lost. It's all been a failure.'"[54] Unfortunately for the country, Westmoreland would never speak those words to his president or fellow citizens, long after nearly everyone knew they were true.

The Tet offensive was an enormous surprise to everyone because of Westmoreland's continual and intentional underestimation of the number of North Vietnamese troops. He had decided to stop counting "Self-Defense" and "Secret Self-Defense" forces (civilian militia in villages). This lowered the number of North Vietnamese troops from about 429,000 to just under 300,000, the magic number palatable to U.S. politicians.

In a later interview Westmoreland said he "did not accept" Major General Joseph McChristian's estimate of 429,000 enemy troops. "I did not accept it. And I didn't accept it because of political reasons—that was—I may have mentioned this, I guess I did—but that was not the fundamental thing: I just didn't accept it."[55] This is a peek into Westmoreland's dishonesty and hubris. Westmoreland operated as though facts required his acceptance for them to be true.

Brigadier General Phillip Davidson (Class of '39) was Westmoreland's chief troop counter, the officer in charge of figures on troop organization and strength. In a memorandum, Davidson, covering Westmoreland's lies, directed his staff: "The figure of combat strength, and particularly of guerrillas, must take a steady and significant downward trend, as I am convinced this reflects true enemy status ... [and] due to the sensitivity of this project, weekly strength figures will hereafter be cleared personally by me."[56] This was out-and-out book-cooking, and there was a paper trail to prove it.

When a troop-counting conference of all the relevant government agencies, a Special National Intelligence Estimate (SNIE), found that the enemy numbered 420,000, Westmoreland's command protested. Davidson told Westmoreland's representative in Washington, Brigadier General George Godding, that the number should be 292,000 North Vietnamese troops, which would mean the army had reached the crossover point. "In view of this reaction," wrote Davidson, "and in view of General Westmoreland's conversations, all of which you have heard, I am sure this headquarters will not accept a figure in excess of the current strength figure carried by the press" (292,000).[57] As is common in the military, the personnel were to give their superiors what was asked of them—to the exclusion of everything else, including the truth. Military officers served up false numbers to justify continuing the war, rather than citing the correct numbers and announcing that America should withdraw.

Meanwhile, at the same conference, the CIA and Defense Intelligence Agency estimated the number of North Vietnamese troops at over 500,000. But the CIA and its director, Richard Helms, who knew Westmoreland was lying, capitulated to his demand for a lower number. In his memoir, Helms writes that "any admission that the Viet Cong were actually gaining strength would obviously have stirred a severe public reaction on the home front."[58]

As one CIA officer described it, the army's underreporting "misrepresented the very nature of the war we were fighting."[59] This prevented

Congress from understanding that the "people's war" against South Vietnam could not be contained through U.S. military force and could or would be lost.[60] In a postwar interview, Westmoreland said his political reason for lowering the number of North Vietnamese troops was that "the people in Washington were not sophisticated enough to understand and evaluate this thing, and neither was the media."[61] Through the misrepresentations and lies of Westmoreland and other high-ranking military officers, the war continued for almost eight more years, eventually taking the lives of over 58,000 U.S. soldiers and 1–3 million Vietnamese people. In 1971 the Pentagon Papers, leaked by defense analyst Daniel Ellsberg, would reveal to the country just how pervasive the lies in Vietnam had been, and how far back they went.

A British correspondent in Vietnam, Max Hastings, wrote, "At every turn, American spokesmen in Washington and Saigon alike sought to deceive the American people and the world about what they were doing. A veteran correspondent warned me before I left on my first trip to Vietnam: 'Remember they lie, they lie, they lie.' He meant the U.S. command, and he was right. Their insane claims about 'body-counts' of enemy dead passed into the legend of the war."[62]

WATERGATE

The military's penchant for deceit does not stay on the battlefield, of course. As the War College study on lying showed, it is everywhere. Two of the United States' most infamous political scandals of the past century showed how military men, once they occupy civilian office, have relied on dishonesty, deception, and blind loyalty to undermine the country's democracy.

Possibly the biggest scandal of the twentieth century was a political operation conducted and overseen by career military men across the board, with a military veteran, President Richard Nixon (U.S. Navy), serving as ringleader. On June 17, 1972, five burglars working on behalf of the Committee for the Re-Election of the President (Nixon) were arrested inside the Watergate apartment complex in Washington, home of the Democratic National Headquarters. Their leader, James W. McCord, was a former CIA officer who had been a lieutenant colonel in the U.S. Air Force Reserve. Two other burglars—Bernard Barker, who had been a second lieutenant bombardier in the U.S. Air Force, and Frank Sturgis, a former marine—were military men. G. Gordon Liddy, the architect of the Watergate plot and Nixon's behind-the-scenes fixer (he had orchestrated the raid on Daniel Ellsberg's psychiatrist's office two years earlier) had been an artillery officer in the army. Liddy's partner in crime, who was also involved in planning both break-ins, was former navy man E. Howard Hunt.

Over the next two years, the president and nearly every one of his top advisors engaged in the cover-up, through lying, threats, misdirection, silence, and bribery. Many of the conspirators were lawyers, but their loyalty to Nixon overwhelmed their oath to uphold the law. The taproots of almost all of their subsequent criminal convictions were conspiracy and perjury—in essence, blind, destructive loyalty to each other. With an exception or two, all of them had one common prior experience: they were military veterans. Some had enjoyed the "victorious response to the challenge of Nazi Germany and imperial Japan," which led to "professional arrogance, lack of imagination, and moral and intellectual insensitivity" and "too much power," as Neil Sheehan described the post–World War II U.S. military in his book *A Bright Shining Lie*.[63] McCord, Liddy, and Hunt were convicted of conspiracy, burglary, and wiretapping, Barker of wiretapping and theft.

Nixon's vice president, Spiro Agnew (Army), resigned his office in 1973 for reasons that had nothing to do with Watergate. He was convicted of not reporting income, the culmination of bribes he took while governor of Maryland. Attorney general Richard Kleindienst (Army Air Corps) pleaded guilty to refusing to testify accurately before the U.S. Senate on a matter unrelated to Watergate. Charles Colson (marines), special counsel to the White House, approved stealing files from the office of Ellsberg's psychiatrist. Colson was convicted of obstruction of justice. Egil Krogh (Navy), a deputy special assistant to Nixon, was convicted of conspiracy for helping to plan the burglary of the psychiatrist's office.

A total of fifty-five people in the Nixon administration were convicted of crimes.[64] These included Nixon's previous attorney general, John Mitchell (Navy), who helped to plan the initial burglary and played a major role in the cover-up. Mitchell was convicted of perjury, obstruction of justice, and conspiracy. Nixon's two closest advisors, John Ehrlichman (Air Force) and H. R. Haldeman (Navy), were convicted of perjury, obstruction of justice, and conspiracy.[65] Nixon resigned the presidency on August 4, 1974. A month later, in an effort to put the nation's "long national nightmare" behind it, President Gerald Ford (Navy) granted him a full pardon.

IRAN-CONTRA

In the 1980s, top security advisors to President Ronald Reagan (Army), almost all of whom were military veterans, worked for over eighteen months to send U.S. weapons to Iran in exchange for money, an illegal transfer that defied the U.S. government's embargo on Iran, a sponsor of terrorism. The advisors on Reagan's National Security Council were overcharging the Iranians for U.S. missiles and using the surplus money to support the Contras, a right-wing rebel group in Nicaragua, the support of which was also illegal.

Reagan also wanted to use his payoffs to Iran to encourage that country to use its influence to help release hostages that had been taken by terrorists in the Middle East. Reagan, of course, did not want anyone to know he was trading arms for hostages, especially that he was trading with a sponsor of terror and enemy of a country, Iraq, that the United States was supporting in its own war against Iran. When the Iran-Contra scheme was exposed in 1986, the administration officials and private contractors tied to it tried to cover up their activities by lying to Congress and federal investigators. Reagan claimed to have no knowledge of the most illegal part of the transaction, but it seemed unlikely that the president would be unaware that his closest advisors, acting in consonance with his beliefs, would be operating without his knowledge or tacit approval.

In 1992, just prior to leaving office, President George H. W. Bush, a former naval officer, pardoned four Reagan administration officials who had been convicted of crimes related to Iran-Contra. They included the former head of the National Security Council, Robert C. McFarlane, a 1959 graduate of the U.S. Naval Academy, as well as the former secretary of defense, Caspar Weinberger (Army), who was awaiting trial. (Bush was to be called as a witness at Weinberger's trial, giving him a personal motive for the pardon.[66])

For his role in Iran-Contra, former admiral John M. Poindexter (Naval Academy, '58), who took over as head of the National Security Council when McFarlane resigned, was convicted of conspiracy, making false statements, destruction of records, and obstruction of Congress.[67] A former lieutenant colonel in the marines and NSC staff member, Oliver North (Naval Academy, '68), was convicted of altering and destroying documents, accepting an illegal gratuity, and aiding and abetting in the obstruction of Congress. Poindexter and North's convictions were reversed on appeal on the grounds that trial witnesses were tainted by their compelled, nationally televised testimony to Congress, and they were not retried. (Sixteen people from the Reagan administration were convicted, compared with one, one, sixteen, and one in the Bush I, Clinton, Bush II, and Obama administrations, respectively.[68])

In 1987 federal investigators asked Weinberger to produce documents and testify to Congress about his knowledge of the scandal. During his testimony, he denied that he kept a diary, a piece of evidence that would have been a goldmine for investigators. In 1991, however, prosecutors from the independent counsel's office discovered that Weinberger had deposited in the Library of Congress thousands of pages of "diary and meeting" notes. "This material showed that, contrary to his sworn testimony, Weinberger knew in advance that the Reagan administration was shipping weapons to Iran in exchange for hostages," David Corn wrote in *Salon*.[69]

The senior military assistant to Secretary Weinberger during Iran-Contra was Colin Powell, at the time a major general in the army. When interviewed in 1987 by congressional investigators, Powell was also asked whether Weinberger kept a diary. Powell said Weinberger did not,[70] and in his 2009 memoir, *My American Dream*, he writes, "I had never seen anything [from Weinberger] that would meet the common understanding of a diary."[71]

The independent counsel, former deputy attorney general Lawrence Walsh, questioned Powell's truthfulness, calling his statements "misleading" and asserting that "Powell actually helped to create Weinberger's daily diary entries for October 10, 1985, the day that U.S. military forces captured the hijackers of the *Achille Lauro* cruise ship in the Mediterranean."[72] (The day was memorable because these hijackers, from the Palestine Liberation Front, had shot and killed a U.S. citizen, Leon Klinghoffer, and pushed his body, in his wheelchair, off the cruise ship they had commandeered.)

In 1992, when Weinberger was under indictment for perjury and obstruction of justice, his attorney submitted a sworn affidavit from Powell, who was then a four-star general. Powell claimed again that, to his knowledge, Weinberger did not keep a diary. In his final report, Walsh concluded, "Powell's vague references to Weinberger's 'notes,' as opposed to his 'diary,' may have been calculated to avoid giving overtly false testimony while providing as little information as possible."[73]

Powell was the chairman of the Joint Chiefs of Staff when the United States and other countries expelled Iraq from Kuwait in 1991 and when he defended Weinberger's note taking. In 1995, *Washington Post* reporter Tom Harwood echoed a common sentiment about Powell: "Of all the people in public life today, Powell is the nearest we have to an icon."[74] In subsequent years, Powell was often mentioned as a presidential candidate. Powell's conflicting statements surrounding Iran-Contra, in which it seemed to me he was covering for Weinberger, did not prevent him from becoming George W. Bush's secretary of state. In that position he again demonstrated his penchant for loyalty over truth by falsely testifying to the United Nations and the world that Iraq possessed weapons of mass destruction.

"STUFF HAPPENS"—IT'S ONLY A WAR

Considering that the Iraq War was launched on a series of fabrications, among them that Saddam Hussein possessed or was producing biological, chemical, or nuclear weapons and that Iraq had a connection to al-Qaeda, it is unsurprising that the Bush administration misrepresented how the war was prosecuted. After journalists' stories and video showed plundering and looting in Iraq after the invasion, the administration told a different story. This was that the looting was minimal (it was not) and that in a war "stuff happens,"[75] according to Secretary of Defense (and former naval officer) Donald Rumsfeld, because "freedom's untidy."[76]

However, Rumsfeld's platitudes couldn't bury the truth. According to Frank Rich in *The Greatest Story Ever Sold*, "When the outrage over the looting story refused to go away . . . the military came up with a new line to explain its lack of preparedness for the civil unrest."[77] The military implied that "as few as 17 items" from the National Museum had been taken, as though this was no big deal. The looting of the artifacts in Iraq, the location of one of the world's first civilizations, the Tigris-Euphrates River Valley, was a colossal blow to the country's—and the world's—cultural history. The museum's looting was one of many occurrences that the invading U.S. generals had not anticipated, despite the nearly eighteen months of run-up time they had to prepare. Actually, up to 14,000 artifacts had been looted, according to one U.S. Marine colonel who was responsible for recovering them, along with possibly one million volumes from the National Library and Archives, according to UNESCO.[78]

On May 1, 2003, six weeks after the start of the war, President Bush appeared in what has to be one of the most premature victory declarations in history. In a military-issued flight suit and riding in the copilot seat of a navy fighter jet, Bush landed on an aircraft carrier, the *Abraham Lincoln*, in front of hundreds of U.S. sailors. The banner behind him read: "Mission Accomplished." The president's—and the military's—theatrics ignored the fact that there was no plan to stop the sectarian war that had broken out between Shia and Sunni Muslims (which should have been a surprise to no one) or the various insurgencies that would arise out of the chaos of the U.S. invasion.

On November 1, 2003, General Ricardo Sanchez, who had replaced Tommy Franks as commander of the coalition ground forces in Iraq, called the insurgency "strategically and operationally insignificant." The very next day, November 2, a U.S. Chinook helicopter was shot down near the insurgency stronghold of Fallujah, killing sixteen U.S. soldiers and wounding twenty-one.[79] General Sanchez didn't have to fear losing his job; as George Packer put it, "relief of command at such a high level would have been an admission of failure, so Sanchez's job was secure."[80]

On the same day the Chinook went down, Bob Schieffer, the moderator of CBS's *Meet the Press*, memorably asked Senator Richard Lugar, "If this is winning, you have to ask the question: How much of this 'winning' can we stand?"[81]

Six months later Bush tried again to muddy the waters by explaining, "That's what you're seeing on your TV screens: desperation by a hateful few."[82] This was consistent with the administration's and the Pentagon's approach toward the public in both wars: don't believe what you're seeing.

The military was finding ways to put out its own information; in current parlance, they were giving the public "alternative facts." Early in the war in Afghanistan, in February 2002, the Pentagon responded to media complaints that the military was restricting reporting by agreeing to facilitate a reality show about soldiers for the entertainment division of ABC. As the public relations officer of Central Command, Rear Admiral Craig R. Quigley, explained, "There's a lot of other ways to convey information to the American people than through news organizations."[83]

LYING ABOUT PAT TILLMAN

One of the reasons for the common dishonesty in the military is an institutionalized disdain for the public, including the civilian command, whom the military treats as an obstacle and a nuisance. Formerly head of Joint Special Operations (JSOC) and once the top U.S. commander in Afghanistan, General Stanley McChrystal (Class of '76) disparaged oversight and those who tried to conduct it. "When it came to observing the formalities of civilian control," wrote former military officer Andrew Bacevich (Class of '69), "the general turned out to be either spectacularly arrogant or stunningly obtuse."[84]

JSOC was particularly autonomous, according to author Mark Bowden: "It was global, operating in secret in more than a dozen countries, and had been freed from strict mission-by-mission oversight from Washington."[85]

In 2010 President Barack Obama fired McChrystal for contributing to and tolerating military officers' disrespect for civilian leadership, the first presidential firing of a general for this reason since Truman sacked MacArthur. McChrystal characterized Obama as being "uncomfortable and intimidated" by top generals at the Pentagon. According to *Rolling Stone*, McChrystal and his staff members ridiculed civilian officials, including Vice President Joe Biden, as well as the ambassador to Afghanistan, Karl Eikenberry (Class of '73), and the national security advisor, James Jones, both of whom were former general officers.[86]

Questions about McChrystal's integrity had arisen years earlier when, as a major general, he facilitated a Silver Star and commendation for deceased army private Pat Tillman to accompany the false story about how Tillman died. On April 22, 2004, Tillman, twenty-seven, was killed by friendly fire while on patrol with his platoon in a remote area in Afghanistan. He happened to be the most recognizable U.S. soldier anywhere because two years earlier he had been an NFL safety for the Arizona Cardinals. In 2002, in the wake of the September 11 attacks, Tillman rejected a contract of $3.6 million and, with his younger brother, enlisted in the army, where both eventually became Rangers.

It was the physical and mental errors of the officers up and down the chain of command that led to Tillman's accidental death and its subsequent cover-up. The first story the army told regarding his death was pure fantasy. In giving Tillman a Silver Star commendation, the army's third highest military decoration, the official record read: "Corporal Tillman put himself in the line of devastating enemy fire as he maneuvered his Fire Team to a covered position from which they could effectively employ their weapons on known enemy positions. While mortally wounded, his audacious leadership and courageous example under fire inspired his men to fight with great risk to their own personal safety, resulting in the enemy's withdrawal and his platoon's safe passage from the ambush kill zone."[87]

Throughout the army chain of command, officers and soldiers knew that Tillman had died from friendly fire, and that the lie was concocted to spare the army embarrassment. Without protest, they allowed subsequent lies surrounding Tillman's death to cascade and be broadcast throughout the world. A heroic death just made for a better story; it had the added benefit of covering up their own mistakes. Importantly, they didn't just sit back while the lies spread; they disseminated them.

In a memo written the day before Tillman's posthumous commendation was released, McChrystal wrote to the head of Central Command, General John Abizaid, and to General Philip Kensinger (the army's commander of Special Operations), and General Bryan Douglas Brown (head of Special Operations Command) that an ongoing investigation would find it "highly possible" that Tillman had been killed by friendly fire. Abizaid claimed that he did not receive McChrystal's cable until "10–20" days later, according to a report in the *San Francisco Chronicle*, referring to a report by the Pentagon's inspector general. Abizaid told investigators that he was in Iraq at the time

McChrystal sent his cable, but the *Chronicle* found that "in fact, he reportedly was at Central Command's forward headquarters in Qatar at the time." A former military prosecutor, John Einwechter, said, "It's certainly possible that Abizaid didn't get the memo because he was busy . . . But it's a personal memorandum from McChrystal, and vice versa. I find it difficult to believe that Abizaid wouldn't make a point of reading anything he got from him."

"I felt that it was essential that you received this information as soon as we detected it in order to preclude any unknowing statements by our country's leaders which might cause public embarrassment if the circumstances of Corporal Tillman's death become public,"[88] McChrystal wrote.

McChrystal's language here is revealing. It shows military leaders and an institution concerned primarily with self-protection and loyalty, not truth. "You should be aware of this lie," not "You should correct it." The warning might ensure that their commander-in-chief would not be embarrassed if the public found out what really happened to Tillman. McChrystal wrote that the president should be apprised "about Corporal Tillman's heroism and his approved Silver Star medal in speeches currently being prepared."[89]

A day later at the National Press Club, President Bush praised Tillman, who he said was "called to defend America," but conspicuously did not mention how Tillman died.[90] Tillman's mother, Mary, wondered why McChrystal, in his memo to the generals, would write "if" rather than "when" the circumstances of her son's death became public.[91]

"To see why the administration wanted to keep the myth going, just look at other events happening in the week before that correspondents' dinner," wrote Frank Rich in the *New York Times*. "On April 28, 2004, CBS broadcast the first photographs from Abu Ghraib; on April 29th a poll on the *New York Times* front page found the president's approval rating on the war was plummeting; on April 30th Ted Koppel challenged the administration's efforts to keep the war dead hidden by reading the names on *Nightline*. Tillman could be useful to help drown out all this bad news, and to an extent he was."[92] The military used Pat Tillman's death as patriotic propaganda for an administration and military having a bad week. A man who had given up his security, his family, and eventually his life was used as a tool to protect the images of army generals and the president.

At Tillman's nationally televised memorial service, Navy SEAL Steve White described how "Pat sacrificed himself so his brothers could live."[93] No one in the military or administration corrected the errors. The story the military concocted served the purpose of offering a heroic narrative to cover for the reality, which was that a series of fatal mistakes by fellow soldiers led to Tillman's death, which was followed by their superiors' efforts to cover up those mistakes.

In 2007 Congress held a hearing on Tillman's death, in which retired generals Abizaid, Brown, and Kensinger, as well as Richard Myers (former chairman of the Joint Chiefs of Staff) and former secretary of defense Donald Rumsfeld, testified. Combined, they answered "I don't recall" or some variation of it eighty-two times.[94] It seems difficult to believe that they would remember relatively few details about the death of the most recognizable American soldier, a story that received wall-to-wall coverage in the press and immediate attention at the highest levels of the U.S. military.

The circumstances surrounding Tillman's death were not accidentally misinterpreted or lost in the "fog of war." There was a wide and concerted cover-up from soldiers, officers, and commanders in and outside of Afghanistan to ensure that the facts of Tillman's death never saw the light of day. According to a 2007 report by the Department of Defense's inspector general, the army's destruction of Tillman's gear began within two or three days of his death, despite many military regulations requiring preservation of evidence.[95] A captain burned Tillman's body armor in a fifty-five-gallon "burn barrel." Soldiers found fragments of U.S. bullets on Tillman's vest and a "flash-bang" grenade, indicating that someone in the platoon had shot him, but a sergeant burned the vest, grenade, and Tillman's uniform. He then washed Tillman's helmet and returned it to the supply clerk for reuse by another soldier. Another sergeant burned a memo pad found in Tillman's gear. Soldiers in Tillman's platoon were ordered not to speak about the killing. The internet and phone connections at Tillman's home base were disabled. His younger brother, Kevin, also a Ranger, was "quarantined" and not told how Pat died, even as he accompanied the body back to the United States.[96]

An army captain, Richard Scott, who began investigating almost immediately, prepared a report that concluded the killing was from friendly fire and resulted from "gross negligence," which could be a basis for criminal charges. "But Scott's conclusions were not, it seemed, what the army wanted to hear," according to the *Telegraph*. Another investigation, by a lieutenant colonel, was ordered. A report of that investigation "emerged" two years later, with Captain Scott's references to "negligent homicide" and a recommendation for a criminal investigation "excised."[97] In its 2007 report, the Pentagon inspector general wrote:

> We concluded that the first two investigations . . . were tainted by the failure to preserve evidence, a lack of thoroughness, the failure to pursue logical investigative leads, and conclusions that were open to challenge based on the evidence provided. More significantly, neither investigator visited the site to visually reenact the incident, secure physical evidence, take photographs, or obtain accurate measurements. In addition, the first investigating officer, with advice from his legal advisor, withheld information concerning suspected fratricide from medical examiners who raised questions based on anomalies they discovered during the autopsy. As a result, the first two investigations lacked credibility and contributed to perceptions that Army officials were purposefully withholding key information concerning CPL Tillman's death.[98]

There's a deeper problem revealed in the tragic story of Pat Tillman. It is one of the prime reasons why the military is a bastion of injustice and corruption: the generals always investigate themselves. Each military service conducts its own investigations and publishes its own reports without the possibility of meaningful external review and oversight. Outside of a few JAG lawyers, a military officer is not trained or competent to conduct a complex investigation. In practice, and in accord with formal rules, a general (or admiral) will order officers under his command to investigate an incident that occurred within his command. The general will then approve, disapprove, or disregard the subsequent report. In contrast, everyone else in America and all other public agencies are subject to review by outsiders, such as independent prosecutors. In the military, only the commanders who order investigations determine whether criminal charges will be brought under military law.

In a court martial (a military criminal case), every judge, juror, prosecutor, and defendant is a member of the military, as is almost every defense attorney.[99] If you want to know of any cases at any military command or know more about a case that everyone knows exists, you can't just go to a computer or a clerk's office and ask for the criminal complaint or the public file, as you can at any clerk's office in every civilian jurisdiction in America. The military will not provide any information unless you file a Freedom of Information Act request. Having to ask for specific materials about cases that may or may not exist and receiving materials (months or years later, if ever) that the military believes you are entitled to makes systematic independent research of the military legal system impossible. From the beginning to the end, the isolation and secrecy of military investigations, in which all the participants have conflicts of interest, solidifies the military's complete separation from civil society. It has its own culture, its own rules, and, most significant, its own understanding of law and justice—in fact, it has its own law.

Following the death of Pat Tillman, the inspector general and the U.S. Army Criminal Investigation Command (CID) viewed a large cache of evidence, as well as the concealment of other evidence, and found that the circumstances surrounding Tillman's killing did not support criminal charges against anyone.[100] In the end, Tillman's stint in the army and his death from friendly fire did not serve the Pentagon's purpose of presenting the war in a positive light. In hindsight, Tillman's death was especially tragic because he had quickly grown disillusioned with the army and dissatisfied with its lack of intellectual stimulation, according to his mother, second-guessing his decision to enlist.

"It disturbed him that the military didn't use people to their full potential and that things were done that seemed to make no sense," she said. Tillman questioned whether the war in Iraq was legal, and when he returned from his first tour, in Iraq, he told his mother the war was "pretty much bullshit."[101]

Ironically, or perhaps fittingly, even in death Tillman was clashing with the military's conception of itself. A total of nine officers, four of them generals, were sanctioned for lying about or misleading the Tillman family or investigators.[102] Three generals received "memorandums of concern." Brigadier General James Nixon made a "well-intentioned but fundamentally incorrect decision" to limit information about the death to his staff. Brigadier General Gary Jones incorrectly characterized why Tillman should receive a Silver Star. Brigadier General Gina Farrisee failed to ensure that the medical examiner's concerns were properly resolved. Lieutenant Colonel Jeff Bailey was criticized "for his handling of the punishment against the Rangers involved in the shooting of Tillman."[103]

The head of Army Special Operations in 2004, Philip Kensinger (Class of '70), was censured and forced to retire for lying about and covering up the facts of Tillman's death. Stanley McChrystal escaped censure, but the inspector general found that he was "accountable for the inaccurate award recommendation" and "for the failure to inform the award approval authority . . . of suspected friendly fire."[104] The soldiers who fired on Tillman received administrative punishments: Sergeant Greg Baker received a more serious punishment, "field grade Article 15" (coming from a higher-ranking officer), than three specialists, Steven Elliott, Stephen Ashpole, and Trevor Alders, who each received a company grade Article 15 and were expelled from the Rangers.[105]

In November 2010, a civilian professor at West Point arranged to have film director Amir Bar-Lev show to the cadets his documentary *The Tillman Story*.[106] The West Point military administration opposed showing the film and consulted with General Abizaid, who had retired from the military and assumed the title of a distinguished civilian chair at West Point. Abizaid (Class of '73) was portrayed in the film as contributing to a cover-up of Tillman's friendly-fire death.[107] Eventually West Point's administration allowed the film to be shown—illustrating its control of information and expression—but it prohibited the media from attending, limited the number of cadets who were permitted to watch the film, and demanded the presence of an army lawyer who could comment on the film during the discussion that followed it.

In an interview after his appearance at West Point, Bar-Lev described the value of dissent and danger of suppression: "Personally, I think his [Tillman's] values and his family's values were something to aspire to—something we should teach cadets and young soldiers . . . We're coming out of a time when a simplistic worldview was seen as proof of moral clarity. The 'you're either with us or against us' mentality. Pat didn't buy into that and I don't buy into that. An overly simplistic view of a complex world is not a good thing, and the lessons of Pat's life are very appropriate for West Point cadets."[108]

Several months later, Colonel Maritza Sáenz Ryan, the head of the Department of Law, notified the civilian law professor who invited Bar-Lev that he would be terminated for budgetary reasons.

LYING IN AFGHANISTAN

Discussing the military's concealment and censorship of information during the war in Afghanistan, John F. Sopko, the special inspector general for Afghanistan, told the *New York Times* in 2017, "The Afghans know what's going on; the Taliban knows what's going on; the U.S. military knows what's going on. The only people who don't know what's going on are the people paying for it."[109] The one institution that has the power to discover and reveal the lies, the U.S. Congress, has been effectively neutered, abdicating its most crucial responsibility concerning oversight of the military and reporting on it to the American public.

"The military's extreme fetish for secrecy and disinformation—the dissemination of plausible but false data—makes a farce of congressional oversight," wrote Chalmers Johnson. "It is impossible for anyone without any extraordinarily high security clearance to make any sense at all of 'defense' appropriations."[110]

This doesn't even address the common fear that every member of Congress has of being painted as "soft" on defense or insufficiently supportive of the United States' armed forces. As former CIA analyst and national security expert Melvin Goodman puts it, "Liberals and conservatives alike declare the defense budget sacrosanct."[111] Going up against the military behemoth, even in aid of a righteous cause, is one of the surest and quickest ways to be voted out of office. It practically writes its own attack ad.

On November 29, 2009, General David Petraeus was trying to convince President Obama to send tens of thousands of U.S. troops to Afghanistan, a "surge" that would increase the U.S. presence by 33,000 troops (fewer than the 48,000 to 90,000 requested).[112] At the White House, Petraeus and Admiral Mike Mullen, chairman of the Joint Chiefs, told Obama that additional troops and a counterinsurgency strategy could turn around the failing war, according to Jonathan Alter in his book *The Promise: President Obama, Year One*.[113]

Obama asked Petraeus, "David, tell me now, I want you to be honest with me. You can do this in 18 months?"

"Sir, I'm confident we can train and hand over to the ANA [Afghan National Army] in that time frame," Petraeus replied.

"Good. No problem," the president said. "If you can't do the things you say you can in 18 months, then no one is going to suggest that we stay, right?"

"Yes, sir, in agreement," said Petraeus.

"Yes, sir," echoed Mullen.

Then Obama asked Secretary of Defense Robert Gates, "Bob, you have any problems?" Gates "was fine with it," according to Alter.

"I'm not asking you to change what you believe," Obama said, "but if you don't agree with me that we can execute this, say so now."

Alter reported that no one in the Oval Office said anything.

Petraeus led Obama to believe that the temporary surge would provide, by July 2011 (eighteen months after the beginning of the surge), a way to decrease the number of troops.[114] But, backtracking just a month after the conversation in the Oval Office, after Obama made his commitment, Petraeus said there could be no clear U.S. "hand-off" of responsibility to the Afghans in July 2011.[115]

"The Petraeus bait-and-switch is a yet another fire-bell in the night—a warning that Petraeus has gained unprecedented power over U.S. war policy," wrote reporter Gareth Porter. "By drawing Obama into a deepening of U.S. military involvement in an unnecessary and self-destructive war on the false pretense that he supported Obama's policy and then turning on that November 2009 policy once he became commander, Petraeus is acting as though he intends to prevent the President from carrying out the policy on which he had decided. Unless Petraeus's bait-and-switch is decisively rebuffed by the White House, the country's descent into de facto military control over war policy will continue and accelerate."[116] Petraeus's status was so elevated that Obama was unable to work around him and the military. Instead, Obama nominated Petraeus as the director of the CIA.

Military personnel commonly believe that inflated optimism—a convoluted description of fabrication—helps the war effort. Military officers deceive their civilian command and the country because they believe they know what is best, a few misrepresentations to rally the president and the public in order to increase support for the military and help achieve victory later.

In a 2014 essay for the Army War College, two former army colonels, Don Snider and Alexander Shine, wrote that the army believes "there are sometimes apparently good reasons for sacrificing objective truth for a 'spin' that seems to serve broader strategic or institutional purposes in the short term."[117] When military officers believe that lying to the president and Americans is an acceptable overall strategy, then the other ethical rules that might constrain them are often tossed aside.

ALTERING INTELLIGENCE ABOUT ISIS

When the wars in Afghanistan and Iraq heated up again in late 2015, the leader of Central Command, which oversees both wars, was General Lloyd Austin (Class of '75). In September of that year, the Pentagon opened a broad investigation to determine the extent to which Central Command had altered intelligence reports to convey false good news to President Obama about the strength of ISIS, the Islamic State. Over fifty analysts at Central Command complained that senior military officers had manipulated intelligence reports to deceive Congress and show success in the bombing of ISIS in Iraq, essentially to impress the Obama administration.[118] The administration's ISIS envoy, John Allen, a retired marine general, had claimed that ISIS had been "checked strategically, operationally, and by and large, tactically. ISIS is losing."[119] In reality, ISIS was growing stronger.

To fight ISIS, the U.S. military promised to produce 15,000 rebel forces at a cost of $500 million and later claimed that the plan was on schedule. By September 2015, however, only fifty-four recruits had been trained, at a cost of $41.8 million. All of them, except for four or five, had been captured or killed by ISIS. At the end of the training in 2015, General Austin told

Congress that the program produced "four or five" rebel fighters in Syria, which members of Congress understandably considered a joke.[120]

In 2015 ISIS consolidated its control over Mosul, the second largest city in Iraq. The terrorist group, known for beheading its captives, seized another key city, Ramadi, and eventually took control of the Sunni heartland in western Iraq. In Syria, ISIS overran the ancient city of Palmyra and destroyed the two-thousand-year-old Temple of Bel, along with other ancient artifacts. ISIS established a position in Libya, an ungoverned state, in the event it began losing ground elsewhere.[121] Intelligence assessments around this time showed that ISIS had expanded into North Africa and Central Asia.[122] This was in addition to high-profile ISIS terrorist attacks, including the killing of 130 people and wounding of hundreds more at restaurants and cultural locations in Paris in November 2015, and three suicide bombers who killed thirty-four people and wounded over three hundred in Brussels, Belgium, in March 2016.

Regarding ISIS's strength and the U.S. military's attempt to contain it, the military's penchant for control kicked into gear. The protesting analysts worked for the Defense Intelligence Agency, which was created to provide an independent perspective, but they reported to Central Command, which was the alleged source of the doctored intelligence.[123] According to two senior analysts who filed a formal complaint with the Pentagon inspector general, some of the altered reports on ISIS were presented to President Obama.[124] The analysts complained that Major General Steven R. Grove and his civilian deputy, Gregory Ryckman, manipulated intelligence, and that Ryckman revised intelligence he believed was overly pessimistic.

In one instance, after ISIS took control of Iraqi cities in 2014, analysts "documented the humiliating retreat of the Iraqi Army," according to a *New York Times* report.[125] But their superiors altered the reports to read that the Iraqi troops had "redeployed," with no mention of retreat.[126] According to a *Daily Beast* report, the analysts accused Grove and Ryckman of "changing their analyses to be more in line with the Obama administration's public contention that the fight against ISIS and Al Qaeda is making progress."[127] They complained that "key elements of intelligence reports were removed" and some negative reports were sent back or not passed to superiors, and that some analysts "self-censored so their reports affirmed already-held beliefs."[128]

After their complaints, some of the analysts were urged to retire and others agreed to leave. By April 2016 the military had removed two senior intelligence analysts from Central Command, one of whom was the senior analyst for Syria, allegedly because they had been skeptical of the reports of U.S. success against ISIS. The Pentagon investigation was spurred by Gregory Hooker, a respected Iraqi expert. Hooker was reassigned to a post in the United Kingdom, although it was unclear whether Hooker requested the move.[129]

In August 2016, under the auspices of the U.S. House of Representatives Intelligence Committee, a joint task force issued an interim report finding that military commanders at Central Command had manipulated the analysts' reports and exaggerated the effects of the U.S. military's campaign against ISIS.[130] The task force found that General Austin had underestimated the danger of ISIS and created a poor working environment where "dozens of analysts viewed the subsequent leadership environment [under Austin] as toxic, with 40% of analysts responding that they had experienced an attempt to distort or suppress intelligence in the past year." Starting in 2014, when ISIS was taking territory in Iraq, Central Command produced "intelligence products that were inconsistent with the judgments of many senior, career analysts" and which "were consistently more optimistic regarding the conduct of U.S. military action than that of the senior analysts" and "also significantly more optimistic than that of other parts of the Intelligence Community (IC) and typically more optimistic than actual events warranted."[131]

The Department of Defense "produced only a portion of requested reports,"[132] according to the task force, and despite whistleblower complaints did not take "any demonstrable steps to improve the analytic climate" within Central Command.[133] The task force concluded that some analysts refused to testify "out of fear of potential reprisals for their testimony."[134]

The task force also implied that Central Command and James Clapper, the director of national intelligence, worked together to present overly optimistic intelligence reports to the president as a means to support the administration's political decisions. Clapper and Major General Grove had several telephone conversations per week. That any conversation occurred was unusual because Clapper, given his elevated standing in the bureaucracy, should have communicated with a higher-ranking officer, and also because high-ranking intelligence officials, including the director of the Defense Intelligence Agency, were excluded. The task force noted, "These frequent interactions are at odds with the DNI James Clapper's testimony to Congress that 'intelligence assessments from CENTCOM . . . come to the national level only through the Defense Intelligence Agency.'"[135]

The alleged deceptions emanating from Central Command harken back to the Vietnam War, when Congress lost or relinquished almost all control of the war in favor of the military. The 2016 report of the Joint Task Force could have been written about General Westmoreland's command in the 1960s. Through the first half of 2015, Central Command's "press releases, statements, and congressional testimonies were significantly more positive than actual events," according to the task force. The task force noted that General Austin testified before the House Armed Services Committee that ISIL (ISIS) was in a "defensive crouch."[136]

In contrast to the task force's conclusions, a Pentagon inspector general report on January 31, 2017, indicated that Grove and his civilian deputy, Ryckman, had not deliberately falsified intelligence reports. As is far too common when the military investigates itself, the focus of the Pentagon inspector general on the mental states of deliberation and intent may function to give everyone a pass. "Early on, MG Grove and Mr. Ryckman did not communicate well with analysts, and they seemed unaware of how their actions and words were perceived," according to the inspector general.[137] "We did not find that anyone *intentionally* attempted to distort intelligence. Nor did we find a systematic distortion of intelligence" (emphasis mine).[138]

One way to mask or minimize misconduct or error is to find that no one acted intentionally, a justification that is frequently cited in military investigation reports. But such a finding, even if valid, does not provide a full analysis of who is responsible for particular actions. An absence of intent does not mean that someone is blameless, because he or she could still have acted with knowledge, recklessness, or negligence. Military investigation reports often claim not to have found intentional misconduct, but then do not include any analysis of whether an officer or soldier acted with any of the other mental states, which are the bases for culpability in the U.S. legal system.

Glenn Fine, the acting inspector general, focused on a lack of intent in his nine pages of written congressional testimony, but he did not mention the additional culpable mental states. Fine told Congress that "we did not find systematic or *intentional* distortion of intelligence by USCENTCOM senior leaders, or that the leaders suppressed or delayed intelligence products."[139]

And "With regard to the specific examples of distortion to which the complainants and other witnesses pointed, we did not find that they [the intelligence leaders at Central Command] demonstrated any systematic or *intentional* distortion of intelligence."

And "We do not believe that this provides evidence of an *intent* to distort intelligence or present a rosier intelligence picture" (emphasis in quotes above mine).[140]

The narrowing of the issue to whether someone acted intentionally allows an incomplete analysis to appear complete. Someone at Central Command, for instance, could have knowingly allowed or recklessly acquiesced to the preparation of false intelligence reports. Without this further analysis, no one can ever know who, if anyone, is responsible.

WHAT ARE WAR CRIMES

On October 3, 2015, four-star general John Campbell was the commander in Afghanistan when U.S. forces flying an AC-130 gunship attacked a hospital, run by Doctors Without Borders, in Kunduz. The soldiers killed forty-two doctors, patients, and staff members and wounded dozens of others. On the day of the attack, army spokesman Brian Tribus (Class of '92) noted, "The strike may have resulted in collateral damage to a nearby medical facility."[141] Tribus's term "medical facility" did not sufficiently describe the fully operational hospital. An investigation later showed that the slow U.S. fixed-wing, four-engine gunship had first circled the hospital for forty-nine minutes—observing no hostile intent—and then, circling repeatedly, attacked the hospital for thirty to sixty minutes. Among the dead were seventeen Afghan doctors and nurses, who were virtually irreplaceable in the impoverished country.

On the second day, Secretary of Defense Ashton Carter claimed that the crew of the gunship acted in self-defense. "And at some point in the course of the events there [*sic*] did report that they, themselves, were coming under attack."[142]

On the third day, General Campbell said the Afghan military had requested the attack. "We have now learned that on Oct. 3, Afghan forces advised that they were taking fire from enemy positions and asked for air support from U.S. forces. An airstrike was then called to eliminate the Taliban threat and several civilians were accidentally struck. This is different from the initial reports which indicated that U.S. forces were threatened and that the airstrike was called on their behalf."[143] Like the previous two statements, this, too, was incorrect. The Afghans had actually provided the United States with the correct coordinates of a real Taliban position, not the hospital.

On the fourth day, Campbell, who was in Washington, said that U.S. forces were not directly engaged in the fighting around the hospital and that the decision to attack was made by U.S. commanders.[144] One U.S. official said, "Campbell's thinking now is that the Americans on the ground did not follow the rules of engagement fully."[145]

The doctors at the hospital did not allow weapons inside, and under no circumstances could the hospital have been considered a lawful military target. Mary Ellen O'Connell, a professor at Notre Dame, said, "Any serious violation of the law of armed conflict, such as attacking a hospital that is immune from intentional attack, is a war crime. Hospitals are immune from attack during an armed conflict unless being used by one party to harm the other and then only after a warning that it will be attacked."[146] The soldiers apparently did not understand they were attacking a hospital, but this alone is not a basis for exonerating them from criminal liability.

Major General William B. Hickman submitted the first army report on the attack to General Campbell. In a memorandum attached to the report Campbell described the "action by the appointing authority," meaning Campbell himself. It is impossible to know the full scope of Hickman's fact-finding, conclusions, and recommendations because Campbell "disapproved" and excised from the report "matters unrelated to the proximate cause of the strike on the MSF Trauma Center," he said in his memorandum. Because proximate cause concerns the acts closest to the result (the deaths), Hickman's report presumably covered soldiers' errors leading up to the actual killings, which is presumably what Campbell excised. Campbell, in an enclosure attached to his memorandum, dictated "substituted command action recommendations." Campbell said "appropriate administrative or disciplinary action" should be considered for sixteen individuals, but he redacted their names from the enclosure.[147]

John Sifton, the Asia advocacy director for Human Rights Watch, ridiculed the military's investigation. "'Mistakes,' 'errors,' 'processes,' 'circumstances'—a lot of potentially accountability shedding verbiage, but the fact is that today's explanations leave open serious questions about whether attackers knowingly or recklessly fired on a functioning hospital."[148] Sifton, unlike Campbell, recognized that officers and soldiers are also responsible for their *knowing* and *reckless* acts, but someone in the military who is acting in good faith must make that analysis for there to be a reliable investigation and report.

To this day, the public has no idea which U.S. military officers and soldiers are responsible for killing forty-two innocent people at the hospital.[149] It appears that Campbell objected to Hickman's inclusion of material that would have portrayed the U.S. attack on the hospital in a broader context. In public, Campbell said the attack "was a tragic and avoidable accident caused primarily by human error," which was "compounded by systems and procedural failures."[150] But that statement is as vague, uninformative, and inconclusive as the vacuum created by Campbell's "disapproved" findings.

"Not long before the attack on the hospital," a *Washington Post* report noted, "a U.S. airstrike pummeled an empty warehouse across the street from the Afghan intelligence headquarters. How U.S. personnel could have confused its location only a few hours later is not clear, nor is it clear why the gunship repeatedly struck the hospital when there was no return fire."[151]

Following a second investigation, the new head of Central Command, General Joseph L. Votel (replacing General Austin), in April 2016, cited "lack of intent" as his reason for concluding that soldiers had not committed war crimes. Votel did not release the names of the sixteen soldiers and officers, including one major general (two stars), who were allegedly disciplined with "suspension and removal from command, reprimands, counseling, and retraining," for the killing of the forty-two people.[152] It is inconceivable that anywhere in American society, except for the military, the identities of sixteen public employees who contributed to the killing of forty-two innocent people would be forever hidden from public view.

But this is how it works in the U.S. military. In a prepared statement, Votel said:

> The label war crimes is typically reserved for *intentional* acts— *intentional* targeting of civilians or *intentionally* targeting protected objects or locations. Again, the investigation found that the incident resulted from a combination of *unintentional* human errors, process errors and equipment failures, and that none of the personnel knew they were striking a hospital . . . In light of the report's conclusion that the errors committed were *unintentional* . . . the measures taken against these individuals were appropriate to address the errors they made . . . There was no *intention* on any of their parts to take a short cut [emphasis mine].[153]

Votel's talking point indicated that a lack of intent prevented the soldiers and officers from being held criminally responsible for the deaths of the civilians. Under U.S. military law, the soldiers could be found guilty of negligent, reckless, or knowing killings. Further, under the laws of war, soldiers are required to distinguish between combatants and noncombatants before attacking. Similarly, an excessive attack, including pounding with howitzers from a gunship a defenseless position like a hospital for thirty to sixty minutes, with no return fire, almost surely violates the requirement that attacks be proportional to the threat that exists and necessary to the mission.

Votel's and Campbell's withholding of the identities of public employees, soldiers and officers, is routine. The military culture—too little attention to what seems like grave misconduct, errors, or crimes—has been allowed to fester because Americans have been unwilling to demand that the military operate under the norms of a democratic society, where public officials are named and accountable. If anything, the light sanctions (suspension, removal, reprimand, counseling, and retraining) for killing dozens of innocent hospital workers signals relative toleration of destructive behavior.

Instead, the only predictable consequences found in the military are actually doled out to those who try to expose wrongdoing. Those who cannot remain silent or toe the party line are ostracized and retaliated against in systemic fashion, an institutional principle and practice that we turn to next.

CHAPTER 5

A Culture of Silence—
Censorship and Retaliation

When even one American—who has done nothing wrong—is forced by fear to shut his mind and close his mouth—then all Americans are in peril.

—Harry Truman

In the spring of 1997, I was a visiting professor teaching courses in international law and human rights at Ural State Law Academy in Yekaterinburg, Russia. During the Soviet era, the city was named Sverdlovsk, and throughout the Cold War it was a center of nuclear, chemical, and biological weapons production. On May 1, 1960, it was the place where a Soviet surface-to-air missile shot down America's CIA pilot Francis Gary Powers and his U-2 spy plane. Sverdlovsk was also the city where an anthrax leak from a military laboratory on April 2, 1979 killed at least sixty-four people.

With a population of about 1.5 million and over a dozen universities, Sverdlovsk became a research hub and one of the most well-educated regions in the Soviet Union. The Russian students in my courses had grown up as Communists but learned quickly after the fall of the Soviet Union (1991) to seek new information, and they were willing to credit the virtues of democracy. They said, for example, that the Soviet Union was at fault for the Cuban missile crisis in October 1962, when it placed nuclear-tipped missiles just ninety miles from the United States. Toward the end of one course, I asked the students what they had learned was the worst thing about the United States. One student, with the others in agreement, replied with a question: "Is every white person in America a member of the Ku Klux Klan?"

Then I asked them what they believed is the best thing about America. They all agreed on the answer: "free speech."

CENSORSHIP AND SILENCE

The Russian students' early learning led to stereotypes about Americans, but, despite the Soviet influence, they developed a willingness to criticize their own country and an understanding of the importance of expression. In contrast, respect for free speech is not a cultural norm or even an aspiration of many of the students and instructors at the U.S. military academies, where almost everyone has grown up in a democracy. This, of course, signals the fragility of democratic practices and government.

The model of learning and education in the military and at the academies is negative reinforcement. At West Point, the officers tell the faculty, staff, and cadets to make "corrections" of each other whenever they spot an infraction. Lurking over every comment and communication is the military's penal code, the Uniform Code of Military Justice, which prohibits students and officers from speaking "disrespectfully" to superior officers or "contemptuously" about civilian leaders. Because these criminal prohibitions are broad and vague, they can be used by commanders to prosecute almost anyone who participates in normal political criticism and commentary. In practice, to protect themselves, officers and students speak only superficially about the most serious and controversial issues. Officers learn to speak of the person who registers meaningful disagreement as not being a "team player," an accusation that will prevent promotion and end a career if ever noted in a yearly evaluation. Officers will say that their silence signifies obedience, respect, teamwork, and humility, but this seems like a denial of a fundamental truth: speech is universally recognized as the most important political right and personal freedom. The officers' silence usually comes from fear they will be stigmatized, punished in career advancement, or even prosecuted criminally for uttering an objectionable opinion, especially if it conflicts with that of someone of a higher rank.

As discussed in the previous chapter, the military culture is tightly insulated because the institution always investigates itself. Consequently, soldiers and officers make a tacit agreement with the institution: silence in exchange for protection. This is what is meant by loyalty. Those who dare to dissent are so routinely and severely punished—lack of promotion, reduction of rank, loss of pension, termination, social ostracism, hazing—that all observers understand the lesson. This retaliatory ethos is imprinted on the students at the academies, fostered in the armed forces, and reinforced by commanders. It is no exaggeration to say that the practice continues to endanger the security of the United States by eroding the most important pillar of democracy.

SILENCE AT WEST POINT

The military academies all have honor codes, and the codes at West Point and the Air Force Academy state that cadets should not tolerate violations of the code. But as the study on lying in the military showed, the hypocrisy in this regard is alarming. Over the last sixty years, surveys from the three military academies "consistently indicate that historically over 50% of these academy graduates have, in retrospect, admitted to having witnessed and tolerated other cadets' and midshipmen's dishonesty at least once," according to one study. "Clearly, these graduates' behaviors and their professed attitudes are disconnected," concluded the authors.[1]

The misconduct at the academies, including sexual assault (discussed in the next chapter), could not proliferate except for this culture of silence. Cadets and midshipmen live and work in close quarters; any wrongdoing would be widely known if not for a significant number of students who minimize abuse, fail to report or stop it, or anticipate trouble for themselves if they decide to report it. For the instructors, West Point regularly wraps its antispeech policies inside threats of retaliation: termination for civilian professors and criminal prosecution for military professors for speaking without the authorization of the public affairs office.

The censorship policy currently in effect at West Point has a title reminiscent of Soviet propaganda: "USMA Local Interpretation Regarding the

Relation of USMA Academic Freedom Policy and Public Affairs Policy and Security Reviews." It was adopted in 2016 by the superintendent, Lieutenant General Robert Caslen. It began with an initiative by the public affairs officer, Lieutenant Colonel Webster Wright, and was supported by West Point's top civilian attorney, Lori Doughty. Wright's idea of controlling speech was buried within a proposal he titled "Media Engagement, Official Speech and Manuscript Clearance." Its purpose, he said, was to "establish policy, assign responsibilities and set procedures for working with external media and clearing manuscripts for presentation or publication." Wright's proposal required professors to submit their papers and speeches based on "official information" for his "review [and] clearance" before the professors could speak in public or publish their work. Wright informed the faculty that Doughty had instructed Wright's office to add to the policy, "Failure to abide by these policies may subject the individual to military and/ or civil penalties, up to and including removal from his/her position."

According to Wright, a primary reason for controlling speech was that at West Point the "respect and status afforded a professor or subject matter expert carries great weight in public debate. For this reason, engagements must be synchronized or USMA personnel risk the possibility of criticizing U.S. policy or policy makers, committing a UCMJ [military penal code] offense or desynchronizing higher-level diplomatic or communications efforts."

Wright made a point to add, "The review and clearance process is not censorship activity." Criticism of government policy is among the most cherished forms of speech, but Wright was threatening termination or criminal prosecution of teachers who dared to speak without approval from Wright or Caslen. Speech that must be explicitly approved in advance is many things, but it is certainly not free. The fact that Wright went out of his way to add what the policy was not made it clear that he knew the academy was paddling deep into the waters of censorship.

DON'T ASK, DON'T TELL, DON'T SPEAK

One example of what happens when retaliatory threats for speaking are enshrined in an institution's policy or norms occurred in 2010. At the time, Congress was considering the abolition of the "Don't ask, don't tell" policy, which prohibited gays and lesbians in the military from revealing their sexual orientations. *Washington Post* reporter Craig Whitlock asked a civilian professor and sociologist at West Point, Morten Ender, for his opinion on the policy. For over a decade, Ender had studied socialization within the military, including during one voluntary deployment to Iraq as a civilian. Obviously, his opinion on the matter was highly relevant.

Ender replied that he'd be happy to talk on the record, but that he had to give the public affairs office (PAO) and his department head, Colonel Tom Kolditz, a "heads-up."

In reply, Kolditz told Ender, "Mort, don't talk to this guy until PAO clears, especially until the repeal vote occurs."

Ender then asked officials in the public affairs office, "Am I good? I'm familiar with Craig's work. He's a legitimate reporter with the WP—unless I'm missing something."

One of the PAO officials, Joseph Tombrello, a retired army major working in a civilian job, told Ender, "Not good to go. This is DOD policy as we speak." Tombrello was apparently referring to a policy that no one may speak publicly about the "Don't ask, don't tell" policy without prior approval.

Tombrello later said, "Bottom line is for DOD to speak with one voice & not get ahead of the process. To say the leadership of DOD & the Army are hypersensitive about the subject would be ... an understatement. We will have the opportunity to participate, just not at this point."

After the *Washington Post* article came out, without any quotes from Ender or anyone at West Point, Ender told Kolditz and Tombrello, "I hope West Point doesn't get besmirched by this. Limiting faculty with knowledge in this area from speaking to the press might BECOME the story—and this will hurt us." He forwarded the *Post* article, which contained a quote from a professor at the Naval Postgraduate School in California. "Guess they didn't get the memo on the west coast," he wryly noted.

After the article appeared, Tombrello replied to Kolditz's questioning of the approach: "I understand your/our issues on this matter. In fact, I discussed the matter yesterday with big Army PA [Public Affairs]. They know we're waiting on the bench, so to speak; however, they (DOD particularly) are not ready for us at this point. We will get into the fight shortly, but have to respect their guidance as we speak ... DOD does not want anyone else talking with the media at this point."

"Ok," Kolditz replied, "just know that we're straining some very hard-fought relationships here. [It's] one thing to ask that no one else speak for the government. It's another thing entirely to become part of the story by attempting to censor academics in their topic areas."

Don Campbell, a professor in the Department of Behavioral Sciences and Leadership, which Kolditz headed and where Ender worked, protested to Kolditz. Kolditz replied to Campbell, "[West Point] is responding to very direct guidance from above Department of the Army level. Under these circumstances there is no way that Supe [superintendent], Dean, or I can approve or endorse media statements. That being said, nothing written has been presented and censored."

Kolditz is doing some mental gymnastics here, recognizing that censorship is wrong, but reasoning that because Ender did not speak or write, then no expression was censored. This ignores the fact that a prohibition on speaking or writing in the first place is just as pernicious as forcing people to clear speech in advance or regulating what they say; the result is no speech or diluted speech.

At a large faculty meeting where Wright's proposed policy was on the agenda, I told the faculty and Wright that "only because of the expanded definition that you've taken do you now devolve onto your office, or onto the department heads, the right and the ability to in fact censor the information that a professor is producing." I told him that "it's particularly troublesome that you would include in your [policy] the threat of civil penalties and removal for someone who violates your policy. I haven't found anybody who's produced any evidence that that exists in any other policy. It makes it seem as though the focus here is on suppressing information and academic freedom, not promoting it."

The next day, the new chair of the Academic Freedom Advisory Committee (yes, *academic freedom*), Colonel Bryndol Sones (Class of '87), wrote to admonish me. Sones ostensibly was most responsible for protecting academic freedom and free speech. "I thought you personally attacked LTC Wright," he told me. "You were unprofessional and mean spirited . . . I was embarrassed for you . . . I wish that you would consider apologizing to LTC Wright."

This kind of backdoor silencing is a hallmark of the U.S. Army, a method of ostracizing dissenters, and I did not respond to it. Wright, the public affairs officer, indeed seemed to be trying to suppress speech.

Eventually, Sones, Wright, Doughty, and several civilian professors, one a former military officer, formed an ad hoc committee to refine Wright's proposal. On the academic freedom committee, eight civilian professors voted to support the revised policy. An economics professor, Dean Dudley, and I voted against it. The reasoning of the eight who voted for it was that if they didn't accept "censorship lite," then Caslen, the superintendent, would impose "censorship full."

Just six months later, on October 12, 2016, Caslen imposed "censorship full." Caslen announced a new policy regarding what faculty, staff, and cadets would be allowed to write online. "Social media can be a powerful and positive tool," Caslen said. "But, as I've discussed many times before, there's an ugly side to it, where individuals take part in inappropriate, disrespectful and potentially harmful interactions online, hiding behind the sense of anonymity and lack of accountability that social media provides . . . In my opinion, postings of this type ['harassment, bullying, hazing, stalking, discrimination, retaliation or any other types of misconduct that undermine dignity and respect'] are cowardly and contrary to who we are as leaders within the public domain."

Under military law, Caslen, at his sole discretion, decides which officers and cadets will be charged with crimes. He alone determines who will serve as their jurors—all of whom, it must be recognized, are military officers under Caslen's command. In essence, Caslen was promising to punish people for speaking or writing words that he viewed as "inappropriate." Like many military officers, he was primarily concerned about the image of the academy and the military. Caslen just did not want to be embarrassed. "Anything posted online," he said, "has the potential to . . . affect the public's perception."

Caslen characterized "online misconduct" as "unacceptable or improper behavior through the use of technology." This is reminiscent of the method of authoritarian societies, defining spoken or written words as behavior or threats to the national order so that penalties or prosecution can seem more palatable and so that speaking can be criminalized. Caslen's terms, *inappropriate, disrespectful, unacceptable*, and *improper behavior*, are so broad and vague that they give him the authority to ban virtually all the expression to which he objects. The ultimate goal seems to be total control over what is said and written about anything. It's a blatant and troubling form of censorship that is the norm at West Point.

Caslen's policy reflected the approach of the military's penal law. Article 89 provides that any soldier "who behaves with disrespect (including 'using certain language' or 'words') toward his superior commissioned officer shall be punished as a court-martial may direct." This provision characterizes speech as behavior and makes disagreeable speech a criminal offense.

An explanatory guide that follows the UCMJ provision expands the concept of disrespect to include virtually anything that offends a superior officer: "a marked disdain, indifference, insolence, impertinence, undue familiarity, or other rudeness in the presence of the superior officer." In elevating loyalty and obedience as the supreme virtues, the explanatory material to Article 89 provides one chilling admonition reminiscent of police states: "The truth is no defense." Once a claim like that is made, it elevates loyalty to the top and elbows out all other values, creating greater distance between the U.S. military and the democratic norms of the United States.

SPEECH AT THE ACADEMIES

At all the military academies, free speech, if considered at all, is viewed as a selfish luxury the schools can't afford, and the few dissenters (that is, those who disagree with a policy) are characterized as unprofessional and mean-spirited, as the colonel who headed the academic freedom committee told me. Time and again, the military shows obsessive-compulsive tendencies toward controlling any words that might be objectionable to a superior officer. In early 2019 the West Point superintendent, Lieutenant General Darryl A. Williams, made a new rule requiring that his office be notified if even a teacher from another college stops by to guest lecture. The long list of visitors Williams wanted information on included: "Social media influencers that could either enhance or detract from the image of USMA [West Point] as the preeminent leader development institution in the world [and any] individual who has the perceived objective of negatively affecting the image of USMA." Williams or his staff could control the content of speech by greasing the wheels of those who would speak favorably of West Point and making entry to West Point logistically difficult or impossible for those whose words he didn't like.

On June 6, 2019, one cadet was killed and nineteen cadets and two soldiers were injured when an army transport truck ferrying the cadets to a summer training exercise rolled over on a hill at a camp near West Point. This followed another accident earlier in the year, when a cadet was killed while skiing on a slope on the West Point grounds. Soon after the truck crashed, Williams's office issued what it called a "blackout order" to West Point personnel: "By order of the Chief of Staff, do not post on social media or contact the media until further notice. The Public Affairs office will provide all public information."

Williams, just hours after the cadet's death, told the media, "You can see by looking around it is very hilly [and] we want to make sure our soldiers and cadets train in realistic training environment, so this is part of our realistic training. I mean, this is the United States Army, we are strong. We are strong here at West Point."[2] Williams's reflexive response was to blame an unnecessary tragedy on realism instead of a driving or other error by a soldier. (In September 2019 the army charged the soldier who was driving with involuntary manslaughter.)

A few months later, on August 31, 2019, a student at West Point's prep school, located on campus, was killed when he fell from a ledge near a popular cliff-diving location in upstate New York. The censorship decree coming from Williams's office this time was even more stringent. His chief of staff, Colonel Mark Bieger (Class of '91), said that West Point "personnel will not engage in discussion about the incident with any media, external organization, family, or friends until the official statement is published." By controlling the flow of information about Americans to Americans—prohibiting family members from speaking to each other—the generals can release a limited number of facts and prevent civilian society from learning what happened and holding the generals and the military accountable.

On October 18, 2019 a cadet at West Point checked out from the armory an operable M5 assault rifle, and then he disappeared. The West Point administration said the cadet was absent without leave, but that he was not dangerous to others and probably had no ammunition. The silencing order came from the dean's office: "Staff and faculty should not communicate about these circumstances on social media or with any external organizations." Four days later, the cadet was found deceased in a dormitory from a self-inflicted gunshot wound, another tragedy in which the facts were controlled and distributed by the military authorities.

Those who voice complaints—including about the restraint of speech itself—are summarily punished. In 2011 the U.S. Office of Special Counsel found that the Naval Academy had "illegally denied ... [an] employee a merit-pay increase because of [his] public statements." The employee was English professor Bruce Fleming, who had been working at the academy for twenty-four years. One Naval Academy official claimed that Fleming should not be rewarded with a salary increase because he complained outside the academy—to a local newspaper—that unqualified students were admitted to populate the school's athletic teams.[3]

Two years later, in 2013, the Naval Academy again pursued Professor Fleming for speech that unsettled the academy, this time in his classes. Fleming said that the military's Sexual Harassment/Assault Response and Prevention (SHARP) program fostered a presumption of guilt against male students. Two female students in different classes objected; one of them accused Fleming of perpetuating "the rape myth."

Fleming emailed one of the women, "I can tell that you were not comfortable with me questioning the givens of sexual assault training ... and I hope that I gave you time to express your POV. Please get used to the fact that there is no assertion that is too sacred for me to question it."

The women said they "felt singled out and harassed" by Fleming and reported him to "sex assault prevention officials."[4]

The academy removed Fleming from his classes, but the English department, chaired by a civilian professor,[5] investigated and exonerated Fleming in two days, concluding that his comments were protected by academic freedom. Fleming then filed a complaint against the women for making unsubstantiated allegations.

Instead of addressing Fleming's complaint, the Naval Academy used the fact that he filed it to punish him. It initiated a new investigation, led by a colonel in the marines, Paul Montanus, who also served in effect as a judge on the matter. Montanus reprimanded Fleming, and the academy again denied him a small pay increase and a research grant. Like Caslen at West Point, Montanus characterized Fleming's speech as "inappropriate conduct" and said that Fleming's complaint against the women was "retaliation" and was "unacceptable and will not be tolerated."[6]

In this upside-down military world, Fleming was reprimanded by the Naval Academy for complaining about the people who had made unsubstantiated complaints about him. The irony in this case is that the academy's vindictive behavior against Fleming, the complainant, is exactly what sexual assault training is supposed to eradicate.[7]

The retaliation against Fleming is consistent with longtime practices at the academies and within the military. In 1996 another civilian professor at the Naval Academy, James Barry, was teaching a class on ethics, which was instituted because of drug use and cheating among its midshipmen. A Vietnam War veteran, Barry taught economics and leadership. In a *Washington Post* opinion piece, Barry wrote that the academy was "plagued by a serious morale problem caused by a culture of hypocrisy, one that tolerates sexual harassment, favoritism, and the covering up of problems."[8]

In response, the academy's superintendent, Admiral Charles Larson, removed Barry from the classroom and directed him to write a report on the problems and recommend solutions within thirty days. In an effort to disparage Barry, Larson held several "public humiliations staged to discredit Barry [and] explicitly targeted his loyalty," according to a former faculty member at the academy.[9] Larson claimed that Barry's op-ed essay contained "half-truths and falsehoods" and that he should have brought his issues to Larson before "going outside the system."[10]

But Professor Barry had done exactly this, trying "for many months and in 11 different memos sent up 'the chain of command' to bring his concerns to the attention of academy leaders," according to Carol Burke, the former professor at the academy. As Burke put it in a *Los Angeles Times* article, a "public institution whose leaders so fear the scrutiny of the public that they would stage pre-emptive denunciations to deter future critics is a fragile one indeed."[11]

At the public denunciations, Larson said that Barry's article "sends a message. It says, 'I don't trust you ... We'll let external forces come in and tell us how to solve this problem.' He's telling me that after 38 years of commissioned service and five years as superintendent, I don't know what's going on here ... I think that's disloyal to me. I think it's very disloyal to the institution, and I never like having people work for me that do that, and I don't think any of you would either ... He betrayed me."[12]

Larson's language—with its focus on himself and loyalty—is enormously revealing. Larson was oblivious to or apathetic about a citizen's constitutional right to free speech. That just got in the way of his authority and maintaining control of everyone at "his" institution.

At one point during a public denunciation, Admiral Larson tried to humiliate Professor Barry by making him stand up and face the faculty and midshipmen. Larson harangued, "That man there is a liar and a traitor."[13] Larson alleged that Barry failed to include in his article changes that he as superintendent had made at the academy, including tightening of the privileges for midshipmen.

"One who has a dissenting opinion can pay a terrible cost," Professor Barry told the *Baltimore Sun*. "What the midshipmen are seeing is what I'm saying in the article."[14] Years later, for an article about Bruce Fleming's case, Barry said, "The midshipmen see guys like me or Bruce stand up and get knocked down. And the lesson to them is they don't want that to happen to them."[15]

The cases of Professors Fleming and Barry reveal what happens when someone breaks the code of silence, even while standing on firm moral and constitutional ground. Silencing dissent anywhere is a threat to democracy, especially when it occurs within institutions as vital to our society as the military and the academies that feed into it. But military officers have learned to believe their positions imbue them with gravitas and, by virtue of their rank, an authority that supplants law.

Admiral Larson said something quite revealing during an interview with military historian and author H. Michael Gelfand for his 2006 book *Sea Change at Annapolis: The United States Naval Academy, 1949–2000*. Always wary of traitors in his midst, Larson said, "There is a society out there right now that is more worried about what is legal than what is right. We don't stand up and say, 'I'm going to do what is right.' I wanted to fix that."[16] This separation between what is right and what is legal, which means loyalty over law, is ostensibly determined by people like Larson. This further solidifies the military's separation from and disdain for democratic practices and constitutional protections.

The only real prospect for improvement at insular institutions like the military academies is to speak up and attempt to implement change from the outside. Professor Barry complained to the American Association of University Professors, a century-old organization whose goal is to protect academic freedom. After public pressure, the Naval Academy returned

Barry to his teaching position,[17] but instead he "found it impossible" to go back to his job. He reached a settlement with the academy and found other work.[18]

In 2004, Congress required a "study and report related to permanent professors" at the Air Force Academy in comparison with the faculties at West Point and the Naval Academy.[19] The "permanent professors" at the academies, the PUSMAs, are military officers who may remain in their positions until mandatory retirement at age sixty-four. In what would be comedic if it weren't a significant waste of government resources, the secretary of the air force hired retired Admiral Larson to evaluate the structure of the Air Force Academy and its faculty model.[20] (The chairperson of the committee for the Middle States Commission on Higher Education, which was responsible for reviewing West Point's academic program for reaccreditation in 2020, was the superintendent of the Air Force Academy, Lieutenant General Jay Silveria.)

Not surprisingly, the academy thought that Larson did a splendid job. The lead article in the official academy newspaper boasted "Larson Report Views Faculty Favorably: Report Finds Academy's Atmosphere for Women Also Improved."[21] Admiral Larson and the newspaper failed to report that at that moment the academy was awash in pervasive cheating, drug dealing, and sexual assaults by its cadets. A secret criminal investigation was under way, using cadets and future air force officers as informants (see chapter 6). This circular accountability system is an echo of what happens when the military investigates itself. It's a closed circle where everyone is approving each other's actions, and it behooves no one to stray from the party line.

The Air Force Academy, like the other academies, tried on two fronts to retaliate against one of its civilian professors after his complaints of wrongdoing by the top two academic officials. David Mullin was an economics professor at the school, and a self-described evangelical Christian. He objected to the academy's alleged violation of the separation of church and state, as enshrined in the First Amendment, a controversy that has festered for years at the academy. Mullin also revealed that a large percentage of military instructors did not have graduate degrees in the academic disciplines they were teaching. In 2011 Mullin complained to the air force that the academic dean, Brigadier General Dana Born, and the vice dean,

Colonel Richard Fullerton, were not correct when they said there were no such instructors at the academy. In fact, Mullin was right about the instructors. Nearly *four dozen* instructors taught courses for which they did not hold a related master's degree.[22]

Mullin believed that Born harbored animosity toward him because he opposed the academy's explicit support for religion, primarily proselytizing by officers and cadets for evangelical Christianity.[23] Allegedly for public expression of her religious beliefs, Born's critics called her "Dana Born-again," according to the local newspaper, the *Colorado Springs Gazette*.[24]

In April 2010 Colonel Fullerton, who was then a department head and Mullin's supervisor, "ordered Mullin to walk around his classroom and climb risers to police student usage of their laptop computers." Professor Mullin objected to scaling heights because this violated an agreement with the academy that he could sit down during classes because of a physical impairment, a pain syndrome that caused dizziness and balance difficulties. Eventually Mullin agreed to climb the risers. He then filed an Equal Opportunity complaint in May 2010. A few months later, on Fullerton's recommendation, Brigadier General Born told Mullin his contract would not be renewed beyond the 2010–2011 academic year.

In January 2011 Mullin and four anonymous air force instructors, who presumbly feared retaliation if they became known, filed a complaint in federal court to suspend a National Prayer Luncheon at the academy. A federal judge dismissed the complaint, ruling that Mullin and the instructors did not have legal standing to sue because the luncheon events would not harm them. In April 2011, three months after Mullin's complaints, Mullin's service dog was poisoned by an unknown culprit.[25] The dog survived, but Mullin is certain that the poisoning, which happened behind his locked office door,[26] was a retaliatory action against him. An air force investigation was "inconclusive."[27]

The air force inspector general investigated both Born and Fullerton and found that they had in fact made false statements about the qualifications of the military faculty to an accreditation agency.[28] Born also made a similar false statement to a local news reporter. But the inspector general found that they made their false statements negligently, not *intentionally*. Born and

Fullerton, the top two academic officers, kept their jobs and received no discipline. As Professor Mullin alleged, the Air Force Academy was using unqualified instructors to teach the cadets, and in 2014 the academy agreed to a settlement with him, but he, like Professor Barry at Navy, did not return to the academy.

EISENHOWER'S OTHER WARNING

Most Americans understand that the protection of freedom, including free expression, is the reason to have a military in the first place. On June 14, 1953, President Dwight D. Eisenhower tried to slap away the heavy hand of censorship when he gave the graduation speech at Dartmouth College. At the time, American institutions were being swept up in the wave of McCarthyism. Pressured by investigators for Senator Joe McCarthy, the U.S. Information Service in Europe, designed to disseminate positive information abroad, had recently removed from its libraries books by alleged Communist sympathizers: Langston Hughes, Dashiell Hammett, and Jean-Paul Sartre. "Don't join the book burners," Eisenhower told the new graduates,

> Don't think you are going to conceal faults by concealing evidence that they ever existed. Don't be afraid to go in your library and read every book, as long as any document does not offend our own ideas of decency . . . And we have got to fight it [communism] with something better, not try to conceal the thinking of our own people. They are part of America. And even if they think ideas that are contrary to ours, their right to say them, their right to record them, and their right to have them at places where they are accessible to others is unquestioned, or it's not America.[29]

LOW WALLS

In the military, censorship is justified by citing national security, a rationale that will always exist, even when the generals assert it without cause. This leaves generals an opening to suppress almost any information, which makes outside control of the military more difficult. Because military leaders regularly move into civilian leadership positions, their model of institutional censorship has seeped into every agency of the government. A former lieutenant general in the air force, James Clapper became the director of national intelligence in 2010 under President Barack Obama. In 2014 he adopted a policy that provided for the termination of federal employees in the agencies he supervised for speaking to reporters without permission.

Clapper was not a rogue agency leader. He represented the U.S. government's practice of routinely restricting or manipulating the press. Americans assume that the First Amendment protects the rights of a free press, but most do not realize how relatively little freedom the press actually enjoys. A 2019 report by Reporters Without Borders ranked the United States last for press freedom among the major English-speaking countries. The nation was ranked forty-eighth of 180 countries, behind every Western European country.[30]

Like the military, the U.S. government's most severe method of restricting information is to prosecute or threaten to prosecute employees who reveal classified information to reporters. It is the heads of government agencies and their designees who have the legal authority to determine what information will be classified. This discretion makes military officers and agency officials broad-based censors, as well as the determiners of the criminal law. Only when they attach the label of "classified" to information can someone be prosecuted, convicted, and imprisoned for releasing it. (An additional cache of vast information is concealed when the military and other public agencies refuse to release data and information requested under the Freedom of Information Act.[31])

In the 1971 Pentagon Papers case (*New York Times v. U.S.*), the Supreme Court ruled that newspapers were allowed to publish a secret Pentagon history of the Vietnam War. But it remains an open constitutional question whether the government may prosecute reporters for releasing classified information obtained from government sources.[32] Throughout U.S. history, any number of government officials and presidential administrations have tolerated the release of classified information to reporters to ensure that the press would not be deterred from investigating the government. In recent years, however, mainly at the insistence of one retired admiral, the government has begun to strong-arm reporters into revealing their sources or not publishing the information the press received from the sources.

On May 23, 2019, the press received word of what it had been spared since the passage of the infamous Alien and Sedition Acts of 1798. The Trump Justice Department charged the founder of WikiLeaks, Julian Assange, under the World War I Espionage Act, with *publishing* classified information.[33] This new government approach—prosecuting a publisher, as well as asking judges to order imprisonment for reporters until they reveal their sources—originated in full in 2009 when retired admiral Dennis Blair morphed into civilian society as the director of national intelligence, a civilian position.

Blair (Naval Academy, '68) helped bring the military ethos of speech restriction and retaliation to civilian government. He bemoaned the lack of criminal prosecutions of those who leaked classified information and convinced attorney general Eric Holder to begin an unprecedented wave of investigations and prosecutions of low-level government employees. "My background is in the Navy," bragged Blair, "and it is good to hang an admiral once in a while as an example to the others. We were hoping to get somebody and make people realize that there are consequences to this and it needed to stop."[34]

Over the previous ninety-two years, the government had prosecuted only three people for releasing classified information to reporters. Following Blair's urging, the Obama administration prosecuted eight in a four-year span.[35] From 2017 to 2019, the Trump administration prosecuted six. In 2014 the government characterized a reporter, James Rosen of Fox News, as a criminal conspirator because he had presumably received classified information about North Korea from a contractor for the State Department. A government affidavit declared that Rosen "aided and abetted" his source's disclosure.[36] The government never prosecuted Rosen.

The prosecution of these low-level employees for releasing classified information illustrates the pernicious hypocrisy inside the U.S. government, especially in favor of high-ranking military officers. A 2005 email from CIA lawyers noted the inconsistency of the CIA's declaring in court documents a critical need to keep "information secret," while at the same time shoveling classified information to reporters to help "sell" their torture program in the early 2000s.[37]

From 1990 to 2004, John Kiriakou was a CIA analyst and one of the eight government employees prosecuted by the Obama administration for disclosing classified information to reporters (the ninth was a soldier, Chelsea [formerly Bradley] Manning, who was prosecuted by the military).[38] Working in Pakistan after 9/11, Kiriakou helped capture Abu Zubaydah, who had trained al-Qaeda fighters. After his CIA career, Kiriakou went on television in 2007 to reveal the CIA's waterboarding of detainees, although he was not completely forthcoming, apparently out of loyalty to other officers. In his interview, Kiriakou said that Abu Zubaydah started talking after only seconds of waterboarding, when in fact he knew that CIA officers had waterboarded Zubaydah eighty-three times. In 2012 Kiriakou pleaded guilty to a felony, admitting that he had provided to a journalist the name of a covert agent who had participated in the brutal interrogations of detainees during the wars. Kiriakou received a sentence of thirty months in prison.[39]

In 2015 CIA officer Jeffrey Sterling was found guilty by a jury of committing nine felonies related to releasing classified information to a *New York Times* reporter, James Risen, about the U.S. failure to stop Iran's nuclear weapons program.[40] Requesting a twenty-year prison term, the government claimed that Sterling, who is black, released the information because he lost a racial discrimination case against the CIA and that his disclosure had endangered a spy. A federal judge sentenced Sterling to three and a half years in prison. In apparently every instance, the federal employees who were prosecuted, like Kiriakou, Sterling, and Manning, received nothing in return for leaking the information, all of which appeared to be true. But there was a bright contrast between the motives of these low-level employees and the motives of one of the most famous leakers of classified information.

LEAKING HYPOCRISY

In 2012 CIA director David Petraeus praised the prosecution of Kiriakou in a memo to the CIA's employees. "It marks an important victory for our agency, for our intelligence community, and for our country," Petraeus wrote. "Oaths do matter, and there are indeed consequences for those who believe they are above the laws that protect our fellow officers and enable American intelligence agencies to operate with the requisite degree of secrecy."[41] Unknown to the world at the time, over a year earlier, in August 2011, Petraeus had passed far more consequential classified information to his lover, who was writing a biography about him.

President Obama nominated General Petraeus to be the director of the CIA and the Senate confirmed him 94–0.[42] A year and a half later, Petraeus resigned as director when his relationship with the married biographer Paula Broadwell, a woman twenty years his junior, became public. Petraeus's affair with Broadwell, a fellow West Point graduate (Class of '95) and lieutenant colonel in the Army Reserve, was discovered during an FBI investigation.[43]

According to federal prosecutors, Petraeus gave Broadwell "black books" containing the names of covert agents, code words, military strategy, quotes from meetings of the National Security Council, and notes of Petraeus's discussions with President Obama. When FBI agents searched Broadwell's house, they found one hundred photographs of the classified information. In 2015 Petraeus pleaded guilty to a misdemeanor, unauthorized removal and retention of classified documents or material, and received a sentence of probation and a fine.[44]

Under the direction of Attorney General Holder, prosecutors did not charge Petraeus with lying to the FBI, despite the fact that he did exactly that when agents asked him whether he had passed classified information to Broadwell.[45] After Petraeus's conviction, the army retained Broadwell as a reservist but rescinded her promotion to lieutenant colonel and revoked her security clearance, which did not include access to the information Petraeus gave her. Broadwell was never prosecuted.[46] The secretary of the army, John McHugh,[47] as well as the secretary of defense, Ashton Carter,[48] decided not to retroactively reduce Petraeus's rank, clearing the way for him to collect a pension of $220,000 per year. It's not that he needed the money. In private life, Petraeus "confided to friends and acquaintances that he's making a hefty sum from his job at a private equity firm [Kohlberg Kravis Roberts] and through speaking fees."[49]

An assistant secretary of defense, Stephen Hedger (Class of '99), reported Carter's decision to senators John McCain and Jack Reed, who had asked Carter not to demote Petraeus. McHugh had been on West Point's Board of Visitors, an advisory body, for fourteen years. McCain was a 1959 graduate of the Naval Academy, while Reed (Class of '71) and Petraeus had attended West Point together.

It does help to have an impressive military title and friends in high places. In 2011, as the vice chief of the Joint Chiefs of Staff, marine general

James "Hoss" Cartwright was the second-highest-ranking military officer in the United States and was considered President Barack Obama's "favorite general."[50] On October 17, 2017, Cartwright pleaded guilty to making false statements to federal investigators, a felony. In an FBI investigation into who leaked classified information to reporters about a U.S. cyberattack on Iranian centrifuges, which help produce nuclear fuel, Cartwright (who was not the leaker) lied to investigators when he denied his conversations with reporters. Prosecutors asked for a sentence of imprisonment of two years, but, with three days remaining in his presidency, Obama pardoned Cartwright on January 17, 2017, just two weeks before he was to be sentenced.

After Petraeus's resignation as CIA director, he became an advisor to the Obama administration.[51] When Petraeus pleaded guilty and received no prison sentence, Stephen Kim, a former State Department employee, was serving a thirteen-month prison sentence for disclosing classified information about North Korea to James Rosen, the Fox News reporter. According to Kim, he wanted the nation to know the dangers of North Korea. The Justice Department had refused Kim's request for a misdemeanor, and he pleaded guilty to a felony. "The reasons that you provided to refuse our misdemeanor offer were grounded in motive and lying to the F.B.I.," Kim's attorney wrote to Eric Holder, the attorney general. "There is no difference between the two cases in that respect." (If anything, General Petraeus's motive was far less noble.)[52]

Even after Petraeus's conduct became known, the cadets and military officers at West Point continued to revere the general. After he resigned as CIA director, Petraeus met with several West Point cadets who were in Washington working in summer internships. A female cadet, concerned about equality for women in the military, asked Petraeus if he had ever known a woman soldier who could qualify for Special Forces. "Yes, Broadwell," said Petraeus, "but I'm not going there."

Like its near deification of General Douglas MacArthur (a statue of him was erected on campus in 1969), West Point's adulation of Petraeus would not suffer a hit at all. In March 2016, as part of their work on civil-military relations, fifteen West Point cadets traveled to New York City to hear Petraeus's lecture at the Union League Club. In that week's *Dean's Weekly*

Significant Activities Report, page 1 as well as page 13 featured a large photograph of Petraeus surrounded by all the cadets in their dress uniforms.[53]

Recruited by the Center for the Study of Civil-Military Operations to share his leadership model with cadets, Petraeus was back at West Point in January 2017 (and again in August 2017). "Petraeus offered guidance, personal anecdotes and leadership skills learned over a 37-year Army career, his experiences as director of the CIA and in his current roles during an hour of invigorating discussion, while leaving time for questions with cadets at the end," according to West Point's Public Affairs Office.[54]

HOW GENERALS KEEP THEIR JOBS

America's generals are almost invincible now, because the president who criticizes or fires one will be characterized as not sufficiently supportive of the military. Before the Korean War, however, this was not the case. General George Marshall, the army's chief of staff and most senior officer in World War II, didn't just promote the next guy in line. Eisenhower did not become general through cronyism or seniority; he earned it. "Eisenhower was put on the fast track to lead Allied forces in Europe over another general who was theoretically next in line,"[55] noted journalist Andrea Stone in her review of Tom Ricks's book *The Generals*. In the old system, Ricks told Stone, "they expected a certain number of their generals to fail—that was seen as the system was working. It was a hard-nosed Darwinian system that allowed smart, new, ambitious, energetic people to rise up in the ranks."[56]

"The Army's shift away from swift dismissal in our recent wars," Ricks writes in *The Generals*, "has gone all but unnoticed, and so major questions about our military have been neglected: How and why did we lose the long-standing practice of relieving generals for failure? Why has accountability declined? . . . Answering these questions promises a way to better understand why our recent wars in Vietnam, Afghanistan, and Iraq have been so long and frustrating."[57]

To answer Ricks, generals don't get to the top of the military hierarchy by questioning anyone of a higher rank. A general who publicly or even privately disagrees with a policy will not last long. Generals get to where they are by remaining silent to advance their careers, even if they believe a policy or action is against the national interests. As author Chris Hedges writes in *War Is a Force That Gives Us Meaning*, "Dissidents who challenge the goodness of our cause, who question the gods of war, who pull back the curtains to expose the lie are usually silenced or ignored."[58]

For example, among the many problems with America's war with Iraq was the conflict between the generals and the secretary of defense, Donald Rumsfeld, over how many troops should be deployed. Rumsfeld wanted fewer, and General Richard Myers, the chairman of the Joint Chiefs of Staff, wanted more. Under the Goldwater-Nichols Act,[59] Myers could have gone directly to President George W. Bush to express his concern that the low number of troops would hinder their ability to win the war and endanger the troops who were there. But he opted to say nothing. "Instead, Myers kept his counsel and his job," writes George Packer in *The Assassins' Gate*. "There was always the example of General Shinseki to dissuade him and other senior officers from excessive candor."[60]

General Eric Shinseki (Class of '65), the army chief of staff from 1999 to 2003, was pushed to retire after testifying—correctly—before Congress that the United States should deploy several hundred thousand troops to Iraq after the invasion, while Rumsfeld wanted far fewer.[61]

General Myers learned his lessons well and kept his job—by keeping his mouth shut. As happens when a military commander in a position to affect a war doesn't speak, the United States deployed too few troops, a sectarian war exploded, Iraq fell into chaos, and people died—at least five hundred thousand in Iraq from 2003 to 2011, according to one study.[62]

Battlefield bravery of lower-ranking soldiers has not translated into moral courage among the generals. In 2011, when President Obama ordered the withdrawal of ten thousand troops from Afghanistan, General Petraeus, who was then commander in Afghanistan, disagreed with the decision. Petraeus was asked by a retired army general, Jack Keane, whether Petraeus felt he should resign if withdrawal "not only protracts the war but risks the mission."

"I don't think quitting would serve our country," Petraeus responded. "More likely to create a crisis. And, I told POTUS I'd support his ultimate decision. Besides, the troops can't quit."[63] Columnist William McGurn noticed the symmetry between Petraeus's response and those of his predecessors. "This was much the same rationale Army Chief of Staff Gen.

Harold Johnson gave for not resigning after LBJ advanced a war policy he believed would fail in Vietnam and weaken the U.S. Army."[64]

From 1964 to 1968, General Harold Johnson (Class of '33) was the army chief of staff when General William Westmoreland was leading the war of attrition in Vietnam. General Johnson believed that Westmoreland's decision to favor large military campaigns against the North Vietnamese and Vietcong—rather than counterinsurgency—would not be successful, but he never said so when it could have mattered. Later in life, Johnson's great regret was that he did not resign in protest and speak up. He told Brigadier General Albion Knight, who was also an ordained priest of the Episcopal Church,

> I remember the day I was ready to go over to the Oval Office and give my four stars to the President and tell him, "You have refused to tell the country they cannot fight a war without mobilization; you have required me to send men into battle with little hope of their ultimate victory; and you have forced us in the military to violate almost every one of the principles of war in Vietnam. Therefore, I resign and will hold a press conference after I walk out of your door." I made the typical mistake of believing I could do more for the country and the Army if I stayed in than if I got out. I am now going to my grave with that lapse in moral courage on my back.[65]

Like Petraeus, Johnson, in revealing his costly error, attributed his inaction to his patriotism, not to the protection of his job.

Johnson was not alone in his silence about the Vietnam War. If he and others of his rank had spoken up, congressional and public support for that war might have collapsed in the mid-1960s, saving tens of thousands of U.S. soldiers' lives and the lives of possibly a million or more Vietnamese. But according to the popular view among professional soldiers, Richard Betts writes, the greatest "sin" in the Vietnam War was that President Lyndon Johnson and Defense Secretary Robert McNamara imposed a "no-win" strategy on the generals. The second greatest sin, after not having a winning strategy, according to Betts, is represented in H. R. McMaster's book *Dereliction of Duty*: "the willingness of the Joint Chiefs of Staff to go along with the misguided plan, keeping quiet in the face of alleged administration duplicity about it, rather than resign or speak frankly in Congress."[66]

In his book's last chapter, "Five Silent Men," McMaster recognized that the lies of a president and the silence of his military advisors are often instrumental in causing wars:

> As American involvement in Vietnam deepened, the gap between the true nature of that commitment and the president's depiction of it to the American people, the Congress, and members of his own administration widened. Lyndon Johnson, with the assistance of Robert S. McNamara and the Joint Chiefs of Staff, had set the stage for America's disaster in Vietnam . . . The failings were many and reinforcing: arrogance, weakness, lying in the pursuit of self-interest, and, above all, the abdication of responsibility to the American people.[67]

The misgivings that retired air force major general Robert Latiff expressed in 2014 about the war in Iraq were similar to Petraeus's, a kind of humble-brag about devotion to duty, an "affectation of modesty," in the words of Leo Tolstoy. If not to protect their positions and pensions, why would generals not shout loudly that a war cannot be won? Why would they put their men and women in danger? A former assistant professor at West Point, Latiff said he considered retiring to protest the war, but a four-star general told him that nobody would notice his retirement.

Latiff remained on active duty until 2006 and lamented the "stop-loss" orders he approved, preventing soldiers from retiring or resigning during the war: "I didn't act on my deeply held disgust. And that still claws at me."[68] But his admission was made long after the time when he was in a position for his words to matter. Back then, he chose to stay silent. The incentive system is clear: when officers are motivated by loyalty or careerism to keep their mouths shut, they put America's military men and women in danger.

Many officers have remained silent and allowed misinformation to become the basis on which America goes to war and how it acts when it gets there. Time and again, the highest-ranking military officers are unwilling to express effectively what they believe to be the truth. If these officers feared threats of criminal prosecution for speaking while on active duty, they could resign and say almost anything the next day. But to the generals, their jobs, rank, and authority just seem too important to sacrifice.

STANDING DOWN

After World War II, newly victorious and arrogant, the U.S. military created a system where dissent, which could reveal errors and misjudgments, was characterized as unpatriotic and disrespectful. This ethos was enforced through criminal prosecution of those who would speak against official policy, a position approved by the Supreme Court in *Parker v. Levy* in 1974 (see the introduction to this book).

Hypocrisy blossomed in the military. Officers claimed they were committed to selfless service and to upholding the Constitution while they remained silent to protect their interests and the image of their employer. Even when they knew they should speak up, officers pointed to their lack of influence as a primary reason for not doing so. It's not clear that nobody would notice, but it's probably correct that a dissenter often begins a journey alone. For some, this is a practical reason to remain silent, but this is also why America needs more moral courage from the generals than from all other officers. For all the talk of self-sacrifice, too many officers are afraid to step forward in this manner. Someone has to be first. True leadership has nothing to do with titles or bars. Often, it is a lonely proposition.

In recent years, retired generals have tried to slip a slender reed of free expression through the military's wall of suppression. Invariably, these initiatives occurred after their service, when the risks were low and their influence was less. In *Why We Lost*, retired lieutenant general Daniel Bolger concludes that the generals have lost their humility. "As for speaking up in public, well, it just didn't happen," Bolger writes. "A serving senior commander who held a press conference or went before Congress and spoke his mind contrary to Bush or Obama administration views might be right, but he'd also be fired . . . Even a misstep in a press interview, a loose phrase or a mistake, often resulted in a reprimand or, in some cases, removal."[69]

Officers repeatedly describe what Bolger observed, but this always leads to the critical question: after taking an oath to defend the Constitution, why do military men and women retreat into silence at the possibility they will be "reprimanded" or "removed" from their jobs for speaking what they believe to be the truth? Especially when it's a truth that could save lives? While often touting their service, they continue to protect themselves at the expense of the nation.

In the spring of 2006 six retired generals—Anthony C. Zinni (four stars) and Gregory Newbold (three stars) from the marines, and John Batiste, Paul D. Eaton, John Riggs, and Charles H. Swannack Jr. (two stars) from the army—demanded the resignation of Secretary of Defense Rumsfeld for his running of the war in Iraq, including providing an insufficient number of troops for the 2003 invasion.[70] Their protest is notable, but it would have been more effective if they had spoken up during the wars, while they were generals on active duty and had greater influence. (Zinni retired in 2000, before the wars began.)

In 2001 Lieutenant General Newbold, on active duty after the invasion of Afghanistan, briefed Rumsfeld on the feasibility of invading Iraq. Also present were the chairman of the Joint Chiefs, General Richard Myers, marine general Peter Pace, navy admiral Edmund Giambastiani Jr., and the deputy secretary of defense, Paul Wolfowitz, a primary architect of the Iraqi War. The military wanted hundreds of thousands of troops, even 500,000, for an invasion, but Rumsfeld dismissed the number, insisting 125,000 or fewer would be sufficient.

In a 2007 article for *Vanity Fair*, David Margolick described the scene, as well as the silence:

> Newbold, who had spent his career commanding infantry and led the Marines into Somalia, believed that Rumsfeld's figure was absurdly, dangerously low; the only question was whether he should say so. True, he'd risk Rumsfeld's famously withering wrath. True, ultimate authority lay with the civilians. True, such objections should ideally come first from the superior officers sitting mutely nearby. And, true, war with Iraq still seemed far-fetched, even preposterous. So he said nothing. And now [2007], billions of dollars and immeasurable heartache and more than 3,000 buried American soldiers later, he has not forgiven himself. "I should have had the gumption to confront

him . . . The right thing to do was to confront, and I didn't. It's something I'll have to live with for a long time."[71]

Major General Batiste was also in a position to affect policy regarding the war, but he too remained silent. On Christmas Eve in 2004 in Iraq, Batiste, who was then the commander of the First Infantry Division, told one hundred soldiers that Rumsfeld is "a man with the courage and conviction to win the war on terrorism." Then, in Batiste's office, with reporters looking on, Rumsfeld asked Batiste whether there was anything he had asked for but not received.

Batiste thought, "My God! Absolutely!" He hesitated and finally said, "We're on the verge of something great here."[72]

After he retired, Batiste said he was aware of the example of General Harold Johnson during the Vietnam War ("going to my grave with that lapse in moral courage"). "Do I wish I'd said something in front of all that press there?" Batiste asked. "Maybe, but we don't air our differences in public. I didn't trust Rumsfeld a bit. I had seen the way he treated other officers and discounted their advice. He wasn't going to listen anyway."[73]

Summarizing the propensity for silence among the generals, Newbold said, "When you look around at how many people were in positions to raise their voices, senior military leaders who had a duty to object, and how many did—I'm having trouble counting how many did. I'm having trouble getting above one. But I know, personally, how many thought this whole thing was crazy. And if the military had said, 'We won't be a part of this,' then it wouldn't have been. They couldn't have done it publicly, but they could have given their best military advice. And it was their duty."[74] The fact that the invasion of Iraq happened at all is exhibit A for the destructive nature of the military's code of silence, for the generals' lack of courage.

In April 2008, in a speech to cadets at West Point, Secretary of Defense Robert Gates said, "More broadly, if as an officer you don't tell blunt truths—or create an environment where candor is encouraged—then you've done yourself and the institution a disservice."[75] A former college president of Texas A&M, Gates discussed the importance of "candor, dissent, and duty." Gates seemed frustrated by conformist thinking and lack of honest expression. But, in the end, Gates could not avoid the very practices he criticized. "Your duties as an officer are . . . to provide blunt, candid advice always; to keep disagreements private; [and] to implement faithfully decisions that go against you."

The approach that Gates prescribes—keep disagreements private and implement decisions that go against you—is exactly the directive that led to the prosecutions of the wrong wars for the wrong reasons. There's a disconnect that is often found among military men and women—you have a duty to serve and protect your country, but under no circumstances should you voice dissent. This reasoning contributed to the wars in Vietnam and Iraq and allowed them to fester for decades, along with the one in Afghanistan. The generals are not being asked here to risk their lives or even experience any physical pain. Instead, where is the general who will step forward and speak up at risk only to his career to save his country? I can't think of one.

All of this leads to an intractable problem: the military culture cannot be fixed from the inside. In its promotion of conformity and blind loyalty, the military sweeps even minor issues under the rug to avoid any kind of dissonance. In its understanding of itself as separate from mainstream society, the military has its own system of rules, law, and justice. Because of its leaders' penchant for retaliation against underlings and their own selfish careerism, military men and women stay silent in the face of anything that might make them or their unit look bad. An examination of the misbehavior and corruption at the academies and in the armed forces reveals what is going on behind these high walls—and how little (almost nothing) is being done to change these destructive practices.

CHAPTER 6

Criminality, Abuse, and Corruption

A cadet will not lie, cheat, steal, or tolerate those who do.

—WEST POINT HONOR CODE

D uring spring break 2016, eighteen-year-old West Point cadet Isaiah Meuchelboeck was arrested in Texas for burglarizing the home of the parents of his former girlfriend, according to media accounts. Shortly before 3:00 A.M., Meuchelboeck, in a ski mask, broke into their house and, with a gun and a knife, skulked through the house and slipped into the sleeping parents' bedroom. The cadet was hovering over the wife when she awoke and started screaming. She called 911 as her husband disarmed and held Meuchelboeck and then waited for the police to arrive.[1] Meuchelboeck would eventually plead guilty to burglary with intent to commit aggravated assault and aggravated assault with a deadly weapon.[2]

According to an army public relations article, while visiting West Point during Parents Weekend just five months earlier, Meuchelboeck's mother said of her son, "He is service oriented so it was not a surprise [that he attended West Point]. He went to private schools, but because his family has military backgrounds he was in that culture early."[3]

Was Meuchelboeck the proverbial bad apple? An outlier? Or was he just an extreme illustration of someone who is "in early" in the military, as his mother attested?

In a 2013 article in *Defense One*, Gregory D. Foster noted that America's founders "had a pronounced fear of and antipathy toward standing armies—large, permanent, professional military establishments—because of the dual temptations for domestic oppression and international adventurism by those in power, the drain on public resources, and, not least, the not-infrequent aberrant behavior of those in uniform."[4] The founders understood that a military ethos, or too many people like Meuchelboeck who are "in the culture," can lead to a host of problems, including abuse, corruption, and criminality.

In his book *The Sorrows of Empire*, author and CIA consultant Chalmers Johnson reported that criminal behavior is "ubiquitous in the military. Although the military invariably tries to portray all reported criminal . . . incidents as unique events, perpetrated by an infinitesimally small number of 'bad apples' and with officers taking determined remedial action, a different reality is apparent at military bases around the globe."[5] The military does a stellar job of presenting a gleaming façade, and thus, as Johnson noted correctly, "rarely do such incidents make it into the mainstream American press."[6] Even with that caveat, Meuchelboeck's case and a peek into other known misbehavior reveal a rickety ethical structure.

FAULTY LEADERS

A survey of the top echelon of military leadership indicates widespread criminality and aberrant behavior. A *USA Today* report found that in a four-year period, from 2013 to 2017, "military investigators . . . documented at least 500 cases of serious misconduct among . . . generals, admirals and senior civilians, almost half of those instances involving personal or ethical lapses."[7] The report found not only an uptick in incidents but also efforts by military authorities to hide or cover up the behavior, an indication of systemic—not isolated—problems. "Despite the widespread abuses," according to the report, "the Pentagon does no trend analysis to determine whether the problem is worsening, nor does it regularly announce punishments for generals and admirals,"[8] if there is any punishment at all.

In only the army, over a period of six years, from 2009 to 2015, two general officers and an additional thirty-nine colonels and lieutenant colonels, the next highest ranks, were court-martialed (prosecuted for alleged crimes), according to Pentagon statistics. From 2008 to 2015, the army relieved seven generals. During that same time span, in all ranks, 1,472 army officers received "nonjudicial" punishments, which are adverse actions other than criminal prosecutions.[9] In 2013 alone, the military "separated" 665 officers from the armed services for failing to meet "military require-ment/behavior/performance standards" and another 79 officers for "legal issues/standards of conduct."[10]

Military leaders' misconduct spreads outward and downward, creating mistrust and resentment through the ranks. Each incident suggests that the leader finds it acceptable to hold others to standards he does not himself meet. For those who have embraced the image of the military leader as a beacon of virtue and service, the number, gravity, and breadth of the offenses among high-ranking officers should give pause about the kind of autonomy America bestows on these officers.

As discussed in chapter 5, David Petraeus, the "greatest general of his generation," some believed, passed critical classified information to his lover and lied to FBI agents about it. He was levied with a fine and given two years of probation for actions that garnered imprisonment for fellow federal employees. The punishment for Petraeus—whose case was heavily covered in the press—was so mild compared with the punishments for everyone else that one can only imagine the kinds of things high-level officers get away with under the public radar.[11] The message to Americans is unmistakable: military leaders make different rules for themselves, and they are held to unique, meaning lower, standards.

Without the digging of reporters, the public would have little knowl-edge of much of the misbehavior committed by high-ranking members of the military, which makes every effort to keep corruption quiet, not only for the protection of the officer-malefactors but also to elevate the status of the military. Reporter Craig Whitlock wrote in 2013 about a "military system that promotes abusive leaders," an "affliction" that "has even infected some civilian leaders at the Pentagon, raising questions about the Defense Department's ability to detect and root out flaws in its command culture."[12] These flaws are the result of the virtually unaccountable power that military officers wield. Within a separate society, this power ensures the officers' immunity from moderating norms. Military officers learn to believe their actions and orders cannot be wrong because they have the authority to execute them, the kind of circular reasoning in the military that never stops spinning. It is reminiscent of President Nixon's infamous and seemingly delusional declaration years after leaving office: "When the president does it, that means that it is not illegal."

ABUSIVE GENERALS

Much of the officers' misconduct concerns abuse of fellow Americans and sexual indiscretions. This is unsurprising, perhaps even expected, given the vast, unchecked authority that officers have over soldiers of lower rank in an institution that does not answer meaningfully to Congress or civilian society. The military seems incapable of attracting and promoting a broad base of ethical high-ranking officers, a proposition that is supported by even the most cursory observations. In 2013, for instance, the army inspector general reported a wide variety of abusive conduct among generals serving throughout the world. How could many officers rise to such high ranks if not for problems inside the system itself? "In the military . . . sexual harassment by the top brass in many cases is considered an open secret, documents show. Yet many stay quiet, and efforts on Capitol Hill to reform the system and call senior officers to account have often failed," according to the 2017 *USA Today* report.[13]

A 2014 army report found that eleven army generals had engaged in misconduct from just 2011 to 2013, including attempts to conceal or downplay malfeasance.[14] In 2014, Major General Michael T. Harrison, the top officer in Japan, shielded a colonel under his command from sexual misconduct complaints, claiming that he'd known the colonel for twenty years and didn't believe the accusations were true.[15] When a Japanese woman claimed that the colonel had sexually assaulted her, Harrison took months to report it. According to the *Washington Post*, "The case provides a textbook example of the Pentagon's persistent struggle to get commanders to take reports of sexual misconduct seriously."[16] Harrison was removed from his post, but he landed a job at the Pentagon prior to retirement, director of program analysis and management.

The army found that Brigadier General Bryan T. Roberts engaged in two inappropriate relationships with women and improperly used government resources, and had a physical altercation and an affair with another woman. Roberts received a $5,000 fine, a reprimand, and a reduction in rank to colonel.[17]

Brigadier General Martin P. Schweitzer failed to "demonstrate exemplary" conduct by sending emails to two officers, in which he called a congresswoman "smoking hot" and told them that he masturbated "3 times over the past 2 hours" after a meeting with her (a comment the army inspector general blacked out from its report).[18]

In 2013 the air force inspector general found that married brigadier general David C. Uhrich had an "inappropriate" romantic relationship with another woman, "repeatedly drank alcohol while on duty," and "regularly kept a bottle of vodka under his desk" at Joint Base Langley-Eustis.[19]

Despite adultery being a criminal offense in the military, its prevalence helps illustrate the impunity with which high-ranking military officers pursue lower-ranking women. In 2012 a civilian female advisor complained that Major General Ralph O. Baker (Class of '82), the commander of the counterterrorism task force for the Horn of Africa, had groped her. Baker was demoted to brigadier general and forced to retire from the army. He denied sexually assaulting the woman and was not criminally charged, a result that seems expected in a military that is dislodged from civilian norms, with generals making the rules that apply to themselves.

"I own the fact that I got intoxicated that night at a social event, and I regret it," said Baker. "It was irresponsible of me. I can understand that in the position of responsibility I had, something had to be done about it."

The woman said that Baker drank wine heavily and that on the way back to the U.S. military base in the back seat of a SUV, he pushed his hand between her legs. The woman said she grabbed his hand to prevent Baker from "putting his hand deeper between my legs." She said that Baker "responded by smiling at me and saying, 'Cat got your tongue.'"[20]

William Ward, a four-star army general and the first head of U.S. Africa Command, was demoted to lieutenant general in 2013 for spending lavishly and ferrying his wife around the world at government expense; they once stopped in Bermuda for unnecessary fueling of their military airplane. (As a retired three-star general, Ward's pension is nearly $209,000 a year.[21]) In November 2015 the secretary of defense, Ashton Carter, fired his top military aide, Lieutenant General Ron Lewis (Class of '87), for using his government credit card at a strip club while traveling with the secretary. Lewis made false official statements about the use of the card, claiming someone else made the charges.[22] Lewis was demoted and retired two years later as a brigadier general.[23]

In May 2016 the army removed a husband and father of four, Major General David Haight, known as the "swinging general," from his position as head of operations and plans at U.S. European Command. Haight had engaged in a decade-long affair with a woman who found sexual partners for him near military bases in the United States. The army believed that Haight's lifestyle made him susceptible to bribery and forced him to resign, stripping him of three ranks. He retired as a lieutenant colonel.[24]

When the military's punishment of an officer is the lowering of his rank, it's like turning the clock back on the officer's career, almost like erasing the misconduct he committed in the higher rank. But if you go back far enough, then you can find that everyone is good and no one is responsible. This is not an argument against redemption, but the military's approach to rank reduction—he was a good officer in a lower rank—prevents recognizing that an officer should not have been in the military in the first place or held a high rank.

In December 2016 the air force demoted a retired four-star general, Arthur Lichte, to major general (two stars) for having coerced sex with a lower-ranking officer three times and telling her he "would deny it until the day he died." Lichte could not be prosecuted because the five-year statute of limitations had lapsed by the time the air force acted.[25]

Major General Joseph Harrington, married, was removed as the commander of U.S. Army Africa in 2017 because of his flirtatious, suggestive texts to the wife of an enlisted soldier under Harrington's command. Harrington met the woman in a gym and told her she was a "hottie" and "looking good for sure."

"U can be my nurse," he texted. "I'd enjoy being in a tent with U . . . you seem to have a great modeling reume [sic]! Truly! Though I hadn't noticed! . . . Where is your hubby tonight? Work?"

Although removed from his command of Africa, Harrington was not truly "fired" in the way that a normal employee might be. The army assigned him to a new position at the Pentagon, the same "punishment" meted out to Major General Harrison.[26] This is reminiscent of the Catholic Church, which moved abusive priests around to different parishes, more interested in protecting its own image than the needs of child victims or the actual integrity of the Catholic institution. One of the differences is that the Catholic Church is at least nominally at the mercy of the civilian judicial system. The armed forces are fortunate enough to have their own.

THE SAGA OF "FAT LEONARD"

Probably the most sensational and widespread investigation ever of high-ranking military officers is still ongoing. Federal agents in 2013 uncovered a raft of criminal and other unseemly activities by naval officers that may have been going on for a decade or more. By late 2019 twenty-six navy officers and sailors, and a few civilians, had pleaded guilty and eleven others remained under indictment. Known by the nickname of the chief informant for federal prosecutors, the "Fat Leonard" investigation may ultimately implicate *sixty admirals* and hundreds of other navy officers in bribery for steering their ships into Asian ports operated by the informant Leonard Glenn Francis in exchange for gifts and the services of prostitutes.[27]

Lured to the United States in a sting set up by the agents, Francis pleaded guilty in 2015 and admitted to bribing "scores" of navy officers. The six-foot-three, 350-pound "Fat Leonard" is cooperating with prosecutors in San Diego, the city where some of the naval ships serviced by Francis's companies, Glenn Defense Marine Asia, were based.[28] Along with providing prostitutes, Francis admitted to bribing naval officers with Cuban cigars, ornamental swords, Kobe beef, Spanish suckling pigs, cash, food, trips, and concert tickets.[29] But to the naval officers, the women Fat Leonard exchanged for military secrets and government money were the most valuable commodity. (This treatment of women goes far beyond this one case, as will be seen.)

On May 17, 2017, the first admiral to be charged criminally, Rear Admiral Robert Gilbeau, received an eighteen-month sentence after pleading guilty to lying to federal agents. Admiral Gilbeau destroyed papers and computer files to conceal his relationship with Francis. Prosecutors alleged that Fat Leonard's business relationship with Gilbeau was similar to those he had with other naval officers. In one incident, Francis provided Gilbeau with two prostitutes, and in return Gilbeau, a supply officer on the carrier *Nimitz*, approved invoices for Glenn Defense Marine Asia that "overcharged the Navy for wastewater removal services."[30]

One navy captain (a rank equal to colonel in the army, marines, and air force), Daniel Dusek, pleaded guilty and in 2016 was sentenced to forty-six and a half months in prison for allowing Francis to overbill the navy for supplies and services in exchange for the services of prostitutes.[31] In a sentencing memorandum in the Dusek case, federal prosecutors asserted that "Francis was able to leverage his way to the top in plain view of generations of senior Naval Officers and Admirals."[32]

From 2006 to 2013, Francis hosted forty-five sex parties for U.S. Navy officers, some of which lasted for days and involved prostitutes rotating among the various officers in attendance. At one 2007 Francis-run bacchanalia at a five-star hotel in Manila, the Philippines, officers committed sex acts using "historical memorabilia" from General Douglas MacArthur's stay at the same hotel in the 1930s. At a "raging multi-day party" the next year at the same hotel, Francis spent more than $50,000 for officers of the *Blue Ridge*, the navy's chief operational ship in the entire Pacific region.[33]

A navy commander and Naval Academy graduate, Michael Vannak Khem Misiewicz, pleaded guilty and was sentenced to six and a half years in prison for his participation in the corruption.[34] The navy's deputy director of operations in Asia, Misiewicz leaked classified information to Francis about planned navy ship movements in return for "cash bribes, plane tickets, flings with prostitutes and Lady Gaga concert tickets."[35]

Another navy commander, Jose Luis Sanchez, pleaded guilty to receiving "cash bribes, luxury hotel rooms, and the services of prostitutes," according to a prosecutor. Complimenting Francis's ability to procure women, Commander Sanchez wrote to Francis, "Yummy . . . daddy like."[36]

In 2013, as part of the investigation, the navy stripped Vice Admiral Ted "Twig" Branch, the director of naval intelligence, and Rear Admiral Bruce Loveless, the director of intelligence operations, of their access to classified information. The navy said that they may have committed misconduct by accepting gifts or services from Francis, which were transactions he could have used to blackmail them.[37] Incredibly, despite not having the required clearance, Admiral Branch kept his post. By January 2016, after more than two years without access to classified information, Branch remained the director of naval intelligence despite being unable to coordinate intelligence activities with any other agencies or even with any employee under his command. He could not enter employees' offices until they "swept" away classified information that might be visible to him. Branch was not prosecuted by either the Department of Justice or the navy, but the navy in September 2017 said it took "appropriate administrative action" in regard to Branch, without naming the action. Branch retired as a vice admiral.

The navy's protection of Branch's job at the expense of national security is as good an indicator as any about where the armed forces' loyalties lie.[38] In March 2017 a federal grand jury indicted then retired Admiral Loveless and "eight other high-ranking Navy officers," including four retired captains, one commander, one colonel, one lieutenant commander, and one retired chief warrant officer, for "accepting luxury travel, elaborate dinners and services of prostitutes from foreign defense contractor Leonard Francis" in exchange for classified information.[39] As of October 2019, Loveless's case appeared to remain open.

As the Fat Leonard investigation progressed, the navy, in 2015, secretly censured and allowed to retire, without prosecution, three additional admirals who had accepted gifts from Francis.[40] The navy did not disclose its action until the media filed a Freedom of Information Act request, and even then it did not release all the requested documents.[41] Vice Admiral Michael Miller, Rear Admiral Terry Kraft, and Rear Admiral David Pimpo served together in lower ranks on the USS *Ronald Reagan* aircraft carrier strike group and accepted "extravagant dinners," ship models, and other gifts from Francis. Two of the admirals gave improper commercial endorsements to Francis's firm. This was Pimpo's second ethics violation, and he was relieved from running the Naval Supply Systems Command.[42]

One extravagant dinner attended by the three admirals cost $23,061 for thirty people, $769 per person. (Each of the admirals paid only from $50 to $70 for the meals.) Pimpo and Miller accepted ship models of the *Ronald Reagan* valued at $870 each and reimbursed Francis for far less than market value. Admiral Kraft was relieved as commander of U.S. Naval Forces Japan and received a letter of censure. Kraft's predecessor as the commander of the *Ronald Reagan*, Rear Admiral Kenneth Norton, received gifts from Fat

Leonard and was given a letter of censure in 2017, but was not prosecuted.[43] Indeed, the military has not prosecuted even one officer involved in the scandal. Civilian attorneys in the Department of Justice initiated every prosecution.

None of these actions kept Admiral Miller from riding the merry-go-round back to the Naval Academy. After his shenanigans with Fat Leonard, Miller was assigned by the navy to be the superintendent at the academy from 2010 to 2014. In 2011 the navy invited Francis to attend the academy's change-of-command ceremony for the outgoing and incoming chief of naval operations (the highest-ranking officer in the navy), Admirals Gary Roughead and Jonathan W. Greenert. Photos showed Francis, Miller, Roughead, and Greenert smiling and embracing each other at their alma mater on the Annapolis campus.[44]

STUPIDITY AND GREED

Regardless of the U.S. military's technological superiority, its hardware and weaponry are useless without software—military officers who surpass their adversaries in intellect, emotional intelligence, situational awareness, humility, and just plain old good judgment. But the military's ethical collapses are not isolated incidents: they infect behavior at home and on the battlefield (through torture and war crimes, the subject of the next chapter). Officers' incompetence and errors can be particularly dangerous to Americans, which was precisely the fear of America's founders. In 2014, for example, Pentagon studies found "systemic problems across the nuclear enterprise," according to a *New York Times* report. In one instance, three military posts that served as nuclear weapons bases sent to each other, via Federal Express, one tool that was necessary for repairs on 450 intercontinental ballistic missiles because no one had checked in years on whether new tools were available. The government spent billions of dollars on emergency repairs of nuclear launching sites.[45]

In 2013 the air force removed Major General Michael J. Carey for drunken behavior while on a trip to Moscow. Carey was responsible for overseeing nuclear-armed intercontinental ballistic missiles. While in Moscow, he spent time with foreign women who might have posed a security risk if Carey had divulged information to them. While drunk in a public area of an airport in Switzerland, according to an air force report, he "talked loudly about the importance of his position ... and that he saves the world from war every day."[46]

In 2014 the air force removed almost its entire command, including its commander, Colonel Robert Stanley, and nine officers from Malmstrom Air Force Base in Montana, where half of the crew members working on nuclear-tipped missiles were cheating on proficiency tests or aware of the cheating, which had been occurring for decades.[47]

When dozens of sailors (later determined to be seventy-eight) were implicated in cheating on tests at a navy nuclear base in Charleston, South Carolina, a reporter for the *New York Times*, Helene Cooper, described a near total loss of confidence in the military. After a press conference given by Admiral John Richardson, then the "director of the Navy's nuclear propulsion programs," Cooper commented: "It was the third such news conference in three weeks, held in the same room at the Pentagon as the previous two, which involved cheating on monthly proficiency tests by Air Force officers with the authority to launch nuclear weapons."[48]

Cooper went on to explain: "But after three weeks of listening to top military officials characterize cheating scandals as failures of integrity instead of *failures in the entire nuclear force*, the Navy officials came under a barrage of questions from skeptical reporters about whether there is something amiss in the country's military system, particularly among the men and women responsible for the country's nuclear arsenal. The officers would not say; they instead reverted to their standard response: 'To say I'm disappointed would be an understatement'" (emphasis mine).[49]

As it habitually does with problems that become public, the military tried to paint massive cheating as the pastime of a few errant sailors, soldiers, and air crews. "We're taking nothing for granted right now," said Richardson (Naval Academy Class of '82). "My team is on board to make sure that we've properly bound this."

A skeptical Cooper reported that "both current and former Air Force missile launch officers say that cheating has been a fact of life among America's nuclear launch officers for decades."[50]

Similar behavior occurred among the part-time backups to those active-duty officers. A huge fraud, possibly reaching $100 million, was discovered in 2014. The plan involved twelve hundred members of the Army National Guard, including two hundred officers, two of whom were generals and dozens of whom were colonels.

The National Guard program allowed soldiers and their relatives, retirees, and civilians (such as high school principals and counselors) to serve as "recruiting assistants" and collect $7,500 for each person they helped convince to join the army. One assistant earned $275,000 and four others earned more than $100,000.[51] Assistants, with the help of army recruiters, would enter into a database the names of people and their birth dates and social security numbers, and then claim (falsely) they had secured a recruit for the army. They'd receive their bonuses and then kick back half the money to the army's recruiters.[52]

The former director of the Army National Guard, Lieutenant General Clyde Vaughn, told a congressional committee that he was aware of the abuses in the program, which began in 2005: "I told them: We got to catch the first peckerwoods to get out here and mess this thing up for everybody, and we got to prosecute them quickly."[53] In 2017, the army found that 492 soldiers were "guilty or suspected of fraud" (without distinguishing between the number guilty and the number suspected), reported the *Washington Times*. The army refused to provide the *Times* with the total cost of the fraud.[54]

ACADEMY LEADERSHIP

Some of the top officers at the U.S. military academies have assumed or remained in their positions after being implicated in and supposedly punished for misconduct. The feedback loop remains intact: officers graduate and then return to those same military academies to teach and indoctrinate new generations of students. One recent superintendent, Lieutenant General David Huntoon (2010 to 2013), began to misuse his subordinates shortly after arriving at West Point in 2010, according to a report by the Pentagon inspector general. Huntoon (Class of '73) had aides work at charity dinners, give free private driving lessons, and feed a friend's cats while she was away. He paid aides who had worked eighteen hours at charity events with $30 and $40 gift cards from Starbucks.[55]

In 2013 Huntoon was replaced[56] by Lieutenant General Robert Caslen (Class of '75), who according to yet another Pentagon inspector general's investigation "violated ethics rules" in 2007 by proselytizing for religion from his office at the Pentagon.[57] Caslen and three other generals allowed Christian Embassy, a private evangelical group, to interview and record them, then post the video online. In uniform, Caslen said in the video, "I'll see a brother in the Lord from these Flag Fellowship Groups [generals and admirals] and I immediately feel like I'm being held accountable because we're the aroma of Jesus Christ."[58] Under Huntoon and Caslen, four (all West Point graduates) of the thirteen colonels who headed the thirteen academic departments were found to have engaged in wrongdoing (including retaliation, nepotism, and sexual harassment) in just one three-year period.

The navy inspector general found that the superintendent of the Naval Academy from 2007 to 2010, Vice Admiral Jeffrey Fowler, presided over an improper slush fund of hundreds of thousands of dollars in government money and contributions from donors. With it, the academy purchased $200 bottles of French wine and Dom Pérignon champagne for select guests, spent $10,000 on food, alcohol, and gifts for the academy's golf association, and spent $18,000 for a party for football coaches. The academy gave athletic coaches clothing, ties, and watches, toys for their children, and jewelry, designer sunglasses, handbags, and coats for their wives, according to the *Navy Times*. Before he resigned, Admiral Fowler described his view of loyalty: "I don't know the technicalities, but the concept of us doing special things for the people who work here in my mind is not a bad thing."[59]

SEXUAL MISCONDUCT

In 1975, when plans were being made in Congress to open the military academies to women, retired general William Westmoreland, who was formerly superintendent at West Point, said "Maybe you could find one woman in 10,000 who could lead combat. But she would be a freak, and we are not running the Military Academy for freaks."[60] This attitude remains embedded in the military decades later, as former defense secretary James Mattis illustrated in a speech at the Virginia Military Institute in September 2018. The "jury is out" on whether women can be successful in combat roles,[61] he said, even though they have been serving in them, in effect, since the beginning of the war in Afghanistan in 2001.

The military has a particularly serious problem with violence against women. A Pentagon survey released in 2019 showed that sexual assault in the military had increased 38 percent from 2016 to 2018. The number of instances of "unwanted sexual contact" among soldiers was 20,500, but this did not reflect more troubling surveys: the 2006 and 2012 surveys showed higher sexual assault rates, but the most recent statistics came after the military had spent $200 million trying to address the problem.

In 2018, despite receiving about six thousand "unrestricted" reports of sexual assaults (in which complainants indicated willingness to participate in prosecutions), military commanders, who control whether charges are brought, prosecuted only about three hundred cases (5 percent). The Pentagon claimed that in 65 percent of the cases, commanders leveled administrative discipline. But these commanders, according to one critic, are "practicing law without a license"; their complete control over cases in which they have personal interests—because every case creates positive or negative perceptions about the conditions at their bases—diminishes the likelihood of a fair, objective disposition in any kind of case.[62]

When the academies first admitted women in 1976, the women began to suffer sexual assault in residential, training, and common areas of the academies. "The issue of consent to a sexual encounter is also more complicated in the military than in civilian life because of hierarchy," Chalmers Johnson wrote. "Both male and female service personnel are indoctrinated to obey the orders of a superior officer or upperclassman."[63]

Abuse and harassment are certainly more common at the academies than at other colleges. Military students, who are labeled "fourth, third, second, and first class" by the academies, must obey or defer to every cadet of a higher class, and cadets within a class must defer to classmates who possess a higher rank. This hierarchal structure relieves perpetrators of having to gain the trust of potential victims and puts them formally in a unique position, one that allows them to more easily control "subordinates" and then sexually assault them. Victimized cadets have no legal ability to leave the academies, or even the physical place where an assault occurred, like their rooms, and they may unavoidably see their accused assailants every day. This type of revictimization can occur only because of the hierarchal structure of the military. A 2014 Rand study showed that 62 percent of the women soldiers who reported unwanted sexual contact "perceived some form of professional or social retaliation, administrative action, and/or punishment associated with their report."[64]

One case at West Point illustrates the powerful and degrading silencing effect of conformity and hierarchy on all people associated with the U.S. military. In 2013 Colonel Matthew Moten was relieved as head of West Point's history department after he "had been accused of trying to kiss and touch female subordinates and wives of subordinate officers."[65] At social events Moten would hold some of the women from behind and whisper that he loved them. The officers felt helpless to confront Moten even as he victimized their wives in public view. That no one complained, even the officer husbands, illustrates a universal belief that their complaints would not be listened to, and that they would likely lead to retaliation. In the end, after years, it was a civilian professor who finally complained about Moten.

Another civilian professor explained how Moten's sexual harassment could have continued over the years: "No one talked because they thought they were alone, that it happened only to them." This was the case even though Moten's behavior occurred at social events. "They thought that when Moten changed their schedules to hurt them they didn't have enough evidence to prove retaliation, and they were scared. It was like water dripping in silence for years, one rumor now and then. But when one professor finally told . . . the drips became a flood when all the other professors told what Moten had done to them."

Sexual harassment is just one expression of disparities in power and methods of control. In hierarchal institutions, harassment stems from power imbalances that create an environment where a supervisor feels free to act unimpeded, and a subordinate is terrified about reporting—or even rejecting—advances. "Consciously or not," Melissa Gira Grant writes in an article about workplace harassment, "we know how rote male dominance is, and that it often feels like nothing. It is the weather, and it is a form of discipline." She goes on to explain, "Our conflict is not over sex, or with men in particular or in general, but over power."[66]

When Air Force cadets chant, while marching, that they will use a "chain saw" to cut a woman "in two" and keep "the bottom half and give the top to you,"[67] they are expressing their worldview.

In March 2018, *Vice* broke a story that a Dropbox folder titled "hoes hoin," filled with hundreds of photos of nude servicewomen, was being shared among men in uniform. *Vice* reported that it was "the latest example of an ongoing problem with revenge porn and online harassment in the U.S. military, one that persists even a year after the revelation of thousands of nude photos of service members shared in a Facebook group called Marines United caused a major scandal."[68]

This kind of institutional norm is another reason why the U.S. military's diligent efforts to separate itself, legally and socially, from American society are singularly dangerous. The separation creates officers and cadets who are shielded from a full range of life events, and from the learning and emotions that come from exposure to people who must be treated as equals. Through separation and self-inflation, cadets at the academies—who will become officers in the field and generals who prosecute wars—learn that control and domination are acceptable. Specifically, they learn that military personnel are not to be evaluated under basic societal standards, that their power grants them privileges unavailable to anyone else.

The *Daily Beast*, citing West Point data, found there were seventy-eight sexual assault complaints in a four-year period (2013–17) at West Point, only ten of which led to criminal charges.[69] Of course sexual assault is a problem in many other institutions, but these have standards in place to deter offenders, foster cultures of openness, and level the playing field to decrease power imbalances—standards not in place at the military academies. All other colleges in the country are required under what is known as Title IX to ensure equal opportunity for students, but the federal military academies are not.[70] All other colleges, under the Clery Act, are also required to report crimes that occur on their campuses—but again, not the academies.[71]

Only after reports of sexual assault grew more frequent at the academies did Congress pass legislation that required surveys of cadets and midshipmen. An investigation from 2003 "found that 20 percent of women enrolled at the [Air Force] academy said they had been sexually assaulted."[72] In a 2004 survey of students at all the military academies, 302 women (10 percent) reported they had been raped, though there had been only 54 official reports of sexual assault.[73]

These numbers indicate both that women are not reporting assaults and that the superintendents of the academies (who are solely responsible for determining whether to bring charges) are not bringing a significant number of cases when women do report.[74] Women may not be reporting because they fear they will be punished with social ostracism or a formal reprimand and harm to their careers. That superintendents do not pursue cases is consistent with the 2019 Pentagon survey, which indicated that the military, in one year, prosecuted only about three hundred of the six thousand unrestricted reports of sexual assault.

In her 2017 lawsuit, a former West Point cadet claimed she had been raped by a male cadet while they were out alone on an early-morning walk. The superintendent and commandant at the time, she charged, "knowingly and intentionally created and enforced a policy and practice" that "tolerated attacks against" female cadets and promoted a "sexually aggressive culture." In a two-to-one decision, a three-judge federal appeals court determined that her lawsuit should be dismissed because under a long-established legal rule, the Feres doctrine, military personnel may not sue the military.

The judge who dissented from the ruling, Denny Chin, noted that the former cadet's complaint contained allegations that the military administrators "created, promoted, and tolerated a misogynistic culture . . . requiring sexually transmitted disease testing for female but not male cadets . . . and permitting sexually explicit, violent, and degrading group chants during team building exercises at West Point, with verses such as the following:

> I wish that all the ladies / were bricks in a pile / and I was a mason / I'd lay them all in style.

> I wish that all the ladies / were holes in the road / and I was a dump truck / I'd fill 'em with my load.

> I wish that all the ladies / were statues of Venus / and I was a sculptor / I'd break 'em with my penis."

The two judges in the majority concluded that federal law does not permit cadets or soldiers to sue superior officers or any other soldiers for money damages, particularly if the "incident is connected to military service," as it is with a cadet enrolled at an academy. This decision was consistent with other court decisions, including the Supreme Court case *Parker v. Levy*, which established that the military is not bound by the Constitution as all other government agencies are. Under the Supreme Court's interpretation of a federal statute, an injured soldier, unlike every other American who is similarly harmed, may not sue the military for cancer caused by Agent Orange in Vietnam, a military surgeon's negligence, or a sexual assault suffered at the hands of another soldier.[75] The system is specifically designed so that the victim, whether cadet, soldier, or officer, has no recourse.

A February 2018 Pentagon study revealed that the number of reported sexual assaults at West Point nearly doubled in just one academic year, 2016–17, compared with the previous year, increasing from twenty-six to fifty. Nonetheless, the superintendent, Lieutenant General Robert Caslen, remained optimistic, even bombastic, attributing the increase in reports to his encouragement of reporting, not an increase in the number of sexual assaults committed. "I'm very encouraged by the [increased] reporting" of sexual assaults, he said. "I've got the steel stomach to take the criticism."[76]

But just a year earlier, in 2017, when another Pentagon study found increasing reports of "unwanted sexual contact" at all three military academies,[77] Caslen had taken a different position, conceding that "we believe our prevention and education programs need modification," according to a West Point press release.

West Point's Public Affairs Office, headed by Lieutenant Colonel Chris Kasker, seemed wholly satisfied with West Point's response to sexual assault. Without citing any evidence, Kasker's office concluded that the rise in reports was a "a good thing . . . as it reflects growing confidence in the system among cadets/victims to address these behaviors and to hold perpetrators accountable."

At the end of each summer, on the return march from training at nearby Camp Buckner, male cadets at West Point, as part of a tradition known as Naked Man, plot how to expose their genitalia without being caught. In another archaic tradition, military officers at West Point designate cadets as "plebes, yearlings or yuks, cows, and firsties." When male firsties (first class), seniors everywhere else in the country, receive metal insignias to wear on their uniforms to indicate their superior rank, many brag, "Firstie brass gets yearling ass."

Some actual cases escape the military's relatively secret legal system—there is no public docket of cases at military commands—and become public trials, such as those during the 2018–19 academic year. In September 2018, an army judge found a West Point cadet guilty of raping a female cadet and sentenced him to two years imprisonment. In February 2019 an air force jury ("panel" members) composed of officers found an air force cadet guilty of sexually assaulting a female cadet and sentenced him to seventy-five days imprisonment.[78] In March 2019 a civilian jury in Pennsylvania found another West Point cadet guilty of raping a female student from a civilian college. The judge sentenced him to three-to-six years imprisonment.[79] The West Point cadets were members of the football team.

In June 2019 an army appellate court comprised of three JAG officers (who serve as judges, prosecutors, and defense attorneys at different times in their careers) dismissed a case against another West Point cadet, who had been found guilty by a jury of other army officers of raping a female cadet and sentenced to twenty-one years imprisonment. The court found that the evidence produced at trial was legally insufficient, and the cadet returned to West Point.[80] The disparity in the length of sentences—two years and twenty-one years for two different West Point cadets who were tried and convicted for the same crime—is perfectly illustrative of the arbitrariness inside the military legal system.

Women students at the military academies appear to be in much greater danger than women students at other colleges. The U.S. Bureau of Justice Statistics, part of the Department of Justice, estimated in its most recent study on the issue that the average annual sexual assault rate between 1995 and 2013 of female college students (all postsecondary, ages eighteen to twenty-four) was 6.1 per 1,000 women.[81]

The academies enroll about 12,900 students (a large majority of them between the ages eighteen and twenty-three) each year, and about 3,200 of them, or 25 percent, are women. According to a 2019 Pentagon study and report mandated by Congress, "The Academies received a total of 117 reports of sexual assault involving cadets and midshipmen in Academic Program Year 2017–2018."[82] The Pentagon did not indicate how many of the reports came from male students, but a previous (2014–15) study found that eleven of ninety-one complainants (12 percent) were males.[83] Assuming that 88 percent of the reports, or 103, in the 2019 study were from women, the current sexual assault rate of women attending the military academies is 32.2 per 1,000 women.

This presents a shocking conclusion: female students' risk of sexual assault increases over five times when they step onto the grounds of Annapolis, Colorado Springs, or West Point: 32.2 women per 1,000 at the academies, compared with 6.1 per 1,000 at civilian colleges. Although sexual assaults occur in many locations, almost 79 percent of the military students (92 of 117) reported that they were assaulted "during military service," indicating the danger of going to work. At West Point, almost 86 percent of the reported sexual assaults occurred during military service.[84]

As part of the 2019 report, the Pentagon included the results of a survey in which students at the academies reported anonymously whether they had experienced "unwanted sexual contact" during the 2017–18 academic year ("attempted oral, anal, or vaginal penetration by a body part or an object and the unwanted touching of genitalia, buttocks, breasts, or inner thighs when the victim did not or could not consent").[85] The report referenced students who chose to respond and is therefore not as reliable an indicator of sexual assault as an actual report by a complainant or a study based on a random selection of people (see below). Compared with the survey two years prior, the number of estimated sexual assaults at West Point skyrocketed from 129 to 273—about one of every four women—an increase of almost 112 percent.[86]

On February 25, 2019, West Point superintendent Lieutenant General Darryl A. Williams mandated a "stand-down," in which all classes and activities were canceled and all five thousand plus cadets, staff, and faculty were required to spend the day discussing the sexual violence at West Point. "We have predators at the United States Military Academy," Williams told everyone; but then, in a curious counterpoint—unless you're at the military academies, where image protection is paramount—he added, "West Point is a higher standard than the University of X ... [You cadets] are the best and brightest ... We have the best coaches ... We have the best professors.... West Point is the holy grail of the Army."

Like his predecessors a graduate of West Point, as well as a former football player, Williams did not address the underlying problem: the destructive authoritarian practices of the military and its academies, and the recruitment of soldiers and military students who, because of their behavior, make persistent sexual abuse possible in the first place.

In response to the 2019 Pentagon report, the House Armed Services Committee, on February 13, 2019, held a hearing requiring the testimony of all the superintendents of the academies and the Pentagon's executive director for "Force Resiliency," Elizabeth P. Van Winkle. After representative Jack Bergman asked Van Winkle whether there was "any comparative data to other non-military colleges," Van Winkle, the military's point person on sexual assault, cited a 2015 study of "twenty-seven colleges across the country." She continued in military verbiage: "We don't typically have a good comparison point in civilian colleges and universities, nor do we compare ourselves with them . . . looking at those rates, comparing them to ours now, which again are slightly apples and oranges in terms of metrics and scientific methods behind it, we're [the academies] *about on par*, but, as I mentioned, we certainly hold ourselves to a higher standard" (emphasis mine).[87]

Van Winkle was apparently comparing the Pentagon survey to a 2015 survey (repeated in 2019) by a private company for the Association of American Universities (AAU), a consortium of sixty research universities. Compared with the actual reporting of sexual assaults by military students noted in the Department of Defense study and the representative national sample of actual interviewees from the Department of Justice study, the surveys on which Van Winkle presumably relied are less reliable. The AAU surveys were distributed via email and completed via the internet, and many students were paid (with Amazon gift cards) for completing the surveys. The respondents in these kinds of surveys are self-selecting and the surveys contain nonresponse bias, in that only those most interested may respond.

The data are available to allow Van Winkle and the military to compare apples and apples. Contrary to Van Winkle's assertion that sexual assault at the academies is "on par" with that at other colleges, at the moment she spoke, women students at the military academies were far more likely to suffer sexual assault than other college students, according to the government's own studies. Worse, West Point reported later that it had received twenty-eight sexual assault complaints in just the first three months of 2019. Extrapolated over a year, the number would be 112; assuming that about 100 of the complaints were from women cadets (in a population of fewer than 1,100 women), then the number of sexual assaults per 1,000 women cadets would be about 91. This would be almost fifteen times the rate per thousand (6.1) among women students at civilian colleges.

DRUGS AND INFORMANTS

Imagine any small college in any small town in America where sexual assault is pervasive and the students are running virtual drug cartels while law enforcement agencies are employing methods used to curb the Mafia to try to catch them. There isn't any such college or large university, but there are three military academies that fit the bill. In 2013, to cite just one instance, the Office of Special Investigations (OSI), part of the air force, was secretly recruiting cadets as informants to combat pervasive sexual assault, drug use, and drug dealing by other cadets at the campus at Colorado Springs, an operation identical to those undertaken by state and federal agents to combat organized crime.

The OSI operation was known to the commandant of cadets, Brigadier General Richard M. Clark, and the academy superintendent, Lieutenant General Michael C. Gould, who allowed cadets to work with OSI, an air force investigation found.[88] The cadet informants were told by OSI investigators to "deceive classmates, professors and commanders while snapping photos, wearing recording devices and filing secret reports," according to an investigative report by Dave Philipps in the *Colorado Springs Gazette*.[89]

The most prominent informant for OSI was cadet Eric Thomas, a member of the air force football and soccer teams. In 2010 "OSI ordered Thomas to infiltrate academy cliques, wearing recorders, setting up drug buys, tailing suspected rapists and feeding information back to OSI," according to the *Colorado Springs Gazette*. Thomas worked in 2011 and 2012 for OSI, which directed him to break the academy's rules.[90] But under a new commandant and superintendent, Brigadier General Gregory Lengyel and Lieutenant General Michelle Johnson, the academy expelled Thomas six weeks prior to his scheduled graduation in 2013, on the grounds that he had violated the honor code and accumulated too many demerit points. This punishment occurred even though Lengyel had been "personally briefed" on "Thomas' help to OSI in investigating multiple drug and sexual assault cases that ended in successful prosecution," according to an air force report.[91]

Many of the demerit points used by the academy to expel Thomas arose from a fight in which he had intervened to protect a female cadet who was unconscious and about to be raped by another cadet. The cadet who Thomas stopped, Stephan Claxton, a recruited basketball player, was found guilty by a military jury of attempted wrongful sexual contact and sentenced to six months in jail.[92] It seems that that the military administrators were looking for a reason to expel Thomas, who had committed the sin of working outside the structure of the academy.

OSI's method in the sting operations was to interview prospective cadet informants for hours without providing an attorney, threatening to punish them for their own infractions if they did not become informants. When finished with the cadets, OSI agents would abandon them, "misleading Air Force commanders and Congress, and withholding documents they are required to release under the Freedom of Information Act," according to the *Colorado Springs Gazette*, a point confirmed in the air force report.[93] One former cadet informer, who is now an air force officer, said that the program "puts you in a horrible situation: Lying, turning on other cadets. I felt like a rat. OSI says they will offer you protection, have your back. Then they don't. Look what happened to Eric." OSI "terminated" Eric Thomas as an informant because he "no longer had access to targets,"[94] and didn't show up to support him at a disciplinary hearing.

The OSI investigator who handled Thomas was Sergeant Brandon Enos. Ordered by a lieutenant colonel, Vasaga Tilo, not to speak to the media, Enos wrote in a letter to Congress that he'd decided to use Thomas as an informant after a female cadet told him that her alleged assailant could "get away with murder" because he played on the football team.[95] Senator John Thune (R-SD) and congressman Randy Neugebauer (R-TX) demanded explanations from the air force, which ultimately admitted the existence of the informant program, but insisted that its academy "stands by their decision that disenrollment [of Thomas] is both appropriate and in the best interest of the Air Force."[96]

The use of cadet informants at the academy occurred about a decade after reports there of drug use, drug dealing, and sexual assault early in the 2000s, when, according to a report from 2003, dozens of women cadets came forward to say they had been raped and then discouraged from reporting the assaults. This led to the forced retirement of the superintendent, Lieutenant General John Dallager, and the removal of three other top officers. Dallager, despite losing a star and being demoted to major general, insisted that he was unaware of the rapes and that he was being "transferred," not removed.[97]

The commandant of cadets at the time of these incidents, Brigadier General S. Taco Gilbert III, exacerbated the crisis. He used the only method he knew—brute but ineffectual coercion—to try to change the cadets' behavior. In an attempt to stop cadets' drug use, possession of child pornography,[98] and trafficking of stolen textbooks, Gilbert focused on petty offenses, targeting cadets for "sloppy marching, dirty dorm rooms and cadets who did not address one another as 'sir' and 'ma'am.'" "I think we are through the storm," he said, after twelve cadets were court-martialed.[99] But his was a simplistic, ineffective approach to endemic corruption, focusing on small transgressions while doing nothing to eliminate the abusive hierarchal structure of the academies fostered by military administrators like himself.

During Gilbert's crackdown, female cadets who complained of sexual assault had to admit their own infractions and subject themselves to Gilbert's stern discipline—despite an earlier policy providing amnesty for women who made such accusations. Gilbert "blamed them for attending raucous parties or otherwise fostering attacks," they said, according to a *New York Times* report.[100] One cadet who was raped received a diagnosis of personality disorder arising from the attack, which would make becoming an officer difficult or near impossible. An air force medical board recommended that she be disenrolled "at the end of the current semester." On the order, Gilbert crossed out "end of semester" and wrote "immediately."[101]

Former cadets who reported rapes said they made frequent requests to speak with the administration. "We were beating down their doors," one said, "trying to get meetings with them. They didn't want to hear about it." Another said, "My rapist is flying planes. I'll never get to."[102]

In 2014 the *Colorado Springs Gazette*, based on air force documents, reported "decades" of sexual assault and substance abuse at the academy, describing parties where cadets smoked synthetic marijuana and allegedly used "date-rape drugs" to incapacitate women. Criminal investigators (OSI) decided against one undercover operation, their own planned party in 2012, because they feared that cadet-informants and *federal agents could not protect women cadets from being raped*. One actual party led to an investigation of thirty-two cadets, of whom sixteen were football players. Three (two football players and a women's basketball player) were court-martialed and sentenced; five (three basketball players and two football players) were dismissed from the academy; six resigned; and three were dismissed for other misconduct.[103]

There were other criminal prosecutions. In June 2012 Stephan Claxton, the basketball player who fought with Eric Thomas, was convicted. In March 2013 another cadet, Anthony Daniels Jr., a prep school graduate recruited to play football, was convicted of attempted sodomy and acquitted of more serious charges and sentenced to eight months in jail. In April 2013 Jamil Cooks, a linebacker on the football team, was convicted of abusive sexual conduct and sentenced to time served.[104]

BLAMING THE VICTIM

Though the military institution is bent on projecting righteousness, people who publicly expose wrongdoing there often suffer more harm than the wrongdoers. Sergeant Enos, the handler who was in a position to exonerate Eric Thomas, was transferred to a job emptying trash cans and vacuuming floors.[105] Senator Kirsten Gillibrand (D-NY), urging a Pentagon investigation of the air force's treatment of Enos and Thomas, said, "The military has shown an inability to police themselves over a 20-year period of proclaimed 'zero tolerance' for sexual assaults. The military brass is failing at their mission, and Congress must demand accountability."[106] But in yet another example of the insulation that allows the military to operate according to its own rules, the Senate failed to pass Gillibrand's bill, which would have made military lawyers rather than base commanders responsible for determining whether to bring criminal charges.

The new superintendent at the Air Force Academy, Lieutenant General Michelle Johnson, said she would consider reinstating the informant program, but not reinstating Eric Thomas.[107] There would remain "a few young people who will make poor choices,"[108] she said, but she refused to release a report on the academy's athletic program and new allegations.[109] For the 2013–14 academic year, the number of reported sexual assaults was twenty-five, down from fifty-one and forty-four the two previous years. But the next academic year, reports of sexual assault at the academy spiked. During the 2014–15 school year, after the informant program stopped, the number of reported sexual assaults was forty-nine (forty-four women and five men), a nearly 100 percent increase under Johnson's leadership.[110]

In June 2017 Johnson, still grasping for answers to the sexual assault problem just months before her retirement, suspended four of the six counselors in the sexual assault prevention office that she had previously hailed as a national model. Just three months earlier the Pentagon had released a report that showed more sexual assaults at the Air Force Academy (thirty-two) for the previous year than at West Point (twenty-six) and the Naval Academy (twenty-eight).[111] Upending the lives of the counselors seemed a lot like Johnson's punitive treatment of Eric Thomas: eliminate the people who are in a position to understand the gravity of the problem.

In June 2018 the academy announced that thirty of the fifty-two members of the men's lacrosse team had engaged in hazing, but refused to reveal what they had done.[112] Eleven cadet swimmers were suspended from their team for hazing.

Among the swimmers, the "hazing took place on Sept. 29, 2017, the same day as a Nerf gunfight at the school that triggered hysteria after it was reported as both an active shooter situation and a terrorist attack," according to the *Colorado Springs Gazette*. Senior swimmers took first-year swimmers to an Olive Garden restaurant and stuffed them with all-you-can-eat pasta. The seniors then blindfolded them and drove them to a field, where they forced them to drink milk and Jell-O with mustard and then run in the woods until they vomited, "spewing chunks," as the senior cadets called it. The senior cadets stripped naked before reblindfolding the first-year cadets, who were led to believe they would have to perform sexual acts on the senior cadets, although none apparently occurred.[113]

Under conditions of rampant criminality and hazing, it seems preposterous that military officers like Lieutenant General Johnson can reject congressional oversight. But the military is popular within U.S. society and has business contractors in every congressional district; members of Congress fear offending the officers they are supposed to be supervising.[114] One source who worked in military contracting for decades told James Fallows of the *Atlantic*, "The system is based on lies and self-interest, purely toward the end of keeping money moving."[115]

In March 2016 the dean of academics at West Point, Brigadier General Tim Trainor, informed a group he called "leaders," mainly the colonels who head the academic departments, of a brand-new criminal investigation of cadets on his campus. Trainor titled his missive, eventually distributed widely, "Investigation of Alleged Drug Use by a Few Cadets." But it turned out to be more than a few cadets. "Leaders," wrote Trainor, "I want to inform you that Special Agents from the U.S. Army Criminal Investigation Command are investigating allegations involving a small number of cadets who may have violated the Uniform Code of Military Justice by being involved in the use and possible distribution of prescription and illegal drugs."

Trainor's "few" were at least two to three dozen cadets reportedly implicated by a drug dealer from a local town after he was arrested for being involved in a regional drug conspiracy. Cadets were selling cocaine and stealing Percocet, a powerful opioid pain medication, from cadets who had received a prescription. One cadet was allegedly found in possession of cocaine valued at $40,000.

By the end of 2017, seven West Point cadets had been charged with major drug felonies, including conspiracy with the intent to distribute controlled substances. Cadets had been advertising and selling drugs to other cadets throughout the dormitories. In response, West Point's officers, while using drug-sniffing dogs frequently in the past, resorted to using the dogs to search not only cadets' rooms but also classrooms for hidden cocaine, oxycodone, oxymorphone, and alprazolam.

At least five of the seven cadets charged with drug felonies played on the athletic teams, and at least four had been admitted through West Point's prep school, the back door through which it often stocks its teams with what it calls "at risk" students. One of the cadets, Christopher Monge, a West Point football player, pleaded guilty to conspiracy to distribute controlled substances. Monge brought cocaine, oxycodone, and Xanax to West Point and sold drugs to more than one hundred cadets, according to Monge's roommate, another football player, who was also charged and testified for the prosecution at Monge's sentencing hearing, according to the *Times Herald*, a local newspaper. A military judge sentenced Monge to thirty months imprisonment.

Rather than criminally charging nearly two dozen additional cadets, Superintendent Robert Caslen, who has sole discretion on whether to bring charges, sent them to lower-level administrative proceedings—misconduct boards, which he newly created—for allegedly using illegal drugs or prescription drugs without a prescription.[116] These misconduct boards are still in operation, and also handle sex-related offenses—private subterranean tribunals in which three military officers who work at West Point sit as jurors, one of them acting simultaneously as a judge, and decide—based on a preponderance of the evidence, not the higher standard of beyond a reasonable doubt—whether a cadet has committed an offense that would otherwise be treated as an alleged crime if the superintendent had instead ordered a court martial. A cadet who has been found guilty at a misconduct board can appeal only to the superintendent who sent him to the board, not to a criminal appellate court, where the proceedings are public. Again, the military's freedom to investigate and police itself allows it to play down what it wants to play down and favor those it wants to favor.

BULLYING INJUSTICE

In an ironic but predictable twist, the military academies, while sparing as many military personnel as possible, attack civilians who simply speak up, usually through threats to their livelihood. The Naval Academy, for example, had for years tried to punish one of its civilian professors, Bruce Fleming, after he criticized its policies in the media. In 2018 the academy fired Fleming, alleging that he exhibited "conduct unbecoming a federal employee," a broad concept carried over from the military penal code. In July 2019 a federal administrative judge rejected every allegation made by the academy and ordered it to reinstate Fleming. In August 2019 the academy resumed paying Fleming's salary but, in apparent defiance of the judge's order, prohibited him from teaching courses or having any contact with cadets. In announcing it would appeal the judge's decision, the academy claimed that Fleming's "presence in the classroom and engaging with midshipmen in any advisory role would be an undue disruption to the academic environment."

This is the military once again flouting any kind of civilian influence, even a judicial order, and working persistently to retaliate against any dissenter. The constant threats induce silence, compliance, obedience, and quiet resignation among people who are supposed to be in a position to provide new thinking. Dedicated to public service, but wanting to protect their careers and families, fearful civilian professors call military officers (who may be decades younger and far less qualified) "sir" and "ma'am" and stand at a civilian version of attention when an officer walks into a room.

One professor who had worked at West Point for over thirty years (hired to teach a specialized course when civilians were almost completely excluded) was flabbergasted when military officers terminated him for "swimming outside his lane." The professor's transgressions, according to his department head, a colonel, and the academic dean, a brigadier general, were dissenting from departmental policy and advocating changes in the operations of a new military academy in Afghanistan, which had been created by civilian and military instructors, including that professor.

Another civilian professor was removed from classes and terminated three days prior to the end of one academic year because the head of the department, a colonel, alleged that the professor was "not a good teacher." The instructor, a foreign national, would be reported immediately to Immigration and Customs Enforcement for deportation, a West Point administrator said. Another professor received a termination notice because the professor was "too opiniated" during classes, according to West Point.

As I've described these kinds of conditions and punishments over the years, a common reaction is that "there must be something more to the story," because the impunity of the military officers seems to be far outside societal norms. There rarely ever is much more to the story, usually nothing more. This kind of treatment is what military officers have learned is an acceptable response to their dissatisfaction with someone. In the hierarchal system, there is little deterrent to acting arbitrarily because there are few meaningful social or legal remedies. The embarrassment coming from the punishment is overwhelming, almost no coworker wants to help and become a target, and most people do not have the will or resources with which to oppose the military.

Once a professor who was in the process of being fired told me he couldn't conceive that military officers would do this to him (termination for disagreeing with their policies). He said he wished that he had not opposed my arguments years earlier for contracts for civilian professors. He believed mistakenly that legal protection, a contract, was not necessary because he could trust that his loyalty to the officers who were terminating him would ensure fair treatment. When others see this, they remain silent about the mistreatment they've received in the hope that the person in charge will not inflict additional or more serious injury on them. The fear and trauma are ever-present but no one knows who else shares these emotions because almost everyone remains silent.

The treatment meted out in this kind of environment ranges from the illogically punitive to the dumbfounding and farcical (though those whose lives and reputations and families are upended and irreparably damaged may not see it that way). In 2010 West Point became a laughingstock when it initiated a federal prosecution of a housekeeper, fifty-six, who had worked for the same contractor for twenty-eight years, for allegedly stealing a bag of meatballs from the cadet dining facility. When apprehended, the housekeeper had meatballs in a garbage bag and was headed to a dumpster. The West Point affidavit used to charge the housekeeper stated that "the defendant revealed a bag of 'completely frozen' meatballs in the defendant's possession," presumably to refute the notion that she was disposing of garbage.[117] West Point did not indicate the number of meatballs she allegedly pilfered. Five months later, civilian prosecutors dropped the charges.[118]

The retaliatory ethos influences every practice in the military. As I entered the main gate at West Point over the years, I noticed that the military police did not appear to have any neutral basis—a legal requirement—for their "random" selection of employees' cars for searches. A neutral basis might include searching every car, every fifth car, or every car with a license plate that ends with an odd or even number.

One day in December 2018, a soldier at the gate took my identification card and told me I'd been "selected for a random vehicle search." When I asked why he'd selected me, he said, "I don't need any reason." I told him I wanted to speak to his supervisor to see if he was correct. Reaching the boiling point in an instant, he snapped, "You're fuckin' right, we'll see."

I drove to the designated search area. Still holding my identification, the soldier then took my driver's license too and walked back to the checkpoint area, about twenty-five yards behind my car. I got out (when cars are searched, drivers have to exit and open the doors, hood, and trunk), walked a few yards, and asked the soldier when the supervisor would arrive. He only shouted, "Get back in your car." As I walked the few steps back to my car, he left the area where he had congregated with civilian guards, pursued me, and shouted again, "I have a better idea. Put your hands against your car and spread your legs."

It's not lawful to single out people because they've asserted a legal right. He searched me and ordered me to remain standing, with my hands against the car, nothing less than a physical assault because it was done without a legal basis, retaliation for relying on the law.

The supervisor arrived, another low-ranking soldier, and spoke with the searching soldier. Apparently they concocted the story that I had "refused a search," which the surveillance camera, of course, would show was false. "Because you refused a search," the supervisor told me, "you can't work at West Point anymore and I'm escorting you off the post." I told him I wanted to see the Provost Marshal, a lieutenant colonel. The supervisor relented, and we drove to the military police building. I told him I wanted to see the paperwork indicating the basis for selecting cars to search. "It's in the office, and I'll show it to you," he said. He never did.

While I was sitting in the lobby, five MPs surrounded me. A new supervisor, another soldier, picked up the yarn. Although I told him several times what had happened, he repeated over and over in front of the others the false story they'd use to try to justify what they probably knew by then was wrongful conduct by another soldier: "You refused a search." When I told my department head, a colonel, about the soldier at the gate, he said, "You questioned his authority." I asked about my legal rights, but, as is often the case in the U.S. military, law was meaningless.

Some soldiers are predisposed to abusive behavior. But assuming that most academy students and soldiers are not genetically wired for malfeasance, the only place from which their crimes can originate is from within the military institution itself. The U.S. military is a world that accepts and encourages abusive behavior. Soldiers and officers learn to believe that they are beyond the control of basic rules, beyond law. It is no surprise that problems fester. Despite being responsible for defending their nation and fellow citizens, soldiers resort to what they know: violence.

CHAPTER 7

Violence, Torture, and War Crimes

Violence is the last refuge of the incompetent.

—ISAAC ASIMOV, *FOUNDATION*

Although one job of the military is obviously to fight when necessary, its most important mission is to preserve the peace without fighting, thereby sparing its soldiers and protecting the populace. However, soldiers' unnecessary or unlawful violence, whether at home or during war in foreign lands, transforms an army into an illegitimate and dangerous occupying institution, the very condition our nation's founders feared. This is why there should be significant concern over the military ethos seeping into civilian society,[1] where 33 percent of all federal employees in executive agencies are military veterans, although they comprise just 6 percent of the U.S. population—partly a result of hiring preferences for veterans.[2]

Outside the military, police officers are most likely to employ government-sanctioned violence, and in their ranks, military veterans comprise a disproportionate presence. Phil Klay, a novelist and former officer in the marines, wrote in 2016, "In Iraq, I knew so many Marines with plans of joining their local police force back home it was almost comical." Klay's intuition was correct. Professors Gregory B. Lewis and Rahul Pathak found that 19 percent of police officers are military veterans.[3]

In conducting possibly the first study of its kind, researchers at the University of Texas in 2018 found that Dallas police officers (a sample of 516) who were military veterans were much more likely to fire their guns while on duty than police officers who were not veterans. The cops who had been deployed—though most deployed soldiers work in support positions and do not see combat—were 2.9 times and the nondeployed cops 1.94 times more likely to have fired their guns. The researchers found that "close to one-third of officers involved in a shooting had a military background," according to the Marshall Project, the criminal justice reform group that sponsored the study.[4]

The American military ethos teaches that threats and violence are early, sometimes first, responses to conflict. Reports indicate that current or former soldiers commit over 33 percent of the mass killings inside the United States. Klay pointed out that the killer of five police officers on July 7, 2016, in Dallas, Texas, "followed standard [military] tactics for a close ambush, which are 'to establish fire superiority and assault through the objective.'"

Though the killer was a veteran of the Afghanistan war, Klay noted that military training and experience don't necessarily lead to violence by veterans.[5] To this, anthropology professor Hugh Gusterson responds, "But the facts speak for themselves. Veterans account for 13 percent of the adult population, but more than a third of the adult perpetrators of the 43 worst mass killings since 1984 had been in the United States military. It is clear that, in the etiology of mass killings, military service is an important risk factor."[6] Commenting on the killings in Dallas, Gusterson writes, "There are obvious reasons why so many mass killers might be military veterans. They may have been drawn to the military in the first place by an attraction to violence. Once in the military, they are trained in the art of killing and, if they have combat experience, they may become disinhibited from killing."[7]

Unnecessary and unchecked aggression and violence, inside and outside America, are some of the consequences of a large standing army.

VIOLENCE AT THE ACADEMIES

Once violence, whether physical or emotional, is accepted as part and parcel of an organization, it does not always stay in its box. The willingness to hurt other people spills over, cascading from person to person, from task to task.

A culture that uses violence cannot always keep a lid on how and when and where it is used. West Point, like similar training grounds, is essentially a laboratory for this very idea.

In August 2015, after a brutal "pillow fight" among West Point cadets got picked up by the national media, the military administration claimed that the ritual was a beloved tradition, a way to teach new cadets how to blow off steam and learn teamwork. It was a bonding ritual that brought the cadets closer together, and all the condemnation from the outside was misguided. But the pillow fight was in fact a new and more violent kind of hazing, germinating from a simplistic view of the world and an archaic model of education, all coming from military officers who seem immature or unaware of modern norms and practices. But they and their old ways are extremely dangerous.

One of the most disturbing aspects of the pillow fight, which was caught on video, was not the pillows at all. It was the fact that some of the 1,270 first-year cadets who participated filled their pillowcases with metal lock-boxes and combat helmets to cause greater injury to their classmates. After only seven weeks at West Point, they had become comfortable hurting each other and were eager to do so, understanding it as part of the world they now inhabited.

This was not the first time this ritual had gotten out of hand. The previous year's pillow fight had caused grave injuries, so the supervising officers were well aware of the danger. In fact, they had ambulances parked and ready just outside the gladiators' arena, an area the size of several football fields, surrounded by dormitories.[8] The most serious injuries from the fights occurred when cadet assailants whipped helmets in pillowcases at victims' heads, a tactic just like "slocking" in U.S. prisons, where inmates stuff padlocks into socks to assault and kill rival inmates.[9]

At the time of the 2015 pillow fight, the West Point commandant of cadets was Brigadier General John Thomson (Class of '86). According to West Point's public relations team, the pillow fights were facilitated by upper-class cadets, to help first-year cadets build unity, but it is unlikely that the administration would not have fully known about and accepted a planned melee of over 1,200 teenagers, with emergency equipment and personnel at the ready.

That academy officials supported this "team-building exercise" was illustrated in one of its first press releases after the fight became public: "West Point applauds the cadets' desire to build esprit and regrets the injuries to our cadets," said head of public affairs Lieutenant Colonel Chris Kasker after the national media reported on the pillow fight. "We are conducting appropriate investigations into the causes of the injuries." In an effort to deflect responsibility from military officers, Kasker maintained that the upperclassmen "allowed the spirit activity to occur out of the desire to enhance the spirit of the class." (West Point's administration uses the word *spirit* for any attempt at motivation, referring to a "spirit activity," a "spirit mission," a "spirit lunch," or "spirit casual dress.") This did not square, of course, with ordering ambulances and setting up a medical tent inside the arena beforehand.[10]

Before it began, one upper-class cadet said to one of the first-year cadets who was about to join the battle, "If you don't come back with a bloody nose, you didn't try hard enough."

"At first the body count, people were joking about it," said one female "firstie" (senior) cadet. "My friends were really excited. And right after, when we learned how many people had gotten hurt, everyone felt totally hard-core. I know it looks *weird from the outside*, but it really bonds us" (emphasis mine).

From the outside, meaning by the standards of normal civil society, *weird* comes nowhere near the right descriptor. A first-year cadet bragged on Twitter: "4 concussions, 1 broken leg, 2 broken arms, 1 dislocated shoulder, and several broken ribs. That's one hell of a pillow fight."[11]

The West Point administration's claim that it was investigating the fight came only after the *New York Times* reported on the brawl, and grisly photographs of cadets with head wounds appeared on Twitter and in *USA Today*.[12] According to the *Times*:

> Video of the fight posted online showed crowds of cadets, some wearing body armor as well as helmets, surging together in a central quad, their yells echoing off the stone walls of the surrounding barracks. As the first-year cadets collided into a boil of white pillows, pummeling one another in the fading light, Army-issued glow sticks flew through the air and an impromptu cavalry of riders in laundry

carts dashed in, cushions swinging. At one point, a smoke grenade
appeared to go off . . . As the scope of injuries became clear, cadets
said in interviews, West Point staff members went door to door in
the barracks [dorms] giving quick concussion checks.[13]

The superintendent, Robert Caslen, responded, "Unfortunately cadets
were injured, with 30 cadets evaluated by medical personnel. Specifically, 24
cadets were diagnosed with concussions, none of them severe. Other injuries sustained included a broken nose, a dislocated shoulder, and a hairline
fracture of a cheekbone for one of the concussed cadets."[14] But an army
orthopedic surgeon at the West Point hospital didn't mince words, calling
the fight what it was: a "mass casualty" event. Just the injuries that Caslen
acknowledged—which certainly weren't all of them—meant that over
2 percent of all first-year cadets suffered significant, possibly lifelong impair-
ments in this bonding exercise.[15]

After the release of an army report on the pillow fight and stung by
public criticism, Caslen changed course and I believe he reverted to his
main goal: deflecting responsibility from himself. "While never officially
sanctioned," Caslen said, "it is now officially banned, and we will take
appropriate action to ensure that all faculty, staff, leaders, the Corps of
Cadets and everyone at West Point knows that it will not be tolerated."
But no "faculty or staff" members were responsible for the pillow fight, only
tactical military officers assigned to safeguard the cadets. "I am taking
appropriate action based on these findings . . . to send a clear message that
this kind of behavior will not be tolerated at our nation's premiere military
academy," said Caslen.[16] He conveniently didn't mention that the academy
had openly sanctioned the melee.

BLOWS TO THE HEAD

Concussions, which are brain injuries, are common at the U.S. military
academies because boxing is part of a required course for every student at
West Point and the Naval Academy and every male student at the Air Force
Academy. In five academic years (from 2011 to 2016), cadets at West Point
suffered 185 concussions from boxing alone, according to West Point's own
data.[17] The Air Force Academy reported 72 boxing concussions, and the

Naval Academy reported 29.[18] The ROTC (Reserve Officers' Training Corps) programs at civilian colleges do not require boxing.

If not for a culture that champions violence—and not the kind necessary to fight just wars—it is impossible rationally to explain the military academies' fixation on boxing. The kinds of skills boxing fosters could be replaced with innumerable other competitions. Additionally, platoons of soldiers will never face off in the ring with Taliban, al-Qaeda, or ISIS fighters. Even if boxing were unique among sports, its value is so infinitesimally small in comparison with its high costs—brain injuries that prevent cadets from becoming officers, and lifetimes of headaches or disability—that it should be abandoned.

At West Point, cadets whose concussions and injuries prevent them from completing a boxing class must retake the class as soon as their brain trauma dissipates. A 2016 study led by researchers at Oxford found that "traumatic brain injury (TBI) [concussion] is the leading cause of disability and mortality in children and young adults worldwide."[19] Nonetheless, that same year, even as other studies showed that women are more susceptible to concussions than men, West Point and Caslen doubled down and expanded the boxing program by requiring all first-year female cadets to take the boxing course and fight male cadets in their weight class.

That boxing is institutionalized at the academies is not only part of a legacy of hazing and abuse but also a badge of distinction, a way to assert proudly that the military is a separate world. Nothing, least of all the reprimands of civilians or the studies of researchers, will impede the academy's traditions. This response is a microcosm of the hubris, arrogance, and ignorance that have plagued the U.S. military since the end of World War II.

By the time Caslen mandated boxing for women cadets, the Pentagon had spent hundreds of millions of dollars on research into and treatment of traumatic brain injuries to soldiers injured by roadside bombs in Afghanistan and Iraq.[20] The Pentagon even declared March to be Brain Injury Awareness Month.[21] But in supporting the required boxing course, Caslen actually provided more evidence of why it should be eliminated.

"I've been knocked out," Caslen said, "given the smelling salts and shoved back in there—that was our concussion protocol back then. I always thought it was a badge of honor when I got a concussion—now you are one of the guys. You get knocked out and keep going."[22] Dr. Robert Cantu, a neurologist at Boston University and an advisor to the army and to professional athletes, said, "No brain trauma is good brain trauma—even if there are not diagnosable concussions, there can still be lasting damage. Maybe you could justify it if there is some crucial lifesaving skill that can't be taught in any other way. But short of that, it's absolutely stupid."[23]

Just twelve days after the 2015 pillow fight was reported in the national media, Caslen met at the Pentagon with the army's surgeon general, Lieutenant General Patricia Horoho. Together, rather than working to eliminate this dangerous activity, they went into self-protection mode, concocting a plan to downplay the danger of concussions. Caslen and Horoho wanted to place an article in the *Wall Street Journal* or *USA Today* based on the research of Colonel Steven Svoboda, a sports medicine physician at West Point. He and his coauthors had published an article in 2014 in *Sports Health* in which they considered the possibility that a reported doubling of concussions among players on the academies' football teams in two consecutive seasons could be attributed to new standards and protocols and might not reflect an actual increase in concussions.[24]

Horoho's and Caslen's plan was outlined in an internal memorandum prepared by one of Caslen's staff officers and leaked to the *New York Times*.[25] In the memorandum, Horoho boasts about her ability to manipulate the press. "Next time, when cadets are injured and it is sensationalized," she directed, "please let me know ahead of time. I can help shape the reaction from my position as surgeon general. I actually learned about this incident from the news."[26] Horoho claimed that she was misquoted in the notes and Caslen claimed that the notes did not accurately reflect the discussion he had with Horoho.

Horoho, the first nurse (rather than physician) to become surgeon general, was the chief medical officer of the army. Her duty to protect everyone's health was overridden by her desire to protect her position and the reputation of officers like Caslen. During Caslen's time as superintendent, a member of the public affairs office said the toughest part of the job was West Point's resistance to and fear of outsiders, especially news reporters. Journalists, who are such a critical element of democracy that they're called the "fourth estate," are treated like adversaries when they visit the West

Point campus, except when the administration is trying to "place an article." Superintendents require journalists to be accompanied by minders from the public affairs office. As is normal at the academies, Caslen and Horoho used subordinates, Kasker from public relations and Svoboda, the physician, to try to avoid embarrassment and protect the military's image.

INSTITUTIONAL VIOLENCE

The hazing and violence of the West Point pillow fight are not anomalies. They have been occurring—in one form or another—at America's *premiere military academy* for over a hundred years. They are a cherished part of the culture and tradition, passed from generation to generation. In his 2000 book *Bullies and Cowards: The West Point Hazing Scandal, 1898–1901*, Philip W. Leon, a former army colonel and senior advisor to the superintendent at West Point, described ritualized brutality there during the late nineteenth century. Leon detailed "scrapping committees," which organized fights that cadets used to haze other cadets.

"Most of the faculty, West Point graduates themselves, knew perfectly well that these fights took place to amend the attitudes of recalcitrant plebes," according to Professor Leon. "The doctors and other staff at the infirmary, or post hospital, regularly saw the boys arriving with bruises, cuts and abrasions, eyes blackened and teeth knocked out."[27]

In 1898 first-year cadet Oscar Booz was hazed mercilessly by other cadets, including having "hot grease poured on him while in bed and Tabasco sauce poured down his throat." The slight and unathletic Booz was forced to engage in a fight that left him beaten badly and was later shocked by having his hands held on a galvanic battery.[28] In agony at his home in Pennsylvania, Booz refused to give up the names of the cadets who tortured him. "I went there expecting to take whatever medicine was given, and it would not be right to complain against the other boys,"[29] he said, and "We take our oaths at West Point, and it is very much like a lodge."[30]

When Booz died of tuberculosis of the larynx eighteen months after the fight, Congress began an investigation and found, according to Professor Leon, "institutionalized forms of torture" of cadets that "shocked the nation when cadets told their stories about the secret suffering taking place behind the walls of the training ground for future soldiers."[31] In the *New York Times*,

Mark Twain himself lodged his opinion on the hazing: "The men who indulge in hazing are bullies and cowards . . . I would make it the duty of a cadet to report to the authorities any case of hazing which came to his notice; make such reports a part of the vaunted West Point 'code of honor' and the beating of young boys by upper class men will be stopped."[32]

Today, more than 120 years since Oscar Booz's horrific treatment, hazing is still common at West Point, with the pillow fight and mandatory boxing being prime examples. Regrettably, the violence has become far more serious. With the admission of women in 1976, it has expanded into the realm of rape and sexual abuse, which has proliferated at West Point and the other academies.

In the early 2000s Colonel Barney Forsythe, vice dean of education, touched on the difficulty of keeping this penchant for violence in check. "I don't know that we've fully sorted all this out yet," he told author David Lipsky. "How to, on one hand, prepare people for the violence of combat, yet equip those same people for the midrange peacekeeping operation and the humanitarian maneuver. Helping cadets not only to learn the sort of traditional warrior spirit—physical courage, obedience to orders in the heat of battle—but also develop a genuine respect for other people and their welfare is a huge challenge."[33] To answer Colonel Forsythe, if not tempered by education and the moderating effects of civil society, the instinct for survival and a yearning for violence impel soldiers to commit all kinds of serious abuse, including torture, war crimes, and murder.

IRAQ AND AFGHANISTAN

One of the most aggressive U.S. Army units in the early days of the Iraq War was commanded by Lieutenant Colonel Nate Sassaman (Class of '85), who had been the starting quarterback of West Point's football team. "When Sassaman spoke of sending his soldiers into Samarra [Iraq], his eyes gleamed," reported Dexter Filkins in the *New York Times*. "We are going to inflict extreme violence," said Sassaman, who led eight hundred soldiers "in the heart of the insurgency-ravaged Sunni Triangle."[34]

Sassaman was so feared by Iraqi civilians that "when mothers put their children to bed at night, they tell them, 'If you aren't a good boy, Colonel Sassaman is going to come and get you,'" an old man in a village told

Filkins. Sassaman was a kind of bogeyman, and he seemed to relish the reputation. "For a whole year, I was the warrior king," Sassaman said.[35]

To coerce Iraqi civilians to inform on their friends, family members, and insurgents, Sassaman's men burned down fields of farmers' crops, destroyed homes with antitank missiles, and gratuitously slapped and roughed up detainees, according to U.S. soldiers. In 2003 Lieutenant Jack Saville (Class of '02), who was working under Sassaman, ordered soldiers to throw into a river two Iraqi cousins who had been hauling plumbing supplies in a truck and driving past curfew. One never made it back to shore. Thirteen days later a body was found a mile downstream, shriveled, decomposed, and unidentifiable. It was thought to be the lost cousin, but the grisly condition of the corpse prevented its positive identification, and thus no one could be charged with manslaughter, according to the army. When confronted about why he covered up for the soldiers who threw the men into the river, Sassaman landed on a distinction without a difference. "I really didn't lie to anybody," he said. "I just didn't come out and say exactly what happened."

Saville, the lieutenant who gave the order to dunk the Iraqis, eventually pleaded guilty to assault and received a forty-five-day sentence. The soldier who pushed the Iraqis into the river was found guilty after a trial and sentenced to six months incarceration. "Both men, in effect, were convicted not of killing Zaydoon," writes Filkins, "but of pushing him and Marwan into the water. Of getting them wet."[36]

Sassaman was not prosecuted at all. Even if any of the soldiers had been charged with more serious crimes, it is likely they would've escaped responsibility. As the New York Times has reported, "The limited data available suggests that even when the military has tried to prosecute troops for murder or manslaughter in a combat zone, the acquittal rate has been significantly higher than it is in the civilian context."[37]

In the view of Tom Ricks, soldiers treated "the Iraqi civilians as the playing field on which the contest occurs."[38] Putting aside the inherent illegality of soldiers' actions against civilians, their violence has led to more intense hatred from their enemies, the coalescing of insurgents, and the enmity of neutrals against America.

"Why does this 'thumbscrew theory of force' hold such sway in decision-making when the evidence is that threats and brutality are not likely to produce compliance, but rather that threats often yield the opposite, more determined resistance?" asks professor Neta Crawford. "The short answer is that these questionable assumptions about the utility of fear and threats of violence are institutionalized . . . an institutionalization of the belief that fear can be productively used to manipulate others."[39]

Violence as a method of dispute resolution has become entrenched in the psyche of U.S. military men and women. In *The Last Full Measure*, author Michael Stephenson delves into psychological tendencies of the soldier: "The power of killing in combat—a sanctioned release for our murderousness—is as though some ancient and psychotic genie that we normally keep stoppered in its civilized bottle has been let loose."[40]

DOING THE ENEMIES' WORK

The methods used to oppose terrorism or fight wars must not be so abject that they turn neutral persons against democracy or undermine the spirit and principles underlying it. But one of the most enduring legacies of America's worldwide war on terror has been to create more terrorists. As veteran foreign affairs journalist Mark Danner writes in his book *Spiral: Trapped in the Forever War*, "33,000 people worldwide died from terrorism in 2014, an increase of 35 percent over the year before—and of 4,000 percent since 2002 . . . We have created in the war on terror a perpetual motion machine."[41] Some of the practices and abuse that inspired terrorists arose from U.S. agents' treatment of captives and their treatment of innocent civilians.

Danner noted that America's enemies in Afghanistan and Iraq, as well as other adversaries in the larger war on terror, understood how to use America's supposed strengths and military superiority against it. The 9/11 attacks baited America into an overreaction, including a foolish invasion of Iraq, which helped to further al-Qaeda's case that America was intent on destroying the Muslim world. Iraqi insurgents picked up this tactic and ran with it, "recognizing the characteristic American quickness to react with overwhelming firepower as their best friend."[42] Danner goes on to explain, "The birth and growth of the Islamic State exemplifies a central theme of the war on terror: that across these fourteen and more years of war the United States through its own actions has done much to aid its enemies and has sometimes helped create them."[43]

The Taliban, al-Qaeda, and later Iraqi insurgents and ISIS were able to garner sympathy for their cause when American soldiers' foibles, blood-thirstiness, and war crimes became public. "In launching the war on terror, eventually occupying two Muslim countries and producing in Guantanamo and Abu Ghraib celebrated images of repression and torture, the United States proved all too happy to oblige," writes Danner.[44] "The United States quickly came to embody the caricature that the jihadist had depicted: a blundering, blasphemous, muscle-bound, violent superpower intent on humiliating, repressing and murdering Muslims."[45] In short, the U.S. military has been doing its enemies' work for them.

SANCTIONED TORTURE

Torture . . . is the state reaching through a person's skin and taking control of his nervous system by force in order to use it as a weapon against him. It is the ultimate destruction, by the state, of human autonomy.

—Mark Danner, *Spiral: Trapped in the Forever War*

Despite the visceral reaction torture provokes among many as an immoral offense, a large percentage of Americans remain comfortable with treating people harshly during war. In 2005, when wars in Afghanistan and Iraq were accelerating, Gallup found that 39 percent of Americans believed torture is justified to prevent terrorism.[46] Even after the details of American inter-rogations (including waterboarding) were made public, many citizens were not fazed. In a 2016 Reuters poll, 63 percent of Americans (82 percent of Republicans and 53 percent of Democrats) felt torture was always or some-times justified in "extracting information from suspected terrorists."[47] The irony in America's use of torture against detainees in the 2000s, approved by the Bush administration, is that it was similar to the methods used by the North Koreans and North Vietnamese on U.S. soldiers who were pris-oners of war and by America's other Cold War Communist enemies, the Soviets and the Chinese, on their own people beginning in the 1950s.[48] America adopted the tactics of its ideological enemies.

In 2002 and 2003, lawyers in President George W. Bush's Justice Depart-ment, led by John Yoo, provided legal cover to support the government's "coercive interrogations" of detainees at Guantanamo Bay, Cuba, in military prisons in Afghanistan (and soon, Iraq), and black sites (secret makeshift CIA prisons) around the world.[49] "The victim must experience intense pain or suffering of the kind that is equivalent to the pain that would be associated with serious physical injury so severe that death, organ failure or permanent damage resulting in a loss of significant body functions will likely result,"[50] wrote Yoo. Essentially, as long as a prisoner didn't die, soldiers and other government agents could pretty much do anything they wanted to his body and mind.

To implement its coercive interrogation program, the CIA hired former military psychologists Bruce Jessen and James Mitchell, who opened a firm and charged the government $81 million for their services.[51] They had never conducted an interrogation, and their methods were based on training for U.S. Air Force personnel who might be captured by countries that had not agreed to provide to prisoners the humane treatment mandated by the Geneva Conventions.[52] Besides the fact that the CIA's methods violated international law, the methods were also ineffective and used on the wrong people. A CIA analyst who conducted interviews at the U.S. military prison at Guantanamo Bay notes that most of the prisoners there were useless for intelligence purposes. There were too many people who didn't belong, old men with dementia, "people lying in their own feces ... If we captured some people who weren't terrorists when we got them," he writes chillingly, "they are now."[53]

The CIA's interrogation policy authorized "stripping" and "hooding" prisoners, and additional treatments included slapping, white noise, loud music, uncomfortably cool environments, sleep deprivation up to forty-eight hours, shackling in upright positions, stress positions (on knees, body slanted forward or backward), waterboarding, and cramped confinement.[54] Detainees could be "sedated" (drugged) during rendition to secret prisons in foreign countries[55] and placed in "rectangular [boxes] ... just over the detainee's height, not much wider than his body, and comparatively shallow, or they can be small cubes allowing little more than a cross-legged sitting position," according to the CIA.[56]

If a prisoner refused liquids, then the CIA's medical officers could force-feed a detainee through "rectal hydration," thrusting a long tube up his rectum.[57] Both the CIA and Army relied on forced nudity, manipulation of sexual organs, and forced feeding to exert control over detainees. These actions would be sexual abuse when considered in any other context, but the CIA and U.S. military considered them legal. The CIA prohibited its detainees from using toilets and placed them in diapers for "prolonged periods."[58] It shackled naked detainees on cold floors, causing one prisoner to die from hypothermia.

CIA officers locked one detainee, Abu Ja'far al-Iraqi, naked, into a standing position for fifty-four hours and then into a sitting position for twenty-four hours. They gave him blood thinner for leg swelling and locked him back into the standing position so that he was deprived of sleep for a total of 102 hours. He was then allowed to sleep for four hours and then deprived of sleep for an additional fifty-two hours. They doused him with cold water (44 degrees Fahrenheit) for eighteen minutes and repeatedly slapped him.[59] Detainees were stripped naked and doused in cold water and wrapped naked in tarps that formed a tub, into which CIA agents poured refrigerated water. Other detainees "were hosed down repeatedly while they were shackled naked, in the standing sleep deprivation position," according to a Senate report.[60]

What kind of Americans do this? Even if unconvinced that "coercive interrogations" violated the Constitution or the Geneva Conventions, advocates of torture would find little evidence of its value. With torture, America diminished its standing and moral authority for no reason. As early as 1989, the CIA had reported to Congress that "inhumane physical or psychological techniques are counterproductive because they do not produce intelligence and will probably result in false answers."[61] A 2009 report prepared for CIA director Leon Panetta concluded that the CIA exaggerated the value of interrogations.[62] According to a Senate report, three directors of the CIA—George Tenet, Porter Goss, and Michael Hayden—impeded White House or congressional oversight or inflated the value of the interrogation program.[63]

By the time of the start of the war on terror in 2001, effective congressional oversight of the CIA and military was absent. Virtual U.S. government agencies were created in other countries to run the wars, and American military officers were the top authorities, the "mayors" in towns in Afghanistan and Iraq. CIA officers ran the secret black sites to conceal the abuse of detainees and to stay outside the jurisdiction of U.S. courts. Later most of the detainees were transferred to the U.S. military prison at Guantanamo Bay, Cuba, which became (and still is) a magnet for terrorist recruitment.[64]

Of the 780 detainees held at Guantanamo since 2002,[65] nine have died in custody there.[66] A Senate report concluded that 26 of the CIA's 119 detainees, or nearly 22 percent, were "wrongfully held," and 39 of them had been subjected to "enhanced interrogation" procedures.[67] None of them had received a trial prior to the CIA's abuse, although the abuse could never be a lawful tactic or punishment anyway. About forty remain in custody; twenty-six of them are being held without being charged and all have been incarcerated for more than ten years.

One U.S. interrogator admitted that he didn't even try to get information from the prisoners. "We didn't know what they were saying . . . ," he said. "I was just having a little fun—playing mind control."[68]

A Pentagon advisor told journalist Seymour Hersh that much of the treatment of detainees in military prisons had nothing to do with obtaining actionable intelligence. The abuse was a way to release soldiers' pent-up emotions. "It's about rage and need to strike back," he said. "It's evil, but it's also stupid."[69]

ABU GHRAIB

In 2004 photographs from Abu Ghraib, the U.S. military prison in Iraq, showing the depredations of U.S. soldiers made their way around the world and turned that prison, like Guantanamo, into a recruitment force for America's enemies. The photographs, taken by a U.S. soldier, showed other soldiers treating Iraqi detainees like dogs, shackled and caged and removed of even their most basic humanity.

Soldiers attached to the Military Police Corps kept the male detainees naked and made them wear women's underwear, under the theory that the degradation would convince them to provide information, and also for fun. American soldiers manipulated almost every part of the naked Iraqi detainees' bodies and celebrated while they did it. They forced hooded detainees to form naked human pyramids and have sexual contact with each other, a particularly humiliating act for Muslim men.

One U.S. soldier is shown smiling and posing with an Iraqi corpse. A smiling female soldier with a cigarette is shown walking in front of a line of naked male detainees who are being forced to masturbate for her as she points at their penises. Soldiers' dogs surround naked, cowering prisoners.[70] The dogs were used to scare detainees into urinating and defecating on themselves, according to a former JAG lawyer, Christopher Graveline, who prosecuted some of the soldiers at military trials.

The most infamous photo shows a male detainee wearing a black hood and shawl and standing on a box with his arms outstretched, with wires connected to his fingers to make him believe he would be electrocuted.[71] "Detainees under American control were raped, beaten, shocked, stripped, starved of food and sleep, hung by their wrists, threatened with death and, in at least one case murdered," according to the *New York Times*. "These are war crimes, punishable under both American and international law."[72]

In the *New Yorker*, Jane Mayer described the homicide of a prisoner at Abu Ghraib at the hands of a CIA officer. During an interrogation, the detainee's "head had been covered with a plastic bag, and he was shackled in a crucifixion-like pose that inhibited his ability to breathe." He later died of asphyxiation, though not a single person was charged.[73]

In another *New Yorker* article about the soldier who took the photographs, Specialist Sabrina Harman, Philip Gourevitch and Errol Morris rejected the expected military response to the scandal: it was aberrant, low-ranking soldiers who committed the crimes. "Yet the abuse of prisoners at Abu Ghraib was de facto United States policy," write the authors. "The authorization of torture and the decriminalization of cruel, inhuman, and degrading treatment of captives in wartime have been among the defining legacies of the current [Bush] Administration ... The Abu Ghraib rules, promulgated by Lieutenant General Ricardo Sanchez, the commander of ground forces in Iraq, elaborated on the interrogation rules for Guantánamo Bay, which had been issued by Secretary of Defense Donald Rumsfeld; they were designed to create far more license than restriction for interrogators who sought to break prisoners."[74]

No officers, but seven enlisted soldiers, including Specialist Harman, the highest ranking among them a staff sergeant, were convicted in military courts for the crimes at Abu Ghraib.[75] Eric Fair, a former soldier and a civilian interrogator in Iraq, described the abuse as not just the action of a few bad apples but rather a systemic and sanctioned part of the U.S. military prison system:

> American authorities continue to insist that the abuse of Iraqi prisoners at Abu Ghraib was an isolated incident in an otherwise well-run detention system. That insistence, however, stands in sharp contrast to my own experiences as an interrogator in Iraq. I watched as detainees were forced to stand naked all night, shivering in their cold cells and pleading with their captors for help. Others were subjected to long periods of isolation in pitch-black rooms. Food and sleep deprivation were common, along with a variety of physical abuse, including punching and kicking . . . While I was appalled by the conduct of my friends and colleagues, I lacked the courage to challenge the status quo . . . but as time passes . . . I'm becoming more ashamed of my silence.[76]

The pictures from Abu Ghraib were also a marketing coup for al-Qaeda and any other burgeoning terrorist group. Army soldiers' abuses of prisoners there will probably inspire terrorist recruitment for generations.[77] Mark Danner memorably framed it as a huge victory for the enemy, one that could not have been better planned: "Had bin Laden gone to Madison Avenue and offered to pay millions for a propaganda poster that would embody his message, could he have found anything more effective?"[78]

Like most of the Guantanamo prisoners, the detainees at Abu Ghraib didn't know anything. "By the fall of 2003 there were several thousand [prisoners], including women and teenagers . . . many of whom had been picked up in random military sweeps and at highway checkpoints,"[79] wrote Seymour Hersh, whose reporting was instrumental in exposing the abuse. According to a later report, "More than 60 percent of the civilian inmates at Abu Ghraib were deemed not to be a threat to a society, which should have enabled them to be released."[80]

The openness and casualness with which the U.S. soldiers posed for pictures revealed something equally disturbing, Hersh recognized. The "abuse of prisoners seemed almost routine—a fact of Army life that the soldier felt no need to hide."[81] The shock of the Abu Ghraib pictures was not the uniqueness of the treatment they depicted. It was the normality of it. Torture and abuse were part of a culture and of a system. One of the officers who served on a task force that investigated U.S. soldiers' murder of civilians at My Lai, Vietnam, was retired brigadier general John H. Johns. In 2006 he said, "If we rationalize it as isolated acts, as we did in Vietnam and as we're doing with Abu Ghraib and similar atrocities, we'll never correct the problem."

At the trial for Army Reserve Specialist Charles Graner, the highest-ranking soldier charged, army judge Colonel James L. Pohl would not allow testimony identifying officers who knew of the abuses, or about the orders that officers had given. Graner "was the ringleader of the horrors seen in the Abu Ghraib snapshots, [but] the entire chain of command above him, including the officers in his immediate proximity at the prison, was spared prosecution," as Frank Rich summarized aptly.[82] The only criminal penalties were reserved for low-ranking soldiers, sacrificed so the military's image could appear unblemished, although the damage to the nation had already been done.

ATTACKING THE MESSENGER

The Bush administration, and later the Obama administration, refused to release what are perhaps hundreds of additional photographs of abuses at Abu Ghraib. In 2009 Congress passed the Protected National Security Documents Act, largely to exempt the photographs from release under the Freedom of Information Act. In August 2018 a federal appeals court rejected the ACLU's demand for the photographs, citing the new law.[83] Without the diligence of the press and the bravery of army major general Antonio Taguba, the extent of detainees' torture by soldiers at Abu Ghraib might have remained secret.

For his report about the abuses at Abu Ghraib, Taguba was treated like a pariah, even a traitor, by his military and civilian superiors. It was a stark example of the retaliation the military engages in when bad news about itself is made public. On May 6, 2004, Taguba reported to Secretary of Defense Donald Rumsfeld that U.S. soldiers had been torturing detainees at Abu Ghraib. At the beginning of the meeting, Rumsfeld mocked Taguba in front of his superior officers—General Richard Myers, chairman of the Joint Chiefs of Staff, General Peter Schoomaker, army chief of staff, and

Lieutenant General Bantz J. Craddock, Rumsfeld's senior military assistant—as well as Rumsfeld's top two civilian deputies, Paul Wolfowitz and Stephen Cambone. "Here . . . comes . . . that famous General Taguba—of the Taguba report!"[84] said Rumsfeld.

A few weeks after his report became public, Taguba was in Kuwait, riding in a car with General John Abizaid, the U.S. commander of Central Command. "You and your report will be investigated," Abizaid warned Taguba, as Taguba told Seymour Hersh in 2007 and repeated to me when he visited West Point later.[85] Abizaid was a company man with bureaucratic experience, and he knew how to instill fear. "I'd been in the Army thirty-two years by then," Taguba told Hersh, "and it was the first time that I thought I was in the Mafia."

Inevitably, Taguba "suffered the fate of all truthtellers," according to Hersh. A retired army general told the veteran reporter that Taguba was "not regarded as a hero in some circles in the Pentagon . . . The leadership does not like to have people make bad news public."[86]

Several months after delivering his report, Taguba was reassigned by the army to the office of an assistant secretary of defense at the Pentagon, a lateral position. Until his report was issued, Taguba had been scheduled to rotate into a position at the Third Army's headquarters, but now he was moved to the Pentagon, "where I could be closely monitored," he said. In 2006 General Richard Cody (Class of '72), the army's vice chief of staff, told Taguba, "I need you to retire by January of 2007."[87]

Looking back on his work, Taguba wrote in 2014 that he had "documented a systemic problem: military personnel had perpetrated 'numerous incidents of sadistic, blatant, and wanton criminal abuses.'"[88] Complaints about prisons at Guantanamo and Bagram (in Afghanistan) were common, but until there were pictures, there was no outcry. Americans need pictures. They have always responded dramatically to pictures.[89]

"I know that my peers in the Army will be mad at me for speaking out," said Taguba, "but the fact is that we violated the laws of land warfare in Abu Ghraib. We violated the tenets of the Geneva Convention. We violated our own principles and we violated the core of our military values. The stress of combat is not an excuse, and I believe, even today, that those civilian and military leaders responsible should be held accountable."[90] The problems at

Abu Ghraib go far deeper than photographs and far beyond individual soldiers' conduct. They revealed a rotten system.

Yet those in the halls of military and civilian power ensured that this would not be the story. They had the same narrative to sell that they have always had: nothing to see here, just some bad apples. "The public talk from the Pentagon and the White House, when contrasted with what was really going on [at Guantanamo and other military prisons] amounted to strategic deception," writes Hersh. "The target of all the duplicity and double talk was not, of course, Al Qaeda and other terrorist groups, but the American press corps, and the American people."[91]

Because the conditions first produced at Guantanamo were replicated in military prisons in Afghanistan and Iraq, a White House official rhetorically asked Hersh, "Why do I take a failed approach at Guantánamo and move it to Iraq?"[92] The answer is that the military knew no other way, for this was its method, going back generations.

KOREA AND VIETNAM

In war, military leaders often believe that "threats and harsh treatment make the fearful and brutalized civilian or political leader capitulate," which is based on the premise that "war is not simply about destroying the other side's military forces but also about affecting the other side's civilians," according to Neta Crawford.[93] But civilians with national identities, as in North Korea, or with fixed ideologies, like organized terrorist groups or local insurgents, rally against their attackers. Excessive or inhumane violence acts as a motivator for the other side.

The atomic bomb represented the largest technological leap ever, and it also marked a point of no return for America. The atomic bombs dropped on Japan saved the lives of thousands (or more) of American soldiers who would have invaded Japan in 1945, but the bombs also killed from 100,000 to 200,000 Japanese civilians. Although based in utilitarianism from the U.S. perspective, the bombs violated the laws of war, which prohibit the targeting of civilians, and signaled that U.S. forces would not be bound by law—that under certain circumstances, they would do anything.

Where does this lead? "To many in the armed forces, particularly the air force, anything short of the massive use of available weaponry to attain

American ends is immoral," writes historian Marilyn B. Young. "The only problem the advocates of unbridled airpower foresaw was the timorousness of a civilian leadership unwilling to use its weapons."[94]

A military's willingness to do anything arises when the generals or soldiers come up intellectually empty or lose control of conditions on the ground. In Korea, where Douglas MacArthur wanted to attack China with atomic weapons, military leaders viewed (and continue to view) civilian oversight as a collection of uninformed opinions that prevent victory. It was President Harry Truman who authorized the use of the bomb, but, once the atomic threshold had been crossed, generals like MacArthur believed they should have discretion in the future to use atomic weapons. From White House and military documents unearthed during his research, historian Michael Beschloss revealed in 2018 that General William Westmoreland and Pacific commander Admiral Ulysses S. Grant Sharp Jr. hatched a secret plan, Operation Fracture Jaw, unknown even to the president, to move nuclear weapons into Vietnam in 1968.

On February 3, 1968, Westmoreland cabled the chairman of the Joint Chiefs, General Earle Wheeler: "We should be prepared to introduce weapons of greater effectiveness against massed forces . . . I visualize that either tactical nuclear weapons or chemical agents would be active candidates for employment."

In a cable on February 10, 1968, Westmoreland wrote to Admiral Sharp, "Fracture Jaw has been approved by me . . . Plan will be dispatched by Armed Forces Courier on 11 Feb." President Lyndon Johnson discovered and rejected their nuclear plan.[95]

American soldiers' mass killings of innocent civilians in the Korean and Vietnam Wars seemed to presage a changing American character, or perhaps a character that had not evolved as rapidly as that of the rest of the Western world. The United Nations Charter and the Geneva Conventions, adopted after World War II, discouraged military incursions and required humane treatment of all combatants and civilians in case of an outbreak of war. But American civilian and military leaders, their thinking dependent on brute, immediate utilitarianism, maintained a tolerance for abuse that they justified by citing countervailing interests. They were often wrong in their calculations about their enemies and what physical force would be effective. But, aside from the deleterious effects of their own hubris, their greatest error was underestimating their enemies' mental and emotional strength, affection for their own way of life, and animosity toward America.

In the Korean War, U.S. soldiers killed civilians pursuant to orders from high-ranking officers and with the acquiescence of civilian government officials, who reasoned that the practice was necessary to protect U.S. soldiers from various threats. "Beginning in Korea, U.S bombing was extended from cities to the countryside with devastating effects," writes Mark Selden in an essay in the anthology *Bombing Civilians: A Twentieth-Century History*. In a particularly callous act of sabotage, "North Korea's main irrigation dams were destroyed [by American forces] shortly after the rice had been transplanted."[96] The long-term goal was apparently to starve the local population. It was this type of behavior that taught the North Koreans that they needed an atomic weapon to defend their nation against America.

Another incident from the Korean War illustrated the inhumanity of some American soldiers, their willingness to follow illegal orders, and the senselessness of intentionally killing civilians that they were ostensibly there to save.

NO GUN RI

The murder of civilians in the Korean War was not an anomaly or an unfortunate type of collateral damage, but a strategy and practice that the U.S. military has tried to hide for decades. In 2011 the BBC reported allegations of "61 separate incidents involving the killing of civilians by U.S. forces . . . logged with the South Korean authorities."[97] For example, Korean "survivors recall 400 civilians killed by U.S. naval artillery on the beaches near the port of Pohang in September 1950."[98] The declassified official diary of a U.S. destroyer, the USS *DeHaven*, revealed that the army insisted that the *DeHaven* fire at a seaside refugee encampment at Pohang. Other Korean survivors reported one hundred to two hundred refugees killed there.[99]

Probably the most disturbing U.S. attack on civilians took place at a South Korean bridge in north-central South Korea, in a village called No Gun Ri in July 1950, a month after the war's outbreak. Trying to find relief from incessant bombing, civilian refugees who were fleeing North Korea eventually sought shelter under and around the bridge. At the time, army generals claimed they could not distinguish who among the civilians fleeing were North Korean soldiers infiltrating the groups of refugees. But this is the opposite of a defense: it is the admission of a war crime. Under the laws of war, soldiers must not attack if they cannot "distinguish" civilians from enemy soldiers.

In what is now beyond dispute, from July 26 to July 29, 1950, U.S. Air Force pilots strafed and U.S. Army soldiers machine-gunned to death up to four hundred civilian refugees, predominantly women, children, and old men. Long denied by the military, the United States did not admit the killings at No Gun Ri until after the Associated Press published an investigative report by Sang-Hun Choe, Charles Hanley, and Martha Mendoza that won a Pulitzer Prize.[100] The killings now can only be characterized as what they were: a massacre.[101]

In their 2001 book *The Bridge at No Gun Ri*, Choe, Hanley, and Mendoza write that in their investigation, "The Pentagon did not report the fact that no hard evidence emerged of infiltration among the group at No Gun Ri."[102] Former U.S. soldier Eugene Hesselman told the reporters, "We didn't know if they were North or South Koreans . . . We were there only a couple of days and we didn't know them from a load of coal."

"Veterans said Capt. Melbourne C. Chandler, after speaking with superior officers by radio, had ordered machine-gunners from his heavy-weapons company to set up near the tunnel mouths and open fire," according to the AP report. "'The hell with all those people. Let's get rid of all of them,'" Chandler said, as Hesselman described it.[103]

The generals in Korea abandoned fact-based judgment and acted on emotion, using the only tactic they understood: massive firepower. The defenseless refugees scraped and scooped hard gravel with their hands, trying to dig holes in which to hide. The living used the corpses of family members and neighbors as shields from the onslaught until they were also killed.

After the AP report confirmed the deaths and spurred a military investigation, a 2001 report by the army inspector general concluded, "The deaths and injuries of civilians, wherever they occurred, were an unfortunate tragedy inherent to war and *not a deliberate* killing" (emphasis mine).[104]

The evidence showed exactly the opposite. The army's method, claiming to find no deliberation, implying the killing was an accident, is a way to minimize the responsibility of soldiers and the military institution, especially the generals over the decades under whom this kind of behavior occurs.

Sometimes, as in the No Gun Ri investigation, the military intentionally conceals evidence or mischaracterizes it. An accidental discovery showed that, in fact, American generals ordered the deliberate and intentional killing of the civilian refugees. In 2006 historian Sahr Conway-Lanz discovered a letter in the National Archives that revealed the official U.S. government reasoning behind the plan to kill the refugees. The letter, dated the day the killings at No Gun Ri began, was written by the U.S. ambassador to South Korea, John Muccio, to the assistant secretary of state, Dean Rusk. After the North Koreans had attacked and made their way into South Korea, Ambassador Muccio described plans designed at a high-level meeting the previous night, which included the top staff officers of the Eighth U.S. Army.[105] "The refugee problem," wrote Muccio, "has developed aspects of a serious and even critical military nature, aside from the welfare aspects . . . If refugees do appear from north of U.S. lines they will receive warning shots, and if they then persist in advancing they will be shot."[106]

Beyond the damning admission in the Muccio letter, the other evidence of orders to kill refugees was also overwhelming. In a 1953 letter to an army historian, Lieutenant General Hobart Gay wrote, referring to himself in the third person, "The Division Commander gave the order to blow the bridge. It was a tough decision because up in the air with the bridge went hundreds of refugees."[107]

The 1999 Associated Press report revealed at least nineteen declassified U.S. military documents showing that commanders ordered or authorized killings of civilians in 1950 and 1951.[108] But in its 2001 report on No Gun Ri, the army excluded evidence of orders to kill. The sources cited in the army's report indicated that its researchers had reviewed the microfilm containing the incriminating Muccio letter, but nowhere in the three-hundred-page report was the letter mentioned. After the Muccio letter became public, Louis Caldera (Class of '78), the secretary of the army when the report was issued in 2001, said "It is certainly possible they may have simply missed it."[109]

In response to the evidence that the AP reporters had amassed, the army denied that the orders to kill were, in fact, orders to kill, claiming that "no policy purporting to authorize soldiers to shoot refugees was ever promulgated to soldiers in the field."[110] The army's defense was that even though its generals wanted to kill civilians, the generals' orders never reached the soldiers. The evidence shows exactly the opposite: at many different places and times, soldiers, following orders, killed civilians. Finally, in 2007, after South Korea requested more information, the Pentagon conceded that the army researchers had reviewed the Muccio letter, but they did not release it because the letter only "outlined a proposed policy" to kill the refugees, according to an army spokesman.[111]

This obviously false statement, regardless of how the spokesman intended to manipulate the press and public perception, ironically does not fit the usual definition of a lie; given the quantum of evidence, almost no one could be deceived into believing that army generals did not give actual orders to kill civilians. The statement is a way for today's generals to say "I don't care about truth and there's nothing you can do about it." In that, the generals are mostly correct. They are largely unaccountable.

Plain as day, the letter describes an already-made decision to kill refugees, and comprises the most compelling evidence in the No Gun Ri investigation. Yet the army knowingly hid it. The killings at No Gun Ri on the date of the letter conformed precisely to what the letter described. The army's reasoning ("no policy to kill was ever promulgated") is ridiculous; it would relieve from responsibility every Mafia chieftain who orders a hit, as well as every superior in any endeavor who orders or directs anything in any business or occupation, because whatever the supervisor said (ordered) can only be called, according to the army's reasoning, a "proposed policy."

Two of the AP reporters, Hanley and Mendoza, reported later that the army excluded from its report over a dozen documents showing that "high-ranking" officers told soldiers that refugees are "fair game," and one order to "shoot all refugees coming across river."[112]

Korean War veteran and former member of Congress Pete McCloskey advised the Pentagon on its report of the killings at No Gun Ri and spoke out against the final report. "I think the American government, the Pentagon and most government agencies don't want to see the truth come out if it will embarrass the government," he told a reporter. "The government will always lie about embarrassing matters ... And I think that the Army just chose to try and down play the terrible character of Army leadership in 1950."[113]

McCloskey gets to the heart of the matter: the airmen and soldiers and officers who killed refugees at No Gun Ri and other places in Korea were not rogue elements. They were dutiful Americans who were following orders. In the next American conflict, U.S. soldiers' murder of civilians would go into overdrive, unmoored from even the thinnest veil of self-protection and military strategy.

KILLING CIVILIANS IN VIETNAM

Basically, I enjoyed Vietnam. It was the most vivid part of my life. I enjoyed the anarchy of it. You know, self-law ... You really appreciate that now when you're getting fucked over all the time dealing with society.

—U.S. marine quoted in Mark Baker, *Nam: The Vietnam War in the Words of the Men and Women Who Fought There*

The premise of the war of attrition, the strategy formulated by America's commanding army generals—Harkins, Westmoreland, and Abrams—in Vietnam, was that if American forces killed more Vietnamese than they could replace, the enemy would admit defeat and somehow join the South in a unified democracy. Aside from the generals' naive and ahistorical thinking, the strategy was impossible to implement; U.S. soldiers often could not identify who among the Vietnamese was an enemy. A reasonable inference is that the soldiers believed they should kill as many people as possible, and this is what happened.

By 1964 the "Viet Cong were so intermingled with the peasantry that the Saigon troops [South Vietnamese] had difficulty distinguishing friend from foe," reported Neil Sheehan. "The American soldiers would soon start to see the whole rural population as the enemy. The Army and the Marine Corps would create a bloody morass into which they and the Vietnamese peasantry would sink."[114] According to Lieutenant Colonel John Paul Vann, who was in Vietnam from 1962 to 1972 as both an officer and also a civilian, "We'd end up shooting at everything—men, women, kids, and the buffalos."[115]

Although soldiers' abuse was common knowledge in Vietnam, reporting it through the chain of command was treacherous. One bracing example is the story of Anthony Herbert, who enlisted in the army in 1947, at age seventeen. Herbert was one of the most decorated soldiers of the Korean War, and as a lieutenant colonel in Vietnam he reported to his army superiors that U.S. and Vietnamese interrogators used electric shocks and water torture on detainees and beat women who were held in metal containers.[116]

Herbert also described U.S. soldiers' abuse of Vietnamese girls in vivid and disturbing detail. "The area was brilliantly lit by floodlights . . . Each of them [girls] was seated with their hands on a table, palms down." The instruments used were "long springy rod[s] of bamboo split into dozens of tight, thin flails on one end. It was a murderous weapon. I'd seen it take the hide off a buffalo. When it was struck down hard, the flails splayed out like a fan, but an instant after impact they returned to their order, pinching whatever was beneath."[117]

In 1969, Herbert said, he reported the abuse to his superiors, Colonel J. Ross Franklin (Class of '50) and Major General John Barnes, but soon after he was relieved of his command for allegedly "unsatisfactory" performance.[118] Barnes claimed that he removed Herbert because he was "a keg of dynamite" who was "completely oriented to killing mercilessly."[119]

In 1971 Herbert filed complaints against both Franklin and Barnes, citing their failure to investigate the abuse that he had reported to them. In an example of how perilous it is for a soldier to report wrongdoing up the chain of command, the two army chiefs of staff who oversaw Herbert's allegations were the former commanders in Vietnam, Generals William Westmoreland and Creighton Abrams. Westmoreland ordered Colonel Henry H. Tufts, commander of the army's Criminal Investigation Division, to investigate Herbert's claims. Tufts confirmed Herbert's allegations of torture, but during the investigative process he also compiled a dossier of inconsistencies in Herbert's public statements to try to discredit him. This is a long-standing army tactic: when the message is damaging, destroy the messenger.

Herbert did exactly what is expected of honorable soldiers, and the consequence was that he was put in his superiors' crosshairs. Pentagon documents showed that Colonel Tufts wrote in 1973 to General Abrams, "This package [the documents] ... provides sufficient material to impeach this man's [Herbert] credibility; should this need arise, I volunteer for the task."[120]

Colonel Tufts was eager to discredit Herbert even after Tufts's agents found truth in Herbert's complaints. Soldiers of "the 173rd Airborne repeatedly beat prisoners, tortured them with electric shocks and forced water down their throats to simulate the sensation of drowning," the agents concluded, according to a 2006 report in the *Los Angeles Times*. Tufts's investigators confirmed 141 incidents of prisoner abuse in Vietnam, and found that twenty-nine soldiers tortured prisoners; fifteen soldiers admitted doing so. But in total, the army sanctioned only three of them with fines or reductions in rank. Tufts and the others in command pursued Herbert not because he was spreading lies, but rather because he was telling the truth.[121]

Over many years the army tried to discredit Herbert, to bury his complaint against Barnes and Franklin, and to attack his claims of a cover-up. The army reported that Herbert's superior officers had not retaliated against him, and in 1972 *Army Magazine* said Herbert's "eminence is undeserved." The next year the Army Public Affairs Office scanned Herbert's new book, *Soldier*, for inconsistencies, and leaked internal reports about Herbert to CBS News. Mike Wallace used these reports in an episode of *60 Minutes* to imply that Herbert was lying about the war crimes he'd witnessed to deflect attention from Herbert's own war crimes, of which there never was any evidence.[122] Wallace and CBS News used Colonel Franklin, who claimed he never received a report of a war crime, to impugn Herbert. (The army later relieved Franklin of his command for throwing a Vietnamese body out of a helicopter.)

Nothing could save Lieutenant Colonel Herbert from retaliation, and he was the best the army could offer the nation. For his work in Korea and Vietnam, Herbert earned "four Silver Stars out of Korea, three Bronze Stars with a V, six battle stars, four Purple Hearts ... he was wounded 14 times—10 by bullets, 3 by bayonet, and once by white phosphorus."[123] Nevertheless, the army systematically tried to destroy his reputation for no other crime than reporting the truth about fellow soldiers' behavior, war crimes that were undermining the American cause overseas and in violation of criminal codes of conduct.

The investigation into Herbert's complaints found that the "abuse of detainees by soldiers of the 173rd Airborne was much more extensive than [Herbert] had alleged," according to the *Los Angeles Times* investigation.[124] In 2006 staff sergeant David Carmon said that abuse of prisoners was widespread in Vietnam and encouraged by officers. He admitted that he had practiced a form of waterboarding on prisoners, the same tactic the CIA would use on detainees during the wars in Afghanistan and Iraq, forty years later. "What I saw were leads hooked to the legs of a metal folding chair," Carmon said. "It was primarily used with the mountain/country detainees that weren't familiar with electricity. They would [tell] them it would make them sterile or something to that nature. When you turned the phone crank, a light tickle of electricity would generally scare them into talking." Carmon was not speaking out of guilt or pangs of conscience. "I am not ashamed of anything I did," he said, "and I would most likely conduct myself in the same manner if placed in a Vietnam-type situation again."[125]

In 2006 Herbert saw correctly a straight line from the war crimes he'd witnessed in Vietnam to the most infamous images of the wars in Iraq and Afghanistan. "If they'd really taken action about the bad apples and been honest about it . . . then they wouldn't be arguing about Abu Ghraib and different places today," he said.[126]

Herbert died in 2014, understanding that what he had uncovered went far beyond bad apples. "War crimes are infinitely easier to overlook than to explain to an investigating committee," he said in 2006. "Nor do they do much for promotion among the 'West Point Protection Society' of the Army's upper-echelon career men. So when I kept bringing up the matter, I kept on making enemies . . . I reported these things and nothing happened . . . I know now it wasn't just the Army. It was General Westmoreland in particular. He did everything he possibly could to keep my case covered up because of the heat being placed on the Army from the My Lai case."[127]

MY LAI

While the bombing of civilian refugees in Korea was tied to some allegedly utilitarian policy objectives, no matter how inhumane, Vietnam is where the bottom fell out. The U.S. soldiers who raped and killed hundreds of women and children in one day in the Vietnam hamlet of My Lai, within the village of Son My, had no military objective at all. They represented a developing venality in the U.S. armed forces.

On March 16, 1968, twenty-six U.S. soldiers in one C Company platoon brutally killed probably 504 innocent children, women, and old men, in what would become known as the My Lai massacre. Five soldiers refused the order of the superior officer on the scene, Lieutenant William Calley, to kill the victims. According to the stalwart Vietnam reporter Neil Sheehan,

> One soldier missed a baby lying on the ground twice with a .45 pistol as his comrades laughed at his marksmanship. He stood over the child and fired a third time. The soldiers beat women with rifle butts and raped some and sodomized others before shooting them. They shot the water buffalos, the pigs, and the chickens. They threw the dead animals into the wells to poison the water. They tossed satchel charges into the bomb shelters under the houses . . . Those who leaped out to escape the explosives were gunned down . . . Lieutenant Calley . . . herded many of his victims into an irrigation ditch and filled it with their corpses.[128]

The U.S. soldiers raped at least twenty women and girls, ages ten to forty-five, and probably many more, and then the soldiers killed their victims in the most gruesome fashion imaginable.[129] In their 1992 book *Four Hours at My Lai*, based on interviews with soldiers at My Lai and U.S. government records, British journalists Michael Bilton and Kevin Sim described the sexual humiliation wrought by the men of C company. Some of the soldiers became "double veterans," the expression used for soldiers who raped and killed the same woman. "Many women were raped and sodomized, mutilated, and had their vaginas ripped open with knives or bayonets," according to Bilton and Sim. "One woman was killed when the muzzle of a rifle barrel was inserted into her vagina and the trigger was pulled."

The soldiers cut off their victim's limbs, beheaded some of them, scalped others, cut the tongues from victims' throats, and slit the throats of others. Soldiers carved into the dead victims "C company" or the ace of spades, a sign of bad luck to the Vietnamese.[130] One former U.S. soldier, Varnado Simpson, described his depravity at My Lai:

> The training came to me and I just started killing . . . We did what we were told, regardless of whether they were civilians. They was the enemy. Period. Kill. If you don't follow a direct order you can be shot yourself. Now what am I supposed to do? I cut their throats, cut off their hands, cut out their tongue, their hair, scalped them. I did it. A lot of people were doing it and I just followed . . . That day in My Lai I was personally responsible for killing about twenty-five people.[131]

This was not unusual behavior for Charlie Company. In the previous weeks, the "normal tactic was for one group of regular rapists to hang back and do their thing" while the rest of the platoon searched the villages. Hearing that a woman had been caught, soldiers would race to the scene and stand in line to wait their turn, including a lieutenant who led one of the platoons.[132]

One boy, about five, had his nose and left hand blown away, and the stump was bleeding heavily. Considering it a mercy killing, a soldier shot the boy three times with a borrowed M-16. "God, what have I done?" the soldier asked after he was done.[133]

The answer was that he was following his orders and training.

COVERING UP THE CRIMES

For eighteen months, the army concealed the horrors of My Lai. But on a tip, journalist Seymour Hersh scoured the United States looking for Lieutenant Calley, who had ordered the murders and alone killed approximately 109 people. Hersh found Calley at a safe house in Georgia, near Fort Benning, where the army had stashed him while trying to decide what to do.[134]

Lieutenant Calley claimed that he had received orders from a captain, Ernest Medina, who was later tried and acquitted. Calley's approach at My Lai was an extension of his generals' strategies, focusing on kill ratios and hoping the North Vietnamese could not replace their dead. Army photographer Ronald Haeberle, who was at My Lai, described the soldiers in the midst of their killing spree. "I asked some soldiers: 'Why?' They more or less shrugged their shoulders and kept on with the killing. It was like they were fixed on one thing—search and destroy, and that meant killing civilians."[135]

At his court-martial in March 1971, Calley testified to the same approach: "Everyone knew ... there was a lot of stress on body count." Asked what kind of body count, he said, "High body count, sir. During the Tet offensive, it was very important so we could tell the people back home we were killing more of them than they were of us. At that time, anything dead went on your body count: VC, buffalo, pigs, cows ... anything. If something was dead, you put it on your body count."[136] When answering a question from his attorney, Calley testified, "I acted as I was directed—I carried out the orders I was given, and do not feel wrong in doing so."[137]

A jury of six army officers found Calley guilty of murdering twenty-two Vietnamese civilians and sentenced him to life in prison. Under military law, military commanders have unreviewable discretion to issue charges, and until 2019 they had unreviewable authority to dismiss convictions and lessen or even altogether eliminate any sentence or punishment.[138] (Notably, commanders were never authorized to increase a punishment.) Even in its current incarnation, this arbitrary system has little relation to justice at all, as evidenced by what ultimately happened to Calley.

Four months after Calley's sentence, the commander of the Third Army, Lieutenant General Albert O. Connor (Class of '37), by virtue of his authority, reduced Calley's life sentence to twenty years.[139] Then, in 1974, Secretary of the Army Howard Callaway (Class of '49) reduced Calley's sentence to ten years. Callaway reasoned, "There are mitigating circumstances indicating that Lt. Calley may have sincerely believed that he was acting in accordance with the orders he had received and that he was not aware of his responsibility to refuse such an illegal order."[140] This was, of course, precisely the reasoning used by the Nazis, a defense that was rejected by the United States and its allies at the trials at Nuremburg, a rejection that was the basis for the convictions and executions of Nazis there.

The army charged twenty-five officers and enlisted men with participating in or covering up the My Lai massacre, but dropped charges against nineteen of them. Of the remaining six who faced a court-martial, only Calley was convicted.[141] After General Connor and Secretary Callaway reduced Calley's sentence, he was eligible for immediate parole. President Nixon ordered Calley transferred from the military prison at Fort Leavenworth to a house at Fort Benning, Georgia. After being convicted of murdering 22 people and probably killing at least 109, William Calley served just five months in detention and three and a half years of house arrest.

According to Neil Sheehan, the massacre at My Lai was "inevitable."[142] Indeed, the line from Korea to Vietnam, and to the modern day, is a straight one, with U.S. soldiers' intentional killings of civilians dotting the way. Perhaps if the soldiers who killed the refugees in Korea had been prosecuted or even disciplined, Lieutenant Calley and the others at My Lai would have learned that they could not act with impunity. This presumes that the military legal system is capable of effectively prosecuting cases. However, the prosecutors and the system are ultimately under the control of commanding military officers who often lack the moral backbone or even external incentive to acknowledge their soldiers' war crimes.

FOLLOWING ORDERS

A beneficiary of this system was army major general Samuel Koster (Class of '42), who was the division commander when Lieutenant Calley and his soldiers killed the civilians at My Lai. Koster was flying over the area in his helicopter at the time of the killings and claimed later that subordinates told him that only about twenty civilians had been "inadvertently killed."[143] Koster did not initiate an investigation or request written reports until two or three days after the killings.[144]

In an army investigation, Koster was interviewed twice and claimed repeatedly that he had carried out a proper formal investigation, and he remembered that written, sworn statements were attached to the report. But it was all a lie. Investigators found no evidence of papers, logs, or destruction certificates, nothing to support Koster's contentions. Rather, in at least twenty-four instances,[145] Koster took actions or failed to take actions that impeded the investigation into the killings, including "countermanding" an order by a subordinate officer to "determine the number of civilian casualties, old men, women, and children."[146]

In 1970, the army concluded that Koster "did not show any *intentional* abrogation of responsibilities" (emphasis mine) and dismissed criminal charges against him.[147] An army inquiry known as the Peers Commission, named after its leader, Lieutenant General William R. Peers, had been launched in 1969. Peers, who had known and served with Koster, called Koster's initial testimony "almost unbelievable."[148] One investigator questioned Koster: "They [soldiers] made no statements, and to further compound the problem, there is no record of such a report ever having arrived at headquarters."

Koster replied, "Yes, sir. I can't explain that."[149]

The commission found that the evidence suggested "that these two individuals [Koster and Brigadier General George H. Young, Jr.] sought to suppress the true facts concerning the events at My Lai."[150] Though Koster never received more than an administrative slap on the wrist, author Tom Ricks concluded that as "the general who presided over the My Lai massacre, Koster had brought more disrepute upon the army than any general in American history since Benedict Arnold,"[151] who, tellingly, worked for the enemy during the Revolutionary War.

The Peers inquiry found that twenty-eight officers and, in addition, one sergeant and one specialist, had taken unlawful actions surrounding the killings (ordering the destruction of the villagers' homes), failed to stop the killings, or, in the aftermath, lied about or covered up the killings.[152] These, of course, do not include the additional soldiers who committed the rapes and murders. The Peers Commission concluded that "the failures of leadership that characterized nearly every aspect of the My Lai incident had their counterpart at the highest level during the attempt to prosecute those responsible."[153]

The soldiers' murders of women and children at My Lai emanated in part from General Westmoreland's body-count strategy, his war of attrition. But, through the arbitrary processes employed by the military—processes that are identical to those employed by generals today—Westmoreland, instead of being the subject of an investigation, directed the My Lai investigation and determined its outcome. The administrative punishment that Westmoreland recommended for Koster consisted of the withdrawal of his temporary appointment as a major general, withdrawal of his Distinguished Service Medal, and the placement of a letter of censure in his file.[154] "When General Westmoreland informed me of the proposed action against General Koster (the letter of censure)," Peers wrote, "I told him, in effect, that it was a travesty of justice and would establish a precedent that would be difficult for the Army to live down."[155]

The army tried to portray the soldiers' atrocities at My Lai as isolated acts, the same rationale it used in the 2000s to try to explain away the killings at No Gun Ri, after failing to get away with denying their existence. But the Peers inquiry concluded that "prior to My Lai 'there had developed . . . a permissive attitude towards the treatment and safeguarding of non-combatants which was exemplified by an almost total disregard for the lives and property of the civilian population . . . on the part of commanders and key staff officers.'"[156]

The Peers report consisted of four volumes. In March 1970 Peers forwarded it to the secretary of the army, Stanley Resor, and the army chief of staff, General Westmoreland. They and their successors kept it secret for more than four years, a cover-up of the report of a cover-up. In November 1974 the army released only volumes 1 and 3.[157]

"In sum, the generals who were running the Army acted less like stewards of their profession and more like the keepers of a guild, accountable only to themselves," writes Tom Ricks in *The Generals*. "This posture would have long-lasting pernicious effects on American generalship."[158] After Vietnam, Koster's next army assignment was as superintendent at West Point, his alma mater, where he became the highest-ranking officer and most prominent role model for cadets.

THE STANFORD PRISON EXPERIMENT
AND THANH PHONG

In 1971 the navy funded what became one of the most famous studies ever in the social sciences, the Stanford Prison Experiment, which documented how captors come to abuse their captives. For the study, Stanford University professor Philip Zimbardo separated a group of students into prisoners and guards in a mock prison setup. The experiment revealed how quickly student subjects took on—and embraced—their roles as abusive prison guards when placed in control of other students. Planned to last for two weeks, the study was halted by Zimbardo after only six days because, he wrote, student guards "became sadistic and our prisoners became depressed and showed signs of extreme stress."[159]

"The Navy and Marine Corps have a direct interest in the conclusions drawn from this study," the study's researchers wrote in 1974, "in as much as parallels can be made between the forces which operated within Dr. Zimbardo's 'prison' and those which spawn disruptive interpersonal conflict in Naval prisons."[160] But the military learned nothing or, more accurately, ignored the study's lessons.

The legacy of Zimbardo's experiment is the understanding that abuse occurs within a context. It is tied to set roles, expectations, and environmental and social conditions. The conditions within an institution can prevent or promote abuse, and people will misuse their power if given too much authority or if their behavior is sanctioned by a higher authority. "All else being equal," Maria Konnikova writes in a *New Yorker* piece looking back on Zimbardo's experiment, "we act as we think we're expected to act—especially if that expectation comes from above."[161]

In 2004 Zimbardo, as an expert witness for one of the soldiers accused of abusing prisoners at Abu Ghraib, concluded that conditions at the prison should lessen the soldier's culpability. In 2018 he wrote that it is "worth noting that . . . [student guards] fully participated in these activities and other offensive behaviors that typified their shift—activities that were strikingly similar to the sexually degrading rituals imposed on Iraqi prisoners by American prison guards in Abu Ghraib Prison."[162]

Abuse and torture can be taught and learned. Zimbardo describes what he terms the "Lucifer Effect" as "the processes of transformation at work when good or ordinary people do bad or evil things."[163] People necessarily learn to view others as less than human, he writes: "Dehumanization is one of the central processes in the transformation of ordinary, normal people into indifferent or even wanton perpetrators of evil. Dehumanization is like a cortical cataract that clouds one's thinking and fosters the perception that other people are less than human. It makes some people come to see those others as enemies deserving of torment, torture, and annihilation."[164]

Indeed, time and again, people at the highest levels of the U.S. military and government have employed the brutality that arises from dehumanization. In 1969 Bob Kerrey, a future governor, senator, and U.S. presidential candidate, was a twenty-five-year-old navy lieutenant commanding six fellow SEALs during their search for a Vietcong leader from Thanh Phong, in the Mekong Delta.

Late one night and early the next morning, Kerrey and his men, known as "Kerrey's Raiders," killed one man, a grandfather; seven women, including a grandmother and another who was pregnant; and thirteen children, ages three to twelve. In announcing to their superiors the success of their mission, the SEALs lied and claimed to have killed twenty-one Vietcong; as a result, Kerrey received a Bronze Star for his supposed heroics at Thanh Phong. For thirty-two years the SEALs remained silent about what really happened inside the village.

Only when word got to Kerrey in 2001 that CBS and the *New York Times* were investigating (and about to reveal) the incident did he admit he had participated in the killing of women and children.[165] In his defense, Kerrey said, "Though it could be justified militarily, I could never make my own peace with what happened that night. I have been haunted by it for 32 years."[166]

One of the SEALs in Kerrey's Raiders, Gerhard Klann, and two surviving Vietnamese witnesses described the killings of unarmed villagers. (The other surviving SEALs offered little information about what happened.) In approaching Thanh Phong, the SEALs were surprised by the presence of one hooch, or thatched hut, which contained five people. In the first of two assaults, the SEALs slit the throats of two grandparents, according to Klann, and stabbed to death their three young grandchildren. Kerrey denied killing any of those family members, but Klann said that Kerrey pushed the grandfather to the ground and kneed him in the chest while Klann slit his throat.[167]

The SEALs then moved to the hut they had targeted from a reconnaissance mission two weeks earlier. Kerrey claimed that at some point the SEALs were shot at with "several rounds" and returned fire with twelve hundred rounds, killing the villagers from a distance of a hundred yards. But in 2001 Kerrey said he could not be certain shots had been fired at his squad. "I don't know if it's noise. In fact, there is some dispute." Kerrey said he found the bodies in a group, evidence of a mass killing at close range, but he did not know why they were together.[168]

In 2001, contradicting Kerrey, Klann and Bui Thi Luom, who was a twelve-year-old girl in 1969, described the slaughter of helpless villagers. Luom said the SEALs killed fifteen of her family members, all women and children; the youngest was three. In her telling, the SEALs ordered them to sit. When a woman coughed, a SEAL put his gun in her mouth. The soldiers talked with each other and then started firing from close range. Luom was wounded in the knee but scurried to safety. Another witness, Pham Thi Lanh, who was the wife of a Vietcong fighter, said she saw the SEALs kill all the victims at close range by slitting their throats or shooting them with automatic weapons.

Klann said the SEALS "rounded up women and children" and "debated" what to do, according to the *Times* report, and then decided to "kill them and get out of there."[169] The SEALs shot others, said Klann, from six to ten feet away with automatic rifle fire, a claim that Kerrey and one other SEAL denied. "The baby was the last one alive," said Klann. "There were blood and guts splattering everywhere."[170]

THE CHARACTER OF NAVY SEALS

Even before the raid by SEAL Team 6 that led to the killing of Osama bin Laden in Pakistan in 2011, the SEALs had long been held in particularly high esteem. The SEAL name was associated with bravery, valor, and dignity. Perhaps that's because only certain SEAL stories—not those like Kerrey's—have been available for public consumption. That abuse by U.S. soldiers' in today's wars continues despite the horror of the killings at No Gun Ri and My Lai illustrates that the culture of the military is unlikely ever to change unless there is intervention from the outside. Predictably, another particularly low moment for Navy SEALs occurred on May 31, 2012, at a remote forward operating base in Kalach, Afghanistan.

On that day, three Navy SEALs seriously beat six Afghan civilians, resulting in the death of one. The navy did not reveal the death or its investigation until a *New York Times* Freedom of Information Act request uncovered internal navy documents. The *Times* article reported that just after dawn on May 31, a bomb exploded at a checkpoint near the small U.S. base where SEALs were training Afghan police. The blast killed one Afghan, resulting in local police detaining at least six suspects, three of them itinerant junk dealers. The men were beaten with rifle butts and car antennas as the police transported them to the American base.

Soldiers reported later that three of the SEALs at the base "stomped on the bound Afghan detainees and dropped heavy stones on their chests" and fired guns near their heads.[171] In one instance, the SEALs spread a detainee's legs and dropped a large rock on his crotch. Another SEAL "jump-kicked" a detainee who was kneeling on the ground. The SEALs stood on the detainees' heads and poured water on their faces to simulate drowning. Finally the SEALS, having apparently gleaned no information, released the men, but one died on the road home from the base.

Soldiers and villagers said that before the beatings, the SEALs, for amusement, had thrown grenades over the walls encircling their position, fired guns at vehicles, and used slingshots to hit children in their heads with hard candy. Afghans said the Americans would shoot the ground around farmers in fields, near almond groves, and on the road to a market. Four other navy personnel described abuse by the SEALs, including a claim that one fired a gun near a detainee's head and another dragged a prisoner by his neck. The army squad leader at the SEALs' base, Staff Sergeant David Roschak, said that one of the SEALs told him, "'Tell your guys not to talk to anyone about what happened outside of this camp. You know, no one needs to know we were involved.'"[172]

Roschak wrote to his superior, "My squad is being involved in a cover-up regarding the possible killing of detainees."[173]

After learning of the incident, the SEALs' superior officer in southeastern Afghanistan, Commander Mike Hayes, informed the Naval Criminal Investigative Service (NCIS) and ordered the SEALs to relinquish their guns. The SEALs were moved to a nearby base, where two of them gave "matching sworn statements" and two others asked for lawyers and did not make statements.[174]

The head of NCIS investigations at the time, Susan C. Raser, said about the accusation of abuse that she "didn't doubt it for a second." A lawyer for the Navy Judge Advocate General's Corps recommended that Captain Robert E. Smith, the equivalent of a colonel in the army, charge the enlisted SEALs with assault and vowed to further investigate the actions of a lieutenant. Commander Hayes, the SEAL's superior officer in Afghanistan, recommended they be removed from their teams.

All branches of the military are bound by the same military penal law, but each branch makes and applies its own administrative rules. These rules can become the informal escape hatches that commanders use to favor their military personnel while pretending to the outside world to have meted out justice. In the navy's processing of the case, a half dozen master chiefs, who are senior enlisted SEALs, recommended not bringing assault charges. Captain Smith, the overall SEAL commander for the U.S. East Coast, agreed. With total control over the criminal justice process, Smith held a Captain's Mast, an informal, secretive closed navy proceeding in which only a captain presides. According to Geoffrey S. Corn, a former army lawyer who was a senior advisor on the law of war, the Captain's Mast "really is like 'The People's Court' with Judge Wapner or whatever, and the commander is the judge. There's no accountability. There's no transparency."

Captain Smith gave the SEALs "letters of instruction," not even reprimands, suggesting that they improve their "leadership and decision making," and sent them to new SEAL teams. Smith would go on to become a top military advisor to the secretary of the navy. By late 2015 two of the enlisted SEALs involved in the alleged abuse, as well as the lieutenant, had been promoted.[175]

As the SEALs became more prominent, their behavior would be more scrutinized. By the end of 2018 over a dozen SEALs were being investigated for criminal acts. In November 2018 two members of SEAL Team 6 and two marines were charged with murder for killing an Army Special Forces (Green Beret) staff sergeant, Logan Melgar, who was a member of their six-man team. Melgar had reported the SEALs and marines to superiors because they had compromised the team's security by bringing back prostitutes to their safe house in Mali, West Africa, and for skimming cash from a fund used to pay informants who would provide information about Islamic militants. What apparently pushed the SEALs and marines over the top was that Melgar was invited to a party at the local U.S. embassy in Bamako, Mali's capital, and he didn't take them.

At 5:00 A.M. they broke through Melgar's locked room door, bound him with duct tape, a method of hazing that SEALs call "taping," and strangled him in his bed.[176] By June 2019 one SEAL and one marine charged with murder had pleaded guilty to conspiracy, lying, and less serious charges; the most severe sentence was four years imprisonment. About killing the soldier, marine sergeant Kevin Maxwell testified during the hearing at which he pleaded guilty, "I was willing to hurt that relationship with him because I was too weak to stand up for him and say, 'I won't do this.' I was trying to fit in with this group . . . I betrayed an American. I betrayed my friend."[177]

The most recent murder case involving a SEAL encapsulates the operational failure inside the U.S. military—incompetence up and down the chain of command and injustice in the legal system. One of the most decorated of all SEALs was Special Operations chief Edward Gallagher, who had been named by the navy as the top platoon leader of SEAL Team 7. In May 2017, during the battle of Mosul, Iraqi forces captured an enemy fighter between twelve and seventeen years old, who had been injured by a bomb. American medics were treating him when Gallagher allegedly pulled out a hunting knife, as he later texted to a friend, and killed the boy by stabbing him several times in the neck and side. Other SEALs and Gallagher, who was holding the dead boy's head upright by pulling his hair, held still for photographs. Gallagher "handed ISIS propaganda manna from heaven," a navy prosecutor said. "His actions are everything ISIS says we are."[178]

Even other SEALs considered Gallagher abusive, and he was eventually charged with the murder of the boy, though the navy delayed taking action for over a year despite other SEALs' allegations against Gallagher. At a pretrial hearing in November 2018 fellow SEALs testified that Gallagher "fired into civilian crowds, gunned down a girl walking along a riverbank and an old man carrying a water jug, and threatened to kill fellow SEALs if they reported his actions," according to a *New York Times* report. At the subsequent trial in 2019 one marine who testified against Gallagher described SEAL snipers who were positioned in a "crowded city of 660,000 along the Tigris River: 'everything on the other side of the river was good to go, was cleared hot, were good targets.'"[179]

Just two weeks prior to his trial, the military judge presiding over the case removed the chief prosecutor, a navy officer, for attaching tracking software to emails he sent to defense attorneys in his quest to try to find who was leaking information about the case to the media. In an astonishing turnabout, at the trial a SEAL medic, Corey Scott, who had been interviewed by navy prosecutors six times previously, said for the first time that he, not Gallagher, had killed the boy, by covering a breathing tube inserted into him after Gallagher stabbed him. Even if Scott was telling the truth by, in effect, admitting to murder, he could not be charged because navy prosecutors had given him immunity in return for his testimony.

In what seems like an incomprehensibly amateurish error, the navy prosecutors apparently did not include in Scott's immunity agreement a provision that would void the agreement and allow him to be prosecuted for all his crimes if he lied to the prosecutors during interviews or at trial or did not disclose a material fact ("I killed the victim"). Further, no immunity agreement should allow a witness to escape prosecution for crimes of which prosecutors are unaware. In July 2019 a jury of five marines and two sailors found Gallagher not guilty of all charges except posing with the corpse. Loyal to Gallagher, Scott had bamboozled the navy lawyers, ensuring that neither he nor Gallagher could ever be held accountable for killing the boy.

President Trump, who had ordered Gallagher released from pretrial confinement and considered pardoning him before the trial, said in a Twitter message: "Congratulations to Navy Seal Eddie Gallagher . . . Glad I could help!"[180]

Then, in rewarding utter failure, the Navy's Judge Advocate General Corps gave its four Gallagher prosecutors a Navy Achievement Medal for their "expert litigation" and "superb results," according to their official citations. (President Trump ordered the medals to be withdrawn.)

Commanders had warned SEALs against speaking out against Gallagher, the son of a West Point graduate.[181] The SEALs who testified against Gallagher received death threats and said they anticipated receiving serious retaliation from rank-and-file SEALs. The morning after his acquittal, Gallagher appeared on the television talk show *Fox and Friends*. He was asked what message he would give to future SEALs. "To future Navy SEALs," he said, "loyalty is a trait that seems to be lost, and I would say, bring that back. You are part of a brotherhood. You are there to watch your brother's back, he's there to watch your back—you just stay loyal."[182]

In August 2019, just over two weeks after Gallagher's television appearance, the top officer in the navy, Admiral John Richardson, dismissed all charges against Lieutenant Jacob Portier, another Navy SEAL. Portier was awaiting trial on charges related to destroying evidence and dereliction of duty for allowing Gallagher to engage in a reenlistment ceremony while posing with the head of the corpse. Richardson also removed the authority of Gallagher prosecutors to investigate Corey Scott for perjury.

Several days later, a media report revealed that the officer in charge of the Gallagher and Portier cases, Rear Admiral Bette Bolivar, had been investigated earlier because of contact she had with Leonard Glenn Francis (of the "Fat Leonard" investigation). Bolivar, when she commanded a navy salvage ship in 1998, "accepted" from Francis "gifts in the form of a hotel room, dinner, drinks, entertainment and a golf outing" in Malaysia, reported the *San Diego Union-Tribune*, based on a 2017 memo by Admiral Philip S. Davidson. "Bolivar's spokesman . . . declined to comment and would not confirm or deny that Bolivar was the subject of the investigation," according to the *Union-Tribune*. The navy report redacted Bolivar's name but, according to the *Union-Tribune*, she was the subject of the report, given the context. "Bolivar's gender and the relatively small size of the salvage community made her identity apparent from the documents," according to the *Union-Tribune*. Both Bolivar and Davison graduated from the Naval Academy. Davidson recommended that Bolivar retain her command position because she "continued to be a significant contributor and valued leader in the Navy."

By late 2019 civilian federal prosecutors in the Fat Leonard case (navy officers receiving the services of prostitutes in return for taking their ships to Francis for maintenance) had brought charges against twenty-two navy officers who were considered the worst offenders and referred the remainder of the cases to the navy. The navy investigated hundreds of officers but did not prosecute even one of them. In fact, navy records, which redacted the names of the officers, showed that navy JAG attorneys had actually told officers they were authorized to attend Francis's lavish dinners, according to the *Union-Tribune*. In this militaristic milieu, loyalty justifies anything, and there is little or nothing currently anyone inside or outside the military can do to hold responsible even the most incompetent officers and serious wrongdoers.

THE WAYS OF WAR

In 2008, with no end in sight to the wars in Afghanistan and Iraq, a group of officers at West Point were discussing the behavior of soldiers overseas. One officer made the argument why soldiers should be constrained by the laws of war. A colonel responded by questioning the value of applying legal principles to U.S. soldiers' actions. "War crimes go on all the time," he said. "You can't expect soldiers to memorize the U.C.M.J. [Uniform Code of Military Justice]. Things are mushy."

Agreeing, a lieutenant colonel said that "the lawyers have hijacked ethics," apparently meaning that law should be more malleable, that it should be made, interpreted, or revised by soldiers in the field. The colonel and lieutenant colonel explained how U.S. soldiers in the wars in Afghanistan and Iraq sometimes try to identify improvised explosive devices (IEDs)—bombs planted in shallow holes in or beside a road—by asking children to walk in an area where they suspect bombs might be planted. The bombs explode when someone walks on them.

This is not a new tactic. In the Vietnam War, Captain Ernest Medina, who led C Company into My Lai, "allowed his troops to use prisoners as human mine detectors," according to professor Christopher J. Levesque.[183] It was unsurprising, then, what happened in the Maywand district of Afghanistan in early 2010. The U.S. soldiers of Bravo Company there had been making plans to form a "kill team" targeting innocent civilians, whom the soldiers called "haji" or "savages," according to reporting by Mark Boal in *Rolling Stone* (calling the activity "bagging savages").[184] The soldiers had no reason to be suspicious of the civilians, a fifteen-year-old boy, a farmer, and a religious leader.

According to Boal, the soldiers contemplated using candy to lure children into the streets, where they could be shot, or throwing candy to the front of a 35,000-pound Stryker military vehicle, presumably so that children would be run over. The soldiers considered using an IED explosion as justification for shooting anyone in the "general area" and getting away with it.[185] These proposed methods were ominously similar to what the officers at West Point described: urging children to walk near suspected roadside bombs.

To conceal their murderous conspiracy, the soldiers planted "drop weapons" or grenades near the bodies of the dead. In their execution of Gul Mudin, the fifteen-year-old Afghan boy, Corporal Jeremy Morlock and Private Andrew Holmes (speaking Pashto, the boy's language) called to the unarmed boy to stop walking toward them. The boy stopped, and the soldiers cowered behind a mud-brick wall. Morlock threw a grenade at the boy, and Holmes shot him at close range with a rifle and a machine gun.

The highest-ranking officer near the scene, Captain Patrick Mitchell (Class of '06), said later, "I just thought it was weird that someone would come up and throw a grenade at us." But Mitchell did not tell soldiers to aid Mudin, whom Mitchell "believed might still be alive. Instead, he ordered

Staff Sgt. Kris Sprague to 'make sure' the boy was dead. Sprague raised his rifle and fired twice," according to Boal.[186]

The soldiers then posed for celebratory photographs, one of which showed Holmes "grabbing the boy's head by the hair as if it were a trophy deer." The platoon's popular squad leader, Staff Sergeant Calvin Gibbs, reportedly manipulated the boy's arms and mouth to pretend the boy was talking. Gibbs then produced a pair of medical shears, cut off one of the boy's pinky fingers, and gave it to Holmes as a trophy of his first kill in Afghanistan. Morlock, who was sentenced to life in prison, said, "None of us in the platoon—the platoon leader, the platoon sergeant—no one gives a fuck about these people."[187]

The Pentagon described the "kill team" as operating covertly, but after dozens of interviews, Boal concluded, "Far from being clandestine, as the Pentagon has implied, the murders of civilians were common knowledge among the unit and understood to be illegal by 'pretty much the whole platoon,' according to one soldier . . . Staged killings were an open topic of conversation."

The soldiers' platoon commander, Captain Matthew Quiggle, and first lieutenant, Roman Ligsay, were found not to be responsible despite failing to report the suspicious killings, according to Boal. In an army report, one soldier said of a speech made by Colonel Harry Tunnell, the brigade commander, "If I were to paraphrase the speech and my impressions about the speech in a single sentence, the phrase would be: 'Let's kill those motherfuckers.'"[188]

The kill team's murders might never have been made public if not for a random occurrence related to another military crime: Private Justin Stoner's sensitivity to the smoke emitted by burning hashish. His fellow soldiers converted his room into a "smoke shack for hash," which he believed could implicate him in drug offenses. "They baked the room many times until it stank constantly,"[189] he said.

Stoner reported the smoking to a sergeant, and then, becoming emotional, told the sergeant that he and other soldiers had executed a civilian. The sergeant did not take Stoner seriously and sent him away.

The next day, when seven soldiers from the kill team discovered that Stoner had contacted the sergeant, they beat and threatened to kill him. Before leaving, they tossed him two fingers, with skin still hanging from the bone, trophies clipped from one of their victims. If Stoner didn't want to end up like "that guy," Morlock said, he better "shut the hell up," according to Boal.

Stoner eventually made his way to army investigators. "They have had a lot of practice staging killings and getting away with it," he told the Army Criminal Investigation Command. Stoner was not charged, but four soldiers were eventually convicted of manslaughter or murder.

In August 2016, after his release from prison, one of the soldiers convicted of manslaughter, Private Adam Winfield, spoke at West Point as part of the showing of the documentary film *Kill Team*. Although he told his father about the killings, Winfield said, he did not try to stop the others because, in part, he feared his own squad leader might kill him. His advice: "You know the right thing to do. Just do it, do the right thing."[190]

But this expression is a vague, meaningless, empty mantra, entirely dependent on context, just as the Stanford Prison Experiment revealed. Where inhumanity or criminality is accepted, "Do the right thing," perversely, can become a rationale to operate outside the law.

ROTATIONAL FIRE

In 2010 two soldiers who had served in Iraq under Lieutenant Colonel Ralph Kauzlarich (Class of '84) came forward to describe Kauzlarich's orders in 2004 in response to IED attacks.[191] The first soldier, Specialist Ethan McCord, said Kauzlarich directed a new standard operating procedure when an IED exploded. "[Kauzlarich] goes, 'If someone in your line gets hit with an IED, 360 rotational fire. You kill every motherfucker on the street,'"[192] McCord said. "I've seen it many times, where people are just walking down the street and an IED goes off and the troops open fire and kill them."[193]

The second former soldier who spoke about Kauzlarich, Specialist Josh Stieber, said "maybe five to ten times" he witnessed "street massacres" when the order was carried out. The standard operating procedure, to "fire in all directions," according to Stieber, "was an order that came from Kauzlarich himself . . . The way we were told to respond was to open fire on anyone in the area, with the philosophy that that would intimidate them, to be proactive in stopping people from making these bombs."[194] Firing indiscriminately violates one of the fundamental laws of war, that a soldier must distinguish enemy combatants from non-combatants.

David Finkel, a *Washington Post* reporter, was embedded with Kauzlarich's battalion for eight months in Iraq for his 2009 book *The Good Soldiers*. Finkel reported that on July 12, 2007, Kauzlarich and his battalion were operating in the city of Al-Amin, Iraq. The events that unfolded that day led to an international uproar three years later, when WikiLeaks released the video and audio of a helicopter attack on what the U.S. military called "insurgents." But the Iraqi men killed in the attack appeared to be locals who were helping two reporters working for the Reuters news agency.

That day, in a densely populated area of Al-Amin, an Apache helicopter and its crew attached to Kauzlarich's battalion were looking for targets. Hearing reports of combat, a photographer for Reuters, Namir Noor-Eldeen, and his driver and assistant, Saeed Chmagh, raced to the scene. Noor-Eldeen walked across a dirt plaza with mud-brick houses on all sides, with a camera slung over his shoulder by a strap.

"Oh yeah. That's a weapon," said one of the Apache's crew members, with eyes on Noor-Eldeen.

"Have individuals with weapons," reported another crew member.[195]

A man with Noor-Eldeen nudged him by the elbow toward a building. Chmagh was carrying a camera and a telephoto lens. Four men were behind him. One of them appeared to be carrying an AK-47, which is common in Iraq, and another seemed to be carrying a rocket-propelled grenade launcher (RPG), according to Finkel's interpretation of the video.

McCord, who arrived on the scene after the killings, said "I did see an RPG and an AK-47, however, my experience in Iraq is when the locals see someone with a camera . . . is they always come out with their weapons, kind of like showing off . . . My personal belief is that I do not believe these guys had anything to do with the attacks we were facing earlier."[196]

The helicopter camera moved from Noor-Eldeen to one of the four men. One of the Apache crewmembers said, "Yup, he's got one too . . . Have five to six individuals with AK-47s. Request permission to engage." (Only one man appeared to have an AK-47.)

The crew received permission to engage, but the circling Apache maneuvered for a better shot. While the Apache was circling, Noor-Eldeen crouched and peered around a corner of a building, where he had been directed, and looked through his camera, with the telephoto lens attached.

"He's got an RPG," said one of the Apache crew members.

"Okay, I got a guy with an RPG."

"I'm gonna fire."[197]

When the Apache completed its circle, there were eight men standing around Noor-Eldeen. Chmagh was a few paces outside the circle of men, talking on his cell phone. The crew started firing the Apache's thundering thirty-millimeter automatic cannon into the circle of men, and within two seconds seven of them were dead or dying.

But Chmagh and Noor-Eldeen were running away. The crew tracked Noor-Eldeen and quickly fired dozens of rounds from the cannon at him, continuing to shoot even after he had collapsed dead into a garbage heap.

Chmagh took cover against a wall, but then he started to run. The Apache fired again, and when the smoke and dust dissipated, Chmagh was down, but alive and trying to crawl, a few inches at most.

The crew hesitated before killing the helpless and unarmed Chmagh, apparently following the rules of engagement. "Come on, buddy," said one of them. But they got impatient and eventually fired anyway.

"All you gotta do is pick up a weapon," said another. But no weapons were in sight.

The Apache circled for several minutes, with the crew looking for another target. Finally, it arrived: a Kia passenger van with two children in the right front passenger seat. The Kia rolled up next to Chmagh. By then, two men had arrived on the scene and appeared to be assisting Chmagh. The van's driver got out and opened the sliding door on the right side of the van, the side with the children. Then the driver returned to the driver's seat, and the two men lifted Chmagh, trying to stuff him through the van's open sliding door. Then the Apache started firing again.

In the sixty seconds leading up to the attack on the van, the Apache's crew members had waited anxiously for permission to engage. One of them radioed to their commander four times, twice asking for "permission to engage." The crew member reported, "We have individuals going to the scene looks like possibly picking up bodies and weapons."

Two other eager crew members became increasingly agitated having to wait for permission.

"Let me engage," said one.

"Can I shoot?" asked another.

"C'mon, let us shoot," said number one.

"They're taking him," said number two.[198]

When they were finally given permission, the crew fired, waited, fired again, waited, and fired again at the van, at Chmagh, and at the men helping him.

The U.S. military would later report eleven dead, including Chmagh and Noor-Eldeen; they counted the other nine as insurgents. When he arrived at the scene of the killings, Specialist McCord carried the children from the van for transport to the hospital. It is unclear whether they survived.

"In a lot of our opinions," Specialist Stieber said, "the stuff we were doing was creating more hatred against us, and yeah, picking fights, and finding more enemies, and actually the only thing that seemed to change that, and the only thing that seemed to prove worthwhile, was actually sitting down and negotiating with and talking with people we knew had at one time or another attacked us."[199]

After an investigation by army major general Vincent Brooks (Class of '80), Central Command concluded that the soldiers had neither committed war crimes nor violated the rules of engagement.[200] Instead, the army relentlessly pursued and prosecuted the soldier who leaked the video of the killings to WikiLeaks, an army private named Chelsea Manning. The army convicted Manning of passing classified information (750,000 pages of other government documents, in addition to the video and audio of the attack), among other charges, and an army judge sentenced Manning to thirty-five years in prison.[201] (In 2017, after Manning had served about seven years, President Obama commuted the sentence.[202])

In the days following the Apache crew's killing of the men, the U.S. military claimed that U.S. troops had been hit by small-arms fire and rocket-propelled grenades and requested the aid of attack helicopters. But there never was any evidence that the dead had fired at U.S. forces or were hostile at all. In law, but often not in practice, as has been seen, soldiers may not kill people unless the soldiers can establish hostile intent, and regardless, they must distinguish hostile forces from civilians before firing. Even if the

Iraqis had been carrying weapons, the soldiers had no legal right to kill them under the laws of war.

A spokesman for multinational forces, U.S. lieutenant colonel Scott Bleichwehl, insisted, "There is no question that coalition forces were clearly engaged in combat operations against a hostile force."[203]

American soldiers on the ground approached the bodies just after the attack on the van. One soldier, Jay March, whose friend and fellow soldier had been killed nearly three weeks earlier, "saw all of the bodies scattered around, blown open, insides exposed," reported Finkel. March reported that he was "happy. It was weird. I was just really very happy. I remember feeling so happy. When I heard they were engaging, when I heard there's thirteen KIA, I was just so happy, because Craig had just died, and it felt like, you know, we got 'em."

One of the men in the heap of bodies was still alive and signaled friendship to March by rubbing two forefingers together, an Iraqi custom. March rubbed the forefingers of his left hand and then dropped it, according to Finkel. March then "extended the middle finger of his right hand" to the man.

When the helicopter crew members realized they had injured two children, perhaps fatally, one of them said, "It's their fault for bringing their kids to a battle."

"That's right," said another.[204]

In commenting later about the soldier who justified the attack on the children, McCord related a chant that U.S. soldiers are taught to sing as they run or march during basic training:

> We went to the market where all the hadji shop,
> pulled out our machetes and we began to chop,
> we went to the playground where all the hadji play,
> pulled out our machine guns and we began to spray,
> we went to the mosque where all the hadji pray,
> threw in a hand grenade and blew them all away.[205]

Stieber and McCord believe the military's training teaches soldiers to "dehumanize" people in occupied countries. "Instead of people being upset at a few soldiers in a video who were doing what they were trained to do," McCord said, "I think people need to be more upset at the system that trained these soldiers. They are doing exactly what the Army wants them to do."[206]

MILITARY JUSTICE

Having separated itself from civil society, not only in America but also throughout the world, the U.S. military operates quite literally outside what most would consider the rule of law. When U.S. soldiers are abroad, they are immune from a country's laws under a status-of-forces agreement between the United States and that country, a condition on which the United States insists. The military has its own penal code, the application of which is based solely on the discretion of military commanders. Congress is the military's nominal boss, but its fear of being perceived as antimilitary or opposing military action has led to its abdication of oversight. In return, generals are wise enough to purchase military goods and services from private contractors in every congressional district in the country. In this arrangement, military commanders operate a type of fiefdom where they possess nearly unlimited discretion.

In changes to the military penal code in 2019, Congress provided military commanders with yet more authority over the criminal justice process. The commanders already had the authority to determine whom to prosecute and what charges to issue. The commanders then literally handpick jurors for the individual they just decided to prosecute from a list of officers and soldiers under their command. The 2019 changes gave the commanders the additional authority to issue subpoenas, just like independent prosecutors and judges in civilian cases. But commanders have no legal training and little competence to determine when the government may take someone's property or demand his testimony, the purpose of a subpoena.

The changes make convictions in serious cases easier to obtain, allowing for a verdict of 6–2, where previously a verdict of 4–1 (still not remotely as protective of individuals as 12–0 verdicts in civilian cases) was required. While most states have abolished the crime of adultery and almost no civilian prosecutor would ever charge anyone with it, Congress, at the military's request, expanded the crime to include oral sex. Extolling the virtues of commanders' additional control over people in the military, the army's chief of legislative training, Colonel Sara Root, gushed, "We're pretty proud that our commanders are at the center of this, and it just gives them some more tools for good order and discipline."[207]

Despite popular perception, this hierarchal culture and hypercharged control over individual behavior creates chaos the world over. American soldiers roam foreign nations and decide for themselves what is right or wrong, without having to moderate their behavior according to the laws of that nation. Military law is a theoretical constraint only. It is not a fair or neutral body of law because it is always—with no exceptions—influenced by commanders who have personal interests in the outcome of every case.

Of the American soldiers who have intentionally killed close to a thousand innocent civilians at No Gun Ri, My Lai, and Haditha, in Iraq (where marines killed twenty-four innocent women, children, and old men in 2005)—three wars spanning fifty-five years—only one soldier, William Calley, was ever convicted of a homicide. And Calley served only five months of imprisonment and just over three years of home confinement, after being found guilty of personally killing twenty-two people.

The absence of fairness and the military's separation from domestic and international norms allow soldiers to feel they are uniquely powerful and righteous. As a result, they wander freely in a mental and geographic landscape where they believe, as Lieutenant Colonel Sassaman boasted, that they are warrior kings. In an attempt to prevent such impunity and the atrocities that stem from it, in 2002 a large majority of nations in the world created the Rome Statute,[208] an international treaty that led to the creation of the International Criminal Court (ICC). When nations will not prosecute their own people or soldiers for committing genocide, crimes against humanity, or war crimes, the statute provides that alleged violators may be accused by international prosecutors. The offending soldiers may then be tried by international judges who sit on the court, which is located in the Netherlands. All Western nations are parties to the treaty—except the United States, which thus joins such human-rights luminaries as China, Russia, Iran, and North Korea.

President Bill Clinton initially supported the court, but "ultimately deferred to the Pentagon and Sen. Jesse Helms (R-NC), who argued that the Court would expose U.S. soldiers to international justice."[209] In every respect, American generals want to be free from laws, except the ones they create with the titular approval of Congress, which they want to be free to enforce in any way they see fit. "Like empires of old," Chalmers Johnson wrote, "ours has its proconsuls, in this case high-ranking military officers who enforce extraterritorial 'status of forces agreements' on host governments to ensure that American troops are not held responsible for crimes they commit against local residents."[210]

In September 2018 President Trump's former hardline national security advisor, John Bolton, gave a scathing speech attacking the International Criminal Court, reiterating that the United States would not recognize or abide by the court's rulings. Bolton even threatened to sanction the court, calling it "ineffective, unaccountable, and indeed, outright dangerous."[211] What was the court's most recent offense, in Bolton's eyes? It was considering an investigation of U.S. soldiers for committing war crimes in Afghanistan.[212] In April 2019, the Trump administration retaliated by revoking the visa of the ICC's chief prosecutor. Days later, ICC judges (who ultimately decide whether to pursue cases) announced that the ICC would not investigate whether war crimes had been committed in Afghanistan.

The separate society, which operates like a separate sovereign within the geographical borders of America and as its own kingdom overseas, cannot be held accountable to such a court. The U.S. military rejects many of the mores, rules, and laws that have evolved over centuries in nations throughout the world. American soldiers' behavior, from torture to intentional killing of civilians, is defended and protected by the highest authority in the land.

CONCLUSION

The Consequences of Separation

A standing military force, with an overgrown Executive will not long be safe companions to liberty.

—JAMES MADISON (1787)

Americans are harder on football coaches who lose games than on generals who lose wars.[1] One of the most backward assumptions in American society is that it is unpatriotic to criticize the military. The seemingly benign notion that we should "Support Our Troops" has morphed into a kind of worship that won't allow for any disapproval or even passing dissent on what the military is doing. If we do care about military men and women, then speaking out and noting the problems in the military are ways to support the troops. But the lack of logic in the notion that dissent weakens the military hasn't prevented it from taking root. The military regularly hides behind this blanket of immunity, which gives the generals a speckled four-star cloak of invisibility and invincibility, despite their inability to win wars.

The U.S. military has possessed the most fearsome weapons ever created, and has often looked unbeatable on paper. However, somehow it has experienced great loss in every war in which it has fought since 1945. With the increasing importance of computers and people to create and operate them—essentially software—the American advantage in weaponry is diminishing as human intellect, knowledge, and judgment become more important and hard weapons like aircraft carriers and tanks become more vulnerable to long-distance missiles, essentially movable computers. One can see in the computer collapse at West Point in 2019 (discussed in the preface to this book), for example, that military failure is centered in human error—a lack of ability to fix technical problems and a lack of judgment among the generals. They've separated from American society, overestimated their ability, disparaged dissenters, and suppressed speech and knowledge. They protect each other when criticism would be better for the nation.

The military's failure circled through the larger American society once again in 2019, and it was represented by even greater computer failure. The National Security Agency (NSA), created in 1952, is part of the Department of Defense and always headed by a high-ranking general or admiral. In 1964 the NSA misinterpreted or mischaracterized the events in the Gulf of Tonkin (a U.S. Navy ship was not really under attack by the North Vietnamese, as the NSA concluded), which led to an additional decade of U.S. war in Vietnam. In that war, the NSA—that is, generals and admirals in the U.S. military—monitored the telephone calls of two U.S. senators (Frank Church, a Democrat, and Howard Baker, a Republican), journalists, and civil rights leaders, including Martin Luther King Jr. In two more wars, in Afghanistan and Iraq, the NSA—once again, America's generals and admirals working in the name of national security and diminishing the civil liberties of citizens *inside the United States*—monitored the telephone usage of tens of millions of Americans.

At some point in 2017, the NSA lost control of EternalBlue, a program that allows the user to plant malware on computers. Whoever stole EternalBlue allowed Shadow Brokers, a hacking group, to post the program online, and it is now being used by Russia, Iran, North Korea, and China, America's most formidable adversaries. In 2019 someone used EternalBlue "to spread malware that has paralyzed hospitals, airports, rail and shipping operators, A.T.M.s and factories that produce critical vaccines," according to a *New York Times* report.

As America's computer systems were under attack from the NSA's product, the Department of Defense remained silent. The generals were helpless, not knowing who stole their weapon or how to stop its use against Americans. A cybersecurity expert at Johns Hopkins University, Thomas Rid, said the loss of the program is "the most destructive and costly N.S.A. breach in history . . . The government has refused to take responsibility, or even to answer the most basic questions . . . Congressional oversight appears to be failing. The American people deserve an answer."[2]

The U.S. military, silent and unaccountable, has provided no answers. As of May 31, 2019, the Pentagon had gone one year without giving a press conference. The U.S. commanders in Afghanistan and Iraq, General Austin "Scott" Miller (Class of '83) and Lieutenant General Paul LaCamera (Class of '85), had not given even one briefing since assuming their critical commands in September 2018. Instead of generals responding to questions about war, the Pentagon allowed its briefing room to be used by Gerard Butler, an actor, to promote a submarine movie, and Gene Simmons, of the rock band Kiss. "The long absence in the Pentagon Briefing Room has deprived journalists of an important part of that access and has removed opportunities to compel officials to answer for decisions they make on behalf of the American people," said Robert Burns, a journalist and president of the Pentagon Press Association.[3]

With *deployment*, *mobilization*, and *killed in action* now part of the lexicon, American children have learned over the decades that collateral damage and overseas wars are part of the American experience, as enduring as museum field trips and high school football games. Of course, this is how it is at West Point as well, where officers reassure cadets that their time for war will come. Cadets look to the generals as the models for the men and women they are to become. General after general shuffles through the academy with his three or four stars pasted on his chest, headgear, shoulders, vehicle, and even the personal flag that hangs behind him when he speaks. With the cadets compelled to attend to his every word, the general tells the next generation of officers that the American soldier is the greatest fighting machine the world has ever produced.

Each general, having never worked outside the army, repeats the same clichés and begins with a wholesome self-effacing joke that is really bragging masked in fake humility. "Academic buildings scared me when I attended West Point, but the army gave me the opportunity to do all right in life." Expecting rousing applause from hundreds or thousands of cadets, the general breathes deeply and readies his subjects. "No one has asked so much from so few. That's you, America's leaders, the protectors of our sons and daughters, the greatest soldiers in the history of our world. Hooah!"

The cadets stir and automatically respond in kind, "Hooah!"

With his fist in the air, the general's oratory is almost finished, but everyone knows what's coming. "Go Army! Beat Navy!"—a reference to the gridiron, not to the battlefield, where the army can't seem to beat anyone.

"Hooah!" the cadets again surge back at him, before quietly slinking off to class.

But something has gone wrong. The North Koreans possess atomic weapons and are a dangerous, treacherous authoritarian regime. Vietnam is similarly Communist and firmly authoritarian, just like China, which supported the Vietnamese and fought Americans on behalf of North Korea. The Taliban are as dangerous and plentiful in Afghanistan, or more so, than when the United States invaded in 2001. Rising from the U.S. invasion of Iraq, ISIS is now also in Afghanistan.

Russia was a ghost in the Middle East until the United States started the war in Iraq that destabilized the region and created refugees throughout the Middle East and Europe. The U.S. now has seventy thousand troops in Afghanistan and the Middle East—and no victory.[4] Russia, backing Bashar al-Assad, who used chemical weapons in the Syrian civil war, now has troops, planes, influence, and control in Syria. Iran and al-Qaeda control more of Iraq than does America.

An Army War College study released in 2019 describes how U.S. "leaders" (read generals) were outsmarted in Iraq. The study, while focused on Iraq, could serve as a coda for the U.S. military's dismal performance over the past seventy-five years: "[Syria and Iran] contributed materially to the killing and wounding of tens of thousands of Iraqis and hundreds, if not thousands, of coalition troops . . . U.S. forces had difficulty keeping up with the evolution of Iranian weapons such as explosively formed penetrators and improvised rocket-assisted munitions (IRAMs). These weapons killed and wounded scores of U.S. troops, but the United States responded to them only at the tactical and operational levels, not the strategic."[5]

Although the army delayed releasing the study for years, the authors—colonels, and lieutenant colonels—described how the generals' decisions had "added up over time to a failure to achieve our strategic objectives."[6] The list of reasons for failure is long, but it bears consideration because it indicates how the generals and the military failed in just about every strategic component of war. The reasons for loss included "a far more sweeping implosion [of Iraq] than U.S. leaders intended"; U.S. overreliance on military technology; poor military tactical coordination with coalition countries; an inability to build domestic law enforcement institutions in Iraq; a lack of understanding that democracy cannot occur quickly, and that the end of fighting is not the end of war; and an inability to understand that nations external to the fighting (Iran), even allies (Jordan and Turkey), will operate against U.S. interests.[7]

Every reason for failure concerned intellectual errors by the generals, or factors they had never thought to consider. The generals did not show competence even in their tactical decisions. "At no point in the war, even during the surge, did U.S. leaders believe the campaign was more than 18 or 24 months from the point when U.S. troops could be withdrawn and responsibility for security handed over to the Iraqis," according to the study.[8] The U.S. had too few troops to accomplish the mission; the army and Department of Defense organized troops on an "ad hoc" basis and relied on too many reserve troops; the commanding generals (George Casey and John Abizaid) engaged in "overly optimistic planning"; the military showed a "limited understanding of the operating environment in Iraq"; the army's one-year operational tours led to short-term planning; the generals did not understand how to measure military success, or what to do with captured enemy fighters; the military showed an overreliance on and inability to organize private contractors, and could not "keep pace with the enemy's strategic communications."[9]

These U.S. military failures concern just about everything having to do with war. Yet, when confronted with dangerous world conditions, the U.S. generals or their defenders blame failure on politicians or the media or really anyone other than themselves. After all, they have exclusive access to military information and can create and control the narrative so the average American doesn't know what to believe. Many Americans are similarly unaware of the wars' cost in lives, and the trillions of wasted dollars. Most do not think of the one hundred thousand dead American soldiers, and hundreds of thousands more who have been injured and maimed, physically, mentally, and emotionally, and the deaths of three to six million people who lived in U.S.-occupied countries.

"Thank you for your service" is the only response many Americans can muster, often an expression of patronizing patriotism. The closest they've ever come to war is walking past a soldier in the airport or seeing one in a parade. Yet fiercely patriotic civilians are quick to vilify anyone who dissents from the military's goals or criticizes its losses or its generals. Most have never worked in public service, provided treatment for injured soldiers, or toured Afghanistan or Iraq. They don't have to—and they'd rather not hear about it. This common reaction—a pat phrase that has come to mean little—is what gives the military such freedom and autonomy. It's why it's difficult to hold any one soldier—or even the institution as a whole—accountable for anything, even the lost wars.

SEPARATION AND ACCOUNTABILITY

The military's loyalty to itself and determined separation from society have produced an authoritarian institution that is contributing to the erosion of American democracy. The hubris, arrogance, and self-righteousness of officers have isolated the military from modern thinking and mores. As a result, the military operates in an intellectual fog, relying on a philosophy and practices that quite literally originated at West Point two hundred years ago. By dint of their rank, officers implicitly trust their own judgment, even when it runs counter to basic facts.

Besides creating a culture based purely on loyalty and fear, the officers' stubbornness affects their performance on the battlefield as well. The generals are more than ready to fight the type of war that would arise in a *Transformers*-like movie. But this is not what they are facing. Defense contractors have a sweet deal, where their expensive new weapons are bought by the armed forces in bulk, whether needed or not. American generals use their big arms to battle insurgents and adversaries with small arms, and then ask for more weapons, vehicles, and soldiers when the greatest need is for more knowledge and better judgment. The generals parrot but don't actually understand how they're locked in a battle over intellect and ideologies of the civilian population, fought on the home turf of adversaries who prevail over the American military with clever thinking under unpredictable conditions.

It's questionable also whether the military is prepared to fight wars against China or Russia using its "biggest" weapons. David Ochmanek, an analyst for the Rand Corporation, which conducts research and war games in conjunction with the Pentagon, said in 2019, "In our games . . . blue [America] gets its ass handed to it" when fighting against "red" (China and Russia).[10] America's "superweapons" have too many "Achilles heels."[11]

"In every case I know of," Robert Work, a former deputy secretary of defense, has said, "the F-35 rules the sky when it's in the sky, but it gets killed on the ground in large numbers" because, except for a fraction of time, the planes are not flying. The U.S. military's large air bases and aircraft carriers, as well as its tank brigades on land, built at enormous cost over decades, can now be destroyed by Chinese and Russian smart missiles from great distance. "Whenever we have an exercise and the red force really destroys our command and control, we stop the exercise," said Work.[12] An August 2019 study from the University of Sydney found that all U.S. bases in the western Pacific could be "rendered useless" in hours by Chinese missiles. The U.S. faces a crisis of "strategic insolvency," according to the study. It seems that the hierarchal U.S. military does not have the flexibility to function effectively in ambiguity because everyone relies on higher-ranking decision-makers, who themselves are prone to poor judgment.

The U.S. military is a slow-moving, top-down, hierarchal organization operating in a fast, flat world. Nimbler local fighters in Afghanistan, Iraq, and elsewhere can outmaneuver and outthink generals who employ plodding processes before making decisions in relative isolation. Rather than cultivating intellect and greater social and cultural awareness in officers and soldiers, the U.S. military's response to conflict has been as blunt, violent, and ineffectual as the machines for which it pleads. This happens on both the battlefield and within the ranks, where lying, retaliation, and cover-up are often officers' standard responses to anything that challenges their personal authority or the institution.

"The United States is no longer seen as a beacon of liberty to the world, but as an imperialistic bully with little respect for international law,"[13] writes former intelligence officer Melvin Goodman, who has blown the whistle on failures in the military and the national security establishment.

"We must guard against the myth of war and the drug of war that can, together, render us as blind and callous as some of those we battle," concludes journalist Chris Hedges.[14]

In the twenty-first century, the United States continues to rely on military intervention and nuclear deterrence against old foes as the ultimate expression of its foreign policy. *Atlantic* writer James Fallows calls America a "chickenhawk nation," one that loves to go to war as long as others are doing the fighting. The U.S., he says, "is more likely to keep going to war, and to keep losing, than [a nation] . . . that wrestles with long-term questions of effectiveness."[15] By permitting the military to function behind its own walls and according to its own rules, Americans, who profess more faith in the military than any other institution, have contributed to the current state of failure.

The full financial cost of the wars in Afghanistan and Iraq and the additional military operations in Pakistan and Syria could cost the United States $13.9 trillion over forty years, when interest costs on the debt used to pay for the wars are included, according to the Watson Institute at Brown University. The war in Afghanistan "has become more expensive, in current dollars, than the Marshall Plan, which helped to rebuild Europe after World War II."[16] The conflict costs $50 billion a year and is now the longest war in American history.[17] What have we achieved? What progress have we made? The very fact that the war continues all these years later gives us some inkling that the answers are nothing and none. But it's hard to know for sure because the primary source of information has a vested interest in selling victory. "Seventeen years into the war in Afghanistan," the *New York Times* claimed in late 2018, "American officials routinely issue inflated assessments of progress that contradict what is actually happening there."[18]

In October 2017, the U.S. commander in Afghanistan, General John Nicholson (Class of '82), at the request of the Afghan government, redacted from a U.S. government report progress about the war.[19] In line with the military's penchant for "bigger and more," Nicholson, who had gotten nowhere, urged the deployment of additional troops, and in 2017, for the first time in U.S. combat history, he used the most powerful non-nuclear bomb in the arsenal, the MOAB (Massive Ordnance Air Blast), allegedly to attack ISIS tunnels.[20] Yet nothing has seemed to work. In fact, *60 Minutes* reported in January 2018 that Kabul was too dangerous for Nicholson to drive even the two miles from the airport to the base, and he regularly required a helicopter to make the trip.[21]

The generals are either incapable of winning wars or are unable to understand that wars cannot be won: in both cases, the only solution is to replace them. The third option, that they know wars cannot be won yet remain silent, is almost too terrible to acknowledge, but the evidence that this is true, as detailed in this book, is overwhelming. After more than sixteen years of war, U.S. or Afghan forces reportedly controlled only about 50 percent of Afghanistan in 2018, but General Nicholson, who was the commander there from 2016 to 2018, still seemed certain of victory. "I'll get to 80 percent in two years," he said, an assertion that Bob Woodward, in his 2018 book *Fear: Trump in the White House*, characterized as "unattainable, even preposterous, to many who had served in Afghanistan."[22]

Nicholson, if he was not exaggerating, somehow deluded himself into believing that the Taliban would "come to the negotiating table"[23] and concede defeat while they controlled 50 percent of the country. It is unclear if this is willful ignorance, inconceivable hubris, or poor judgment on the part of the man in charge. But it really doesn't matter.

The U.S. inspector general for Afghanistan, John F. Sopko, completed a quarterly report in January 2018 that described the progress and number of Afghan security forces, the primary beneficiaries of the $120 billion the United States spent on reconstruction in Afghanistan. In an unprecedented move, the U.S. military command decided to remove from Sopko's report unclassified information regarding the number of Afghan soldiers and police officers, the number of killed and wounded, and the condition of their equipment. The military also removed data concerning "the number of districts, and the population living in them, controlled or influenced by the Afghan government or by the insurgents, or contested by both," a key indicator of whether the U.S. and Afghanistan were making any progress against the Taliban.[24]

This is how democracy can be destroyed, concealing vital information from the people. As Sopko complained, "the number of districts controlled or influenced by the Afghan government had been one of the last remaining publicly available indicators for members of Congress . . . and for the American public of how the 16-year-long U.S. effort to secure Afghanistan is faring."[25] By hiding basic facts and numbers—even from members of Congress—behind the shroud of national security, the military illustrated once again how it operates as a separate sovereign, out of range of any kind of oversight. In cases like this, the military's reasoning doesn't seem connected to national security at all. The real reason for its censorship is that it is embarrassed that the facts indicate its failure.

President Donald Trump's solution to the grinding war on the ground in Afghanistan was to stop talking about it altogether, further insulating the military from public scrutiny. "We will not talk about numbers of troops or our plans for further military," Trump said in August 2017. As Bob Woodward writes, "With that, Trump dodged Bush's and Obama's Achilles' heel. His strategy had the effect of pushing the Afghanistan War debate away, off the front page and out of the news unless there was a major act of violence."[26] Trump's claim was that any explanation of the plans for Afghanistan gave away important intelligence. What it really accomplished—and perhaps its ultimate goal—was to give the military free rein, which on more than one occasion Trump was all too willing to do.

In August 2019 the Taliban and the United States agreed tentatively to a future ceasefire in which the United States would withdraw most of its fourteen thousand troops from Afghanistan and the Taliban would prevent terrorist attacks on the United States and its allies. Several days later, the Taliban killed 14 and wounded 145 people in one of its most lethal attacks of 2019. The next week, on the same road, the result was worse: a Taliban suicide bomber killed 63 and wounded 182 people at a wedding hall. After additional Taliban attacks, the U.S. secretary of state, Mike Pompeo, apparently wary of comparisons to General William Westmoreland's war of attrition in Vietnam more than fifty years earlier, said on September 8, 2019, "You should know in the last ten days we've killed over a thousand Taliban. And while this is not a war of attrition, I want the American people to know that President Trump is taking it to the Taliban in an effort to make sure that we protect America's interests." The next day, President Trump rejected the tentative agreement, and the war in Afghanistan continued, now in its nineteenth year.

The confusion inherent in war and the complexity of modern enemies and political alliances mean that the public is at the mercy of its messenger, the American generals who are in sole possession of critical information that is needed to run a democracy. And evidence has shown that these people cannot be trusted. As the Army War College study on lying among officers illustrates, reports on the inner workings of the military and its external effectiveness come from untrustworthy people. Officers who are in a position to benefit from false reports of progress are the very ones tasked with preparing and sharing such reports.

Reforming the military from the inside is not possible. The generals (and other officers) who benefit from the status quo would have to admit the problems and lead the charge for reform. They enjoy the perks of their status, and then additional perks after their time is done. "Retired generals play a shadowy but important role in the U.S. military establishment, and especially in the Army," Tom Ricks explains. "They are part Greek chorus and part shadow board of directors, watching and commenting on their successors' work. They tend to be well informed about current operations, because some are hired as consultants and mentors in war games and war college seminars, and others maintain friendships with former subordinates who have risen to the top."[27]

If the military has not implemented reform after seventy-five years of failure and losses, there is no reason to believe the generals have the intellectual capacity, courage, humility, and moral judgment necessary to undertake reform now. They view themselves as royalty, according to one former military prosecutor,[28] and if history teaches anything, it's that almost no regal person or institution will ever voluntarily give up power. Change will have to come from the outside, although it is not clear whether Americans have the willingness and fortitude to undertake this considerable task.

MILITARY PASS

I felt very bad for him. He had his shortcomings, but he was a hell of a nice guy and I admired him. As you know, I love military guys.

—President Trump on former national security advisor Michael Flynn,
who pleaded guilty to a felony

The problems discussed here extend further and wider than the armed forces, because the military ethos has effectively consumed the highest civilian offices of government. "President Trump had concentrated ever more power in the Pentagon, granting it nearly unilateral authority in areas of policy once orchestrated across multiple agencies, including the State Department," according to Ronan Farrow in his 2018 book *War on Peace: The End of Diplomacy and the Decline of American Influence*, sounding the alarm about the Defense Department's takeover of matters once handled by the State Department and its considerable collection of experienced diplomats. Many of these diplomats are underutilized and leaving in frustration. It has been a hollowing-out of the intellectual core of America's civilian government—where 33 percent of the civilian employees in executive agencies are military veterans—in favor of blunt military thinking. To illustrate, in November 2019, when its workings were drawn into the Trump impeachment hearings surrounding Ukraine, the State Department's secretary was Mike Pompeo (West Point Class of '86); his top two aides were Ulrich Brechbuhl and Brian Bulatao (friends of his from the Class of '86); the diplomat Pompeo had selected to head the U.S. embassy in Ukraine was William B. Taylor (Class of '69); and the secretary of defense was Mark Esper (another friend from the Class of '86).

Farrow describes how a military net has captured nearly every international policy and practice:

> In Iraq and Syria, the White House quietly delegated more decisions on troop deployments to the military. In Yemen and Somalia, field commanders were given authority to launch raids without White House approval. In Afghanistan, Trump granted the secretary of defense, General James Mattis, sweeping authority to set troop levels. In public statements, the White House downplayed the move, saying the Pentagon still had to adhere to the broad strokes of policies set by the White House. But in practice, the fate of thousands of troops in a diplomatic tinderbox of a conflict had, for the

first time in recent history, been placed solely in military hands. Diplomats were no longer losing the argument on Afghanistan: they weren't in it.[29]

Farrow explains how the process of military personnel moving or retiring into civilian oversight positions has amped up in recent years, especially in the Trump administration.[30] "Back home, the White House itself has become overcrowded with military voices," he writes. "A few months into the Trump administration, at least ten of twenty-five senior leadership positions on the president's National Security Council were held by current or retired military officials . . . [which] grew to include the White House chief of staff, a position given to former general John Kelly."[31] The military is no longer limited to prosecuting wars. It is in charge of running much of the civilian U.S. government, which makes the need for change even more urgent.

CONTROLLING THE MESSAGE

As America continues its armed conflicts throughout the world, its generals continue to misrepresent the facts surrounding war. "The American military," according to a 2018 *New York Times* report, "says the Afghan government effectively 'controls or influences' 56 percent of the country. But that assessment relies on statistical sleight of hand. In many districts, the Afghan government controls only the district headquarters and military barracks, while the Taliban control the rest." The U.S. government reports that Afghanistan has 314,000 forces, while Afghanistan itself claims only 207,000, and one-third of these may be "ghosts," men who have left or deserted. The U.S. claims 25,000 to 60,000 Taliban fighters, but the Afghan government counts 77,000.[32]

In 2017 the Pentagon claimed that "the ratio of civilian deaths to airstrikes in the operation against the Islamic State in Iraq is one for every 157 strikes."[33] The military is comfortable controlling the flow of information and rarely has to contend with anyone else digging for facts. But some news and nongovernmental organizations that have the wherewithal are attempting to counter the military's fabrications.

In November 2017 the *New York Times* editorial board wrote, "A half-century ago, the Pentagon's misleading claims about civilian deaths in

Vietnam eroded public trust and, ultimately, support for the war. The United States military today claims to have learned the hard lessons of that and subsequent wars . . . It turns out this is all, at least partly, an illusion."[34] In contrast to the Pentagon's contentions, a *Times* investigation found one civilian death for every five U.S. airstrikes against ISIS, a rate thirty-one times greater than stated in the Pentagon's reports. To verify its conclusions, the *Times* explained, its reporters "provided the first systematic, ground-based sample of airstrikes in Iraq since the operation began in 2014." The reporters visited 150 locations that had been bombed, mapped destruction with satellite imagery, interviewed hundreds of witnesses, and collected bomb fragments that were examined by experts.[35]

In April 2019 Amnesty International reported on its investigation into the U.S.-led coalition airstrikes and bombing of ISIS forces in Raqqa, Syria, in 2017. Amnesty concluded that the number of civilian deaths was ten times greater than that claimed by the coalition (over 1,600 actual dead, but only 159 claimed). Using the same obtuse approach that U.S. forces used in Korea (bombing cities) and Vietnam (attrition), as well as in Afghanistan and Iraq, coalition forces destroyed eleven thousand buildings in Raqqa. "One U.S. military official boasted about firing 30,000 artillery rounds during the campaign—the equivalent of a strike every six minutes, for four months straight—surpassing the amount of artillery used in any conflict since the Viet Nam war," Amnesty reported. "With a margin of error of more than 100 metres, unguided artillery is notoriously imprecise and its use in populated areas constitutes indiscriminate attacks."

For the investigation (by Amnesty and Airwars), "more than 3,000 digital activists in 124 countries took part, analyzing a total of more than 2 million satellite image frames. The organization's Digital Verification Corps, based at six universities around the world, analyzed and authenticated video footage captured during the battle . . . [and researchers] gathered names for more than 1,000 of the victims," directly verifying 641 of those, with "very strong multiple source reports for the rest." In contrast, the coalition estimate of only 159 civilian deaths was made despite a failure to conduct "site investigations."[36] But the media and nongovernmental organizations can rarely muster the resources to make this kind of analysis, often leaving the military generals as the only source of reporting on themselves.

PROTECTING THE BOSS

Despite the perception that the military is a disciplined organization, many of its operations and decision-making processes are chaotic because law and rules are applied at the discretion and pleasure of individual officers who rotate constantly through different assignments every year or two. This model fits perfectly with the punitive personality of President Trump, who advanced an authoritarian ethos and selected as his top aides former and current military officers who appeared to be willing to lie, exaggerate, or remain silent when witnessing wrongdoing. That this behavior has spread to the civilian command can be seen in the craven ways that Trump's military guys in civilian jobs protect him no matter the cost. After retired lieutenant general Michael Flynn, who pleaded guilty to a felony for lying to the FBI, Trump's second national security advisor was Lieutenant General H. R. McMaster. McMaster's defenses of Trump seemed particularly disappointing, given his reputation for integrity.

In one instance, on May 10, 2017, the day after the president fired FBI director James Comey, who was investigating Russia's support of Trump in the 2016 election, Trump and McMaster met at the White House with the Russian foreign minister and ambassador to the United States. Comey, who had not worked in the military, would not buckle under to Trump's demand for loyalty. Trump's military aides would. In disclosing what was almost surely classified information, Trump told the Russians how ISIS might try to plant bombs in laptop computers for detonation on airplanes. After the controversy that arose, McMaster spoke to the media at the White House. "At no time were intelligence sources or methods discussed and the President did not disclose any military operations that weren't already publicly known," he said. "I was in the room. It didn't happen."[37]

But this was a deception, according to one former intelligence officer. "It sounds like [the] White House is parsing words by saying 'didn't discuss sources or methods' as a weak cover your [ass] ... That's a technicality. If the information itself was specific enough, it implicitly discloses sources and methods."[38]

McMaster, a West Point graduate (Class of '84) and former instructor there, flushed his hard-won and sterling reputation away in an effort to remain loyal to his commander-in-chief. He defended Trump's disclosures to the Russians as if the release of classified information to an adversary was a routine presidential prerogative. "It is wholly appropriate for the president to share whatever information he thinks is to the advancement of the security of the American people," McMaster claimed, and then he condemned the messenger while using patriotism as his sword: "Our national security has been put at risk by those violating confidentiality, and those releasing information to the press that could [be] connected with other information available to make American citizens and others more vulnerable."[39]

The lack of self-awareness and hypocrisy from McMaster was staggering. He was warning against exactly what Trump had done and what he was defending, delivering inside information to the Russians. Then he defended Trump by vilifying the White House aides and reporters who had disclosed what Trump told the Russians.

McMaster seems to have fallen from what was once a noble perch. In his book *Dereliction of Duty* (1997), he warns of the dangers of blind loyalty of military officers and condemns the duplicity of the chairman of the Joint Chiefs of Staff, General Maxwell Taylor, during the Vietnam War. "When he found it expedient to do so," McMaster writes, "he [Taylor] misled the JCS, the press, and the NSC ... Ever loyal to the president ... Taylor shielded him from the views of his less politically sensitive colleagues."[40] Two decades later, overwhelmed by the blind loyalty he learned in the chain of command, McMaster engaged in the behavior that he once condemned.

President Trump's second chief of staff, retired four-star marine general John "I Am an American Flag" Kelly, is an illustration of the intellectual (and physical) violence inherent in the military ethos, which became prominent in the Trump White House. When Kelly took over for Reince Priebus in late July 2017, he would supposedly bring needed "discipline" to Trump and the White House. As secretary of homeland security, Kelly had been highly regarded, given a kind of automatic pass because of his military pedigree. However, I believe he shared Trump's authoritarian demeanor, bullying temperament, and looseness with the truth.

The first red flag appeared when Kelly appeared to lie while trying to cover up one of Trump's blunders. On October 16, 2017, Trump called the widow of a slain soldier, La David Johnson, one of four U.S. soldiers killed during an operation in Niger. (Almost no one, including members of

Congress, knew of the military's operations in the African country. Trump later falsely claimed that the raid was a success, and garnered valuable intelligence. It did not.)

The Pentagon reported that the soldiers were on a "low-risk reconnaissance mission," but Niger's defense secretary said the soldiers were searching for Islamist militants.[41] Complaining about the secrecy inside the Trump White House, Senator John McCain (R-AZ) said, "There's a mind-set over there that they're a unicameral government . . . We are coequal branches of government; we should be informed at all times. We're just not getting the information in the timely fashion that we need."[42]

When Trump called Johnson's widow, Myeshia, she was in a car on the way to meet her husband's body, accompanied by a Democratic congresswoman, Frederica Wilson. Wilson listened to the call on the speakerphone and later criticized Trump for forgetting La David Johnson's name and saying that Johnson "knew what he signed up for," a particularly heartless thing for a president to tell a military widow. This account was confirmed by Johnson's mother, who was also in the car. Trump objected to Wilson's listening in on the conversation and enlisted retired general Kelly, using Kelly's credibility to attack and falsely disparage Wilson.

During the dustup, Trump even used the death of Kelly's son, who died in Afghanistan in 2010, to attack President Obama by claiming he had not called Kelly to express condolences. Then Trump hid behind the four stars of his chief of staff, who aggressively attacked Congresswoman Wilson on behalf of President Trump.

In a rare press conference for a White House chief of staff, Kelly praised Trump for his telephone conversations with the families of the four soldiers killed in Niger. Expressing his disgust with Wilson, Kelly said, "It stuns me that a member of Congress would have listened in on that conversation . . . And I thought at least that was sacred. You know, when I was a kid growing up, a lot of things were sacred in our country. Women were sacred, looked upon with great honor. That's obviously not the case anymore as we see from recent cases. Life—the dignity of life—is sacred. That's gone. Religion, that seems to be gone as well."

Despite Kelly's revealing his own biases and retrograde ideas about women, his main point was to attack someone who had apparently wronged his boss. Kelly continued to demean and berate Wilson, calling her an "empty barrel." The retired general then told a false story about Wilson's bragging about obtaining funding for a federal building in Florida that was named after two FBI agents who had been killed in a shootout. Kelly, by coincidence, apparently even attended the dedication of the building when Wilson spoke:

> And a congresswoman stood up and in the long tradition of empty barrels making the most noise, stood up there and all of that and talked about how she was instrumental in getting the funding for that building, and how she took care of her constituents because she got the money, and she just called up President Obama, and on that phone call he gave the money—the $20 million—to build the building. And she sat down, and we were stunned. Stunned that she had done it. Even for someone that is that empty a barrel, we were stunned.[43]

Everything Kelly alleged about Wilson was false. There was proof. Wilson was not yet even a member of Congress when the funding for the building was approved in 2009. The *Fort Lauderdale Sun Sentinel* unearthed a video of the 2015 dedication of the FBI building in Miramar, Florida. Wilson said little of what Kelly had attributed to her. Instead, she praised fellow members of Congress and devoted most of her speech to recognizing the deceased FBI agents and others in law enforcement.[44]

But Kelly—like his boss—was not swayed by facts. He showed no interest in admitting an error or apologizing. The White House press secretary, Sarah Huckabee Sanders, in her own defense of Kelly, perfectly illustrated the invincibility and unaccountability of men in uniform. "If you want to go after General Kelly," she said, "that's up to you. If you want to get into a debate with a four-star Marine general, I think that's something highly inappropriate," said Sanders, as if Kelly were a demigod who should not be questioned.[45]

Huckabee Sanders, like many Americans, illustrated her "slavish veneration" of the military, according to commentator Richard Cohen.[46] Kelly showed himself to be a Trump-like authoritarian, self-righteous and unapologetic in the face of countervailing facts. The incident was a textbook example of troops falling into line, sacrificing their dignity and honesty to show loyalty to their leader.

In an interview a few weeks later, Kelly offered even more of the antiquated ideas he had hinted at during the Congresswoman Wilson episode. "I would tell you that Robert E. Lee was an honorable man," he said in a television interview. "He was a man that gave up his country to fight for his state, which 150 years ago was more important than country. It was always loyalty to state first back in those days. Now it's different today. But the lack of an ability to compromise led to the Civil War, and men and women of good faith on both sides made their stand where their conscience had them make their stand."[47]

Kelly's remarks seemed grounded in antebellum pride, and they were even more troubling considering the recent context. Two months earlier, a far-right rally in Charlottesville, Virginia, ostensibly about protecting Confederate statues (including one of Lee), had left one person dead. The president received near universal scorn after he condemned "both sides" of the conflict, equating the marching neo-Nazis with the counterprotesters.

Essentially, Kelly was echoing the Confederate rationale for the Civil War. Columbia professor Stephanie McCurry called it "the Jim Crow version of the causes of the Civil War."[48] Yale professor David Blight called it "profound ignorance. I mean, it's one thing to hear it from Trump, who, let's be honest, just really doesn't know any history and has demonstrated it over and over and over. But General Kelly has a long history in the American military."[49]

According to Professor Blight, Kelly's statement "reflects a very old set of ideas about the meaning of the Civil War. Everybody was right, and nobody was wrong . . . It takes away all responsibility."[50] The ideas might be old, but there's little question where Kelly learned them. The southern tradition is ever-present in the military, where Kelly spent forty-six years (1970–2016). It's a place where—in 2001—"the premiere leadership institution in the world" decided to name a refurbished area "Reconciliation Plaza," just across from Grant Hall and Lee Barracks. West Point has long honored the Confederate general, with Lee Road, Lee Gate, Lee Barracks, and a Robert E. Lee portrait unveiled in 1954,[51] at the height of the civil rights movement.

It was possible to observe General Kelly's real attitudes and aggressive behavior only when he was outside the military cocoon, when he had to interact with people who were not intimidated by his rank and whom he could not browbeat into fear and submission. In November 2017 he scuffled physically with a Chinese security official in Beijing.[52] In February 2018, after a disagreement with a Trump advisor, Corey Lewandowski, he grabbed Lewandowski, who offered no resistance, by the collar and pushed him against a wall, *in the White House*.[53] In October 2018 he engaged in a profane argument over immigration policy with the new national security advisor, John Bolton, again inside the White House.[54] One former Trump official said that Kelly is "demonstrating his personality now, the way he really is."[55]

In October 2018, writing in *New York Magazine*, Olivia Nuzzi reported that members of Kelly's staff, who called him "general" or "chief," were disappointed in how he handled the resignation of Rob Porter, who was the president's staff secretary before Porter's two ex-wives accused him of physically abusing them. A former White House official said of Kelly, "Not only did he lie, he tried to get everybody else to lie. People had deferred to him because he was a four-star Marine general, served his country, Gold Star father—all of these things that made you think, What a patriotic upstanding American serving his country! I viewed him as this giant, four-star general, everything that goes along with that. He's very petty. He's a small man."[56]

In John Kelly, one finds the manifestation of the ignorance, hubris, and prejudice that are too common among American military leaders. General Kelly, the disciplinarian, and Lieutenant General McMaster, the former Vietnam truth-teller, were among the best the military could offer the nation. But they are well trained. Under pressure, their insecurity and arrogance catapults them into their comfort zone—loyalty over all else and, with Kelly, physical aggression: close ranks and attack the outsiders.

MILITARY INJUSTICE

The U.S. military has not shown that it can evolve to support the rule of law or free speech, which are the central girders of democracy. The officers' worship of hierarchy and the generals' thirst for control over other people are unlikely ever to change. That no two democratic nations have ever fought a war with each other, yet over the past seventy-five years America has become one of the most militaristic nations in history, indicates that the authoritarian U.S. military ethos cannot produce success in the modern world. The U.S. military's hierarchal structure and authoritarianism are abject relics, destructive in the extreme, ineffectual in a world where wars will be prevented or, if necessary, won or lost and democracies will be sustained or usurped depending on the ingenuity and equality of the people and their access to information.

On the way toward a military that reflects modernity and is respectful of humanitarian principles, with humility and reserve in its people and interventions, several significant steps should be taken to lessen the military's autonomy and its erosion of democratic principles and practices, all with a view toward bringing the military back to civilian society. The first obligation is with the people. America should ensure that it fights wars only in self-defense, which under modern norms and law means an imminent or actual attack on the nation. Adherence to this principle would have prevented U.S. involvement in Korea, Vietnam, and Iraq. The military action in Korea was authorized by the United Nations, but the primary reason the United States participated and provided over 80 percent of the troops was to oppose communism, not to prevent an attack on America. The war in Afghanistan would have ended within a year or two after 2001. Today the military uses broad congressional resolutions to decide for itself where to initiate combat, drone strikes, and targeted killings around the world. If those actions are necessary for America's security, then the people should approve the necessity, legality, and morality of them through their representatives' declaration of war. A declaration, instead of a mundane-sounding "resolution," would help everyone understand that the upcoming war will result in the deaths of hundreds of thousands or millions of people, as in America's most recent wars.

The return of such important decisions to the people cannot occur if generals remain standing at the pinnacle of the hierarchal military pyramid. No institution in the modern world can function effectively—and certainly not evolve to keep pace with change—with a few people with near absolute authority standing over everyone else.

Therefore, second, the hierarchal structure of the military should be dismantled. The number of variables that lead to success and the complexity of the challenges today cannot be assimilated, understood, and resolved by a few decision-makers. The military can no longer ignore the evidence-based research, thinking, operations, and norms of civilian society. The military institution should become flatter. Generals and officers, like head surgeons, who in a career directly confront far more life-and-death decisions than any military officer, should have higher levels of authority during actual (occurring) combat, but far less authority during planning stages and even less authority in garrison and everywhere else.

This reallocation of authority would make planning and decision-making more inclusive and therefore better utilize the abilities of soldiers and officers, instead of their having to wait around to implement the predilections of generals who make decisions with too little information and under conditions that do not allow for dissent or even discussion. The additional reforms noted below would help diminish groupthink and fear by redistributing authority. Thus, the third reform would remove commanders from the military legal system. Like everywhere else in American society, the legal system should be run by independent civilian professionals, with all citizens eligible to sit as jurors.

The Uniform Code of Military Justice, the military's penal law, should be abolished. Like everyone else, soldiers should be prosecuted in the courts of the state where they allegedly committed a crime. For alleged crimes in other countries or at sea, soldiers can be prosecuted under the general federal penal code or a code like that created for Washington, D.C., a federal enclave, with independent judges, prosecutors, and defense attorneys. In a modern world, battlefield trials and trials on ships are not necessary. The trial of Lieutenant William Calley, convicted of murdering twenty-two people in Vietnam, was held in 1971 at Fort Benning, Georgia. Nobody should have the right or disadvantage of being judged only by the people who work for the same employer, the condition that exists now for military personnel. Equality under law promotes democracy; a separate legal code for the military ensures separation from it.

In the current military legal system, commanders are hopelessly conflicted, compromised, and naturally biased, overseeing the entire process while possessing no legal expertise or experience, all the while wanting to protect their prestige and that of their units. Commanders or other high-ranking officers control judges, jurors, prosecutors, and defense attorneys; everyone is answerable to a military officer of higher rank who controls her or his career. The military culture even influences the top judges. The highest military court is the Court of Appeals for the Armed Forces, which, by having only civilian judges, is supposed to provide a buffer between accused soldiers and their commanders. However, it's the recommendation of the secretary of defense that is most influential in convincing the Senate whether to confirm judges to this court. This is a judicial system where everything is oriented around hierarchy. In 2019 all five "civilian" judges on the court were former military officers.

Contrast this with the civilian system, where authority and responsibility are dispersed among independent, freestanding juridical institutions (prosecutors, judges, jurors, and defense), none answerable for their livelihood to anyone within the others. In the military commanders alone determine whether any charge will be brought against any soldier. Commanders even select the particular soldiers and officers who will be jurors, and those jurors are dependent in their careers on pleasing their commander or his underlings. The commanders' authority and discretion are far too vast to be exercised by one person. This conflicted system is structured for arbitrariness and abuse. Indeed, on November 15, 2019, President Trump, illustrating the consequences of near worship of the military, reversed the Navy's discipline of SEAL Edward Gallagher for posing with a corpse; pardoned an army lieutenant who had been convicted of murder for ordering the killing of two civilians in Afghanistan; and pardoned an army major, Mathew L. Golsteyn (Class of '02), who was awaiting trial on a charge of murdering an unarmed Afghan. After the secretary of the navy, Richard V. Spencer, objected to Trump's lenient treatment of Gallagher, the secretary of defense, Mark Esper (Class of '86), at Trump's direction, forced Spencer to resign.

Fourth, the Judge Advocate General's Corps should be abolished across all branches and replaced with civilian attorneys from the Department of Justice. The JAGs are the military attorneys who provide legal authorizations to military commanders to do everything, including spending billions of dollars on weapons systems and conducting bombing runs. Calling it "operational law," the JAGs give commanders the go-ahead to drop bombs after concluding that the value of the bombing outweighs the number of innocent civilians who will be *unavoidably* killed. These kinds of decisions should be more reflective of the mores and values in all U.S. society, not those of people in the military, who represent a narrow swath of society.

No matter how competent, the JAG attorneys are also hopelessly conflicted; they are advising the very superior officers who have significant influence over their careers. Compressed by the weight of hierarchy, conformity, and obedience, these military lawyers do not press the application of law as zealously as do civilian lawyers. The incentives are not in place for them to do so, and they are as vulnerable to retaliation as anyone else in the military.

Moreover, all other American subcultures are accountable to democratically constituted prosecution offices, and there is no compelling reason why the military should be different. Police officers might argue that they are at great risk when called to a location where suspects are armed. But almost everyone would think it ridiculous if police departments had a separate corps of police-officer lawyers who only practice "police law" and only prosecute and defend police officers. But this is the military way, and it creates gross injustice. Instead, a cadre of civilian lawyers should be attached to the military. This would help integrate the military into civilian society and ensure that the generals and their decisions are more representative of American values and law.

NEW LEADERS

One of the most prominent reform-minded commentators on the military is author Tom Ricks, who has written well-regarded books on the modern and historical military. In his epilogue in *The Generals*, Ricks offers several recommendations.[57] Hovering over all of them is the sobering conclusion that the generals are more focused on their own careers, on bestowing favors or protecting fellow officers, and on shielding the military establishment from embarrassment than on defending the nation. In a book dedicated to "those who died following poor leaders," Ricks's final conclusion is perhaps the most disturbing in what it suggests is absent in the psyches of military officers: he recommends that military men and women should have to "abide by the belief that the lives of soldiers are more important than the careers of officers—and that winning wars is more important than either."[58]

Ricks's proposal to fire incompetent generals is on the mark as far as it goes, but it does not address the fundamental problem with military personnel today: the military does not contain officers capable of winning wars. The men and women who become generals and admirals are selected from a narrow, insular segment of society, and they receive conformist educations at the military academies and later at military schools. Of equal or greater importance, as a 2017 study on the decline of the "cognitive" abilities of officers in the army illustrates (discussed in the introduction and below), is that the intellectual capacity of army officers has deteriorated over the past hundred years, especially, and almost tragically, as the military institution has exploded in size and influence. "Between 1900 and 2016, the population of the United States increased threefold, while the size of the officer corps increased almost twenty-fivefold," according to the authors of the study, three social scientists on the faculty at West Point (Arthur T. Coumbe, Steven J. Condly, and William L. Skimmyhorn).[59]

"More than any single factor," the scientists argued, "intelligence ... predicts success or achievement in learning, training, education, workplace performance, health, income, and wealth."[60] Alarmingly, "the rigor of [the army's] intellectual screening mechanisms to control entry into the officer corps is low—and continues to decline," and its entry "standards have never been lower, at least in peacetime."[61] It's not exactly peacetime, but a hundred-year decline in the intellectual ability of army officers helps explain military failure in every war over the past seventy-five years.

The scientists chronicle the way intellectual standards at West Point have crumbled. "At West Point, the race to the bottom began immediately after the war [World War II] when ... the rigor in admissions tests was reduced."[62] Up until that time, the military-officer faculty at West Point had not been "elite" for over a hundred years, and in the 1940s and 1950s the student body began to join the faculty in their lack of ability. On academic achievement and aptitude tests, the cadets scored below the students at large state universities.[63]

Even as the collective intellectual ability of the cadets decreased, a November 2019 study—facilitated by West Point, coauthored by one of its psychology professors, and using ten years of West Point's own data—found that "cognitive ability [in cadets] emerged as the strongest predictor of academic and military grades . . . Cognitive ability was an especially strong predictor of academic GPA . . . and also, the best pretraining predictor of military GPA." Especially in recent years, West Point has been admitting lower-performing students despite knowing that other students with more ability would provide a greater benefit to the army and the nation.[64]

In the 1960s West Point "had to lower its academic standards to secure enough students,"[65] and in the early 1970s it "had to accept virtually every qualified candidate in order to make its enrollment quota."[66] From the 1970s into the 1990s, "West Point continued its qualitative decline."[67] Eventually the intellectual capacity of the student body at West Point hit bottom, and it remains there today. Some cadets produce test scores so low that they would barely qualify the cadets to enlist at the lowest ranks. "The worst year for the academy in this regard was 2006, when about 25 percent of its ASVAB [Armed Services Vocational Aptitude Battery] test takers fell below the minimum OCS [officer candidate school] mark." West Point accepted students "who scored in the Category IV range" on the test, "which in enlisted recruiting is the lowest allowable qualifying score."[68]

This is astonishing and frightening. Students admitted to West Point, who are barely qualified to enlist in the military, would seem to have little or no capacity as generals to make the tactical and strategic decisions necessary to win a war. With less competition from the poorer students, the top students will develop more slowly and will never fully actualize their potential, even as generals leading the prosecutions of wars. Equally alarming is that instead of raising its standards, West Point lowered the value of intelligence tests in admissions and increased the value of "non-cognitive" factors, amorphous measures that can be easily manipulated and are often created to favor someone or some group. The weight that West Point "accorded measures of mental ability or achievement (such as SAT scores and high school GPA)," according to Coumbe, Condly, and Skimmyhorn, "dropped from 60 to 55 percent while the weight attached to physical measures rose from 10 to 15 percent. It was a relatively small but very significant change."[69]

As the intellectual ability of officers in the army had been declining for a hundred years, West Point decided to allow the quality of the cadets to decline further. This occurred in part, according to Coumbe, Condly, and

Skimmyhorn as well as Joel Jebb—the director of English at the prep school, whose doctoral dissertation reported the same—because West Point wanted to increase the diversity of the student body, bring enlisted soldiers into the academy, and stock its athletic teams with players. The one single thing that military administrators at West Point could have done to improve the army—increasing the number of officers with greater intellectual capacity—they consciously decided not to do. This obviously makes no sense unless the officers who make these decisions are more concerned with protecting their and the military's image and their interests than in benefiting the nation.

America has been losing wars without realizing why. "This trend of deteriorating mental standards, strangely enough, has generally escaped the notice of social scientists and historians," the scientists from West Point comment.[70] Instead of reporting the intellectual hollowing-out of West Point and the military and turning to Americans for a solution, the military academies have lied about the problem. To pretend they were selective institutions and, thereby, to continue the massive financial support they receive from Congress, they claimed and continue to claim that their admissions acceptance rates are in the single or low double digits. The academies have been, in fact, admitting over 50 percent of their applicants, many of them exceptionally low academic performers. During the transition to lower standards and intellect, the military obtained unprecedented control over American life while its officers, who came from the narrowest segment of society, possessed ever-decreasing ability. It is a tyranny not of the elite but of some of the least capable.

CRIMINAL CADETS

The structure that creates the generals should be abandoned, the fifth necessary reform. The military academies should be transformed into national civilian universities. As currently constituted, they foster hubris, arrogance, favoritism, and mediocrity in the highest ranks of the military. The deficiency of the academies can be illustrated starkly by how many of their students are engaged in criminal activity, as well as the severity of the crimes.

The past and current superintendents of West Point, for example, had as their number-one priorities, respectively, the prevention of sexual assault by cadets and "force protection," identifying who among the cadets, professors, and staff members (or outsiders) might become "active shooters." In November 2018, in his first initiative, Lieutenant General Darryl A. Williams, who had become superintendent the previous summer, made mandatory a meeting where all faculty and staff were required to watch videos of actual murders in a restaurant and at a Walmart store, as well as a reenactment of mass murder in an office building. The academies are starting at such a low level—trying to prevent rape and homicide by cadets on campus—that it seems impossible they could evolve into institutions that recruit and develop top students and officers.

In 2017, at the Air Force Academy, sixteen criminal investigators were looking into sexual abuse, drug use, and hazing by cadets on the lacrosse team, after decades of the same behavior across the academy. Just a few months earlier, the superintendent at the time, Lieutenant General Michelle Johnson, had said that problems with academy athletes were in the rearview mirror, based on another, previous investigation. "Now they are our shining stars," said Johnson.[71] But yet a third investigation was under way at the academy concerning thirteen first-year cadets who allegedly cheated on "knowledge" tests. The tests were so simple and superficial (naming well-known military leaders) that the tests were not even counted when calculating grade-point averages. A spokesman for the academy said the investigations were necessary because "we develop leaders who will lead Airmen in the future."[72]

At the same time, West Point—and maybe this is the real reason why everyone there must watch videos of murders—appeared to have dodged a mass murder by one of its cadets. On November 16, 2017, in the early morning hours, a custodian found an empty weapons-storage box in a latrine on the sixth floor of Eisenhower "Ike" Hall. It contained a gun holster and empty boxes for bullets. Just hours earlier, in the auditorium of Ike Hall on the evening of November 15, the senior cadets had celebrated Branch Night—along with graduation day, one of the two most celebratory occasions of their four years at the academy.

On Branch Night, seniors receive a lecture from a prominent officer and then, with great fanfare, are permitted to open envelopes they have received from their tactical officers. The envelopes contain letters assigning the cadets to one of the seventeen branches in the army, such as infantry, aviation, armor, and field artillery. This assignment determines where they will live in the world, what role, if any, they will play in combat operations, and what people they will meet along the way and sometimes marry. It is a big deal.

The euphoria of Branch Night could not usually be dissipated by the 6:50 A.M. mandatory formation the next day. But on the morning of November 16, when the cadets wandered outside for formation, they were met by a phalanx of military police patrolling the grounds with loaded rifles. With no evidence as to who had left the weapons container in Ike Hall, the tactical officers did not know what cadets, if any, to trust or fear. The officers ordered the cadets into lines and marched them into the mess at Washington Hall. At least one cadet with murderous thoughts was marching and eating among them, and after breakfast he silently slipped into his usual seat in class.

Later in the day, after inspections and the execution of a search authorization (warrant), criminal investigators identified the owner of the weapons container, a senior who the night before had apparently enjoyed the Branch Night celebration while packing significant firepower. During a search, investigators found in his room two loaded handguns and fifteen hundred live rounds of ammunition, according to multiple sources. There was some speculation that the cadet would have opened fire in the auditorium if he had not received the branch assignment he requested. That theory dissipated some when investigators found the cadet's to-do list: a kill list in which he identified for assassination other cadets and at least one civilian athletic coach.

Not until five days later did the West Point chief of staff, Colonel Mark Bieger, open his letter to some in the West Point community with a familiar salutation: "Ladies and Gentlemen, I want to bring to your attention an ongoing criminal investigation involving a West Point cadet." Colonel Beiger did not mention the handguns, ammunition, or kill list. Publicly, Beiger apparently never referred to the cadet again, but a source indicated that the cadet pleaded guilty and received years in prison, a proceeding that was, of course, kept secret.

Just ten days before Branch Night, late in the morning on Sunday, November 5, 2017, air force veteran Devin Patrick Kelley, walked into a church in Sutherland Springs, Texas, and opened fire with an assault rifle. He killed twenty-six worshippers, shooting many of them in the back. In 2012, while in the air force, Kelley had been convicted of assaulting his wife and cracking the skull of his stepson, for which he served twelve months confinement.

Contrary to federal law, the air force did not report Kelley's domestic-assault conviction to a national database that, if checked, would have prevented Kelley from purchasing his assault rifle and other guns.[73] In a report after the mass killing at the church, the *New York Times* found, "The problem dates back decades. In 1996, the inspector general found that the Army, Navy and Air Force were failing to report the vast majority of convictions to the F.B.I. Federal agencies, unlike state and local ones, are required by law to report criminal records to the F.B.I. But in 2014, the inspector general found that the Defense Department still was not doing so."[74]

THE PROBLEM OF THE ACADEMIES

In a 2009 article, Tom Ricks recommended the elimination of military academies altogether. In "Why We Should Get Rid of West Point," an article in the *Washington Post*, he proposed: "Shut down West Point, Annapolis and the Air Force Academy, and use some of the savings to expand ROTC scholarships. After covering the U.S. military for nearly two decades, I've concluded that graduates of the service academies don't stand out compared to other officers . . . These institutions [including the military's war colleges] strike me as second-rate."[75]

While the current model at West Point and the academies should be abandoned, America is unlikely to find better officers through ROTC programs at other colleges; the standards to become an army officer, regardless of the source, have been declining for over a hundred years, as Arthur T. Coumbe and his social scientist colleagues at West Point have found.[76] The standards at West Point and in ROTC plummeted even further in the 2000s as they adopted "developmental" models, in which they accepted deficient, "at risk" students for any number of reasons. "The number of waivers for medical and physical reasons [through which to gain admission despite deficiencies] shot up sharply while test scores, especially the test scores of cadets on the lower edge of the quality distribution, sank [in

ROTC] . . . The Department of the Army became so concerned with the dropping quality of officer aspirants that it even considered converting the USMA [West Point] from a 4-year to a 3-year institution."[77] As Coumbe and his colleagues write in their summary, "The size of the Army, changing economic paradigms and the consequent decline of the prestige of an Army career, expansion of college aid, unbalanced college growth, competition from the other services, increasing emphasis placed on officer retention, and diversity considerations all help explain this trend."[78]

Amid the scientists' soft words is a sharp point: the officers currently in the U.S. military are not as competent as officers of past generations, and they are not capable, for lack of individual capacity or moral courage, of keeping America out of wars or winning the wars for which they are responsible.

Tom Ricks is not the first to argue that West Point is second-rate and should be closed. Edward L. King, a retired army lieutenant colonel and Korean War veteran who was disgusted with the Vietnam War and with the My Lai massacre and its cover-up, wrote in 1972 a book titled *The Death of the Army: A Pre-Mortem* and an opinion piece published in the *New York Times*. With reasoning that is as apt today as it was then, King argues that West Point "has played a primary role in creating an institutional system that has brought about the moral decay of the army and the failure of Vietnam. If public apathy lets this system remain largely unchanged, then we must be prepared for more Mylais probably both at home and abroad."[79]

Of course, as evidenced by U.S. soldiers' killing of innocent civilians in the new wars, in Haditha, Iraq, and the Maywand district in Afghanistan, for example, King's prediction has come true. His perspective was even more insightful in that when he wrote, he was unaware of the massacre of civilians at No Gun Ri in Korea and the SEALs' murders of women, children, and grandparents at Thanh Phong, in Vietnam, which did not become public knowledge until 1999 and 2001. Like Colonel Tony Herbert, whose career was destroyed by fellow army officers after he reported U.S. soldiers' war crimes in Vietnam, King recognized the destructive West Point culture:

The amorphous W.P.P.A. (West Point Protective Association)—the nickname applied in the Army officer corps to all West Point graduates working together to promote and protect each other's careers—has been in operation for decades . . . The corps has grown to the point where West Point graduates comprise slightly less than 4 per cent of the total active officer corps (yet make up more than 50 per cent of all general officers). All but two of the sixteen Army four-star generals now on active duty are West Pointers. It was not by accident that in 1968 [when My Lai occurred] . . . 22 of the 24 principal commanders and staff officers of the United States Army were graduates of West Point.[80]

The reasons for the diminution of quality in the military academies are many, but one primary reason is that their faculties are laden with unqualified teachers who are insiders: short-term military instructors without doctoral degrees who graduated from the academies to which they return and teach; civilian instructors who are former military officers hired by their friends; and military administrators consisting entirely of academy alumni, none of whom has ever held any job outside the military or worked in education. That this myopic, crony-inspired educational system has not changed since King wrote in 1972—in fact, it has changed little since the early 1800s—is ratification of West Point's role in disabling the American military: zero wins in nearly seventy-five years of continuous conflict. King describes the futility of this system:

West Point . . . has become an educational anachronism. The sterile educational environment and the narrow viewpoint of a chiefly alumni military faculty has served to continue the inbred characteristic of the West Point graduate. Most West Point officer-instructors hold only master's degrees . . . and teach only two or three years before being rotated to other Army duties . . . The major purpose of the West Point curriculum and the military faculty is more to indoctrinate loyal future members of the W.P.P.A. than to broadly educate them to be innovative thinkers. The United States Military Academy should be closed.[81]

The West Point that King describes in 1972 is identical to the one that exists today. In a four-year academic career, most cadets will be taught by civilian instructors in only a handful of the minimum of forty courses they will take. In all their other courses, the instructors will be inexperienced military officers who have never held a job outside the military. This cronyism has cascaded for generations and relies on outdated thinking and methods buried in the nineteenth century.

The academies should be repurposed and renamed to reflect broader missions (e.g. U.S. National University, West Point). The transformation could be completed in several years, after which all the students, admitted on the basis of merit and reflective of America, would be civilians who would receive broad educations, absent military training. In return, they would be obligated to work in government for five years, and some of them would be free to complete a year of military training, like the model used in the United Kingdom, before becoming an officer. The back-door prep schools discussed in chapter 2 of this volume should be eliminated altogether. Administrators and instructors in the new national universities should be selected solely on the basis of merit, not military experience. Finally, and obviously, in accord with the Constitution, national universities should be under civilian control.

America's generals and admirals do not possess and have not developed the requisite judgment, decision-making ability, and moral courage to sustain long-term success. This is why they keep losing. The Pentagon does not generally identify generals and admirals who have engaged in wrongdoing, and often permits them to retire with full honors. We don't even know how bad the situation is, although the unsuccessful and lost wars are pretty good indicators. The American military needs new leaders, leaders who will not come from within the old military establishment or its academies.

FREEDOM OF SPEECH

As the recent Devin Patrick Kelley tragedy at the church in Texas and the Branch Night scare demonstrated, even when the stakes are the lives of other people, the military adheres to its destructive code of silence. Military men and women are trained not to speak to the public or up the chain of command, even when circumstances demand it. In 2003 the United States invaded Iraq with absolutely no plan for how to maintain the peace after its "shock and awe" first act. Is it that no one had thought about it? Of course not. Many had. It's that no one felt comfortable questioning the military leadership about the lack of a plan. In this silence, the war moved forward.

In August and September of 2019 James Mattis, the former general and first secretary of defense under President Trump, was promoting his book *Call Sign Chaos: Learning to Lead.* Mattis, just eight months removed from government, was in a unique position to offer insight into the Trump administration. But he portrayed his reluctance to write and speak freely and fully as the product of a restrained and moderate military man. His unwillingness to reveal all he knew about President Trump's behavior and competence (positive or negative) left the nation with a less complete understanding of America's strengths and weaknesses. Mattis's philosophy seemed to be represented by one word: silence.

During an interview, Mattis asked a writer for *Vanity Fair* whether he knew "the French concept of *devoir de réserve* . . . the duty of silence," Mattis said, answering his own question. "If you leave an administration, you owe some silence."

The *Vanity Fair* writer, Jeffrey Goldberg, said, "But duty manifests in other ways. You have a First Amendment guarantee to speak your mind . . . And don't you have a duty to warn the country if it is endangered by its leader?"

Mattis said, "I didn't cook up a convenient tradition here. You don't endanger the country by attacking the elected commander in chief."

Mattis did not provide convincing support that silence is beneficial, but he seemed to have learned that loyalty in the form of silence is more important than full disclosure. This belief among military men and women is almost inalterable because they justify it as the natural extension of their patriotism and duty. Especially when the silence is from within someone like Mattis, who was entrusted with critical responsibilities, Americans are left bereft of many facts that they could otherwise use to operate their democracy.

Inside the current military system, the additional great impediments to success are the conformity and fear induced by the promise of criminal prosecution or threats to end the careers of those who dissent or speak up. Of course, this presupposes that military officers care more for their careers than their country, remaining silent and keeping their jobs rather than uttering the truth and possibly losing them. Therefore, sixth, this silence of the selfish should be ameliorated with a federal law requiring generals and admirals formally and publicly to register their dissent when they believe a war should not be fought or should be abandoned. This would signal to everyone that speaking up is a greater virtue than remaining silent. If Congress could not muster the will to require public disclosure, it could require the generals and admirals to register their dissent in closed congressional hearings, which are used today in other matters. In circumstances where speaking up could create a risk to lives (almost never), the publication of dissent could be delayed for a short time.

Some will argue that a law requiring generals and admirals to speak from their conscience will upset the regal military "chain of command," implying some greater but amorphous harm emanating from free speech. This criticism is an inapt remnant of an age when people desiring to control others would set up kingdoms, militaries, and religions to frighten people senseless and coerce obedience, as the U.S. military does today. America's generals have failed the nation for generations and should have their unmerited, career-advancing arrangements dismantled. Their systemic suppression of speech and truth to avoid embarrassment and to elevate their status should be ended.

Probably most generals and admirals knew the futility of fighting in Vietnam and invading Iraq, as well as continuing the war in Afghanistan. They remained and continue to remain silent today to protect their careers. With this new rule, the careers of generals would be protected, but for a better reason. Encouraging discussion and thereby limiting wars, rather than featherbedding the careers of generals and increasing the number and duration of wars, would benefit the nation. With military officers finally reporting to the nation instead of only to their direct superiors, Americans would become more aware of the facts for and against war. With that information, they could decide whether to start, fight, or end a war. This is what democracy looks like.

Without the freedom to speak, the commonplace retaliation that exists inside the military is so detrimental to the communication of truth that it should be made a criminal offense, the seventh necessary reform. In taking extraordinary steps to protect their status, many officers will hurt others who tell the truth. "Careerism is a potent force that serves as a catalyst for dishonesty," according to the authors of the 2015 study *Lying to Ourselves: Dishonesty in the Army Profession*.[82] A broader law than the one prohibiting retaliation against witnesses in criminal matters is necessary to encourage people to speak without fear they will lose their jobs and livelihoods for doing so. This would lead to more speech and more truthfulness.

In *Lying to Ourselves*, Leonard Wong and Stephen Gerras describe in their study the harm created by the conformist culture of the U.S. armed forces, particularly the army. In effect, they circle back to the beginning of the dysfunction in the military. As this archaic, authoritarian culture becomes more entrenched, the military has less ability to confront flexible adversaries who employ modern thinking, which increases the likelihood of losing more wars: "Unfortunately, the boundaries of this parallel ethical universe are slowly expanding into more and more of the [Army] profession. Ethical fading and rampant rationalizations have allowed leaders to espouse lofty professional values while slogging through the mire of dishonesty and deceit. The end result is a corrosive ethical culture that few acknowledge and even fewer discuss or work to correct. The Army urgently needs to address the corrupting influence of dishonesty in the Army profession."[83]

One army major quoted in the study described his discomfort with falsification and the harm it portended: "It's getting to the point where you're almost rewarded for being somebody you're not . . . We're creating an environment where everything is too rosy because everyone is afraid to paint the true picture. You just wonder where it will break, when it will fall apart."[84]

We need not wonder any longer. The time has arrived.

Even after generations of lost wars in which several million people have been killed when the United States intervened, the public continues to accept failure within the American military. This presages greater loss in the future. The remedy is for the people to reassert control over the military and reintegrate it into civil society. It's time for the nation to take back its armed forces—which are supposed to be protecting the citizens and their democracy. If civil society doesn't act to reform the military institution, we will all remain at the mercy of its failure.

ACKNOWLEDGMENTS

In writing this book, I have been supported by exceptional professionals. Bloomsbury executive editor Anton Mueller believed in the importance of this book and, more precisely than anyone, could see how the large number of variables that lead to military or government failure can be isolated and organized. With patience, persistence, and commitment, Anton showed me how to explain what is truly difficult to understand: how things that happen inside America affect whether the nation's wars are won or lost. On more than one occasion, Anton showed the way, and without him I would not have made it to the finish.

I'm enormously grateful that I can entrust my most important work to my agent, Jeff Ourvan of the Jennifer Lyons Literary Agency. Jeff's superb judgment, mentorship, and friendship along the way have meant everything to me. He had the highest expectations for the book and offered encouragement and solutions whenever I needed them. Along with his expertise in just about everything related to writing and publishing, Jeff's determination, good will, and spirit inspired me, and I want to express my deepest appreciation.

I was the beneficiary of the remarkable analytic and organizational skill of the book's editorial consultant, Jon Sternfeld. He marshalled the facts and showed where they should be placed and which of them should be discarded. Jon is an extraordinary teacher. Learning from Jon was one of the bright moments in my career.

Laura Phillips, the managing editor, brought the book and everyone together in the end and ensured it represented what I wanted to say. Her clarity and resolve brought us to the end of this project, and I am enormously grateful.

Miranda Ottewell, the book's copy editor, made the art of writing seem like a science, in the best possible way. When Miranda said a sentence should be clarified, I knew she must be correct. Miranda helped me become confident that the reader will understand the meaning I was trying to convey.

I am grateful to Morgan Jones, the editorial assistant, who cared about this book and ensured we met our goals. Morgan moved us from point to point, saving all of us a great deal of time while ensuring we were headed in the right direction.

I also want to thank the Bloomsbury creative, art, public relations, and marketing teams for their commitment to bringing this book to the reader.

NOTES

Some of the internet links in the endnotes may have been broken, and some websites may have been taken down or revised. The views expressed in this book are those of the author and do not reflect the official policy or position of the Department of the Army, the Department of Defense, or the U.S. government. The information in this book is from open sources.

INTRODUCTION: BREAKING THE MYTH

1. George Packer, *The Assassins' Gate: America in Iraq* (New York: Farrar, Straus and Giroux, 2005), 148.

2. James Fallows, "The Tragedy of the American Military," *Atlantic*, January/February 2015, http://www.theatlantic.com/features/archive/2014/12/the-tragedy-of-the-american-military/383516.

3. Eyder Peralta, "Pentagon Paid Sports Teams Millions For 'Paid Patriotism' Events," *The Two-Way* (blog), NPR, November 5, 2015, https://www.npr.org/sections/thetwo-way/2015/11/05/454834662/pentagon-paid-sports-teams-millions-for-paid-patriotism-events.

4. James McCartney with Molly Sinclair McCartney, *America's War Machine: Vested Interests, Endless Conflicts* (New York: Thomas Dunne, 2015), 20.

5. Noah Shachtman, "27,000 Work in Pentagon PR and Recruiting," *Wired*, February 5, 2009, https://www.wired.com/2009/02/27000-work-in-p (quoting an Associated Press report).

6. Chalmers Johnson, *Nemesis: The Last Days of the American Republic* (New York: Metropolitan Books, 2006), 138.

7. David Vine, "Where in the World Is the U.S. Military?" *Politico*, July/August 2015, https://www.politico.com/magazine/story/2015/06/us-military-bases-around-the-world-119321; Daniel Brown and Skye Gould, "The U.S. Has 1.3 Million Troops Stationed around the World—Here Are the Major Hotspots," *Business Insider*, August 31, 2017, http://www.businessinsider.com/us-military-deployments-may-2017-5.

8. Linda J. Bilmes, "The Military Budget Needs a True Accountability Assessment," *New York Times*, September 6, 2012, https://www.nytimes.com/roomfordebate/2011/05/08/how-to-cut-the-military/the-military-budget-needs-a-true-accountability-assessment.

9. Roxana Tiron, "Trump Seeks $639 Billion for Defense Department, Up 10%," *Bloomberg*, March 16, 2017, https://www.bloomberg.com/news/articles/2017-03-16/trump-seeks-639-billion-for-defense-department-a-10-increase.

10. Adam Taylor and Laris Karklis, "This Remarkable Chart Shows How U.S. Defense Spending Dwarfs the Rest of the World," *Washington Post*, February 9, 2016, https://www.washingtonpost.com/news/worldviews/wp/2016/02/09/this-remarkable-chart-shows-how-u-s-defense-spending-dwarfs-the-rest-of-the-world.

11. Todd Harrison, *Analysis of the FY 2017 Defense Budget* (Washington, D.C.: Center for Strategic and International Studies, 2016), 1, https://defense360.csis.org/wp-content/uploads/2016/08/Analysis-of-the-FY-2017-Budget.pdf.

12. John Mueller, "War Has Almost Ceased to Exist: An Assessment," *Political Science Quarterly* 124, no. 2 (2009): 298, https://politicalscience.osu.edu/faculty/jmueller/THISPSQ.pdf.

13. Andrew Bacevich, *Breach of Trust: How Americans Failed Their Soldiers and Their Country* (New York: Metropolitan Books, 2013), 111.

14. John Mueller, "War Has Almost Ceased to Exist," 312.

15. David E. Cunningham and Douglas Lemke, "Combining Civil and Interstate Wars," *International Organization* 67 (2013): 611, 623–25.

16. Dominic Tierney, *How We Fight: Crusades, Quagmires, and the American Way of War* (New York: Little, Brown, 2010), 41.

17. John W. Dower, *The Violent American Century: War and Terror since World War II* (Chicago: Haymarket Books, 2017), 103.

18. Tierney, *How We Fight*, 41.

19. Dower, *Violent American Century*, 104.

20. Andrew Bacevich, *The Limits of Power: The End of American Exceptionalism* (New York: Metropolitan Books, 2008), 130.

21. Dower, *Violent American Century*, 90.

22. Michael R. Gordon, "Pentagon Inquiry Blames ISIS for Civilian Deaths in Mosul Strike," *New York Times*, May 25, 2017, https://www.nytimes.com/2017/05/25/us/politics/mosul-us-airstrike-civilian-deaths-isis-pentagon.html.

23. Bacevich, *Limits of Power*, 147–48.

24. Arthur T. Coumbe, Steven J. Condly, and William L. Skimmyhorn, *Still Soldiers and Scholars? An Analysis of Army Officer Testing* (Carlisle, PA: U.S. Army War College Press, 2017), xix–xx, 6, https://ssi.armywarcollege.edu/pdffiles/PUB1374.pdf.

25. Ibid., 354, 351.

26. Neil Sheehan, *A Bright Shining Lie: John Paul Vann and America in Vietnam* (New York: Random House, 1988), 452.

27. Anna Fifield, "Why Does North Korea Hate the United States? Let's Go Back to the Korean War," *Washington Post*, May 17, 2017, https://www.washingtonpost.com/news/worldviews/wp/2017/05/17/why-does-north-korea-hate-the-united-states-lets-go-back-to-the-korean-war/?utm_term=.c82908d2bf4a.

28. Blaine Harden, "Rocket Man Knows Better," *New York Times*, September 23, 2017, https://www.nytimes.com/2017/09/23/opinion/sunday/trump-kim-jong-un.html.

29. Tom O'Connor, "What War with North Korea Looked Like in the 1950s and Why It Matters Now," *Newsweek*, May 4, 2017, http://www.newsweek.com/us-forget-korean-war-led-crisis-north-592630.

30. Justin McCurry, "Why Are North Korea's Leaders Specifically Threatening U.S. Bombers?" *Guardian*, September 26, 2017, https://www.theguardian.com/world/2017/sep/26/why-are-north-koreas-leaders-specifically-threatening-us-bombers.

31. Mark H. Odonoghue, "Professors Claim Invasion Violated International Law," *Harvard Crimson*, May 4, 1970, http://www.thecrimson.com/article/1970/5/4/professors-claim-invasion-violated-international-law.

32. Neil Sheehan, *Bright Shining Lie*, 285.

33. U.S. National Archives, "Vietnam War U.S. Military Fatal Casualty Statistics," August 2013, https://www.archives.gov/research/military/vietnam-war /casualty-statistics.

34. Neta C. Crawford, "What Is War Good For? Background Ideas and Assumptions about the Legitimacy, Utility, and Costs of Offensive War," *British Journal of Politics and International Relations* 18, no. 2 (2016): 283, 282–99.

35. Associated Press, "A Timeline of U.S. Troop Levels in Afghanistan since 2001," *Military Times*, July 6, 2016, https://www.militarytimes.com/news/your-military /2016/07/06/a-timeline-of-u-s-troop-levels-in-afghanistan-since-2001.

36. Andreas Wimmer, *Waves of War: Nationalism, State Formation, and Ethnic Exclusion in the Modern World* (Cambridge, UK: Cambridge University Press, 2013), 34.

37. This was the same day that Bush announced the end of major combat operations in Iraq, a widely mocked event.

38. "The U.S. War in Afghanistan, 1999–2019," Council on Foreign Relations, https://www.cfr.org/timeline/us-war-afghanistan.

39. National Intelligence Council, *National Intelligence Estimate: The Terrorist Threat to the U.S. Homeland* (Washington, D.C.: National Intelligence Council, 2007), https://www.dni.gov/files/documents/Newsroom/Press%20Releases /2007%20Press%20Releases/20070717_release.pdf.

40. Griff Witte, "Afghanistan War, 2001–2014," Encyclopaedia Britannica Online, https://www.britannica.com/event/Afghanistan-War.

41. Rod Nordland and Joseph Goldstein, "Afghan Taliban's Reach Is Widest since 2001, U.N. Say," *New York Times*, October 11, 2015, http://www.nytimes.com /2015/10/12/world/asia/afghanistan-taliban-united-nations.html; and Mark Mazzetti and Matt Apuzzo, "Inquiry Weighs Whether ISIS Analysis Was Distorted," *New York Times*, August 25, 2015, http://www.nytimes.com/2015/08 /26/world/middleeast/pentagon-investigates-allegations-of-skewed-intelligence -reports-on-isis.html.

42. Greg Jaffe and Missy Ryan, "The U.S. Was Supposed to Leave Afghanistan by 2017. Now It Might Take Decades," *Washington Post*, January 26, 2016, https://www.washingtonpost.com/news/checkpoint/wp/2016/01/26/the-u-s -was-supposed-to-leave-afghanistan-by-2017-now-it-might-take-decades.

43. Mark Landler, Eric Schmitt, and Michael R. Gordon, "Trump Aides Recruited Businessmen to Devise Options for Afghanistan," *New York Times*, July 10, 2017, https://www.nytimes.com/2017/07/10/world/asia/trump-afghanistan -policy-erik-prince-stephen-feinberg.html.

44. "Full Transcript and Video: Trump's Speech on Afghanistan," *New York Times*, August 21, 2017, https://www.nytimes.com/2017/08/21/world/asia/trump -speech-afghanistan.html.

45. Richard A. Clarke, *Against All Enemies* (New York: Free Press, 2004), 30–31.

46. Thomas E. Ricks, *Fiasco: The American Military Adventure in Iraq* (New York: Penguin, 2006), 15.

47. "Colin Powell Tops 4th of July List of Most Admired Americans According to New Poll Commissioned by the Fraternal Order of the Eagles (FOE)," *CISION*, July 3, 2014, https://www.prweb.com/releases/2014/07/prweb11995226.htm.

48. Jonathan Schwarz, "Lie after Lie after Lie: What Colin Powell Knew Ten Years Ago Today and What He Said," *Huffington Post*, April 7, 2013, http://www .huffingtonpost.com/jonathan-schwarz/colin-powell-wmd-iraq-war_b_ 2624620.html.

49. Ibid.

50. Ricks, *Fiasco*, 90.

51. "Factbox: Iraq War, the Notable Quotes," Reuters, March 11, 2008, https://www .reuters.com/article/us-iraq-war-quotes/factbox-iraq-war-the-notable-quotes -idUSL2127625200803110.

52. Frank Rich, *The Greatest Story Ever Sold: The Decline and Fall of Truth from 9/11 to Katrina* (New York: Penguin, 2006), 75.

53. Bob Woodward, *Plan of Attack* (New York: Simon & Schuster, 2004), 414.

54. Ricks, *Fiasco*, 115.

55. Packer, *Assassins' Gate*, 166.

56. Melvin A. Goodman, *National Insecurity: The Cost of American Militarism* (San Francisco: City Lights, 2013), 15.

57. "U.S. and Allied Killed and Wounded," Costs of War, Watson Institute, Brown University, 2018, https://watson.brown.edu/costsofwar/costs/human/military.

58. "Casualty Status," U.S. Department of Defense, https://dod.defense.gov/News /Casualty-Status. See also "Casualties in Iraq," Antiwar.com, http://antiwar .com/casualties, and "Operation Iraqi Freedom" and "Operation Enduring Freedom," icasualties.org, http://www.icasualties.org.

59. Rosa Brooks, *How Everything Became War and the Military Became Everything: Tales from the Pentagon* (New York: Simon & Schuster, 2016), 99.

60. Captain Sara Knutson (Afghanistan) was in criminal law. Lieutenants Benjamin Britt and Dennis Zilinski (Iraq) were in constitutional and military law. Captains Jonathan Edds (Iraq) and Andrew Pedersen-Keel (Afghanistan) and Lieutenant Phil Neel (Iraq) were in the thesis course, which I directed; other instructors were their advisors.

61. Richard K. Betts, *American Force: Dangers, Delusions, and Dilemmas in National Security* (New York: Columbia University Press, 2012), 5.

62. Ibid., 148.

63. Linda J. Bilmes, "The Financial Legacy of Iraq and Afghanistan: How Wartime Spending Decisions Will Constrain Future National Security Budgets" (HKS Faculty Research Working Paper Series RWP13-006, Harvard Kennedy School, Cambridge, MA, 2013), https://www.hks.harvard.edu/publications/financial -legacy-iraq-and-afghanistan-how-wartime-spending-decisions-will-constrain.

64. Associated Press, "Polls Finds [sic] Many View Afghan, Iraq Wars as Failures," *Boston Globe*, August 2, 2014, http://www.bostonglobe.com/news/nation/2014 /08/01/polls-finds-many-view-afghan-iraq-wars-failures/hFfH2aMpV19lr VIOZMBuwL/story.html.

65. National Intelligence Council, *Mapping the Global Future: Report of the National Intelligence Council's 2020 Project Based on Consultations with Nongovernmental Experts around the World* (Washington, D.C.: National Intelligence Council, 2004), 83, https://www.dni.gov/files/documents/Global%20Trends_Mapping%20 the%20Global%20Future%202020%20Project.pdf.

66. Tim Arango, "Iran Dominates in Iraq After U.S. 'Handed the Country Over,'" *New York Times*, July 15, 2017, https://www.nytimes.com/2017/07/15/world /middleeast/iran-iraq-iranian-power.html.

67. *Parker v. Levy*, 417 U.S. 733, 736–37 (1974).

68. Ibid., 743.

69. *Goldman v. Weinberger*, 475 U.S. 503, 507 (1986).

70. *Solorio v. U.S.*, 483 U.S. 435 (1987).

71. Francis Fukuyama, *Political Order and Political Decay* (New York: Farrar, Straus and Giroux, 2014), 518–19.

72. Harry Truman, "Radio and Television Address to the American People on the Situation in Korea," July 19, 1950, in the American Presidency Project archives, UC Santa Barbara, https://www.presidency.ucsb.edu/documents/radio-and -television-address-the-american-people-the-situation-korea.

73. Adrian R. Lewis, *The American Culture of War: The History of U.S. Military Force from World War II to Operation Iraqi Freedom* (New York: Routledge, 2007), 377, cited in Richard Swain, "Review," *Journal of Military History* 71, no. 4 (2007): 1329–30, https://muse.jhu.edu/article/222558.

74. George W. Bush, Presidential News Conference, October 11, 2001, CSPAN video clip, https://www.c-span.org/video/?c4552776/bush-shopping-quote.

75. Bacevich, *Breach of Trust*, 33.

76. Tom Shanker, "At West Point, a Focus on Trust," *New York Times*, May 21, 2011, https://www.nytimes.com/2011/05/22/us/22mullen.html.

77. Rosa Brooks, "Generals Are from Mars: Their Bosses Are from Venus," *Foreign Policy*, July 25, 2012, https://foreignpolicy.com/2012/07/25/generals-are-from -mars-their-bosses-are-from-venus.

CHAPTER 1: THE ORIGINS OF THE SEPARATE WORLD

1. Robert Kagan, *Of Paradise and Power* (New York: Alfred A. Knopf, 2003), 10.

2. Christopher Hamner, "American Resistance to a Standing Army," National History Education Clearinghouse, 2018, http://teachinghistory.org/history -content/ask-a-historian/24671.

3. Lawrence Hunter, "Both James Madison and the Anti-Federalists Were Right about Standing Armies," *Forbes*, July 29, 2012, https://www.forbes.com/sites

/lawrencehunter/2012/07/29/both-james-madison-and-the-anti-federalists
-were-right-about-standing-armies/#16ddf89375a0.

4. David Leonhardt, "The Monopolization of America," *New York Times*,
November 25, 2018, https://www.nytimes.com/2018/11/25/opinion/monopolies
-in-the-us.html.

5. Jesse Greenspan, "9 Things You May Not Know about the U.S. Armed Forces,"
History, September 29, 2014, https://www.history.com/news/9-things-you
-may-not-know-about-the-u-s-armed-forces.

6. Department of Defense, Selected Manpower Statistics, Fiscal Year 1997, 46–53,
table 2-11, http://www.alternatewars.com/BBOW/Stats/DOD_SelectedStats_
FY97.pdf.

7. James Madison, speech before the Constitutional Convention, June 29, 1787,
Avalon Project, http://avalon.law.yale.edu/18th_century/debates_629.asp.

8. Andrew Bacevich, *Breach of Trust: How Americans Failed Their Soldiers and Their
Country* (New York: Metropolitan Books, 2013), 81.

9. David Coleman, "U.S. Military Personnel, 1954–2014," https://historyinpieces
.com/research/us-military-personnel-1954-2014#fnref-5821-fn1; and U.S.
Department of Defense, Selected Manpower Statistics, 46–53.

10. Richard F. Grimmett, *Instances of Use of United States Armed Forces Abroad,
1798–1999*, CRS Report R41677 (Washington, D.C.: Congressional Research
Service, 1999), 3, https://www.pegc.us/archive/DoD/docs/RL30172.pdf.

11. Ronan Farrow, *War on Peace: The End of Diplomacy and the Decline of American
Influence* (New York: W.W. Norton, 2018), xxi.

12. Ibid., xxi.

13. Barbara Torreon, *Instances of Use of United States Armed Forces Abroad, 1798–
2017*, CRS Report R42738 (Washington, D.C.: Congressional Research Service,
2017), https://www.everycrsreport.com/reports/R42738.html.

14. "About the U.S. Department of Defense," U.S. Department of Defense,
January 27, 2017, https://www.defense.gov/About.

15. Ibid. See also K. K. Rebecca Lai, Troy Griggs, Max Fisher, and Audrey Carlsen,
"Is America's Military Big Enough?" *New York Times*, March 22, 2017,

https://www.nytimes.com/interactive/2017/03/22/us/is-americas-military-big
-enough.html.

16. Christopher Mann and Hannah Fischer, *Recent Trends in Active-Duty Military Deaths, CRS In Focus IF10899* (Washington, D.C.: Congressional Research Service, 2018), updated May 20, 2019, https://fas.org/sgp/crs/natsec/IF10899.pdf.

17. Chris Whipple, *The Gatekeepers: How the White House Chiefs of Staff Define Every Presidency* (New York: Crown, 2017), 274.

18. James Madison, "Political Observations," National Archives, April 20, 1795, https://founders.archives.gov/documents/Madison/01-15-02-0423.

19. Missy Ryan, "'There Have to Be Limits': Guantanamo Attorneys Challenge Lifetime Imprisonment without Charge," *Washington Post*, July 11, 2018, https://www.washingtonpost.com/world/national-security/there-have-to-be -limits-lawyers-for-guantanamo-inmates-challenge-lifetime-imprisonment -without-charge/2018/07/11/f3933faa-8533-11e8-9e80-403a221946a7_story.html.

20. Ellen Mitchell, "The Pentagon's Battle of the Bands," *Politico*, May 22, 2016, https://www.politico.com/story/2016/05/pentagons-bands-battle-223435.

21. The entire program for a cadet could be completed in a few months, which enabled the first class to graduate in 1802.

22. One exception in World War II might be George Marshall, who graduated from the Virginia Military Institute. See Mark Atwood Lawrence, "'George Marshall,' by Debi and Irwin Unger with Stanley Hirshson," *New York Times*, November 26, 2014, http://www.nytimes.com/2014/11/30/books/review/george -marshall-by-debi-and-irwin-unger-with-stanley-hirshson.html. The Marshall Plan, which helped reinvigorate Europe after World War II, was possibly America's greatest foreign policy success. On the other hand, Marshall was also behind one of America's greatest foreign policy failures, "the 1946 Marshall Mission to China, which attempted to mediate between the Communists and the Nationalists." See Chalmers Johnson, *The Sorrows of Empire: Militarism, Secrecy, and the End of the Republic* (New York: Henry Holt, 2004), 53–54.

23. Michael S. Rosenwald, "The Truth about Confederate Gen. Robert E. Lee: He Wasn't Very Good at His Job," *Washington Post*, October 13, 2018, https://www .washingtonpost.com/news/retropolis/wp/2017/05/19/the-truth-about -confederate-gen-robert-e-lee-he-wasnt-very-good-at-his-job.

24. Mark Greenbaum, "Lincoln's Do-Nothing Generals," *New York Times*, November 27, 2011, http://opinionator.blogs.nytimes.com/2011/11/27/lincolns -do-nothing-generals.

25. Wayne A. Hall, "Point's Reconciliation Plaza Honors Army's War Dead," *Times Herald-Record*, October 6, 2001, http://www.recordonline.com/article /20011006/news/310069988.

26. The Air Force Academy was founded in 1954.

27. Bruce Fleming, "The Academies' March toward Mediocrity," *New York Times*, May 20, 2010, https://www.nytimes.com/2010/05/21/opinion/21fleming .html.

28. See Theodore J. Crackel, *West Point: A Bicentennial History* (Lawrence: University Press of Kansas, 2002), 277–80; and Association of Graduates, USMA Leadership (West Point, NY: U.S. Military Academy, 2013), https://www .westpointaog.org/document.doc?id=5614.

29. There were a few exceptions to the schedule in that time.

30. See *Tim Bakken v. Department of the Army*, United States of American Merit Systems Protection Board, July 5, 2012, 7, http://mspbwatch.files.wordpress .com/2013/03/bakken-v-army-initial-decision.pdf. See also Michael Randall, "Ruling: Point Retaliated against Professor Alleging Improper Compensation," *Times Herald Record*, July 19, 2012, http://www.recordonline.com/apps /pbcs.dll/article?AID=/20120719/NEWS/207190326; and Joan Johnson-Freese, *Educating America's Military* (New York: Routledge, 2013), 73.

31. *Bakken v. Army*, 7.

32. Ibid., 11.

33. As far as I know, I'm the only civilian instructor ever to litigate against the academy.

34. *Bakken v. Army*, 11. In 2015, a new army inspector general issued a report removing "adverse information" against Ryan from its database on the ground that the administrative judge had found only that West Point retaliated, given that Ryan was not listed in the case title as a party. The Merit Systems Protection Board prohibits listing the names of individuals. U.S. Army Inspector General Reconsideration Review, Case 15-00042, May 29, 2015.

35. Bob Woodward, *Plan of Attack* (New York: Simon & Schuster, 2004), 17.

36. *Hohri v. U.S.*, 782 F.2d 227, 231 (D.C. Cir. 1986), vacated; *U.S. v. Hohri*, 482 U.S. 64 (1987).

37. Johnson, *Sorrows of Empire*, 53. Johnson wrote before President Barack Obama relieved General Stanley McChrystal in 2010.

38. Avalon Project, "Military-Industrial Complex Speech, Dwight D. Eisenhower, 1961," Yale Law School, http://avalon.law.yale.edu/20th_century /eisenhower001.asp.

39. David Barstow, "Behind TV Analysts, Pentagon's Hidden Hand," *New York Times*, April 20, 2008, https://www.nytimes.com/2008/04/20/us/20generals .html.

40. Bryan Bender, "From the Pentagon to the Private Sector," *Boston Globe*, December 26, 2010, http://archive.boston.com/news/nation/articles/2010/12 /26/defense_firms_lure_retired_generals.

41. Stephen Daggett, *Costs of Major U.S. Wars* (Washington, D.C.: Congressional Research Service, 2010), 2, https://fas.org/sgp/crs/natsec/RS22926.pdf.

42. "NCI Budget and Appropriations," National Cancer Institute, https://www .cancer.gov/about-nci/budget#current-year.

43. "Cancer Statistics," National Cancer Institute, https://www.cancer.gov/about -cancer/understanding/statistics.

44. Dina Rasor, "The Pentagon's Biggest Overrun: Way Too Many Generals," *Truthout*, January 5, 2012, http://www.truth-out.org/opinion/item/5920:the -pentagons-biggest-overrun-way-too-many-generals.

45. James McCartney with Molly Sinclair McCartney, *America's War Machine: Vested Interests, Endless Conflicts* (New York: Thomas Dunne, 2015), 87.

46. James Fallows, "The Tragedy of the American Military," *Atlantic*, January/ February 2015, http://www.theatlantic.com/features/archive/2014/12/the -tragedy-of-the-american-military/383516.

47. McCartney, *America's War Machine*, 135.

48. Lee Fang, "Emails Show Close Ties Between Heritage Foundation and Lock-heed Martin," *The Intercept*, September 15, 2015, https://theintercept.com/2015 /09/15/heritage-foundation.

49. Valerie Insinna, "Inside America's Dysfunctional Trillion-Dollar Fighter-Jet Program," *New York Times*, August 21, 2019, https://www.nytimes.com/2019/08/21/magazine/f35-joint-strike-fighter-program.html.

50. McCartney, *America's War Machine*, 7.

51. Great Lakes Systems and Technology, "GLS&T a United States Military Academy Project Day Sponsor," http://www.gl-systems-technology.net/united-states-military-academy-project-day-sponsor.html. See also Association of Graduates, West Point Donor Stories (West Point, NY: U.S. Military Academy, 2012), https://www.westpointaog.org/WestPointDonorStories.

52. "Proposed Course of Action re: Vietnam," draft memorandum from McNaughton to Robert McNamara, March 24, 1965, *The Pentagon Papers*, Mike Gravel, ed., 3: 694–702, available at https://www.mtholyoke.edu/acad/intrel/pentagon3/doc253.htm.

53. Whipple, *Gatekeepers*, 17–18.

54. Ibid., 20.

55. Robert Scheer, "McNamara's Evil Lives On," *Huffington Post*, July 8, 2009, http://www.huffingtonpost.com/robert-scheer/mcnamaras-evil-lives-on_b_227522.html.

56. Thomas E. Ricks, *The Generals: American Military Command from World War II to Today* (New York: Penguin, 2012), 13.

57. See generally George Packer, *The Assassins' Gate* (New York: Farrar, Straus and Giroux, 2005).

58. Kevin Gosztola, "MSNBC's 'Hubris' Documentary: Overlooking the Role of Media in Selling the Iraq War," *Dissenter*, February 19, 2013, http://dissenter.firedoglake.com/2013/02/19/msnbcs-hoax-documentary-overlooking-the-role-of-media-in-selling-iraq-war. See also David Corn, "'Hubris': New Documentary Reexamines the Iraq War 'Hoax,'" *Mother Jones*, February 16, 2013, https://www.motherjones.com/politics/2013/02/hubris-rachel-maddow-documentary-iraq-war-david-corn.

59. Frank Rich, *The Greatest Story Ever Sold: The Decline and Fall of Truth from 9/11 to Katrina* (New York: Penguin, 2006), 13.

60. "A Timeline of the Iraq War," *ThinkProgress*, May 17, 2006, https://thinkprogress
.org/a-timeline-of-the-iraq-war-6622633720be.

61. George Bush, "President's Remarks in 'Focus on Education with President
Bush' Event," White House press release, September 27, 2004, https://george
wbush-whitehouse.archives.gov/news/releases/2004/09/20040927-4.html.

62. Mujib Mashal and Eric Schmitt, "White House Orders Direct Taliban Talks to
Jump-Start Afghan Negotiations," *New York Times*, July 15, 2018, https://www
.nytimes.com/2018/07/15/world/asia/afghanistan-taliban-direct-negotiations.html.

63. "Operation Iraqi Freedom" and "Operation Enduring Freedom," icasualties
.org, http://www.icasualties.org.

64. Thomas E. Ricks, *Fiasco: The American Military Adventure in Iraq* (New York:
Penguin, 2006), 33.

65. Ibid.

66. Woodward, *Plan of Attack*, 413.

67. George Bush, "Bush Delivers Graduation Speech at West Point," White
House press release, June 1, 2002, https://georgewbush-whitehouse.archives
.gov/news/releases/2002/06/20020601-3.html.

68. Walter Pincus, "Dick Cheney Wants to Forget History and Write His Own
Version," *Washington Post*, June 19, 2014, https://www.washingtonpost.com
/world/national-security/dick-cheney-wants-to-forget-history-and-write-his
-own-version/2014/06/19/9accbaaa-f71a-11e3-a3a5-42be35962a52_story.html.

69. Kerry Sheridan, "Iraq Death Toll Reaches 500,000 Since Start of U.S.-Led
Invasion, New Study Says," *Huffington Post*, October 15, 2013, https://www
.huffingtonpost.com/2013/10/15/iraq-death-toll_n_4102855.html.

70. Ricks, *Fiasco*, 68–69.

71. Richard K. Betts, *American Force: Dangers, Delusions, and Dilemmas in National
Security* (New York: Columbia University Press, 2012), 202.

72. Farrow, *War on Peace*, 67.

73. Ibid., xxvi.

74. Robert Costa and Philip Rucker, "Military Leaders Consolidate Power in
Trump Administration," *Washington Post*, August 22, 2017, https://www

.washingtonpost.com/politics/military-leaders-consolidate-power-in-trump
-administration/2017/08/22/db4f7bee-875e-11e7-a94f-3139abce39f5_story
.html.

75. Lee Fang, "Meet Mike Pompeo: The Congressional Candidate Spawned by
the 'Kochtopus,'" *ThinkProgress*, September 21, 2010, https://thinkprogress.org
/meet-mike-pompeo-the-congressional-candidate-spawned-by-the-kochtopus
-2b5530a2e2ac.

76. Costa and Rucker, "Military Leaders Consolidate Power."

77. Michael R. Gordon, "Trump Shifting Authority over Military Operations
Back to Pentagon," *New York Times*, March 19, 2017, https://www.nytimes.com
/2017/03/19/us/trump-shifting-authority-over-military-operations-back-to
-pentagon.html.

78. Ibid.

79. Barbara Starr and Ryan Browne, "Mattis Confirms White House Has Given
Him Authority to Set Afghanistan Troop Levels," CNN, June 14, 2017,
https://www.cnn.com/2017/06/13/politics/pentagon-afghanistan-troop-levels
/index.html.

80. Charlie Savage and Eric Schmitt, "Trump Poised to Drop Some Limits on
Drone Strikes and Commando Raids," *New York Times*, September 21, 2017,
https://www.nytimes.com/2017/09/21/us/politics/trump-drone-strikes
-commando-raids-rules.html.

81. "What Went Wrong in the Deadly Raid on al-Qaida in Yemen?" *PBS News-
Hour*, February 2, 2017, https://www.pbs.org/newshour/show/went-wrong
-deadly-raid-al-qaida-yemen.

82. Ayesha Rascoe, "U.S. Military Probing More Possible Civilian Deaths in
Yemen Raid," Reuters, February 1, 2017, https://www.reuters.com/article/us
-usa-trump-commando-idUSKBN15G5RX.

83. Cynthia McFadden, William M. Arkin, Ken Dilanian, and Robert
Windrem, "Yemen SEAL Raid Has Yielded No Significant Intelligence:
Officials," NBC News, February 27, 2017, https://www.nbcnews.com/news
/investigations/yemen-seal-raid-yielded-no-significant-intelligence-say
-officials-n726451.

84. Matt Flegenheimer, "How Long Can John Kelly Hang On?" *New York Times*, February 26, 2017, https://www.nytimes.com/2018/02/26/magazine/how-long-can-john-kelly-hang-on.html.

CHAPTER 2: UNFOUNDED HUBRIS

1. "Confidence in Institutions," Gallup, http://www.gallup.com/poll/1597/confidence-institutions.aspx#1.

2. Phil Klay, "Two Decades of War Have Eroded the Morale of America's Troops," *Atlantic*, May 2018, https://www.theatlantic.com/magazine/archive/2018/05/left-behind/556844.

3. "Confidence in Institutions."

4. Leonard Wong and Stephen Gerras, *Lying to Ourselves: Dishonesty in the Army Profession* (Carlisle, PA: U.S. Army War College Press, 2015), 30, http://ssi.armywarcollege.edu/pdffiles/pub1250.pdf.

5. Steven D. Levitt and Stephen J. Dubner, "Can You Be Too Smart for Your Own Good?" *Freakonomics* (blog), May 23, 2013, http://freakonomics.com/2013/05/23/can-you-be-too-smart-for-your-own-good-and-other-freak-quently-asked-questions-full-transcript.

6. Joan Johnson-Freese, *Educating America's Military* (New York: Routledge, 2013), 81.

7. Andrew Bacevich, *Breach of Trust: How Americans Failed Their Soldiers and Their Country* (New York: Metropolitan Books, 2013), 95.

8. Neil Sheehan, *A Bright Shining Lie: John Paul Vann and America in Vietnam* (Random House: New York, 1988), 285.

9. David Halberstam, "MacArthur's Grand Delusion," *Vanity Fair*, September 24, 2007, http://www.vanityfair.com/news/2007/10/halberstam200710. See also William Stueck, *The Korean War: An International History* (Princeton, NJ: Princeton University Press, 1995).

10. Halberstam, "MacArthur's Grand Delusion."

11. Thomas E. Ricks, *The Generals: American Military Command from World War II to Today* (New York: Penguin, 2012), 96.

12. Halberstam, "MacArthur's Grand Delusion."

13. Ian Hunter, *Malcolm Muggeridge: A Life* (Vancouver: Regent College Publishing, 1980), 161.

14. Halberstam, "MacArthur's Grand Delusion."

15. Ibid.

16. Ricks, *The Generals*, 197.

17. Ibid., 127.

18. Ibid., 131.

19. Ibid., 202.

20. Lewis Sorley, *Westmoreland: The General Who Lost Vietnam* (Boston: Houghton Mifflin, 2011), 68.

21. Sheehan, *Bright Shining Lie*, 558.

22. Sorley, *Westmoreland*, 89–90.

23. Sheehan, *Bright Shining Lie*, 693.

24. Peter Davis, dir., *Hearts and Minds* (BBS Productions, 1974; distributed in the U.S. by Warner Brothers, 1975), 1:33:00–1:33:32, https://vimeo.com/126567345.

25. Sorley, *Westmoreland*, 109.

26. Ibid., 212.

27. Ibid., 105.

28. Lewis Sorley, "To Change a War: General Harold K. Johnson and the PROVN Study," *Parameters*, Spring 1998, 93–109, http://ssi.armywarcollege.edu/pubs/parameters/Articles/98spring/sorley.htm.

29. Sorley, *Westmoreland*, xix.

30. Sheehan, *Bright Shining Lie*, 557.

31. Gregory Daddis, *Westmoreland's War: Reassessing Strategy in Vietnam* (New York: Oxford University Press, 2014), IX.

32. Ibid., xx.

33. Ibid., 183.

34. Chalmers Johnson, *The Sorrows of Empire: Militarism, Secrecy, and the End of the Republic* (New York: Henry Holt, 2004), 5.

35. Craig Whitlock, "Pentagon to Review Perks for Its Leaders," *Washington Post*, December 7, 2012, https://www.washingtonpost.com/world/national-security /pentagon-to-review-perks-for-its-leaders/2012/12/07/1ae7aa7c-4099-11e2-b9a1 -7ad17c5c7b86_story.html. See also Laura Gottesdiener, "7 Absurd Ways the Military Wastes Taxpayer Dollars," *Salon*, December 12, 2012, http://www.salon .com/2012/12/12/7_absurd_ways_the_military_wastes_taxpayer_dollars.

36. Rajiv Chandrasekaran and Greg Jaffe, "Petraeus Scandal Puts Four-Star General Lifestyle under Scrutiny," *Washington Post*, November 17, 2012, https://www.washingtonpost.com/world/national-security/petraeus-scandal -puts-four-star-general-lifestyle-under-scrutiny/2012/11/17/33a14f48-3043-11e2 -a30e-5ca76eeec857_story.html.

37. Seymour M. Hersh, *Chain of Command: The Road from 9/11 to Abu Ghraib* (New York: HarperCollins, 2004), 42.

38. Dina Rasor, "The Pentagon's Biggest Overrun: Way Too Many Generals," *Truthout*, January 5, 2012, http://www.truth-out.org/opinion/item/5920:the -pentagons-biggest-overrun-way-too-many-generals.

39. SIGinsidesource, Colonel Bernard Banks, West Point Academy, May 10, 2012, YouTube video, 4:40–4:50 and 12:44–13:06, https://www.youtube.com/watch ?v=6r5uioAO7mQ.

40. David Burge, "Lt. Gen. Sean B. MacFarland, Former Fort Bliss Commander, Retiring after Three Decades," *El Paso Times*, February 27, 2018, https://www .elpasotimes.com/story/news/military/ft-bliss/2018/02/27/lt-gen-sean-b -macfarland-former-fort-bliss-commander-retiring-after-three-decades /375221002.

41. Sean MacFarland, "Fight, Kill, Die, Buddy," *Military Review*, September 2011, https://www.armyupress.army.mil/Portals/7/military-review/Archives/English /MilitaryReview_20110930PofA_art013.pdf, 55, 51-55.

42. James Fallows, "The Tragedy of the American Military," *Atlantic*, January/ February 2015, http://www.theatlantic.com/features/archive/2014/12/the -tragedy-of-the-american-military/383516.

43. Charlie Dunlap, "'Duty: Memoirs of a Secretary at War,' by Robert M. Gates," *Lawfare* (blog), July 18, 2014, https://www.lawfareblog.com/duty-memoirs -secretary-war-robert-m-gates.

44. Dan Lamothe, "West Point Criticized after Cadets Wear Sombreros at Army Football Game near Mexico," *Washington Post*, September 22, 2016, https://www.washingtonpost.com/news/checkpoint/wp/2016/09/22/west -point-criticized-after-cadets-wear-sombreros-at-army-football-game-near -mexico.

45. Mark Hemingway, "What Is Happening at West Point?" *Weekly Standard*, October 11, 2017, http://www.weeklystandard.com/what-is-happening-at-west -point/article/2010027.

46. Editorial Staff and Melissa Leon, "Exclusive: Former West Point Professor's Letter Exposes Corruption, Cheating and Failing Standards (Full Letter)," Robert Heffington, *American Military News*, October 11, 2017, https:// americanmilitarynews.com/2017/10/exclusive-former-west-point-professors -letter-exposes-corruption-cheating-and-failing-standards-full-letter.

47. U.S. General Accounting Office, *DOD Needs to Enhance Performance Goals and Measures to Improve Oversight of Military Academies*, GAO-03-1000 (Washington, D.C.: U.S. General Accounting Office, 2003), https://www.gao.gov /new.items/d031000.pdf. See also U.S. Government Accountability Office, *Military Education: Additional DOD Guidance Is Needed to Enhance Oversight of the Service Academies and Their Preparatory Schools*, GAO-12-327R (Washington, D.C.: U.S. Government Accountability Office, 2012), https://www.gao .gov/assets/590/588832.pdf.

48. Brandon O'Connor, "Class of 2019: 'Class Dismissed, Next Stop Army Career,'" *Army Public Affairs*, May 26, 2019, https://www.army.mil/article/222369 /class_of_2019_graduation_class_dismissed_next_stop_army_career.

49. National Institute of Cancer, Fact Book, 2003, xiii, https://www.cancer.gov /about-nci/budget/fact-book/archive/2003-fact-book.pdf.

50. Michael Hill, "West Point Names Barracks for Black Graduate Who Was Shunned," *Military Times*, May 10, 2015, https://www.militarytimes.com/news /your-military/2015/05/10/west-point-names-barracks-for-black-graduate -who-was-shunned.

51. West Point Admissions, "Getting Started: Your Path to Success Starts Here," United States Military Academy, https://westpoint.edu/admissions/getting -started.

52. David Lipsky, *Absolutely American: Four Years at West Point* (Boston: Houghton Mifflin, 2003), 57.

53. Gregory Korte and Fredreka Schouten, "Pride and Patronage," *USA Today*, September 15, 2014, https://www.usatoday.com/story/news/politics/2014/09/15 /service-academies-congress-nomination-army-navy/15452669.

54. Ibid.

55. The other 20–25 percent are admitted through special prep schools, discussed later in this chapter.

56. "Mail Fraud and Wire Fraud," U.S. Department of Justice, https://www.justice .gov/usam/usam-9-43000-mail-fraud-and-wire-fraud.

57. "America's Top Colleges," *Forbes*, 2018, https://www.forbes.com/top-colleges /list/#tab:rank.

58. Carter Coudriet, "Top Colleges 2017: The Methodology," *Forbes*, August 2, 2017, https://www.forbes.com/sites/cartercoudriet/2017/08/02/top-colleges-2017 -the-methodology/#34a076d7e44a.

59. J. Wai, "1,339 U.S. Colleges Ranked by Average Student Brainpower," *Psychology Today*, October 2014, https://www.psychologytoday.com/files/attachments /56143/1339-us-colleges-ranked-average-student-brainpower.pdf.

60. Bruce Fleming, "Let's Abolish West Point: Military Academies Serve No One, Squander Millions of Tax Dollars," *Salon*, January 5, 2017, https://www.salon .com/2015/01/05/lets_abolish_west_point_military_academies_serve_no _one_squander_millions_of_tax_dollars.

61. Ibid.

62. National Center for Education Statistics, "Admissions Full Instructions," 2019– 2020, U.S. Department of Education, https://surveys.nces.ed.gov/ipeds /VisInstructions.aspx?survey=14&id=30102&show=all.

63. Robert Morse, Eric Brooks, and Matt Mason, "How U.S. News Calculated the 2019 Best Colleges Rankings," *U.S. News and World Report*, September 9, 2018,

https://www.usnews.com/education/best-colleges/articles/how-us-news
-calculated-the-rankings.

64. "Navigator," National Center for Education Statistics, Fall 2018, https://nces
.ed.gov/collegenavigator/?q=u+s+military+academy&s=NY&l=93&id=19703
6#admsns (West Point); https://nces.ed.gov/collegenavigator/?q=u+s+naval+
academy&s=MD&l=93&id=164155#admsns (Naval Academy); https://nces.ed
.gov/collegenavigator/?q=u+s+air+force+academy&s=CO&l=93&id=128328#
admsns (Air Force Academy).

65. From 2009 to 2014 the Naval Academy reported acceptance rates ranging from
a low of 6.80 percent to a high of 9.50 percent. The Air Force Academy reported
acceptance rates ranging from a low of 9.90 percent to a high of 16.80 percent.

66. 18 U.S. Code, sections 1931 and 1343. See also U.S. Department of Justice, Justice
Manual, Criminal Resource Manual section 942, "The Scheme and Artifice to
Defraud," https://www.justice.gov/usam/criminal-resource-manual-942
-scheme-and-artifice-defraud; and *U.S. v. Carpenter*, 484 U.S. 19 (1987).

67. Daniel de Vise, "Naval Academy Professor: A Veneer of Selectivity," *Washington Post*, December 30, 2011, https://www.washingtonpost.com/blogs
/college-inc/post/naval-academy-professor-a-veneer-of-selectivity/2011/12/29
/gIQA9droQP_blog.html.

68. Joe Nocera, "Navy Opens a Backdoor, and In Come Athletes and Victories,"
New York Times, December 9, 2016, http://www.nytimes.com/2016/12/09
/sports/ncaafootball/navy-midshipmen-army-football.html. (The Naval
Academy reported in 2016 that its prep school costs $14 million per year.)

69. Joel Jebb, "USMAPS English: Needless Detour, or Pathway to Success?" (PhD
diss., Columbia University, 2016), 5, http://academiccommons.columbia.edu
/catalog/ac%3A198542.

70. Fleming, "Let's Abolish West Point."

71. "United States Military Academy Preparatory School," *Journal of the American
Institute of Architects*, May 13, 2013, http://www.architectmagazine.com/project
-gallery/united-states-military-academy-preparatory-school.

72. There are two other federal academies, Coast Guard and Merchant Marine,
contained within the departments of Homeland Security and Transportation,
rather than Defense.

73. "West Point Preparatory Scholarship Program of the West Point Association of Graduates," Association of Graduates, February 15, 2017, http://www .westpointaog.org/document.doc?id=3351.

74. Jebb, "USMAPS English," 291.

75. Ibid., 301.

76. Ibid., 304.

77. Ibid., 5.

78. "Fast Facts," National Center for Education Statistics, 2017, https://nces.ed.gov /fastfacts/display.asp?id=171.

79. Daniel de Vise, "Naval Academy Prep School: Asset or Liability?" *Washington Post*, October 19, 2011, https://www.washingtonpost.com/blogs/college-inc/post /naval-academy-prep-school-asset-or-liability/2011/10/19/gIQAlDLPyL_blog .html.

80. Tom Roeder, "Military Academies, Including AFA, Face Criticism for using Prep Schools to Fill Athletic Teams," *Colorado Springs Gazette*, September 8, 2014, http://gazette.com/gazette-exclusive-military-academies-including-afa -face-criticism-for-using-prep-schools-to-fill-athletic-teams/article/1537071.

81. Lance Betros, *Carved from Granite: West Point since 1902* (College Station: Texas A&M University Press, 2012), 309.

82. These were combined averages for first-year students from 2004, 2005, and 2006.

83. Betros, *Carved from Granite*, 103.

84. "Compare [SAT] scores," College Board, 2017, https://collegereadiness .collegeboard.org/sat-scoring-before-march-2016. The maximum SAT score was 2400, although the SAT received a new scoring system in 2016. See Nick Anderson, "SAT Scores at Lowest Level in 10 Years, Fueling Worries about High Schools," *Washington Post*, September 3, 2015, http://www.washingtonpost .com/local/education/sat-scores-at-lowest-level-in-10-years-fueling-worries -about-high-schools/2015/09/02/6b73ec66-5190-11e5-9812-92d5948a40f8_story .html.

85. Betros, *Carved in Granite*, 106–7.

86. "Army Black Knights School History," Sports-Reference.com, http://www
.sports-reference.com/cfb/schools/army.

87. Brandy Zadrozny and James LaPorta, "West Point Let Football Star Break
Rules before Drunk Driving Death, Investigation Found," *Daily Beast*,
December 22, 2017, https://www.thedailybeast.com/west-point-let-football
-star-break-rules-before-drunk-driving-death-investigation-found.

88. Brandy Zadrozny and James LaPorta, "Cadet Run Out of West Point after
Accusing Army's Star Quarterback of Rape," *Daily Beast*, December 8, 2018,
https://www.thedailybeast.com/cadet-run-out-of-west-point-after-accusing
-armys-star-quarterback-of-rape.

89. Ibid.

90. Michelle Eberhart, "The Class of 2016 Becomes Second Lieutenants," *Pointer
View*, May 26, 2016, http://www.pointerview.com/2016/05/26/the-class-of
-2016-becomes-second-lieutenants.

91. Arthur T. Coumbe, Steven J. Condly, and William L. Skimmyhorn, *Still
Soldiers and Scholars? An Analysis of Army Officer Testing* (Carlisle, PA: U.S.
Army War College Press, 2017), ix–xx, https://ssi.armywarcollege.edu/pdffiles
/PUB1374.pdf.

92. Jason W. Warren, "The Centurion Mindset and the Army's Strategic Leader
Paradigm," *Parameters* 45 (2015): 30, http://ssi.armywarcollege.edu/pubs
/Parameters/issues/Autumn_2015/6_Warren.pdf.

93. Ibid., 38.

94. Thomas E. Ricks, "General Failure," *Atlantic*, November 2012, http://www
.theatlantic.com/magazine/archive/2012/11/general-failure/309148.

95. George Packer, *The Assassins' Gate* (New York: Farrar, Straus and Giroux, 2005),
298.

96. Michael R. Gordon, "The Conflict in Iraq: Road to War; The Strategy to
Secure Iraq Did Not Foresee a 2nd War," *New York Times*, October 19, 2004,
https://www.nytimes.com/2004/10/19/washington/the-conflict-in-iraq-road
-to-war-the-strategy-to-secure-iraq-did.html.

97. Thomas E. Ricks, *Fiasco: The American Military Adventure in Iraq* (New York:
Penguin, 2006), 38.

98. Ibid., 70.

99. Daniel P. Bolger, *Why We Lost: A General's Inside Account of the Iraq and Afghanistan Wars* (Boston: Houghton Mifflin, 2014), 431.

CHAPTER 3: CONFORMITY AND CRONYISM

1. "By the Numbers: Today's Military," NPR, March 31, 2010, https://www.npr.org/2011/07/03/137536111/by-the-numbers-todays-military.

2. David Lipsky, *Absolutely American: Four Years at West Point* (Boston: Houghton Mifflin, 2003), 43.

3. All these statistics include "strongly agree," "agree," or "somewhat agree." All decimal points are rounded up or down.

4. David Aaronovitch, *Voodoo Histories: The Role of the Conspiracy in Shaping Modern History* (New York: Riverhead, 2010), 331.

5. Joan Johnson-Freese, *Educating America's Military* (New York: Routledge, 2013), 30.

6. Thomas E. Ricks, *The Generals: American Military Command from World War II to Today* (New York: Penguin, 2012), 127.

7. Lucian K. Truscott IV, "The Not-So-Long Gray Line," *New York Times*, June 28, 2005, http://www.nytimes.com/2005/06/28/opinion/the-notsolong-gray-line.html.

8. Laurence Knell, "Managing the 'Creativity Conundrum'—the Conflict between Creativity and Conformity in Organisations," Linked in, January 31, 2016, https://www.linkedin.com/pulse/managing-creativity-conundrum-conflict-between-conformity-knell.

9. Heidi Urben, "Civil-Military Relations in a Time of War" (PhD diss., Georgetown University, 2010), http://timemilitary.files.wordpress.com/2012/11/urben-diss-1-5.pdf, 54.

10. Ibid., 11.

11. Mark Thompson, "Does the Military Vote Really Lean Republican?" *Time*, November 5, 2012, http://swampland.time.com/2012/11/05/does-the-military-vote-really-lean-republican.

12. Jason K. Dempsey, *Our Army: Soldiers, Politics, and American Civil-Military Relations* (Princeton, NJ: Princeton University Press, 2009), 72.

13. Urben, "Civil-Military Relations," 41.

14. David Zucchino and David S. Cloud, "U.S. Military and Civilians Are Increasingly Divided," *Los Angeles Times*, May 23, 2015, http://www.latimes.com /nation/la-na-warrior-main-20150524-story.html. See also Pew Research Center, "The Military-Civilian Gap: Fewer Family Connections," November 23, 2011, http://www.pewsocialtrends.org/2011/11/23/the-military-civilian-gap -fewer-family-connections.

15. Zucchino and Cloud, "U.S. Military and Civilians."

16. John R. Hibbing, Kevin B. Smith, and John R. Alford, "Differences in Negativity Bias Underlie Variations in Political Ideology," *Behavioral and Brain Sciences* 37 (2014): 306, https://motyl.people.uic.edu/NegativityBiasCommentary .pdf.

17. Ibid.

18. Ibid.

19. Ibid., 303.

20. See generally Richard Hofstadter, *Anti-Intellectualism in American Life* (New York: Alfred A. Knopf, 1963), 134–35.

21. Stephen J. Gerras and Leonard Wong, *Changing Minds in the Army: Why It Is So Difficult and What to Do About It* (Carlisle, PA: U.S. Army War College Press, 2013), 9, https://ssi.armywarcollege.edu/pdffiles/PUB1179.pdf.

22. David C. Gompert, Hans Binnendijk, and Bonny Lin, *Blinders, Blunders, and Wars: What America and China Can Learn* (Santa Monica, CA: Rand, 2014), 247, http://www.rand.org/content/dam/rand/pubs/research_reports/RR700 /RR768/RAND_RR768.pdf.

23. Bob Woodward, *Plan of Attack* (New York: Simon & Schuster, 2004), 6.

24. James Stavridis, "Professionals Write, Whispers on a Wall," *Marine Corps Gazette*, May 2011, 83; cited in Johnson-Freese, *Educating America's Military*, 37.

25. Johnson-Freese, *Educating America's Military*, 23.

26. George Packer, *The Assassins' Gate* (New York: Farrar, Straus and Giroux, 2005), 304.

27. Gompert, Binnendijk, and Lin, *Blinders, Blunders, and Wars*, 174.

28. Ibid., 248–49.

29. Ibid., xv.

30. Thomas E. Ricks, "Why We Should Get Rid of West Point," *Washington Post*, April 19, 2009, http://www.washingtonpost.com/wp-dyn/content/article/2009 /04/16/AR2009041603483.html.

31. Dominic Tierney, *How We Fight: Crusades, Quagmires, and the American Way of War* (New York: Little, Brown, 2010), 9.

32. Johnson-Freese, *Educating America's Military*, 23.

33. Ibid., 11.

34. Diego Gambetta and Steffen Hertog, "Why Are There So Many Engineers among Islamic Radicals?" *European Journal of Sociology* 50 (2009): 221, https:// orientemiedo.files.wordpress.com/2010/01/diego-gambetta-steffen-hertog -why-are-there-so-many-engineers-among-islamic-radicals.pdf.

35. Ibid., 216.

36. Ibid., 227.

37. Ibid., 222.

38. Ibid., 225.

39. "Admissions Frequently Asked Questions (FAQs)," under category "Academics," U.S. Military Academy, 2019, https://westpoint.edu/admissions /frequently-asked-questions.

40. See Matthew Harwood, "Air Force Academy Whistleblower Alleges Dog Poisoned in Retaliation," *Truthout*, March 12, 2012, http://www.truth-out.org /news/item/7214:air-force-academy-whistleblower-alleges-dog-poisoned-in -retaliation; and Inspector General of the Air Force, *Report of Investigation Concerning Brigadier Gen. Dana H. Born and Colonel Richard L. Fullerton*, January 2012, http://posting.csindy.com/images/blogimages/2012/07/03 /1341354549-ltr_fr_john_taylor_6-20-12.pdf.

41. Harwood, "Air Force Academy Whistleblower."

42. Scott E. Carrell and James E. West, "Does Professor Quality Matter? Evidence from Random Assignment of Students to Professors," *Journal of Political Economy* 118 (2010): 421, http://faculty.econ.ucdavis.edu/faculty/scarrell/profqual2.pdf.

43. Harwood, "Air Force Academy Whistleblower."

44. Kirsten Keller, Nelson Lim, Lisa Harrington, Kevin O'Neill, and Abigail Haddad, *The Mix of Military and Civilian Faculty at the United States Air Force Academy: Finding a Sustainable Balance for Enduring Success* (Santa Monica, CA: Rand, 2013), 53–67, http://www.rand.org/content/dam/rand/pubs/monographs/MG1200/MG1237/RAND_MG1237.pdf.

45. Harwood, "Air Force Academy Whistleblower."

46. Lipsky, *Absolutely American*, 36.

47. Ibid., 35.

48. See Theodore J. Crackel, *West Point: A Bicentennial History* (Lawrence: University Press of Kansas, 2002), 277–80; and Association of Graduates, USMA Leadership (West Point, NY: U.S. Military Academy, 2013), https://www.westpointaog.org/document.doc?id=5614.

49. 10 U.S. Code, section 3962.

50. Arroyo Center, *Identifying Civilian Labor Market Realities for Army Officers Making Stay/Leave Decisions* (Santa Monica, CA: Rand, 2012), 1, http://www.rand.org/content/dam/rand/pubs/research_briefs/2012/RAND_RB9653.pdf.

51. "About ABET," Accreditation Board for Engineering and Technology, http://www.abet.org/about-abet.

52. "United States Military Academy," Accreditation Board for Engineering and Technology, http://main.abet.org/aps/AccreditedProgramsDetails.aspx?OrganizationID=714&ProgramIDs=.

53. Erin A. Cech, "Culture of Disengagement in Engineering Education?" *Science, Technology, & Human Values* 39, no. 1 (2014): 63–64, http://sth.sagepub.com/content/39/1/42.full.pdf+html.

54. Lipsky, *Absolutely American*, 34.

55. "Academics: Majors," U.S. Naval Academy, http://www.usna.edu/Academics
/Majors-and-Courses.

56. Crackel, *West Point*, 377–78.

57. Ibid., 281–91.

58. Ibid., 234.

59. *Commissioned Officer Professional Development and Career Management*, Department of the Army pamphlet 600–3, pp. 35–36, https://www.army.mil/e2/c
/downloads/376665.pdf.

60. Tim Kane, "Why Our Best Officers Are Leaving," *Atlantic*, January/
February 2011, http://www.theatlantic.com/magazine/archive/2011/01/why-our
-best-officers-are-leaving/308346.

61. Commissioned Officer Professional Development, 36.

62. Casey Wardynski, David S. Lyle, and Michael J. Colarusso, *Toward a U.S. Army
Officer Corps Strategy for Success: Retaining Talent* (Carlisle, PA: U.S. Army War
College Press, 2010), v, https://ssi.armywarcollege.edu/pdffiles/PUB965.pdf.

63. Packer, *Assassins' Gate*, 247–48.

64. Paul Yingling, "A Failure in Generalship," *Armed Forces Journal*, May 1, 2007,
http://www.armedforcesjournal.com/a-failure-in-generalship.

65. Paul Yingling, "Why an Army Colonel Is Retiring Early—to Become a High
School Teacher," *Washington Post*, December 2, 2011, https://www
.washingtonpost.com/opinions/why-an-army-colonel-is-retiring-early—to
-become-a-high-school-teacher/2011/12/02/gIQAB2wAMO_story.html.

66. Megan McArdle, "Why Companies Fail," *Atlantic*, March 2012, https://www
.theatlantic.com/magazine/archive/2012/03/why-companies-fail/308887.

CHAPTER 4: SUPREME VALUES

1. "The Army Values," Army.mil Features, https://www.army.mil/values.

2. Ibid.

3. Samuel P. Huntington, *The Soldier and the State: The Theory and Politics of Civil-
Military Relations* (Cambridge, MA: Harvard University Press, 1959), 304.

4. "Army Values."

5. "Eleven Offenses Punishable by Death in United States Army," *Sausalito News*, April 20, 1918, 5, https://cdnc.ucr.edu/cgi-bin/cdnc?a=d&d=SN19180420.2.56.

6. Article 91, Punitive Articles of the Uniform Code of Military Justice, http://www.ucmj.us/sub-chapter-10-punitive-articles/891-article-91-insubord inate-conduct-toward-warrant-officer-noncommissioned-officer-or-petty -officer.

7. Thomas E. Ricks, *The Generals: American Military Command from World War II to Today* (New York: Penguin, 2012), 309–10.

8. Leonard Wong and Stephen Gerras, *Lying to Ourselves: Dishonesty in the Army Profession* (Carlisle, PA: U.S. Army War College Press, 2015), 7, 8, 12, http://ssi .armywarcollege.edu/pdffiles/pub1250.pdf.

9. Ibid., ix.

10. Ibid., 12.

11. Ibid., 5–6.

12. Ibid., 1.

13. Ibid., 26–27.

14. Ibid., 13.

15. Ibid., 14.

16. Ibid., 27.

17. Ibid., 28.

18. Ibid., 33.

19. Synopsis of Wong and Gerras, *Lying to Ourselves*, Strategic Studies Institute website, https://ssi.armywarcollege.edu/pubs/display.cfm?pubID=1250.

20. Wong and Gerras, *Lying to Ourselves*, 25.

21. Ibid., 17.

22. Joe Doty and Pete Hoffman, "Admit It—Lying Is a Problem in the Military," *Army Magazine* 64 (July 2014): 19, https://lscpagepro.mydigitalpublication.com /publication/?i=213587#{"issue_id":213587,"page":20}.

23. Christian Swezey, "Dark Days for the Black Knights," *Washington Post*, December 10, 2005, http://www.washingtonpost.com/wp-dyn/content/article /2005/12/09/AR2005120901899.html.

24. Michelle Eberhart, "Campo Explains His Trials to Cadets, Overcoming Obstacles," *Pointer View*, September 22, 2016, 4, http://www.pointerview.com /2016/09/22/campo-explains-his-trials-to-cadets-overcoming-obstacles.

25. Robert Coyne and Robert Thorup, "West Point Honor Code Separations: Duty, Honor, Country . . . Fairness?" *American University Law Review* 27 (1977): 823.

26. Malcolm Carter, "Cheating Scandal Hits West Point," *Park City Daily News*, May 30, 1976, http://news.google.com/newspapers?nid=1697&dat=19760530& id=OyMqAAAAIBAJ&sjid=okYEAAAAIBAJ&pg=6736,4251742.

27. Associated Press, "Study: Cheating Scandal 'Bigger,'" *Bakersfield Californian*, December 15, 1976, https://newspaperarchive.com/bakersfield-californian-dec -15-1976-p-1. See also Frank Borman et al., *Report to the Secretary of the Army by the Special Commission on the United States Military Academy,* December 15, 1976 (West Point, NY: U.S. Military Academy, 1976), n.p. [3], http://www.west -point.org/users/usma1983/40768/docs/borman.pdf.

28. Theodore J. Crackel, *West Point: A Bicentennial History* (Lawrence: University Press of Kansas, 2002), 243–46.

29. Associated Press, "86 Survivors of 1976 Scandal among West Point Graduates," *Toledo Blade,* June 8, 1978, http://news.google.com/newspapers?nid=1350&dat =19780607&id=fhhPAAAAIBAJ&sjid=bAIEAAAAIBAJ&pg=4931,3511547.

30. "Coast Guard Cadets 'Guilty' of Cheating," *Eugene [OR] Register-Guard*, June 2, 1976, http://news.google.com/newspapers?nid=1310&dat=19760602&id =_KtVAAAAIBAJ&sjid=K-EDAAAAIBAJ&pg=6066,267529.

31. Eric Schmitt, "An Inquiry Finds 125 Cheated on a Naval Academy Exam," *New York Times,* January 13, 1994, http://www.nytimes.com/1994/01/13/us/an-inquiry -finds-125-cheated-on-a-naval-academy-exam.html.

32. Michael O'Brien, *America's Failure in Iraq* (Bloomington, IN: Author House, 2010), 357.

33. Ricks, *Generals*, 221.

34. Ibid., 219–21.

35. Ibid., 222.

36. H. R. McMaster, *Dereliction of Duty: Lyndon Johnson, Robert McNamara, the Joint Chiefs of Staff, and the Lies That Led to Vietnam* (New York: Harper, 1997), 106.

37. Lloyd C. Gardner and Marilyn B. Young, eds., *Iraq and the Lessons of Vietnam; or, How Not to Learn from the Past* (New York: New Press, 2007), 6.

38. Robert J. Hanyok, "Spartans in Darkness: American SIGINT and the Indochina War, 1945-1975," Center for Cryptologic History, National Security Agency (2002), https://fas.org/irp/nsa/spartans, chap. 5, https://fas.org/irp/nsa/spartans/chapter5.pdf, 177.

39. Hanyok, "Spartans in Darkness," 177.

40. James McCartney with Molly Sinclair McCartney, *America's War Machine: Vested Interests, Endless Conflicts* (New York: Thomas Dunne, 2015), 181.

41. Robert J. Hanyok, "Skunks, Bogies, Silent Hounds, and the Flying Fish: The Gulf of Tonkin Mystery, 2-4 August 1964," *Naval History and Heritage Command*, November 2, 2017, https://www.history.navy.mil/research/library/online-reading-room/title-list-alphabetically/s/skunks-bogies-silent-hounds-flying-fish.html, 38.

42. Hanyok, "Skunks," 38.

43. Robert J. Hanyok, "Spartans in Darkness," 213.

44. Lewis Sorley, *Westmoreland: The General Who Lost Vietnam* (Boston: Houghton Mifflin, 2011), 94.

45. Ibid., 94.

46. Ibid., 143.

47. Ibid., 144.

48. Hanyok, "Spartans in Darkness," 312.

49. Sorley, *Westmoreland*, 144.

50. Ibid., 144–45.

51. James M. Lindsay, "TWE Remembers: General Westmoreland Says the 'End Begins to Come Into View,'" *Foreign Policy* (blog), November 21, 2017,

https://www.cfr.org/blog/twe-remembers-general-westmoreland-says-end
-begins-come-view-vietnam.

52. Neil Sheehan, *A Bright Shining Lie: John Paul Vann and America in Vietnam* (New York: Random House, 1988), 699.

53. Lindsay, "TWE Remembers."

54. Sorley, *Westmoreland*, 179.

55. Ibid., 163.

56. Ibid., 164.

57. Ibid., 166.

58. Ibid., 165.

59. Ibid., 161–62.

60. Ibid., 162.

61. Ibid., 163.

62. Max Hastings, "Eyewitness to Apocalypse: Fifty Years Ago This Week, US Troops Went into Vietnam," *Daily Mail*, March 11, 2015, http://www.dailymail.co.uk/news/article-2990655/Eyewitness-apocalypse-Fifty-years-ago-week-troops-went-Vietnam-MAX-HASTINGS-saw-humbled-army-peasant-fanatics-amid-horrors-haunt-day.html.

63. Sheehan, *Bright Shining Lie*, 285.

64. RoyalScribe, "Comparing Presidential Administrations by Arrests and Convictions," *Daily Kos*, January 11, 2017, https://www.dailykos.com/stories/2017/1/11/1619079/-Comparing-Presidential-Administrations-by-Arrests-and-Convictions-A-Warning-for-Trump-Appointees.

65. David Stout, "John D. Ehrlichman, Nixon Aide Jailed for Watergate, Dies at 73," *New York Times*, February 16, 1999, http://www.nytimes.com/1999/02/16/us/john-d-ehrlichman-nixon-aide-jailed-for-watergate-dies-at-73.html.

66. David Johnston, "Bush Pardons 6 in Iran Affair, Aborting a Weinberger Trial; Prosecutor Assails 'Cover-Up,'" *New York Times*, December 24, 1992, http://www.nytimes.com/learning/general/onthisday/big/1224.html#article.

67. As an admiral, Poindexter would never be completely banished by the military community. After 9/11 he was tapped to run a surveillance program called Total Information Awareness, which never got off the ground—partly because of the

Orwellian name. Poindexter resigned after being found to be running "a terrorist futures-trading market" out of the Pentagon in 2003.

68. RoyalScribe, "Comparing Presidential Administrations." This source indicates zero for the Obama administration, but it should have counted the conviction of David Petraeus, who was Obama's CIA director.

69. David Corn, "Colin Powell the Untouchable," *Salon*, March 20, 2000, http://www.salon.com/2000/03/20/powell_3.

70. Lawrence E. Walsh, "Officers of the Department of Defense (*U.S. v. Caspar W. Weinberger* and Related Investigations)," in Final Report of the Independent Counsel for Iran/Contra Matters, August 4, 1993, https://fas.org/irp/offdocs /walsh/part_viii.htm.

71. Colin Powell, *My American Journey* (New York: Random House, 2009), 342.

72. Walsh, "Officers of the Department of Defense."

73. Ibid.

74. Richard Harwood, "Damned If You Don't," *Washington Post*, April 10, 1995, https://www.washingtonpost.com/archive/opinions/1995/04/10/damned-if -you-dont/fe7ae398-f0c5-480d-a898-a81bccc773ab.

75. Greg Mitchell, "6 Years Ago: 'Stuff Happens,' Rumsfeld said, Amid Chaos in Iraq," *Huffpost*, May 25, 2011, https://www.huffpost.com/entry/6-years-ago -stuff-happens_b_185691.

76. Ibid.

77. Frank Rich, *The Greatest Story Ever Sold: The Decline and Fall of Truth from 9/11 to Katrina* (New York: Penguin, 2006), 85.

78. Ibid.

79. Reuters, "Highest Death Toll Since April," *New York Times*, November 2, 2003, https://www.nytimes.com/2003/11/02/international/middleeast/highest-us -death-toll-since-april.html.

80. George Packer, *The Assassins' Gate* (New York: Farrar, Straus and Giroux, 2005), 305.

81. Tim Graham and Rich Noyes, "Meet Bob Schieffer, CBS's Dan Rather Echo," Media Research Center, November 2, 2003, https://www.mrc.org/media -reality-check/meet-bob-schieffer-cbss-dan-rather-echo.

82. George Bush, "Remarks to the American Israeli Political Action Committee, U.S. State Department, May 18, 2004," https://2001-2009.state.gov/p/nea/rls/rm/32761.htm.

83. Felicity Barringer, "A Nation Challenged: Media; 'Reality TV' About G.I.'s On War Duty," *New York Times*, February 21, 2002, https://www.nytimes.com/2002/02/21/world/a-nation-challenged-media-reality-tv-about-gi-s-on-war-duty.html.

84. Andrew Bacevich, *Breach of Trust: How Americans Failed Their Soldiers and Their Country* (New York: Metropolitan Books, 2013), 121.

85. Mark Bowden, *The Finish: The Killing of Osama Bin Laden* (New York: Atlantic Monthly Press, 2012), 150.

86. Michael Hastings, "The Runaway General," *Rolling Stone*, June 22, 2010, http://www.rollingstone.com/politics/news/the-runaway-general-20100622.

87. Mike Fish, *An Un-American Tragedy*, part 2, ESPN, http://www.espn.com/espn/eticket/story?page=tillmanpart2.

88. Associated Press, "Full Text of Tillman Memo to Top Generals," NBC News, August 3, 2007, http://www.nbcnews.com/id/20113601/ns/us_news-military/t/full-text-tillman-memo-top-generals/#.W2TJZC2ZOL8.

89. Ibid.

90. Mick Brown, "Betrayal of an All-American Hero," *Telegraph*, October 7, 2010, http://www.telegraph.co.uk/culture/8046658/Betrayal-of-an-all-American-hero.html.

91. Ibid.

92. Frank Rich, "All the President's Press," *New York Times*, April 29, 2007, http://www.nytimes.com/2007/04/29/opinion/29rich.html.

93. Mike Fish, *An Un-American Tragedy*.

94. Ibid.

95. Office of the Inspector General, Department of Defense, *Review of Matters Related to the Death of Corporal Patrick Tillman*, U.S. Army report IP02007E001, March 26, 2007, 24, http://www.npr.org/documents/2007/mar/tillman/tillman_dod_ig.pdf.

96. Ibid., 21–23.

97. Brown, "Betrayal."

98. Inspector General, *Death of Corporal Patrick Tillman*, 2.

99. Accused soldiers may retain private defense attorneys.

100. Inspector General, *Death of Corporal Patrick Tillman*, appendix A.

101. Brown, "Betrayal."

102. David S. Cloud, "9 Officers Faulted for Aftermath of Tillman Death," *New York Times*, March 27, 2017, http://www.nytimes.com/2007/03/27/washing ton/27tillman.html.

103. Associated Press, "Panel to Decide Whether Kensinger Has Rank Reduced," ESPN, July 31, 2007, http://sports.espn.go.com/espn/news/story?id=2956053.

104. Inspector General, *Death of Corporal Patrick Tillman*, 54–55.

105. Associated Press, "Possible Charges and Punishments So Far in Pat Tillman's Death," *Times Herald Record*, November 10, 2006, http://www.recordonline .com/article/20061110/News/611090350.

106. *The Tillman Story*, directed by Amir Bar-Lev (New York: Passion Pictures, 2010), http://www.imdb.com/title/tt1568334.

107. Josh White, "Army Withheld Details about Tillman's Death," *Washington Post*, May 4, 2005, http://www.washingtonpost.com/wp-dyn/content/article /2005/05/03/AR2005050301502.html.

108. Linda Flanagan, "An Interview with Amir Bar-Lev, Director of The Tillman Story," *Huffington Post*, December 15, 2010, http://www.huffingtonpost.com /linda-flanagan/an-interview-with-amir-ba_b_797142.html.

109. Thomas Gibbons-Neff, "Afghan War Data, Once Public, Is Censored in U.S. Military Report," *New York Times*, October 30, 2017, https://www.nytimes .com/2017/10/30/world/asia/afghanistan-war-redacted-report.html.

110. Chalmers Johnson, *The Sorrows of Empire: Militarism, Secrecy, and the End of the Republic* (New York: Henry Holt, 2004), 119.

111. Melvin A. Goodman, *National Insecurity: The Cost of American Militarism* (San Francisco: City Lights, 2013), 9.

112. Rajiv Chandrasekaran, "The Afghan Surge Is Over: So Did It Work?" *Foreign Policy*, September 25, 2012, http://foreignpolicy.com/2012/09/25/the-afghan -surge-is-over.

113. Jonathan Alter, *The Promise: President Obama, Year One* (New York: Simon & Schuster, 2010), 390.

114. Ibid.

115. Gareth Porter, "Bait-and-Switch in Afghanistan," *Counterpunch*, September 20, 2010, http://www.counterpunch.org/2010/09/20/bait-and-switch-in-afgha nistan.

116. Ibid.

117. Don Snider and Alexander Shine, *A Soldier's Morality, Religion, and Our Professional Ethic: Does the Army's Culture Facilitate Integration, Character Development, and Trust in the Profession?* (Carlisle, PA: U.S. Army War College Press, 2014), 23, https://ssi.armywarcollege.edu/pubs/display.cfm?pubID=1203.

118. Mark Mazzetti and Matt Apuzzo, "Analysts Detail Claims That Reports on ISIS Were Distorted," *New York Times*, September 15, 2015, http://www .nytimes.com/2015/09/16/us/politics/analysts-said-to-provide-evidence-of -distorted-reports-on-isis.html.

119. Ibid.

120. After Austin retired in 2016, West Point named him its Leadership Chair for the Study of Leadership, the most prominent position in the Department of Behavioral Studies and Leadership.

121. David D. Kirkpatrick, Ben Hubbard and Eric Schmitt, "ISIS' Grip on Libyan City Gives It a Fallback Option," *New York Times*, November 28, 2015, http://www.nytimes.com/2015/11/29/world/middleeast/isis-grip-on-libyan -city-gives-it-a-fallback-option.html.

122. Mark Mazzetti and Matt Apuzzo, "Inquiry Weighs Whether ISIS Analysis was Distorted," *New York Times*, August 25, 2015, http://www.nytimes.com /2015/08/26/world/middleeast/pentagon-investigates-allegations-of-skewed -intelligence-reports-on-isis.html.

123. Mazzetti and Apuzzo, "Analysts Detail Claims."

124. Shane Harris and Nancy A. Youssef, "Exclusive: 50 Spies Say ISIS Intelligence Was Cooked," *Daily Beast*, September 9, 2015, http://www.thedailybeast .com/articles/2015/09/09/exclusive-50-spies-say-isis-intelligence-was-cooked .html.

125. Matt Apuzzo, Mark Mazzetti, and Michael S. Schmidt, "Pentagon Expands Inquiry into Intelligence on ISIS Surge," *New York Times*, November 21, 2015, http://www.nytimes.com/2015/11/22/us/politics/military-reviews-us-response -to-isis-rise.html.

126. Ibid.

127. Harris and Youssef, "ISIS Intelligence Was Cooked."

128. Ibid.

129. Shane Harris and Nancy A. Youssef, "Intel Analysts: We Were Forced Out for Telling the Truth about Obama's ISIS War," *Daily Beast*, April 3, 2016, http://www.thedailybeast.com/articles/2016/04/03/intel-analysts-we-were -punished-for-telling-the-truth-about-obama-s-isis-war.html.

130. House Joint Task Force on CENTCOM Intelligence Analysis, *Initial Findings of the U.S. House of Representatives Joint Task Force on U.S. Central Command Intelligence Analysis*, August 10, 2016, https://assets.document cloud.org/documents/3010857/Initial-Findings-of-the-U-S-House-of.pdf.

131. Ibid., 1.

132. Ibid., 4.

133. Ibid., 2.

134. Ibid., 4.

135. Ibid., 10.

136. Ibid., 10.

137. Rowan Scarborough, "Pentagon Backs Accuracy of Intelligence Reports in Progress of War against Islamic State," *Washington Times*, February 1, 2017, http://www.washingtontimes.com/news/2017/feb/1/centcom-didnt-distort -reports-isis-war-pentagon.

138. Mark Mazzetti and Michael S. Schmidt, "Pentagon Clears Officials of Skewing Data in ISIS Reports," *New York Times*, February 1, 2017, https://www .nytimes.com/2017/02/01/world/middleeast/pentagon-isis-reports.html.

139. Department of Defense Office of Inspector General Report, "Investigation of Allegations Related to USCENTCOM Intelligence Products": Testimony before the House Armed Services Committee Subcommittee on Oversight

and Investigations, February 28, 2017, 115th Cong. 27 (2017) (statement of Glenn A. Fine), https://fas.org/irp/congress/2017_hr/dodig-centcom.pdf.

140. Ibid., 30.

141. Thomas Gibbons-Neff, "From 'Collateral Damage' to 'Deeply Regrets': How the Pentagon Has Shifted on the Afghan Hospital Attack," *Washington Post*, October 6, 2015, https://www.washingtonpost.com/news/checkpoint/wp /2015/10/06/how-the-pentagon-shifted-from-collateral-damage-to-deepest -regrets-on-afghan-hospital-attack.

142. Ibid.

143. Robert Burns, "Kunduz Airstrike Was Requested by Afghans, U.S. Commander Says," *U.S. News and World Report*, October 5, 2015, http://www .usnews.com/news/politics/articles/2015/10/05/us-commander-afghans -requested-deadly-us-airstrike.

144. John F. Campbell, "Department of Defense Press Briefing by Gen. Campbell in the Pentagon Briefing Room," October 5, 2015, U.S. Department of Defense, https://www.defense.gov/News/Transcripts/Transcript-View /Article/621848/department-of-defense-press-briefing-by-gen-campbell-in -the-pentagon-briefing-r.

145. Eric Schmitt and Matthew Rosenberg, "General Is Said to Think Afghan Hospital Airstrike Broke U.S. Rules," *New York Times*, October 6, 2015, http://www.nytimes.com/2015/10/07/world/middleeast/doctors-without -borders-airstrike-kunduz.html.

146. Spencer Ackerman, "Doctors Without Borders Airstrike: U.S. Alters Story for Fourth Time in Four Days," *Guardian*, October 6, 2015, http://www .theguardian.com/us-news/2015/oct/06/doctors-without-borders-airstrike -afghanistan-us-account-changes-again.

147. John F. Campbell, "Investigation Report of the Airstrike on the Médecin Sans Frontières/Doctors Without Borders Trauma Center in Kunduz, Afghanistan on 3 October 2015," Headquarters, United States Forces— Afghanistan, November 21, 2015, 002-006, http://fpp.cc/wp-content/uploads /01.-AR-15-6-Inv-Rpt-Doctors-Without-Borders-3-Oct-15_CLEAR.pdf.

148. Sudarsan Raghavan, "U.S. Cites Errors and Technical Failures in Report on Afghan Hospital Attack," *Washington Post*, November 25, 2015, https://www .washingtonpost.com/world/us-suspends-military-personnel-over-attack-in -kunduz/2015/11/25/8446688e-92c9-11e5-befa-99ceebcbb272_story.html.

149. Campbell, "Investigation Report of the Airstrike."

150. Raghavan, "U.S. Cites Errors."

151. Ibid.

152. U.S. Central Command, Summary of the Airstrike on the MSF Trauma Center in Kunduz, Afghanistan on October 3, 2015; Investigation and Follow-on Actions, 4, https://info.publicintelligence.net/CENTCOM-Kunduz HospitalAttack.pdf.

153. Joseph Votel, "Department of Defense Press Briefing by Army General Joseph Votel, Commander, U.S. Central Command," Department of Defense Press Operations, April 29, 2016, https://dod.defense.gov/News/Transcripts /Transcript-View/Article/746686/department-of-defense-press-briefing-by -army-general-joseph-votel-commander-us.

CHAPTER 5: A CULTURE OF SILENCE

1. Frederick V. Malstrom and R. David Mullin, "Dishonesty and Cheating in a Federal Service Academy: Toleration Is the Main Ingredient," *Research in Higher Education Journal* 19 (2013): 3, http://www.aabri.com/manuscripts/121416 .pdf.

2. "Deadly West Point Accident Rare but Not Unprecedented," *CBS This Morning*, June 7, 2019, https://www.cbsnews.com/news/west-point-deadly -accident-rare-but-not-unprecedented.

3. Peter Schmidt, "Investigators Say Naval Academy Punished Professor Who Criticized Affirmative Action," *Chronicle of Higher Education*, January 26, 2011, http://chronicle.com/article/Investigators-Say-Naval/126064.

4. Annys Shin, "A Naval Academy Professor Comes Under Fire for His Interactions with Two Students," *Washington Post*, November 2, 2014, http://www .washingtonpost.com/local/a-naval-academy-professor-comes-under-fire -for-his-interactions-with-two-students/2014/11/02/7f1df05c-6048-11e4-8b9e -2ccdac31a031_story.html.

5. Unlike West Point and the Air Force Academy, the Naval Academy permits civilians to chair departments and become dean. About 50 percent of its instructors are civilians.

6. Shin, "Naval Academy Professor Comes Under Fire."

7. In August 2018, the academy terminated Fleming, sixty-four. Fleming appealed his dismissal. A federal administration judge, in July 2019, rejected the academy's allegations and ordered the academy to return Fleming to his job.

8. Tom Bowman, "Naval Academy Teacher Ousted from Class for Critical Article; Admiral Larson Attacks 'Falsehoods' in Piece," *Baltimore Sun*, April 3, 1996, http://articles.baltimoresun.com/1996-04-03/news/1996094031_1_academy-barry-harassment.

9. Carol Burke, "The Naval Academy Brass Still Don't Get It," *Los Angeles Times*, May 6, 1996, http://articles.latimes.com/1996-05-06/local/me-1017_1_naval-academy.

10. Bowman, "Naval Academy Teacher Ousted."

11. Burke, "Naval Academy Brass Still Don't Get It."

12. Ibid.

13. Shin, "Naval Academy Professor Comes Under Fire."

14. Bowman, "Naval Academy Teacher Ousted."

15. Shin, "Naval Academy Professor Comes Under Fire."

16. Paul Vitello, "Adm. Charles R. Larson, 77, Dies; Twice Led Naval Academy," *New York Times*, August 3, 2014, http://www.nytimes.com/2014/08/04/us/adm-charles-r-larson-who-twice-led-naval-academy-is-dead-at-77.html.

17. Tom Bowman, "Removed Naval Instructor Will Return to Classroom; Superintendent Reverses Action Against Critic," *Baltimore Sun*, April 6, 1996, http://articles.baltimoresun.com/1996-04-06/news/1996097104_1_barry-larson-academy.

18. Shin, "A Naval Academy Professor Comes Under Fire."

19. Inspector General of the Air Force, *Report of Investigation Concerning Brig. Gen. Dana H. Born and Col. Richard L. Fullerton*, January 2012, 4, http://posting.csindy.com/images/blogimages/2012/07/03/1341354549-ltr_fr_john_taylor_6-20-12.pdf.

20. Ibid., 4. See also Scott Elliott, "Report Focuses on Air Force Academy Instructors," Air Force Print News, September 2, 2004, http://www.af.mil/News/Article Display/tabid/223/Article/136166/report-focuses-on-air-force-academy-instructors.aspx.

21. Academy Spirit staff, "Larson Report Views Faculty Favorably," *Academy Spirit*, September 17, 2004, http://csmng.com/wp-files/archiveissues/academyspirit /academyspirit_2004-09-17.pdf.

22. See Matthew Harwood, "Air Force Academy Whistleblower Alleges Dog Poisoned in Retaliation," *Truthout*, March 12, 2012, http://www.truth-out.org /news/item/7214:air-force-academy-whistleblower-alleges-dog-poisoned-in -retaliation; and Inspector General of the Air Force, *Report of Investigation Concerning Born and Fullerton*.

23. Chris Lisee, "Debate Reignites over Religion at Air Force Academy," *Washington Post*, July 16, 2012, https://www.washingtonpost.com/national/on-faith /debate-reignites-over-religion-at-air-force-academy/2012/07/16/gJQAv BoPpW_story.html. See also Pam Zubeck, "Air Force Academy Endowment Chief Wears Religion on His Necktie," *Colorado Springs Independent*, March 7, 2018, https://www.csindy.com/TheWire/archives/2018/03/07/air-force -academy-endowment-chief-wears-religion-on-his-necktie.

24. Tom Roeder, "Academy Dean Dana Born Retires 34 Years after She Arrived for AFA Basic Training," *Colorado Springs Gazette*, June 30, 2013, http://gazette .com/academy-dean-dana-born-retires-34-years-after-she-arrived-for-afa -basic-training/article/1503233.

25. Harwood, "Air Force Academy Whistleblower."

26. Ibid.

27. Pam Zubeck, "Air Force Clears Born in COIN Allegation," *Colorado Springs Independent*, June 12, 2012, http://www.csindy.com/IndyBlog/archives/2012/06 /12/air-force-clears-born-in-coin-allegation.

28. Inspector General of the Air Force, *Report of Investigation Concerning Born and Fullerton*.

29. "Eisenhower at Dartmouth," June 14, 1953, YouTube video embedded in Richard C. Cahn, "Don't Join the Book Burners," *Dartmouth Alumni Magazine*, July–August 2016, at 29:20–30:10, https://dartmouthalumnimagazine.com /articles/%E2%80%9Cdon%E2%80%99t-join-book-burners%E2%80%9D.

30. "2019 World Press Freedom Index," Reporters Without Borders, https://rsf.org /en/ranking_table.

31. Tim Bakken, "The Prosecution of Newspapers, Reporters, and Sources for Disclosing Classified Information: The Government's Softening of the First Amendment," *University of Toledo Law Review* 45 (2013): 1.

32. *New York Times v. U.S.*, 403 U.S. 713 (1971).

33. Charlie Savage, "Assange Indicted under Espionage Act, Raising First Amendment Issues," *New York Times*, May 23, 2019, https://www.nytimes.com/2019 /05/23/us/politics/assange-indictment.html. See *U.S. v. Julian Paul Assange*, Indictment, May 23, 2019, https://int.nyt.com/data/documenthelper/1037 -julian-assange-espionage-act-indictment/426b4e534ab60553ba6c/optimized /full.pdf#page=1.

34. Sharon LaFraniere, "Math behind Leak Crackdown: 153 Cases, 4 Years, 0 Indictments," *New York Times*, July 20, 2013, http://www.nytimes.com/2013/07 /21/us/politics/math-behind-leak-crackdown-153-cases-4-years-0-indictments .html.

35. One of the prosecutions began during the George W. Bush administration.

36. Charlie Savage, "Holder Hints Reporter May Be Spared Jail in Leak," *New York Times*, May 27, 2014, http://www.nytimes.com/2014/05/28/us/holder-hints -reporter-may-be-spared-jail-in-leak.html.

37. Noam Cohen and Ravi Somaiya, "Report Says C.I.A. Used Media Leaks to Advantage," *New York Times*, December 9, 2014, http://www.nytimes.com/2014 /12/10/us/politics/report-says-cia-used-media-leaks-to-advantage.html.

38. In 2016 Bradley Manning transitioned into a woman and is now known as Chelsea Manning.

39. Scott Shane, "Former C.I.A. Officer Released after Nearly Two Years in Prison for Leak Case," *New York Times*, February 9, 2015, http://www.nytimes.com /2015/02/10/us/former-cia-officer-released-after-nearly-two-years-in-prison -for-leak-case.html?ref=us.

40. Matt Apuzzo, "C.I.A. Officer Is Found Guilty in Leak Tied to Times Reporter," *New York Times*, January 26, 2015, http://www.nytimes.com/2015/01 /27/us/politics/cia-officer-in-leak-case-jeffrey-sterling-is-convicted-of -espionage.html.

41. Associated Press, "CIA 'Whistleblower' John Kiriakou Jailed for Two Years for Identity Leak," *Guardian*, October 23, 2012, http://www.theguardian.com /world/2012/oct/23/cia-whistleblower-john-kiriakou-leak.

42. Kathleen Hennessey, "Senate Confirms David Petraeus as CIA Director," *Los Angeles Times*, June 30, 2011, http://articles.latimes.com/2011/jun/30/news/la -pn-petraeus-confirmed-20110630.

43. One month after graduating from West Point in 1974, Petraeus married Holly Knowlton, the daughter of the West Point superintendent, Lieutenant General William A. Knowlton. Petraeus was still married to her when he began his relationship with Broadwell.

44. 18 U.S.C. section 1924, "Unauthorized Removal and Retention of Classified Documents or Material," Legal Information Institute, https://www.law.cornell.edu/uscode/text/18/1924.

45. *U.S. v. David Howell Petraeus*, "Factual Basis," March 3, 2015, 13, http://www.justice.gov/sites/default/files/opa/press-releases/attachments/2015/03/03/petraeus-factual-basis.pdf.

46. Jessica Bennett, "Paula Broadwell, David Petraeus and the Afterlife of a Scandal," *New York Times*, May 28, 2016, http://www.nytimes.com/2016/05/29/fashion/david-petraeus-paula-broadwell-scandal-affair.html.

47. Nancy A. Youssef and Shane Harris, "Exclusive: Pentagon May Demote David Petraeus," *Daily Beast*, January 18, 2016, http://www.thedailybeast.com/articles/2016/01/18/exclusive-pentagon-may-demote-david-petraeus.html.

48. Phil Stewart and Idrees Ali, "Retired General, ex-CIA Chief David Petraeus to Receive No Further Punishment," Reuters, January 30, 2016, http://in.reuters.com/article/usa-pentagon-petraeus-idINKCN0V9044.

49. Youssef and Harris, "Pentagon May Demote Petraeus."

50. Charlie Savage, "James Cartwright, Ex-General, Pleads Guilty in Leak Case," *New York Times*, October 17, 2016, http://www.nytimes.com/2016/10/18/us/marine-general-james-cartwright-leak-fbi.html. See also *U.S. v. Cartwright*, "Plea Agreement," October 16, 2016, 12–13, https://www.justice.gov/opa/file/903501/download.

51. Matt Apuzzo, "Ex-C.I.A. Officer Sentenced in Leak Case Tied to Times Reporter," *New York Times*, May 11, 2015, http://www.nytimes.com/2015/05/12/us/ex-cia-officer-sentenced-in-leak-case-tied-to-times-reporter.html.

52. Matt Apuzzo, "Letter Calls Plea Deal for David Petraeus a 'Profound Double Standard,'" *New York Times*, March 16, 2015, http://mobile.nytimes.com/2015/03/16/us/politics/letter-calls-plea-deal-for-david-petraeus-a-profound-double-standard.html.

53. Dean's Institute of Innovation and Development, *Dean's Weekly Significant Activities Report*, March 2, 2016 (West Point, NY: U.S. Military Academy,

2016), 1, 13, https://www.usma.edu/centers/Deans%20Weekly%20Activity%20
Report%20Past%20Issues/Dean%27s%20Weekly%20Significant%20Activi-
ties%20Report%202%20March%202016.pdf.

54. Michelle Eberhart, "Petraeus Offers Advice, Leadership Skills to Cadets,"
Pointer View, January 12, 2017, http://www.pointerview.com/2017/01/12/petraeus
-offers-advice-leadership-skills-to-cadets.

55. Andrea Stone, "Tom Ricks' 'The Generals' Explores How Hard It Is to Get
Rid of Bad Military Leaders," *Huffington Post*, November 2, 2012, https://www
.huffingtonpost.com/2012/11/02/the-generals-tom-ricks_n_1979201.html.

56. Ibid.

57. Thomas E. Ricks, *The Generals: American Military Command from World War II
to Today* (New York: Penguin, 2012), 12.

58. Chris Hedges, *War Is a Force That Gives Us Meaning* (New York: Public Affairs,
2002), 14.

59. This 1986 act made the Chairman of the Joint Chiefs of Staff the principal
military advisor to the president.

60. George Packer, *The Assassins' Gate* (New York: Farrar, Straus and Giroux, 2005),
246.

61. Thomas E. Ricks, *Fiasco: The American Military Adventure in Iraq* (New York:
Penguin, 2006), 69.

62. Dan Vergano, "Half-Million Iraqis Died in the War, New Study Says," *National
Geographic*, October 16, 2013, https://news.nationalgeographic.com/news/2013
/10/131015-iraq-war-deaths-survey-2013.

63. William McGurn, "Silence of the Generals: Should Someone Resign?" *New
York Post*, June 5, 2014, https://nypost.com/2014/06/05/silence-of-the-generals
-should-someone-resign.

64. Ibid.

65. Lewis Sorley, "To Change a War: General Harold K. Johnson and the PROVN
Study," *Parameters* 28, no. 1 (Spring 1998): 93–109, http://ssi.armywarcollege
.edu/pubs/parameters/Articles/98spring/sorley.htm.

66. Richard K. Betts, *American Force: Dangers, Delusions, and Dilemmas in National
Security* (New York: Columbia University Press, 2012), 207.

67. H. R. McMaster, *Dereliction of Duty: Lyndon Johnson, Robert McNamara, the Joint Chiefs of Staff, and the Lies That Led to Vietnam* (New York: Harper, 1997), 322, 334.

68. Samuel Freedman, "A General in a Classroom Takes on the Ethics of War," *New York Times*, February 8, 2014, http://www.nytimes.com/2014/02/08/us/a -general-in-a-classroom-takes-on-the-ethics-of-war.html.

69. Daniel P. Bolger, *Why We Lost: A General's Inside Account of the Iraq and Afghanistan Wars* (New York: First Mariner Books, 2015), 423–24.

70. David S. Cloud and Eric Schmitt, "More Retired Generals Call for Rumsfeld's Resignation," *New York Times*, April 14, 2006, https://www.nytimes.com/2006 /04/14/washington/more-retired-generals-call-for-rumsfelds-resignation .html.

71. David Margolick, "The Night of the Generals," *Vanity Fair*, March 5, 2007, http://www.vanityfair.com/news/2007/04/iraqgenerals200704.

72. Ibid.

73. Ibid.

74. Ibid.

75. Robert Gates, "West Point Evening Lecture, U.S. Military Academy, April 1, 2008," in *Stars and Stripes*, April 22, 2008, http://www.stripes.com/news/text -of-secretary-of-defense-robert-gates-speech-at-west-point-1.77986.

CHAPTER 6: CRIMINALITY, ABUSE, AND CORRUPTION

1. Amanda Weber, "West Point Cadet Armed with Gun Breaks into Former Girlfriend's House," News4SA.Com., March 17, 2016, http://news4sanantonio .com/news/local/sheriffs-office-west-point-cadet-armed-with-gun-breaks -into-former-girlfriends-house.

2. Dalondo Moultrie, "Former West Point Cadet Pleads Guilty to 2016 Burglary," *New Braunfels Herald-Zeitung*, August 16, 2018, http://herald-zeitung.com /news/article_eec028ee-a0e0-11e8-89d3-c369d212e88b.html.

3. Kathy Easwood, "USMA Parents Weekend a Success as Family and Friends Visit Cadets," U.S. Army (website), October 15, 2016, http://www.army.mil /article/157171/USMA_Parents_Weekend_a_success_as_family_and_friends _visit_cadets.

4. Gregory D. Foster, "Why the Founding Fathers Would Object to Today's Military," *Defense One*, July 15, 2013, http://www.defenseone.com/ideas/2013/07/why-founding-fathers-would-object-todays-military/66668.

5. Chalmers Johnson, *The Sorrows of Empire: Militarism, Secrecy, and the End of the Republic* (New York: Henry Holt, 2004), 107. Johnson included racism with criminality.

6. Ibid., 107.

7. Tom Vanden Brook, "Senior Military Officials Sanctioned for More Than 500 Cases of Serious Misconduct," *USA Today*, October 24, 2017, https://www.usatoday.com/story/news/politics/2017/10/24/generals-sex-misconduct-pentagon-army-sanctions-hagel-gillibrand/794770001. The 508 violations concerned misconduct and unethical behavior (234); personnel matters (109); government resources (60); travel violations (55); and 50 others.

8. Ibid.

9. Michelle Tan, "129 Army Battalion, Brigade Commanders Fired since 2003," *Army Times*, February 2, 2015, http://www.armytimes.com/story/military/careers/army/officer/2015/02/02/129-army-battalion-brigade-commanders-fired-since-2003/22531897.

10. U.S. Department of Defense, *2013 Demographics: Profile of the Military Community* (Washington, D.C.: Office of the Deputy Assistant Secretary of Defense, 2014), 52, http://download.militaryonesource.mil/12038/MOS/Reports/2013-Demographics-Report.pdf.

11. "Petraeus Sentenced to 2 Years' Probation, Fine for Sharing Classified Info," NPR, April 23, 2015, https://www.npr.org/sections/thetwo-way/2015/04/23/401672264/gen-david-petraeus-will-be-sentenced-thursday-over-secret-notebooks.

12. Craig Whitlock, "Pentagon Investigations Point to Military System That Promotes Abusive Leaders," *Washington Post*, January 28, 2014, http://www.washingtonpost.com/world/national-security/pentagon-investigations-point-to-military-system-that-promotes-abusive-leaders/2014/01/28/3e1be1f0-8799-11e3-916e-e01534b1e132_story.html.

13. Vanden Brook, "Senior Military Officials Sanctioned."

14. Office of the Inspector General, Department of the Army, *Reports of Army Inspector General (OIG) Investigations into Senior Official Misconduct as Provided to the Washington Post Newspaper, 2011–13*, Governmentattic.org, http://www .governmentattic.org/13docs/ArmyOIGincsSeniorOfficials_2011-2013.pdf.

15. Office of the Inspector General, Department of the Army, *Report of Investigation by the Army Inspector General into Maj. Gen. Michael T. Harrison Sr., August 28, 2013*, document embedded in Craig Whitlock, "Army General Disciplined over Mishandling of Sexual-Assault Case in Japan," *Washington Post*, April 22, 2014, https://www.washingtonpost.com/world/national-security /army-general-disciplined-over-mishandling-of-sexual-assault-case-in-japan /2014/04/22/6339f268-ca2b-11e3-a75e-463587891b57_story.html.

16. Whitlock, "Army General Disciplined."

17. Ernesto Londoño, "Army General Suspended after Fight with Mistress," *Washington Post*, May 21, 2013, https://www.washingtonpost.com/world /national-security/army-general-suspended-after-fight-with-mistress/2013/05 /21/60d12840-c25f-11e2-914f-a7aba60512a7_story.html.

18. Craig Whitlock, "Military Brass, Behaving Badly: Files Detail a Spate of Misconduct Dogging Armed Forces," *Washington Post*, January 26, 2014, https://www.washingtonpost.com/world/national-security/military-brass -behaving-badly-files-detail-a-spate-of-misconduct-dogging-armed-forces /2014/01/26/4d06c770-843d-11e3-bbe5-6a2a3141e3a9_story.html; and Office of the Inspector General, Department of the Army, *Report of Investigation by the Army Inspector General into Brig. Gen. Martin P. Schweitzer, August 23, 2013*, posted on *Washington Post* website, http://apps.washingtonpost.com/g/page /world/martin-p-schweitzer-investigation/770.

19. Office of the Inspector General, Department of the Air Force, *Report of Investigation into Brig. Gen. David C. Uhrich, September 2013*, posted on *Washington Post* website, http://apps.washingtonpost.com/g/page/world/report-on-gen -david-c-uhrich/769.

20. Dan Lamothe, "Army General, Accused of Sexual Assault by Senior Adviser, Retired Quietly with Demotion," *Washington Post*, October 1, 2014, https://www .washingtonpost.com/news/checkpoint/wp/2014/10/01/army-general-accused -of-sexual-assault-by-senior-adviser-retired-quietly-with-demotion.

21. Spencer Ackerman, "Top General Undone by Spa Treatments, Snickers, Broadway Show," *Wired*, August 17, 2012, https://www.wired.com/2012/08

/william-ward. See also Associated Press, "General William Ward Demoted for Lavish Travel, Spending," *Politico*, November 13, 2012; Lolita Baldur, "William Ward, Four Star General, Demoted For Lavish Spending, Ordered To Repay \$82,000," *Huffington Post*, November 13, 2012, http://www.huffington post.com/2012/11/13/william-ward_n_2122379.html.

22. Office of the Inspector General, Department of Defense, *Report of Investigation: Ronald F. Lewis Major General, U.S. Army*, October 4, 2016, https://www.stripes.com/polopoly_fs/1.432732.1475764858!/menu/standard/file /lewis.pdf.

23. Phil McCausland and Courtney Kube, "Former Major General Demoted in Retirement for Using Credit Card at Strip Clubs," NBC News, February 9, 2017, https://www.nbcnews.com/news/us-news/former-major-general -demoted-retirement-using-credit-card-strip-clubs-n719156.

24. Tom Vanden Brook, "Army Demotes 'Swinging General' after Investigation into Affairs, Lifestyle," *USA Today*, December 16, 2016, http://www.usatoday .com/story/news/politics/2016/12/16/army-demotes-swinging-general-david -haight/95493058.

25. Tom Vanden Brook, "Air Force Busts Retired Four-Star General Down Two Ranks for Coerced Sex," *USA Today*, February 1, 2017, http://www.usatoday .com/story/news/politics/2017/02/01/air-force-busts-retired-four-star-general -down-two-ranks-coerced-sex/97356020.

26. Denis Slattery, "Army Boss Axed over Alleged Lewd Messages Sent to Soldier's Wife," *New York Daily News*, October 13, 2017, http://www .nydailynews.com/news/national/army-boss-axed-alleged-lewd-messages -soldier-wife-article-1.3561575.

27. Craig Whitlock, "'Fat Leonard' Probe Expands to Ensnare More Than 60 Admirals," *Washington Post*, November 5, 2017, https://www.washingtonpost .com/investigations/fat-leonard-scandal-expands-to-ensnare-more-than-60 -admirals/2017/11/05/f6a12678-be5d-11e7-97d9-bdab5a0ab381_story.html.

28. Craig Whitlock, "Navy Censures 3 Admirals in Far-Reaching Bribery Investigation," *Washington Post*, February 10, 2015, http://www.washingtonpost.com /world/national-security/navy-censures-3-admirals-for-accepting-gifts-amid -corruption-probe/2015/02/10/4f7a1612-b17b-11e4-886b-c22184f27c35_story .html.

29. Tony Perry, "Navy Officer Becomes 5th Person to Plead Guilty in Bribery Case," *Los Angeles Times*, January 6, 2015, http://www.latimes.com/local/lanow /la-me-ln-officer-navy-bribery-20150106-story.html.

30. Kristina Davis, "Former Navy Admiral Gets Prison in 'Fat Leonard' Bribery Scam," *San Diego Union-Tribune*, May 17, 2017, http://www.sandiegouniontribune .com/news/courts/sd-me-gilbeau-sentence-20170517-story.html.

31. Craig Whitlock, "Highest-Ranking Navy Officer Yet Sentenced in Sex-for-Secrets Scandal," *Washington Post*, March 25, 2016, https://www.washingtonpost .com/news/checkpoint/wp/2016/03/25/highest-ranking-navy-officer-yet -facing-prison-time-in-sex-for-secrets-scandal.

32. Craig Whitlock, "Leaks, Feasts and Sex Parties: How 'Fat Leonard' Infiltrated the Navy's Floating Headquarters in Asia," *Washington Post*, January 31, 2018, https://www.washingtonpost.com/investigations/leaks-feasts-and-sex-parties -how-fat-leonard-infiltrated-the-navys-floating-headquarters-in-asia/2018/01 /23/4d31555c-efdd-11e7-97bf-bba379b809ab_story.html.

33. Ibid.

34. Craig Whitlock, "'Fat Leonard' Bribery Scandal Claims Navy Officer Who Escaped Cambodia's Killing Fields as a Child," *Washington Post*, April 29, 2016, https://www.washingtonpost.com/news/checkpoint/wp/2016/04/29/fat -leonard-bribery-scandal-claims-navy-officer-who-escaped-cambodias -killing-fields-as-a-child.

35. Craig Whitlock, "Navy Commander to Plead Guilty in Corruption Case Involving Lady Gaga Tickets, Prostitutes and Military Secrets," *Washington Post*, January 28, 2016, https://www.washingtonpost.com/news/checkpoint/wp /2016/01/28/navy-commander-to-plead-guilty-in-corruption-case-involving -lady-gaga-tickets-prostitutes-and-military-secrets.

36. Justin Wm. Moyer, "Navy Commander Pleads Guilty to Taking Cash, Luxury Hotel Rooms and Prostitutes as Bribes from 'Fat Leonard,'" *Washington Post*, January 7, 2015, https://www.washingtonpost.com/news/morning-mix/wp/2015 /01/07/navy-commander-pleads-guilty-to-taking-cash-luxury-hotel-rooms -and-prostitutes-as-bribes-from-fat-leonard.

37. Steve Kenny and Christopher Drew, "Contracting Case Implicates 2 Admirals," *New York Times*, November 8, 2013, http://www.nytimes.com/2013/11/09 /us/bribery-case-implicates-2-admirals.html.

38. Craig Whitlock, "The Admiral in Charge of Navy Intelligence Has Not Been Allowed to See Military Secrets for Years," *Washington Post*, January 28, 2016, https://www.washingtonpost.com/news/checkpoint/wp/2016/01/27/the -admiral-in-charge-of-navy-intelligence-has-not-been-allowed-to-see -military-secrets-for-years.

39. "U.S. Navy Admiral and Eight Other Officers Indicted for Trading Classified Information in Massive International Fraud and Bribery Scheme," U.S. Department of Justice, March 14, 2017, https://www.justice.gov/opa/pr/us-navy -admiral-and-eight-other-officers-indicted-trading-classified-information -massive.

40. Craig Whitlock, "Three U.S. Naval Officers Censured in 'Fat Leonard' Corruption Probe," *Washington Post*, July 17, 2015, https://www.washingtonpost.com /world/national-security/three-us-admirals-censured-in-fat-leonard -corruption-probe/2015/07/17/7f29ca1a-2b1f-11e5-a5ea-cf74396e59ec_story.html.

41. Ibid. See also Jeanette Steele, "Admiral Loses Star in 'Fat Leonard' Scandal," *San Diego Union-Tribune*, July 20, 2015, http://www.sandiegouniontribune.com /military/sdut-fat-leonard-censure-letters-2015jul20-htmlstory.html.

42. Whitlock, "Three U.S. Naval Officers Censured."

43. Craig Whitlock, "Navy Censures Retired Admiral for Taking Gifts from 'Fat Leonard,'" *Washington Post*, November 29, 2017, https://www.washingtonpost .com/news/checkpoint/wp/2017/11/29/navy-censures-retired-admiral-for -taking-gifts-from-fat-leonard.

44. Whitlock, "'Fat Leonard' Probe Expands."

45. David Sanger and William Broad, "Pentagon Studies Reveal Major Nuclear Problems," *New York Times*, November 13, 2014, http://www.nytimes.com/2014 /11/14/us/politics/pentagon-studies-reveal-major-nuclear-problems.html.

46. Max Fisher, "Amazing Details from the Drunken Moscow Bender That Got an Air Force General Fired," *Washington Post*, December 19, 2013, https://www .washingtonpost.com/news/worldviews/wp/2013/12/19/amazing-details-from -the-drunken-moscow-bender-that-got-an-air-force-general-fired.

47. Helene Cooper, "Air Force Fires 9 Officers in Scandal over Cheating on Proficiency Tests," *New York Times*, March 27, 2014, https://www.nytimes.com/2014 /03/28/us/air-force-fires-9-officers-accused-in-cheating-scandal.html.

48. Helene Cooper, "Navy Opens Inquiry into Cheating in Reactor Training," *New York Times*, February 4, 2014, http://www.nytimes.com/2014/02/05/us/politics /navy-is-investigating-reports-of-sailors-cheating-on-tests.html.

49. Ibid.

50. Ibid.

51. Helene Cooper, "Fraud in Army Recruiting Bonus Program May Cost Nearly $100 million," *New York Times*, February 4, 2014, http://www.nytimes.com/2014 /02/05/us/politics/wide-reaching-army-recruiting-fraud-described-by -investigators.html.

52. Lisa Rein, "Army Recruiting Scandal Nets New Indictments as Long Probe of Kickbacks Continues," *Washington Post*, October 23, 2015, https://www .washingtonpost.com/news/federal-eye/wp/2015/10/23/army-recruiting -scandal-nets-new-indictments-as-probe-of-kickbacks-continues.

53. Cooper, "Fraud May Cost Nearly $100 Million."

54. Rowan Scarborough, "Army Finishes 5-Year Investigation, but National Guard Troops' Careers Still Left in Limbo," *Washington Times*, August 30, 2017, https://www.washingtontimes.com/news/2017/aug/30/army-finishes -investigation-of-national-guard-recr.

55. Office of the Inspector General, Department of Defense, *Report of Investigation: Lieutenant General David Huntoon, U.S. Army, Superintendent, United States Military Academy, West Point, New York*, May 1, 2012, 28, https://media .defense.gov/2018/Jul/25/2001946758/-1/-1/1/H11L120171242.PDF. See also Craig Whitlock, "West Point Superintendent Misused His Office, Pentagon Report Says," *Washington Post*, June 14, 2013, https://www.washingtonpost.com /world/national-security/west-point-superintendent-misused-his-office-ig -says/2013/06/14/10bff076-d51e-11e2-bc43-c404c3269c73_story.html.

56. Most superintendents serve for five years. Huntoon served as superintendent at the rank of lieutenant general for three years—July 15, 2010, to July 15, 2013—presumably because he was required to serve three years as a three-star general to qualify for a pension increase.

57. Josh White, "Officers' Roles in Christian Video Are Called Ethics Breach," *Washington Post*, August 4, 2007, http://www.washingtonpost.com/wp-dyn /content/article/2007/08/03/AR2007080301907.html.

58. Office of the Inspector General, Department of Defense, *Alleged Misconduct by DOD Officials Concerning Christian Embassy*, July 20, 2007, 26, http://www .militaryreligiousfreedom.org/press-releases/christian_embassy_report.pdf; and Bruce Wilson, "DOD: Pentagon Officers Promoted Right Wing Christian Group," *Talk to Action*, August 3, 2007, http://www.talk2action.org/story/2007/8/3/144028 /7864/Dominionism_in_the_military/DOD_Pentagon_Officers_Promoted _Right_Wing_Christian_Group.

59. "IG: 'Slush Fund' Used at Academy," *Military Times*, March 26, 2013, https://www.militarytimes.com/2013/03/26/ig-slush-fund-used-at-academy.

60. David Lipsky, *Absolutely American: Four Years at West Point* (Boston: Houghton Mifflin, 2003), 50.

61. Sophie Tatum, "Mattis: 'The Jury Is Out' on Whether Women Will Be Successful in Combat Roles," CNN, September 25, 2018, https://www.cnn.com /2018/09/25/politics/james-mattis-women-military-combat/index.html.

62. Dave Philipps, "'This Is Unacceptable': Military Reports a Surge of Sexual Assaults in the Ranks," *New York Times*, May 2, 2019, https://www.nytimes.com /2019/05/02/us/military-sexual-assault.html.

63. Chalmers Johnson, *The Sorrows of Empire: Militarism, Secrecy, and the End of the Republic* (New York: Henry Holt, 2004), 106.

64. Department of Defense, *Annual Report on Sexual Assault in the Military, Fiscal Year 2014*, 10, http://sapr.mil/public/docs/reports/FY14_Annual/FY14_DoD_ SAPRO_Annual_Report_on_Sexual_Assault_Full.pdf.

65. "Report: West Point Department Head Quits after Sexual Harassment Investigation," *Stars and Stripes*, September 9, 2013, https://www.stripes.com/news /army/report-west-point-department-head-quits-after-sexual-harassment -investigation-1.240145#.WUoxzsaZOL8.

66. Melissa Gira Grant, "The Unsexy Truth about Harassment," *New York Review of Books*, December 8, 2017, https://www.nybooks.com/daily/2017/12/08/the -unsexy-truth-about-harassment.

67. Ashley Anderson and Elizabeth Deutsch, "Stop Assaults on Military Campuses," *New York Times*, May 12, 2015, http://www.nytimes.com/2015/05/12 /opinion/stop-assaults-on-military-campuses.html.

68. Alexa Liautaud, "Explicit Photos of Female Service Members Are Being Shared in a Dropbox Folder Called 'Hoes Hoin,'" *Vice News*, March 9, 2018, https://news.vice.com/en_us/article/ywq8py/explicit-photos-of-female -service-members-are-being-shared-in-a-dropbox-folder-called-hoes-hoin.

69. Brandy Zadrozny and James LaPorta, "Cadet Run Out of West Point after Accusing Army's Star Quarterback of Rape," *Daily Beast*, December 9, 2017, https://www.thedailybeast.com/cadet-run-out-of-west-point-after-accusing -armys-star-quarterback-of-rape.

70. 20 U.S.C., sections 1681–1688 (1972).

71. Ibid., section 1092(f).

72. Jake New, "Still Exempt From Title IX," *Inside Higher Education*, August 12, 2014, https://www.insidehighered.com/news/2014/08/12/forty-years-after-first -female-cadets-service-academies-still-exempt-title-ix.

73. Ibid.

74. Ibid.

75. *Feres v. U.S.*, 340 U.S. 135 (1950).

76. Lolita Baldor, "Sexual Assault Reports Double at West Point Military Academy," *Chicago Tribune*, February 7, 2018, http://www.chicagotribune.com /news/nationworld/ct-sexual-assault-reports-double-at-west-point-20180207 -story.html.

77. "DoD Releases Report on Sexual Harassment and Violence at Military Service Academies," U.S. Department of Defense, March 15, 2017, https://dod.defense .gov/News/News-Releases/News-Release-View/Article/1114265/dod-releases -report-on-sexual-harassment-and-violence-at-military-service-acade.

78. Stephen Losey, "Air Force Academy Cadet Sentenced to 75 Days for Sexual Assault," *Air Force Times*, February 7, 2019, https://www.airforcetimes.com /news/your-air-force/2019/02/07/air-force-academy-cadet-sentenced-to-75 -days-for-sexual-assault.

79. Michael P. Rellahan, "West Point Cadet Guilty of Rape in Chester County Trial," Chester County (Pennsylvania) *Daily Local News*, October 12, 2018, https://www.dailylocal.com/news/west-point-cadet-guilty-of-rape-in-chester -county-trial/article_9c503a46-ce3e-11e8-8d8f-cf18a84b747e.html.

80. Derrick Bryson Taylor, "West Point Cadet's Rape Conviction Is Overturned, Drawing Criticism," *New York Times*, June 9, 2019, https://www.nytimes.com /2019/06/09/nyregion/west-point-cadet-rape-case.html.

81. Sofi Sinozich and Lynn Langton, "Rape and Sexual Assault Victimization among College-Age Females, 1995–2013," U.S. Department of Justice, Bureau of Justice Statistics, December 2014, 4, https://www.bjs.gov/content/pub/pdf /rsavcaf9513.pdf.

82. Department of Defense, *Annual Report on Sexual Harassment and Violence at the Military Service Academies, Academic Program Year, 2017–2018*, January 25, 2019, 4, https://www.evawintl.org/Library/DocumentLibraryHandler.ashx ?id=1165.

83. Department of Defense, *Annual Report on Sexual Harassment and Violence at the Military Service Academies, Academic Program Year, 2014–2015*, 10–12, http:// sapr.mil/public/docs/reports/MSA/APY_14-15/APY_14-15_MSA_Full_ Report.pdf.

84. Department of Defense, *Annual Report on Sexual Harassment, 2017–2018*, 8–10.

85. Ibid., 4.

86. Ibid., 8.

87. "Military Service Academy Officials Testify Before House Hearing on Sexual Assault," *PBS NewsHour*, February 13, 2019, 3:54:10–3:56:10, https://www.pbs .org/newshour/nation/watch-live-military-service-academy-officials-testify -before-house-hearing-on-sexual-assault.

88. Air Force Inspector General, *Report of Inquiry Concerning the Air Force Office of Special Investigations' Use of Cadets as Confidential Informants at the Air Force Academy*, February 2014, 8, http://s3.amazonaws.com/content.gazette /Redacted%20ROI%20into%20AFOSI.pdf.

89. Dave Philipps, "Honor and Deception: A Secretive Air Force Program Recruits Academy Students to Inform on Fellow Cadets and Disavows Them Afterward," *Colorado Springs Gazette*, December 1, 2013, http://gazette.com/honor-and -deception-a-secretive-air-force-program-recruits-academy-students-to-inform -on-fellow-cadets-and-disavows-them-afterward/article/1510262.

90. Ibid.

91. Air Force Inspector General, *Cadets as Confidential Informants at the Air Force Academy*, 9.

92. Philipps, "Honor and Deception." See also Dave Philipps, "Cadet Informant at AFA 'Failed' His Mission, Air Force Report Says," *Colorado Springs Gazette*, March 20, 2014, http://gazette.com/cadet-informant-at-afa-failed -his-mission-air-force-report-says/article/1516806.

93. Philipps, "Honor and Deception."

94. Philipps, "Honor and Deception."

95. Dave Philipps, "Informant Debate Renewed as Air Force Revisits Cadet Misconduct," *New York Times*, August 9, 2014, http://www.nytimes.com/2014 /08/10/us/informant-debate-renewed-as-air-force-revisits-cadet-miscon duct.html.

96. Dave Philipps, "Honor and Deception."

97. Diana Jean Schemo, "Ex-Superintendent of Air Force Academy Is Demoted in Wake of Rape Scandal," *New York Times*, July 12, 2003, http://www.nytimes .com/2003/07/12/us/ex-superintendent-of-air-force-academy-is-demoted-in -wake-of-rape-scandal.html.

98. On January 6, 2016, a federal judge sentenced West Point cadet Ricky Hester, twenty-six, to eight years in prison after a jury found him guilty of receipt, distribution, and possession of child pornography. Hester, who supervised a local Sunday school program and participated in the Marines' Toys for Tots program, kept twelve hundred images and videos of children as young as four being forced into sexual activity on his cell phone that, according to the judge, depicted "torture of children." Steve Lieberman, "West Point Cadet Gets 8 Years in Child Pornography Case," *Journal News*, January 7, 2016, http://www .armytimes.com/story/military/crime/2016/01/07/west-point-cadet-gets-8 -years-child-pornography-case/78403790.

99. Michael Moss, "General's Crackdown Faulted in Rapes," *New York Times*, March 26, 2003, http://www.nytimes.com/2003/03/26/us/general-s -crackdown-faulted-in-rapes.html.

100. Ibid.

101. Ibid.

102. Schemo, "Ex-Superintendent of Air Force Academy Is Demoted."

103. Tom Roeder, "Broken Code: AFA Superintendent Calls for Investigation of Athletic Transgressions," *Colorado Springs Gazette*, August 2, 2014, http://gazette.com/broken-code-a-year-long-gazette-investigation-showed-a-trend-of-athlete-misconduct-at-the-air-force-academy-where-despite-the-sacred-honor-code-leaders-and-coaches-recruited-questionable-players-in-order-to-win-on-the-gridiron./article/1534978.

104. Ibid.

105. Philipps, "Informant Debate Renewed."

106. Dave Philipps, "Inquiry Urged on Air Force Academy's Handling of Sexual Assault Cases," *New York Times*, August 20, 2014, http://www.nytimes.com/2014/08/21/us/senators-urge-review-in-handling-of-air-force-academy-sex-assault-cases.html.

107. Philipps, "Informant Debate Renewed."

108. Roeder, "Broken Code."

109. Tom Roeder, "Air Force Academy to Remain Silent on Athletic Department Issues," *Colorado Springs Gazette*, October 21, 2014, http://m.gazette.com/article/1539814.

110. Department of Defense, *Annual Report on Sexual Harassment and Violence at the Military Service Academies*, January 6, 2016, 12, http://sapr.mil/public/docs/reports/MSA/APY_14-15/APY_14-15_MSA_Report.pdf.

111. Tom Roeder, "Air Force Academy Suspends Sexual Assault Counselors amid Probe," *Colorado Springs Gazette*, June 30, 2017, http://gazette.com/air-force-academy-suspends-sexual-assault-counselors-amid-probe/article/1606232.

112. Stephen Losey, "Air Force Academy Busts Dozens of Athletes for Hazing—Now Some of Them May Not Graduate," *Air Force Times*, June 6, 2018, https://www.airforcetimes.com/news/your-air-force/2018/06/06/air-force-academy-busts-dozens-of-athletes-for-hazing-now-some-of-them-may-not-graduate.

113. Tom Roeder, "That Air Force Academy Hazing Ritual Was Like Something out of a Bad Fraternity Movie," *Colorado Springs Gazette*, September 14, https://taskandpurpose.com/air-force-academy-hazing-ritual.

114. James Fallows, "The Tragedy of the American Military," *Atlantic*, January/ February 2015, http://www.theatlantic.com/features/archive/2014/12/the-tra gedy-of-the-american-military/383516.

115. Ibid.

116. Associated Press, "6 West Point Cadets Face Drug Conspiracy Charges," *Army Times*, November 11, 2016, https://www.armytimes.com/news/your -army/2016/11/11/6-west-point-cadets-face-drug-conspiracy-charges. See also Michael Randall, "West Point Cadet Gets 30 Months of Confinement for Drug Conspiracy," *Times Herald-Record*, May 10, 2017, https://www.record online.com/news/20170510/west-point-cadet-gets-30-months-of-confinment -for-drug-conspiracy.

117. Lee Higgins and Richard Liebson, "West Point Meatball Mystery Prompts Federal Charges," *USA Today*, March 21, 2013, http://www.usatoday.com/story /news/nation/2013/03/21/west-point-meatball-charges/2007159.

118. Associated Press, "Charges Dropped in Alleged Meatball Theft at West Point," *Times Herald-Record*, August 24, 2013, http://www.recordonline.com /apps/pbcs.dll/article?AID=/20130824/NEWS/308240323/-.

CHAPTER 7: VIOLENCE, TORTURE, AND WAR CRIMES

1. U.S. Office of Personnel Management, *Employment of Veterans in the Federal Executive Branch, Fiscal Year 2014*, 8, https://www.fedshirevets.gov/veterans -council/veteran-employment-data/employment-of-veterans-in-the-federal -executive-branch-fy2014.pdf.

2. "Veteran Population Projections: FY2015 to FY2045," National Center for Veterans Analysis and Statistics, September 2018, https://www.va.gov/vetdata /docs/QuickFacts/Population_quickfacts_2018.PDF; and "U.S. and World Population Clock," U.S. Census Bureau, 2019, https://www.census.gov/popclock.

3. Simone Weichselbaum, Beth Schwartzapfel, and Tom Meagher, "When Warriors Put on the Badge," Marshall Project, March 30, 2017, https://www .themarshallproject.org/2017/03/30/when-warriors-put-on-the-badge.

4. Simone Weichselbaum, "Police with Military Experience More Likely to Shoot," Marshall Project, October 15, 2018, https://www.themarshallproject .org/2018/10/15/police-with-military-experience-more-likely-to-shoot.

5. Phil Klay, "Don't Confuse Veterans and Violence," *New York Times*, July 19, 2016, https://www.nytimes.com/2016/07/19/opinion/dont-confuse-veterans -and-violence.html.

6. Hugh Gusterson, "Veterans and Mass Shootings," *New York Times*, July 21, 2019, https://www.nytimes.com/2016/07/22/opinion/veterans-and-mass -shootings.html.

7. Hugh Gusterson, "Understanding Mass Killings," *Sapiens*, July 18, 2016, https://www.sapiens.org/column/conflicted/mass-killers-military-service.

8. Crap Reporter, "Annual West Point Pillow Fight Gone Wild—Fight, Weapons, Blood," September 4, 2015, Youtube video, https://www.youtube .com/watch?v=UOMb2FOwIgM.

9. Katharine Q. Seelye, William K. Rashbaum, and Danielle Ivory, "Whitey Bulger's Fatal Prison Beating: 'He Was Unrecognizable,'" *New York Times*, October 31, 2018, https://www.nytimes.com/2018/10/31/us/who-killed-whitey -bulger.html. See also Kyle Smith, "A Democratic Politician Goes to Jail, Now Advocates for Prison Reform," *New York Post*, September 6, 2015, http://nypost .com/2015/09/06/a-democratic-politician-goes-to-jail-now-advocates-for -prison-reform.

10. Dave Philipps, "At West Point, Annual Pillow Fight Becomes Weaponized," *New York Times*, September 4, 2015, https://www.nytimes.com/2015/09/05/us /at-west-point-annual-pillow-fight-becomes-weaponized.html.

11. Ibid.

12. Mary Bowerman, "30 Cadets Injured in Bloody Pillow Fight at West Point," *USA Today*, September 6, 2015, http://www.usatoday.com/story/news/nation -now/2015/09/05/bloody-pillow-fight-west-point-military-cadets-injured /71766336.

13. Philipps, "Pillow Fight Becomes Weaponized."

14. Robert Caslen, "Statement from the 59th Superintendent, United States Military Academy," Service Academy Forums, September 5, 2015, https://www .serviceacademyforums.com/index.php?threads/plebe-pillow-pugilists.44578 /page-2.

15. In a similar ritual at the Air Force Academy in Colorado Springs, in 2012, first-year cadets threw their cadet leaders into the snow after the first winter storm.

A brawl broke out, and twenty-seven cadets suffered "concussions, cuts, broken bones and a bite wound." A spokesman for the Air Force called the assaults a "teachable moment." Philipps, "Pillow Fight Becomes Weaponized."

16. Associated Press, "West Point Bans Annual Pillow Fight after Dozens Are Injured," *New York Post*, November 25, 2015, http://nypost.com/2015/11/25/west -point-bans-annual-pillow-fight-after-dozens-are-injured.

17. Dan Lamothe, "West Point Women Have a New, Bloody Requirement as the Army Completes Gender Integration," *Washington Post*, September 21, 2016, https://www.washingtonpost.com/news/checkpoint/wp/2016/09/21/west -point-women-have-a-new-bloody-requirement-as-the-army-completes -gender-integration.

18. Dave Philipps, "Concussions in a Required Class: Boxing at Military Acade-mies," *New York Times*, September 29, 2015, http://www.nytimes.com/2015/09 /30/us/despite-concussions-boxing-is-still-required-for-military-cadets.html.

19. Amir Sariaslan, David J. Sharp, Brian M. D'Onofrio, Henrik Larsson, and Seena Fazel, "Long-Term Outcomes Associated with Traumatic Brain Injury in Child-hood and Adolescence: A Nationwide Swedish Cohort Study of a Wide Range of Medical and Social Outcomes," *PLOS Medicine*, October 23, 2016, http:// journals.plos.org/plosmedicine/article?id=10.1371/journal.pmed.1002103.

20. Philipps, "Concussions in a Required Class."

21. "Traumatic Brain Injury," Department of Defense, https://www.defense.gov /News/Special-Reports/0315_tbi.

22. Philipps, "Concussions in a Required Class."

23. Philipps, "Pillow Fight Becomes Weaponized."

24. Kelly G. Kilcoyne, Jonathan F. Dickens, Steven J. Svoboda, Brett D. Owens, Kenneth L. Cameron, Robert T. Sullivan, and John-Paul Rue, "Reported Concussion Rates for Three Division I Football Programs: An Evaluation of the New NCAA Concussion Policy," *Sports Health: A Multidisciplinary Approach* 6, no. 5 (September 2014): 402–5, https://www.ncbi.nlm.nih.gov/pmc /articles/PMC4137672.

25. Dave Philipps, "Generals Sought More Positive Coverage on Head Injuries, Document Shows," *New York Times*, September 30, 2015, http://www.nytimes

.com/2015/09/30/us/generals-sought-more-positive-coverage-document
-shows.html.

26. U.S. Military Academy, Superintendent Trip Exsum, Pentagon, September 16, 2015, document embedded in "Summary of a Meeting at the Pentagon," *New York Times*, https://www.nytimes.com/interactive/2015/09/29/us/west-point-document-summarizes-a-meeting-of-army-generals.html.

27. Philip W. Leon, *Bullies and Cowards: The West Point Hazing Scandal, 1898–1901* (Westport, CT: Greenwood Press, 2000), 21–22.

28. Ibid., 48.

29. "Former Cadet Booze Dies in Great Agony," *San Francisco Call*, December 4, 1900, https://cdnc.ucr.edu/cgi-bin/cdnc?a=d&d=SFC19001204.2.38.

30. Leon, *Bullies and Cowards*, 48.

31. Ibid., 71.

32. Ibid., x.

33. David Lipsky, *Absolutely American: Four Years at West Point* (Boston: Houghton Mifflin, 2003), 20–21.

34. Dexter Filkins, "The Fall of the Warrior King," *New York Times*, October 23, 2005, http://www.nytimes.com/2005/10/23/magazine/23sassaman.html.

35. Sassaman would go on to write a memoir titled *Warrior King: The Triumph and Betrayal of an American Commander in Iraq* (New York: St. Martin's Press, 2008).

36. Filkins, "Warrior King."

37. Charlie Savage and Elisabeth Bumiller, "An Iraqi Massacre, a Light Sentence and a Question of Military Justice," *New York Times*, January 27, 2012, https://www.nytimes.com/2012/01/28/us/an-iraqi-massacre-a-light-sentence-and-a-question-of-military-justice.html.

38. Thomas E. Ricks, *The Gamble: General David Petraeus and the American Military Adventure in Iraq, 2006–2008* (New York: Penguin, 2009), 5.

39. Neta C. Crawford, "What Is War Good For? Background Ideas and Assumptions about the Legitimacy, Utility, and Costs of Offensive War," *British Journal of Politics and International Relations* 18, no. 2 (2016): 290.

40. Michael Stephenson, *The Last Full Measure: How Soldiers Die in Battle* (New York: Crown, 2012), 383.

41. Mark Danner, *Spiral: Trapped in the Forever War* (New York: Simon & Schuster, 2016), 6.

42. Ibid., 2.

43. Ibid., 6.

44. Ibid., 58.

45. Ibid., 57.

46. Darren K. Carlson, "Would Americans Fight Terrorism by Any Means Necessary?" Gallup, March 1, 2005, http://news.gallup.com/poll/15073/would-americans-fight-terrorism-any-means-necessary.aspx.

47. Chris Kahn, "Exclusive: Most Americans Support Torture Against Terror Suspects—Reuters/Ipsos Poll," Reuters, March 30, 2016, https://www.reuters.com/article/us-usa-election-torture-exclusive-idUSKCN0WW0Y3.

48. Danner, *Spiral*, 63.

49. Neil Lewis and the *New York Times*, "A Guide to the Memos on Torture," *New York Times*, https://www.nytimes.com/ref/international/24MEMO-GUIDE.html. See also Wilson Andrews and Alicia Parlapiano, "A History of the C.I.A.'s Secret Interrogation Program," *New York Times*, December 9, 2014, http://www.nytimes.com/interactive/2014/12/09/world/timeline-of-cias-secret-interrogation-program.html.

50. John Yoo, U.S. Department of Justice, Memorandum for William J. Haynes II, General Counsel of the Department of Defense, "Re: Military Interrogation of Alien Unlawful Combatants Held Outside the United States," March 14, 2003, 45, https://www.aclu.org/files/pdfs/safefree/yoo_army_torture_memo.pdf.

51. Scott Shane, "Report Portrays a Broken C.I.A. Devoted to a Failed Approach," *New York Times*, December 9, 2014, http://www.nytimes.com/2014/12/10/world/senate-torture-report-shows-cia-infighting-over-interrogation-program.html. See also Senate Select Committee on Intelligence, Committee Study of the Central Intelligence Agency's Detention and Interrogation Program,

December 3, 2014, document embedded in "The Senate Committee's Report on the C.I.A.'s Use of Torture," *New York Times*, December 9, 2014, 9–11, https://www.nytimes.com/interactive/2014/12/09/world/cia-torture-report -document.html.

52. Committee on Intelligence, Central Intelligence Agency's Detention and Interrogation Program, 9–10; and Spencer Ackerman, "Torture by Another Name: CIA Used 'Water Dousing' on at Least 12 Detainees," *Guardian*, October 16, 2015, http://www.theguardian.com/law/2015/oct/16/cia-torture -water-dousing-waterboard-like-technique.

53. Seymour M. Hersh, *Chain of Command: The Road from 9/11 to Abu Ghraib* (New York: HarperCollins, 2004), 2–3.

54. Central Intelligence Agency, OMS Guidelines on Medical and Psychological Support to Detainee Rendition, Interrogation, and Detention, December 2004, 8, https://www.cia.gov/library/readingroom/docs/0006541536.pdf.

55. Ibid., 4.

56. Ibid., 16.

57. Ibid., 10.

58. Committee on Intelligence, Central Intelligence Agency's Detention and Interrogation Program, 63.

59. Ibid., 149n901.

60. Ibid., 105.

61. Ibid., 18; and Shane, "Report Portrays a Broken C.I.A."

62. Mark Mazzetti, "C.I.A. Report Found Value of Brutal Interrogation Was Inflated," *New York Times*, January 20, 2015, http://www.nytimes.com/2015 /01/21/world/cia-report-found-value-of-brutal-interrogation-was-inflated .html.

63. Mark Mazzetti, "Panel Faults C.I.A. Over Brutality and Deceit in Terrorism Interrogations," *New York Times*, December 9, 2014, http://www.nytimes.com /2014/12/10/world/senate-intelligence-committee-cia-torture-report.html.

64. Cliff Sloan, "The Path to Closing Guantánamo," *New York Times*, January 5, 2015, http://www.nytimes.com/2015/01/06/opinion/the-path-to-closing -guantanamo.html.

65. Marina Koren, "Who Is Left at Guantanamo?" *Atlantic*, May 12, 2016, http://www.theatlantic.com/politics/archive/2016/05/guanatanamo-bay -forever-prisoners/482289.

66. "The Guantánamo Docket," *New York Times*, data updated May 2, 2018, http://projects.nytimes.com/guantanamo. See also Human Rights First, Fact Sheet: Guantánamo by the Numbers, updated October 10, 2018, https://www .humanrightsfirst.org/sites/default/files/gtmo-by-the-numbers.pdf.

67. Committee on Intelligence, Central Intelligence Agency's Detention and Interrogation Program, 12.

68. Hersh, *Chain of Command*, 12–13.

69. Ibid., 14.

70. Wired.com staff, "Disturbing New Photos from Abu Ghraib," *Wired*, March 28, 2008, https://www.wired.com/2008/03/gallery-abu-ghraib.

71. Philip Gourevitch and Errol Morris, "Exposure: The Woman behind the Camera at Abu Ghraib," *New Yorker*, March 24, 2008, https://www.newyorker .com/magazine/2008/03/24/exposure-5.

72. Editorial Board, "Will Anyone Pay for Abu Ghraib?" *New York Times*, February 5, 2015, http://www.nytimes.com/2015/02/05/opinion/will-anyone -pay-for-abu-ghraib.html.

73. Jane Mayer, "A Deadly Interrogation: Can the C.I.A. Legally Kill a Prisoner?" *New Yorker*, November 14, 2005, http://www.newyorker.com/magazine/2005/11 /14/a-deadly-interrogation.

74. Gourevitch and Morris, "Exposure."

75. "Iraq Prison Abuse Scandal Fast Facts," CNN, March 4, 2019, http://www.cnn .com/2013/10/30/world/meast/iraq-prison-abuse-scandal-fast-facts.

76. Eric Fair, "An Iraq Interrogator's Nightmare," *Washington Post*, February 9, 2007, http://www.washingtonpost.com/wp-dyn/content/article/2007/02/08 /AR2007020801680.html.

77. Phillip Carter, "The Road to Abu Ghraib: The Biggest Scandal of the Bush Administration Began at the Top," *Washington Monthly*, November 1, 2004, https://washingtonmonthly.com/2004/11/01/the-road-to-abu-ghraib.

78. Danner, *Spiral*, 60.

79. Hersh, *Chain of Command*, 21.

80. Ibid., 40.

81. Ibid., 24.

82. Frank Rich, *The Greatest Story Ever Sold: The Decline and Fall of Truth from 9/11 to Katrina* (New York: Penguin, 2006), 155.

83. Ashley Rundell, "Federal Appeals Court Rejects Release of Abu Ghraib Photographs," *Jurist*, August 22, 2018, https://www.jurist.org/news/2018/08 /federal-appeals-court-rejects-release-of-abu-ghraib-photographs.

84. Seymour Hersh, "The General's Report," *New Yorker*, June 25, 2007, http://www .newyorker.com/magazine/2007/06/25/the-generals-report.

85. Hersh, "General's Report."

86. Hersh, *Chain of Command*, 43.

87. Antonio M. Taguba, "Stop the C.I.A. Spin on the Senate Torture Report," *New York Times*, August 5, 2014, http://www.nytimes.com/2014/08/06/opinion /stop-the-cia-spin-on-the-senate-torture-report.html.

88. Taguba, "Stop the C.I.A. Spin."

89. Hersh, *Chain of Command*, 18.

90. Hersh, "General's Report."

91. Hersh, *Chain of Command*, 15.

92. Ibid., 20.

93. Crawford, "What Is War Good For?," 289.

94. Marilyn B. Young, "Bombing Civilians from the Twentieth to the Twenty-First Centuries," in *Bombing Civilians: A Twentieth Century History*, edited by Yuki Tanaka and Marilyn B. Young (New York: New Press, 2009), 154–55.

95. David Sanger, "U.S. General Considered Nuclear Response in Vietnam War, Cables Show," *New York Times*, October 6, 2018, https://www.nytimes.com /2018/10/06/world/asia/vietnam-war-nuclear-weapons.html.

96. Mark Selden, "A Forgotten Holocaust: U.S. Bombing Strategy, the Destruction of Japanese Cities, and the American Way of War from the Pacific War to Iraq," in Tanaka and Young, *Bombing Civilians*, 93.

97. Jeremy Williams, "'Kill 'Em All': The American Military in Korea," *BBC History*, February 17, 2011, http://www.bbc.co.uk/history/worldwars/coldwar /korea_usa_01.shtml.

98. Williams, "'Kill 'Em All.'"

99. Charles J. Hanley and Martha Mendoza, "'Shoot Refugees' Korean War Letter Went Undisclosed," *USA Today*, April 13, 2007, http://usatoday30 .usatoday.com/news/world/2007-04-13-korea-refugees_N.htm.

100. Sang-Hun Choe, Charles J. Hanley, and Martha Mendoza, "Bridge at No Gun Ri," Associated Press Special Report, September 29, 1999, https:// msuweb.montclair.edu/~furrg/vietnam/aponnogunri.pdf.

101. Rachel Mullin, "July 26, 1950: No Gun Ri Massacre," Teaching People's History, Zinn Education Project, https://www.zinnedproject.org/news/tdih /no-gun-ri-massacre.

102. Charles J. Hanley, Sang-Hun Choe, and Martha Mendoza, *The Bridge at No Gun Ri: A Hidden Nightmare from the Korean War* (New York: Henry Holt, 2001), 287.

103. Choe, Hanley, and Mendoza, "Bridge at No Gun Ri."

104. Army Inspector General, "No Gun Ri Review," January 2001, x, https:// msuweb.montclair.edu/~furrg/vietnam/aponnogunri.pdf.

105. Charles J. Hanley and Martha Mendoza, "Letter on Korean War Massacre Reveals Plan to Shoot Refugees," *Washington Post*, May 30, 2006, http://www .washingtonpost.com/wp-dyn/content/article/2006/05/29/AR2006052900914 .html.

106. Hanley and Mendoza, "'Shoot Refugees' Korean War Letter."

107. Choe, Hanley, and Mendoza, "Bridge at No Gun Ri."

108. Hanley and Mendoza, "Letter on Korean War Massacre."

109. Ibid.

110. Hanley and Mendoza, "'Shoot Refugees' Korean War Letter."

111. Charles J. Hanley and Martha Mendoza, "Pentagon Withheld Document from Report on No Gun Ri Killings," *New York Times*, April 15, 2007, https:// www.nytimes.com/2007/04/15/world/americas/15iht-military.1.5293259.html ?_r=0.

112.   Hanley and Mendoza, "'Shoot Refugees' Korean War Letter."

113.   Williams, "'Kill 'Em All.'"

114.   Neil Sheehan, *A Bright Shining Lie: John Paul Vann and America in Vietnam* (New York: Random House, 1988), 383.

115.   Ibid., 383.

116.   Deborah Nelson and Nick Turse, "A Tortured Past," *Los Angeles Times*, April 20, 2006, http://articles.latimes.com/2006/aug/20/nation/na-viet nam20.

117.   Joe Bageant, "Remembering Colonel Tony Herbert," April 12, 2007, https://bageant.typepad.com/joe/2007/04/remembering_col.html.

118.   Nelson and Turse, "Tortured Past."

119.   Ibid.

120.   Ibid.

121.   Ibid.

122.   Ibid. See also Sam Roberts, "Anthony B. Herbert, Decorated War Hero Turned Army Whistleblower, Dies at 84," *New York Times*, February 25, 2015, https://www.nytimes.com/2015/02/26/us/anthony-b-herbert-decorated-war -hero-turned-army-whistleblower-dies-at-84.html.

123.   Bageant, "Remembering Colonel Tony Herbert."

124.   Nelson and Turse, "Tortured Past."

125.   Ibid.

126.   Ibid.

127.   Bageant, "Remembering Colonel Tony Herbert."

128.   Sheehan, *Bright Shining Lie*, 689.

129.   Valerie Wieskamp, "My Lai, Sexual Assault and the Black Blouse Girl: Forty-Five Years Later, One of America's Most Iconic Photos Hides Truth in Plain Sight," Reading the Pictures, October 29, 2013, http://www.readingthepictures .org/2013/10/my-lai-sexual-assault-and-the-black-blouse-girl-forty-five-years -later-one-of-americas-most-iconic-photos-hides-truth-in-plain-sight.

130. Michael Bilton and Kevin Sim, *Four Hours in My Lai* (New York: Penguin, 1992), 128–29.

131. Ibid., 130–31.

132. Ibid., 129–30.

133. Ibid., 127–28. See also William Thomas Allison, *My Lai: An American Atrocity in the Vietnam War* (Baltimore: John Hopkins, 2012), 45–46.

134. Investigating Power, "My Lai Massacre," interview with Seymour Hersh, YouTube video, https://www.youtube.com/watch?v=VWchy6ykNnQ.

135. Bilton and Sim, *Four Hours in My Lai*, 132–33.

136. Lucian K. Truscott IV, "The Good Lieutenant Calley," *Village Voice*, March 4, 1971, reprinted in Tony Ortega, "Lt. William Calley at His My Lai Trial: 'I Carried Out the Orders I Was Given,'" *Village Voice*, November 23, 2010, http://www.villagevoice.com/news/lt-william-calley-at-his-my-lai-trial-i -carried-out-the-orders-i-was-given-6679932.

137. Ibid.

138. The one exception prior to 2019 was that commanders could not reduce sentences for sexual assault, but this had been in place for only a few years.

139. Allison, *My Lai*, 114.

140. Tony Adams, "Bo Callaway Dies at Age 86," *Columbus (Georgia) Ledger-Enquirer*, March 15, 2014, https://www.ledger-enquirer.com/news/local /article29324335.html.

141. Michael T. Kaufman, "Oran Henderson, 77, Dies; Acquitted in My Lai Case," *New York Times*, June 5, 1998, http://www.nytimes.com/1998/06/05/world /oran-henderson-77-dies-acquitted-in-my-lai-case.html.

142. Sheehan, *Bright Shining Lie*, 690.

143. David Stout, "Gen. S. W. Koster, 86, Who Was Demoted after My Lai, Dies," *New York Times*, February 11, 2006, http://www.nytimes.com/2006/02/11 /national/11koster.html.

144. Allison, *My Lai*, 64–66.

145. Peers Commission, *Report of the Department of the Army Review of the Preliminary Investigations into the My Lai Incident*, Volume I (hereafter *Peers*

Commission Report), March 14, 1970, 12-9 to 12-12, https://www.loc.gov/rr/frd /Military_Law/pdf/RDAR-Vol-I.pdf.

146. Ibid., 12-9.

147. Stout, "Gen. S. W. Koster."

148. Thomas E. Ricks, *The Generals: American Military Command from World War II to Today* (Penguin: New York, 2012), 305.

149. Ibid.

150. *Peers Commission Report*, 10-16.

151. Ricks, *Generals*, 307.

152. *Peers Commission Report*, 12–9 to 12–35.

153. Lewis Sorley, *Westmoreland: The General Who Lost Vietnam* (New York: Houghton Mifflin Harcourt, 2011), 214.

154. Fred L. Borch, "*Samuel W. Koster v. The United States*: A Forgotten Legal Episode from the Massacre at My Lai," *Army Lawyer*, November 2015, 2–3, https://www.loc.gov/rr/frd/Military_Law/pdf/11-2015.pdf.

155. Sorley, *Westmoreland*, 214.

156. Joseph Goldstein, Burke Marshall, and Jack Schwartz, eds., *The My Lai Massacre and Its Cover-up: Beyond the Reach of Law* (New York: Free Press, 1976), 7, 314–15.

157. Ibid., 2.

158. Ricks, *Generals*, 309.

159. Philip G. Zimbardo, quote on Stanford Prison Experiment home page, http://www.prisonexp.org.

160. Craig Haney, Curtis Banks, and Philip Zimbardo, "A Study of Prisoners and Guards in a Simulated Prison," *Naval Research Reviews*, September 1973, 1, http://www.zimbardo.com/downloads/1973%20A%20Study%20of%20Prisoners%20and%20Guards,%20Naval%20Research%20Reviews.pdf.

161. Maria Konnikova, "The Real Lesson of the Stanford Prison Experiment," June 12, 2015, *New Yorker*, http://www.newyorker.com/science/maria -konnikova/the-real-lesson-of-the-stanford-prison-experiment.

162. "Philip Zimbardo's Response to Recent Criticisms of the Stanford Prison Experiment," Stanford Prison Experiment, http://www.prisonexp.org /response.

163. Philip Zimbardo, *The Lucifer Effect: Understanding How Good People Turn Evil* (New York: Random House, 2007), 5.

164. Ibid., xii.

165. Richard C. Paddock, "Bob Kerrey's War Record Fuels Debate in Vietnam on His Role at New University," *New York Times*, June 2, 2016, http://www.ny times.com/2016/06/03/world/asia/vietnam-fulbright-university-kerrey.html.

166. Richard C. Paddock, "Two Survivors Say U.S. Unit Killed Villagers 'in Cold Blood,'" *Los Angeles Times*, April 29, 2001, http://articles.latimes.com/2001 /apr/29/news/mn-57238.

167. Gregory L. Vistica, "One Awful Night in Thanh Phong," *New York Times*, April 25, 2001, http://www.nytimes.com/2001/04/25/magazine/one-awful -night-in-thanh-phong.html.

168. Ibid.

169. Ibid.

170. Ibid.

171. Nicholas Kulish, Christopher Drew, and Matthew Rosenberg, "Navy SEALs, a Beating Death and Claims of a Cover-Up," *New York Times*, December 17, 2015, https://www.nytimes.com/2015/12/17/world/asia/navy-seal-team-2 -afghanistan-beating-death.html.

172. Sarah Kaplan, "Report: Navy SEALs Covered Up Accusations of Deadly Abuse," *Washington Post*, December 17, 2015 https://www.washingtonpost .com/news/morning-mix/wp/2015/12/17/report-navy-seals-covered-up -accusations-of-deadly-abuse.

173. Kulish, Drew, and Rosenberg, "Navy SEALs, a Beating Death."

174. Ibid.

175. Ibid.

176. Kevin Maurer and Spencer Ackerman, "Navy SEALs, Marines Charged with Green Beret Logan Melgar's Murder," *Daily Beast*, November 15, 2018,

https://www.thedailybeast.com/seals-marines-charged-with-green-beret
-logan-melgars-murder.

177. Kate Andrews, "Marine Pleads Guilty to Hazing Death of Green Beret in
     Mali," *New York Times*, June 6, 2019, https://www.nytimes.com/2019/06/06/us
     /politics/green-beret-death-mali.html. See also Dan Lamothe, "Navy SEAL
     Pleads Guilty in Hazing Death of Special Forces Soldier in Mali," *Washington
     Post*, May 16, 2019, https://www.washingtonpost.com/world/national-security
     /navy-seal-pleads-guilty-in-hazing-death-of-special-forces-soldier-in-mali
     /2019/05/16/9482ad52-77f9-11e9-b3f5-5673edf2d127_story.html.

178. Dave Philipps, "Decorated Navy SEAL Is Accused of War Crimes in Iraq,"
     New York Times, November 15, 2018, https://www.nytimes.com/2018/11/15/us
     /navy-seal-edward-gallagher-isis.html.

179. Dave Philipps, "Navy SEAL Chief Accused of War Crimes Is Found Not
     Guilty of Murder," *New York Times*, July 2, 2019, https://www.nytimes.com
     /2019/07/02/us/navy-seal-trial-verdict.html.

180. Dave Philipps, "Acquittal of Navy SEAL May Deter Others from Reporting
     Crimes, Some Officials Worry," *New York Times*, July 3, 2019, https://www
     .nytimes.com/2019/07/03/us/Edward-Gallagher-acquitted.html.

181. Dave Philipps, "Navy SEAL War Crimes Witness Says He Was the Killer,"
     New York Times, June 20, 2019, https://www.nytimes.com/2019/06/20/us/navy
     -seal-edward-gallagher-corey-scott.html.

182. Philipps, "Acquittal of Navy SEAL."

183. Christopher J. Levesque, "The Truth behind My Lai," *New York Times*,
     March 16, 2018, https://www.nytimes.com/2018/03/16/opinion/the-truth
     -behind-my-lai.html.

184. Mark Boal, "The Kill Team: How U.S. Soldiers in Afghanistan Murdered
     Innocent Civilians," *Rolling Stone*, March 28, 2011, http://www.rollingstone
     .com/politics/news/the-kill-team-20110327.

185. Ibid.

186. Ibid.

187. Ibid.

188. Karin Assmann, John Goetz, and Marc Hujer, "'Let's Kill': Report Reveals Discipline Breakdown in Kill Team Brigade," *Spiegel*, April 4, 2011, http://www.spiegel.de/international/world/let-s-kill-report-reveals-discipline-break down-in-kill-team-brigade-a-754952.html.

189. Boal, "Kill Team."

190. Caleb Phillips, "MWI and SCPME Screen 'Kill Team' to More Than 500 Cadets," *Pointer View*, August 25, 2016, 7, http://www.usma.edu/pv/Pointer %20View%20Archive/16AUG25.pdf.

191. Ralph Lopez, "Second Soldier Alleges Former Tillman Commander Ordered '360 Rotational Fire' in Iraq," *Truthout*, September 12, 2010, http://truth-out .org/archive/component/k2/item/91728:second-soldier-alleges-former -tillman-commander-ordered-360-rotational-fire-in-iraq.

192. Ibid.

193. Ibid.

194. Ibid.

195. David Finkel, "U.S. Gunfire Kills Two Reuters Employees in Baghdad," excerpt from Finkel, *The Good Soldiers* (New York: Farrar, Straus and Giroux, 2009), in *Washington Post*, April 6, 2010, 4, http://www.washingtonpost.com /wp-dyn/content/article/2010/04/06/AR2010040601368_4.html.

196. Ralph Lopez, "Soldier at WikiLeaks Scene Says No Attack Was Being Planned," *Truthout*, August 16, 2010, https://truthout.org/articles/soldier-at -wikileaks-scene-says-no-attack-was-being-planned.

197. Finkel, "U.S. Gunfire," 5.

198. Ibid. See also Finkel, *The Good Soldiers*, 97–105.

199. Lopez, "Second Soldier."

200. Peter Grier, "Killings of Iraqi Journalists: U.S. Says They Were Not War Crimes," *Christian Science Monitor*, April 7, 2010, https://www.csmonitor.com /USA/Military/2010/0407/Killings-of-Iraqi-journalists-US-says-they-were -not-war-crimes.

201. Julie Tate, "Bradley Manning Sentenced to 35 Years in WikiLeaks Case," *Washington Post*, August 21, 2013, https://www.washingtonpost.com/world

/national-security/judge-to-sentence-bradley-manning-today/2013/08/20
/85bee184-09d0-11e3-b87c-476db8ac34cd_story.html.

202. Laura Jarrett and Gloria Borger, "Obama Commutes Sentence of Chelsea Manning," CNN, January 18, 2017, http://www.cnn.com/2017/01/17/politics /chelsea-manning-sentence-commuted/index.html.

203. Alissa J. Rubin, "2 Iraqi Journalists Killed as U.S. Forces Clash with Militias," *New York Times*, July 13, 2007, http://www.nytimes.com/2007/07/13/world /middleeast/13iraq.html.

204. Finkel, "U.S. Gunfire," 5.

205. Lopez, "Soldier at WikiLeaks Scene."

206. Lopez, "Second Soldier."

207. Gary Sheftick, "Host of Changes to UCMJ Take Effect," *Pointer View*, January 17, 2019, 2.

208. In 2019, 122 of the world's 195 countries were members of the International Criminal Court.

209. Melvin A. Goodman, *National Insecurity: The Cost of American Militarism* (San Francisco: City Lights Books, 2013), 12.

210. Chalmers Johnson, *The Sorrows of Empire: Militarism, Secrecy, and the End of the Republic* (New York: Henry Holt, 2004), 5.

211. Mark Landler, "Bolton Expands on His Boss's Views, Except on North Korea," *New York Times*, September 10, 2018, https://www.nytimes.com /2018/09/10/us/politics/trump-plo-bolton-international-criminal-court .html.

212. Murtaza Hussain, "The U.S. Goes to War against the ICC to Cover Up Alleged War Crimes in Afghanistan," *Intercept*, September 12, 2018, https:// theintercept.com/2018/09/12/john-bolton-icc-afghanistan-war-crimes.

CONCLUSION: THE CONSEQUENCES OF SEPARATION

1. When he was a lieutenant colonel, Paul Yingling said that in the military a private who loses a rifle is punished more than a general who contributes to losing a war. Thomas E. Ricks, "General Failure," *Atlantic*,

November 2012, https://www.theatlantic.com/magazine/archive/2012/11 /general-failure/309148.

2. Nicole Perlroth and Scott Shane, "In Baltimore and Beyond, a Stolen N.S.A. Tool Wreaks Havoc," *New York Times*, May 25, 2019, https://www.nytimes.com /2019/05/25/us/nsa-hacking-tool-baltimore.html.

3. Missy Ryan, Dan Lamothe, and Paul Sonne, "Pentagon Marks a Year without Press Secretary Briefings," *Washington Post*, May 31, 2019, https://www .washingtonpost.com/world/national-security/pentagon-marks-a-year -without-press-secretary-briefing/2019/05/31/dd6c299e-1289-4a19-bde7 -09bbc1b2c480_story.html.

4. Phil Stewart, Idrees Ali, and Roberta Rampton, "U.S. Deploys More Troops to Middle East, Blames Iran for Tanker Attacks," Reuters, May 24, 2019, https://www.reuters.com/article/us-usa-iran-military/us-deploys-more-troops -to-middle-east-blames-iran-for-tanker-attacks-idUSKCN1SU1VQ.

5. Joel D. Rayburn and Frank K. Sobchak, eds., with Jeanne F. Godfroy, Matthew D. Morton, James S. Powell, and Matthew M. Zais, *The U.S. Army in the Iraq War*, vol. 2, Surge and Withdrawal, 2007–2011 (Carlisle, PA: U.S. Army War College Press, January 2019), 620, https://ssi.armywarcollege.edu /pubs/display.cfm?pubID=1376.

6. Ibid., 615.

7. Ibid., 615–21.

8. Ibid., 622.

9. Ibid., 622–39.

10. Sydney J. Freedberg Jr., "US 'Gets Its Ass Handed to It' in Wargames: Here's a $24 Billion Fix," *Breaking Defense*, March 7, 2019, https://breakingdefense .com/2019/03/us-gets-its-ass-handed-to-it-in-wargames-heres-a-24-billion -fix.

11. Ibid.

12. Ibid.

13. Melvin A. Goodman, *National Insecurity: The Cost of American Militarism* (San Francisco: City Lights, 2013), 15.

14. Chris Hedges, *War Is a Force That Gives Us Meaning* (New York: Public Affairs, 2002), 17.

15. James Fallows, "The Tragedy of the American Military," *Atlantic*, January/February 2015, http://www.theatlantic.com/features/archive/2014/12/the-tragedy-of-the-american-military/383516.

16. Rod Nordland, Ash Ngu, and Fahim Abed, "How the U.S. Government Misleads the Public on Afghanistan," *New York Times*, September 8, 2018, https://www.nytimes.com/interactive/2018/09/08/world/asia/us-misleads-on-afghanistan.html.

17. Bob Woodward, *Fear: Trump in the White House* (New York: Simon & Schuster, 2018), 119.

18. Nordland, Ngu, and Abed, "How the U.S. Government Misleads the Public."

19. Thomas Gibbons-Neff, "Afghan War Data, Once Public, Is Censored in U.S. Military Report," *New York Times*, October 30, 2017, https://www.nytimes.com/2017/10/30/world/asia/afghanistan-war-redacted-report.html.

20. Barbara Starr, "Is the Top US Commander in Afghanistan in Trump's Crosshairs?" CNN, August 4, 2017, https://www.cnn.com/2017/08/03/politics/nicholson-afghanistan-trump/index.html.

21. "16 Years Later, Afghan Capital Under Siege," *60 Minutes*, January 11, 2018, https://www.cbsnews.com/news/16-years-later-afghan-capital-under-siege.

22. Woodward, *Fear*, 312.

23. Ibid.

24. Alex Johnson, "Inspector General Accuses Pentagon of Censoring Afghanistan Data," NBC News, January 30, 2018, https://www.nbcnews.com/news/world/inspector-general-accuses-pentagon-censoring-afghanistan-data-n842481.

25. Ibid.

26. Woodward, *Fear*, 260.

27. Thomas E. Ricks, *Fiasco: The American Military Adventure in Iraq* (New York: Penguin, 2006), 81.

28. Tom Vanden Brook, "Senior Military Officials Sanctioned for More Than 500 Cases of Serious Misconduct," *USA Today*, October 24, 2017, https://www

.usatoday.com/story/news/politics/2017/10/24/generals-sex-misconduct
-pentagon-army-sanctions-hagel-gillibrand/794770001.

29. Ronan Farrow, *War on Peace: The End of Diplomacy and the Decline of American Influence* (New York: W.W. Norton, 2018), 156.

30. Former West Point superintendent Robert Caslen was on the short list to replace national security advisor Michael Flynn before Trump ultimately selected another military general, H. R. McMaster.

31. Farrow, *War on Peace*, 156.

32. Nordland, Ngu, and Abed, "How the U.S. Government Misleads the Public."

33. Editorial Board, "Telling the Truth about the Cost of War," *New York Times*, November 23, 2017, https://www.nytimes.com/2017/11/23/opinion/america-war
-casualties-soldiers.html.

34. Ibid.

35. Ibid.

36. "Syria: Unprecedented Investigation Reveals US-Led Coalition Killed More Than 1,600 Civilians in Raqqa 'Death Trap,'" Amnesty International, April 25, 2019, https://www.amnesty.org/en/latest/news/2019/04/syria-unprecedented
-investigation-reveals-us-led-coalition-killed-more-than-1600-civilians-in
-raqqa-death-trap.

37. Dan Merica, Jake Tapper, and Jim Sciutto, "Sources: Trump Shared Classified Info with Russians," CNN, May 16, 2017, http://www.cnn.com/2017/05/15
/politics/trump-russia-classified-information/index.html.

38. Ibid.

39. Michael A. Memoli and Noah Bierman, "McMaster: It Was 'Wholly Appropriate' for Trump to Share Intelligence with Russians," *Baltimore Sun*, May 16, 2017, https://www.baltimoresun.com/la-na-essential-washington-updates
-mcmaster-it-was-wholly-approrpriate-1494951421-htmlstory.html.

40. H. R. McMaster, *Dereliction of Duty: Lyndon Johnson, Robert McNamara, the Joint Chiefs of Staff, and the Lies That Led to Vietnam* (New York: Harper, 1997), 106.

41. Sudarsan Raghavan, "Hours before Death in Niger, U.S. Soldiers Were Targeting Militants in Mali," *Washington Post*, November 5, 2017, https://www .washingtonpost.com/world/africa/hours-before-death-in-niger-us-soldiers -were-targeting-militants-in-mali/2017/11/05/57861ad2-c243-11e7-9922 -4151f5ca6168_story.html.

42. Eugene Scott, "Accusations of Racism and Grandstanding Fly between Wilson and Kelly, Overtaking Big Questions about Niger Attack," *Washington Post*, October 20, 2017, https://www.washingtonpost.com/news/the-fix/wp/2017/10 /20/accusations-of-racism-and-grandstanding-fly-between-wilson-and-kelly -overtaking-big-questions-about-niger-attack.

43. "Full Transcript and Video: Kelly Defends Trump's Handling of Soldier's Death and Call to Widow," *New York Times*, October 19, 2017, https://www .nytimes.com/2017/10/19/us/politics/statement-kelly-gold-star.html.

44. Larry Barszewski, "Frederica Wilson 2015 Video Shows John Kelly Got It Wrong," *Fort Lauderdale Sun Sentinel*, October 21, 2017, http://www.sun -sentinel.com/local/broward/fl-reg-wilson-kelly-tape-of-speech-20171020 -story.html.

45. Richard Cohen, "Sarah Huckabee Sanders Is Wrong about John Kelly," *Washington Post*, October 23, 2017, https://www.washingtonpost.com/opinions/sarah -huckabee-sanders-is-wrong-about-john-kelly/2017/10/23/9c3223ca-b824-11e7 -9e58-e6288544af98_story.html.

46. Ibid.

47. Bob Fredericks, "White House Backs Kelly's Controversial Civil War Comments," *New York Post*, October 31, 2017, http://nypost.com/2017/10/31 /white-house-backs-kellys-controversial-civil-war-comments.

48. Philip Bump, "Historians Respond to John F. Kelly's Civil War Remarks: 'Strange,' 'Sad,' 'Wrong,'" *Washington Post*, October 31, 2017, https://www .washingtonpost.com/news/politics/wp/2017/10/31/historians-respond-to -john-kellys-civil-war-remarks-strange-sad-wrong.

49. Ibid.

50. Jennifer Schuessler, "A Refusal to Compromise? Civil War Historians Beg to Differ," *New York Times*, October 31, 2017, https://www.nytimes.com/2017/10/31 /arts/a-refusal-to-compromise-civil-war-historians-beg-to-differ.html.

51. "Unveiling Portrait of Gen. Robert E. Lee, West Point Military Academy, New York," January 19, 1954, National Archives Catalogue, https://catalog.archives.gov/id/25593.

52. Jonathan Swan, "Scoop: Skirmish in Beijing over the Nuclear Football," Axios, February 18, 2018, https://www.axios.com/scoop-skirmish-in-beijing-over-the-nuclear-football-1518992774-1e7a513d-4190-459d-ad4f-2c8746fecc6f.html.

53. Maggie Haberman and Katie Rogers, "The Day John Kelly and Corey Lewandowski Squared Off Outside the Oval Office," *New York Times*, October 22, 2018, https://www.nytimes.com/2018/10/22/us/politics/john-kelly-lewandowski-fight-secret-service.html.

54. Julie Hirschfeld and Maggie Haberman, "John Kelly and John Bolton Have Shouting Match over Immigration," *New York Times*, October 18, 2018, https://www.nytimes.com/2018/10/18/us/politics/immigration-kelly-bolton-shouting-match.html.

55. Felicia Sonmez, "John Kelly Has 'Hissy Fits' and Is Hurting White House Morale, Scaramucci Says," *Washington Post*, October 21, 2018, https://www.washingtonpost.com/politics/scaramucci-blasts-john-kellys-hissy-fits-says-hes-hurting-white-house-morale/2018/10/21/b45cdba2-d551-11e8-83a2-d1c3da28d6b6_story.html.

56. Olivia Nuzzi, "My Private Oval Office Press Conference with Donald Trump, Mike Pence, John Kelly, and Mike Pompeo," *New York Magazine*, October 10, 2018, http://nymag.com/intelligencer/2018/10/my-private-oval-office-press-conference-with-donald-trump.html.

57. Thomas E. Ricks, *The Generals: American Military Command from World War II to Today* (New York: Penguin, 2012), 447–62.

58. Ibid., 461.

59. Arthur T. Coumbe, Steven J. Condly, and William L. Skimmyhorn, *Still Soldiers and Scholars? An Analysis of Army Officer Testing* (Carlisle, PA: U.S. Army War College Press, 2017), 333, https://ssi.armywarcollege.edu/pdffiles/PUB1374.pdf.

60. Ibid., 12.

61. Ibid., 8–9.

62. Ibid., 351.

63. Ibid., 10.

64. Angela L. Duckworth, Abigail Quirk, Robert Gallop, Rick H. Hoyle, Dennis R. Kelly, and Michael D. Matthews, "Cognitive and Noncognitive Predictors of Success," *Proceedings of the National Academy of Sciences*, November 4, 2019, https://www.pnas.org/content/early/2019/10/29/1910510116.

65. Coumbe, Condly, and Skimmyhorn, *Still Soldiers*, 204.

66. Ibid., 240.

67. Ibid., 280.

68. Ibid., 308.

69. Ibid., 313.

70. Ibid., 354.

71. Tom Roeder, "Air Force Academy Probes Alleged Frosh Cheating, Athlete Misconduct," *Colorado Springs Gazette*, October 17, 2017, http://gazette.com/air-force-academy-probes-alleged-frosh-cheating-athlete-misconduct/article/1613351.

72. Colleen Sikora, "Authorities Investigate Allegations of Hazing, Cheating at USAFA," KRDO NewsChannel 13, October 17, 2017, http://www.krdo.com/news/military/authorities-investigate-allegations-of-hazing-cheating-at-usafa/638916497.

73. Charles S. Clark, "Air Force Security Had Four Chances to Block Firearms of Texas Church Shooter," *Government Executive*, December 7, 2018, https://www.govexec.com/defense/2018/12/air-force-security-had-four-chances-block-firearms-texas-church-shooter/153381/?oref=river.

74. Shaila Dewan and Richard A. Oppel Jr., "For the Military, a Long History of Failure to Report Crimes," *New York Times*, November 7, 2017, https://www.nytimes.com/2017/11/07/us/texas-shooting-background-checks.html.

75. Thomas E. Ricks, "Why We Should Get Rid of West Point," *Washington Post*, April 19, 2009, http://www.washingtonpost.com/wp-dyn/content/article/2009/04/16/AR2009041603483.html.

76. Coumbe, Condly, and Skimmyhorn, *Still Soldiers*, 125, 179, 239.

77. Ibid., 307–8.

78. Ibid., xx.

79. Edward L. King, "Who Needs West Point?" *New York Times*, April 29, 1972, https://www.nytimes.com/1972/04/29/archives/who-needs-west-point.html.

80. Ibid.

81. Ibid.

82. Leonard Wong and Stephen Gerras, *Lying to Ourselves: Dishonesty in the Army Profession* (Carlisle, PA: Strategic Studies Institute and U.S. Army War College Press, 2015), 26, https://ssi.armywarcollege.edu/pdffiles/pub1250.pdf.

83. Ibid., 33.

84. Ibid., 27–28.

INDEX

A NOTE ON THE AUTHOR

Tim Bakken is the first civilian promoted to professor of law in West Point's history. He created the Department of Law at the National Military Academy of Afghanistan in Kabul. He became a federal whistleblower after reporting what he believed was corruption at West Point and, after the army retaliated against him, became one of the few federal employees to win a retaliation case against the U.S. military. Bakken received law degrees from Columbia University and the University of Wisconsin and practiced law in New York, including as a homicide prosecutor in Brooklyn. He is still teaching at West Point and lives in New York.